LAND, MEMORY, RECONSTRUCTION, AND JUSTICE

Perspectives on Land Claims in South Africa

EDITED BY **CHERRYL WALKER, ANNA BOHLIN, RUTH HALL, AND THEMBELA KEPE**

OHIO UNIVERSITY PRESS
ATHENS

Ohio University Press, Athens, Ohio 45701
www.ohioswallow.com
© 2010 by Ohio University Press
All rights reserved

To obtain permission to quote, reprint, or otherwise reproduce or distribute material from Ohio University Press publications, please contact our rights and permissions department at (740) 593-1154 or (740) 593-4536 (fax).

Printed in the United States of America
Ohio University Press books are printed on acid-free paper ⊚ ™

17 16 15 14 13 12 11 10   5 4 3 2 1

Library of Congress Cataloging-in-Publication Data

Land, memory, reconstruction, and justice : perspectives on land claims in South Africa / edited by Cherryl Walker ... [et al.].
  p. cm.
Includes bibliographical references and index.
ISBN 978-0-8214-1927-4 (pb : alk. paper) — ISBN 978-0-8214-4354-5 (electronic)
 1. Land reform—South Africa. 2. Land reform—Social aspects—South Africa. 3. Land tenure—South Africa. 4. Restitution—South Africa. I. Walker, Cherryl.
 HD1333.S6L3575 2010
 333.3'168—dc22
                       2010017347

Contents

List of Illustrations   vii
Acknowledgments   ix
Abbreviations   xi

Introduction   1
   Cherryl Walker, Anna Bohlin, Ruth Hall, and Thembela Kepe

PART 1   CONTEXTUAL, COMPARATIVE, AND LEGAL PERSPECTIVES

ONE   Reconciling the Past, Present, and Future
The Parameters and Practices of Land Restitution in South Africa   17
   Ruth Hall

TWO   Giving Land Back or Righting Wrongs?
Comparative Issues in the Study of Land Restitution   41
   Derick Fay and Deborah James

THREE   Change through Jurisprudence
The Role of the Courts in Broadening the Scope of Restitution   61
   Hanri Mostert

PART 2   RESTITUTION VOICES: MEMORY, CONTESTATION, RECONSTRUCTION

FOUR   Urban Restitution Narratives
Black River, Cape Town   83
   Uma Dhupelia-Mesthrie

FIVE   The Right to Land Restitution as Inspiration for Mobilization   100
   Marc Wegerif

SIX   Choosing Cash over Land in Kalk Bay and Knysna
The Time Factor in Urban Land Claims   116
   Anna Bohlin

SEVEN   Securing Postsettlement Support toward Sustainable Restitution
Lessons from Covie   131
   Angela Conway and Tim Xipu

PART 3 RESTITUTING COMMUNITY: POLITICS, IDENTITY, DEVELOPMENT

EIGHT Acrimonious Stakeholder Politics
Reconciliation and Redevelopment in District Six 143
  Christiaan Beyers

NINE "Model Tribes" and Iconic Conservationists?
Tracking the Makuleke Restitution Case in Kruger National Park 163
  Steven Robins and Kees van der Waal

TEN The ≠Khomani San Land Claim against the Kalahari Gemsbok National Park
Requiring and Acquiring Authenticity 181
  William Ellis

ELEVEN The Ambiguities of Using Betterment Restitution as a Vehicle for Development
An Eastern Cape Case Study 198
  Chris de Wet and Eric Mgujulwa

TWELVE Land Restitution and Community Politics
The Case of Roosboom in KwaZulu-Natal 215
  Chizuko Sato

PART 4 RESTITUTION POLICY: LIMITS AND POSSIBILITIES

THIRTEEN Land Claims and Comanagement of Protected Areas in South Africa
Exploring the Challenges 235
  Thembela Kepe

FOURTEEN Restitution in Default
Land Claims and the Redevelopment of Cato Manor, Durban 255
  Cherryl Walker

FIFTEEN Unfinished Business
The Role of Governmental Institutions after Restitution of Land Rights 273
  Alan Dodson

SIXTEEN Restitution, Agriculture, and Livelihoods
National Debates and Case Studies from Limpopo Province 288
  Michael Aliber, Themba Maluleke, Mpfariseni Thagwana, and Tshililo Manenzhe

SEVENTEEN Strategic Questions about Strategic Partners
Challenges and Pitfalls in South Africa's New Model of Land Restitution 306
  Bill Derman, Edward Lahiff, and Espen Sjaastad

Contributors 325
Index 327

Illustrations

MAPS

1. South Africa, showing the locality of major case studies   xiii
2. South Africa's bantustans, 1989   xiii
3. Cape Town and the Group Areas Act   xiv
4. Mkambati Nature Reserve and surrounds   238

TABLES

1. Claims lodged by province   28
2. Settled claims by province as of December 2006   29
3. Settled rural claims involving land restoration as of 31 March 2006   31

FIGURE

1. Restitution budget allocation, 1995–2008   32

Acknowledgments

The editors thank the Ford Foundation (South Africa) for its generous support of both the 2006 conference that gave rise to this publication and the production of the publication itself. The larger project of which the conference and publication are components was originally developed within the Human Sciences Research Council, whose institutional support for this work is also appreciated. So too is the support of the University of Toronto's "Connaught New Staff Matching Grant" for Thembela Kepe's participation in the project. We also thank Royden Yates for his help with the preparation of some of the maps.

Abbreviations

ACLA	Advisory Commission on Land Allocation
AFRA	Association for Rural Advancement
ANC	African National Congress
BRC	Border Rural Committee
BRRA	Black River Ratepayers' and Residents' Association
CASE	Community Agency for Social Enquiry
CBNRM	community-based natural resources management
CLCC	chief land claims commissioner
CLRA	Communal Land Rights Act
CMDA	Cato Manor Development Association
COLA	Commission on Land Allocation
CPA	communal property association
CRLR	Commission on Restitution of Land Rights (commonly known as the Land Claims Commission)
DA	Democratic Alliance
DEAT	Department of Environmental Affairs and Tourism
DLA	Department of Land Affairs (renamed the Department of Rural Development and Land Reform in 2009)
DPWLA	Department of Public Works and Land Affairs (pre-1994)
DWAF	Department of Water Affairs and Forestry
GEAR	Growth, Employment, and Redistribution (macroeconomic strategy)
GLTP	Great Limpopo Transfrontier Park
HSRC	Human Sciences Research Council
IDP	integrated development plan

IFP	Inkatha Freedom Party
IUCN	International Union for Conservation of Nature
KNP	Kruger National Park
LCC	Land Claims Court
LRC	Legal Resources Centre
MOU	memorandum of understanding
NGO	nongovernmental organization
NP	National Party
NNP	New National Party
PDOA	Provincial Department of Agriculture
PLAAS	Institute for Poverty, Land and Agrarian Studies (formerly Programme for Land and Agrarian Studies) (University of the Western Cape)
PPF	Peace Parks Foundation
RBO	Roosboom Board of Overseers
RDP	Reconstruction and Development Programme (socioeconomic policy framework)
RLCC	regional land claims commissioner
SAFCOL	South African Forestry Company Limited
SANParks	South African National Parks
SCLC	Southern Cape Land Committee
SDI	spatial development initiative
SKKLRF	Southern Cape and Karoo Land Restitution Forum
TRALSO	Transkei Land Service Organisation
TRC	Truth and Reconciliation Commission
UDF	United Democratic Front
UDM	United Democratic Movement
VOC	Voice of the Cape (community radio station and Web site)

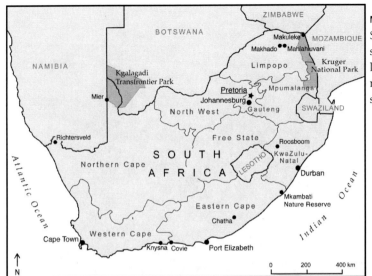

MAP 1. South Africa, showing the locality of major case studies

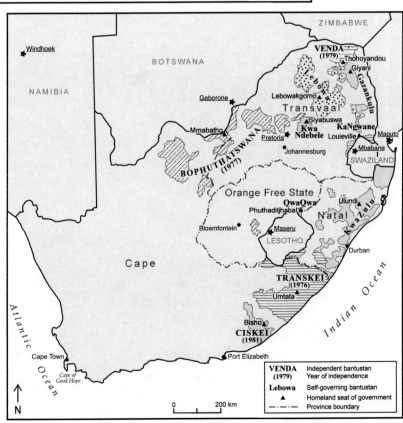

MAP 2. South Africa's bantustans, 1989

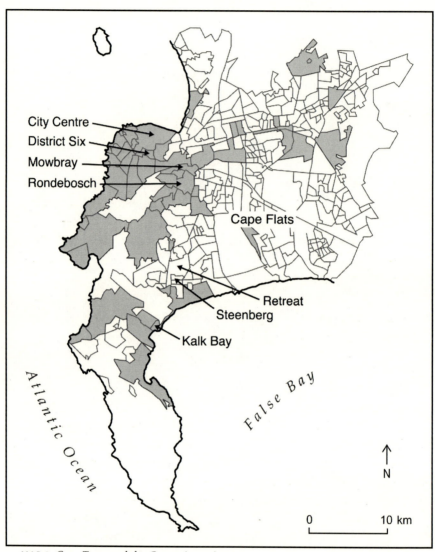

MAP 3. Cape Town and the Group Areas Act

Introduction

CHERRYL WALKER, ANNA BOHLIN,
RUTH HALL, AND THEMBELA KEPE

This collection of articles explores the conflicted terrain of land claims and land restitution in postapartheid South Africa. The volume comprises thematic overviews and detailed case studies in which the authors wrestle with the many meanings and complex outcomes of the state's official program of redress.[1] This introduction provides background reflections on major issues as well as a brief overview of the individual chapters within each of the four parts into which the collection is divided. An in-depth account of the history and scope of the program follows in chapter 1.

LAND CLAIMS IN SOUTH AFRICA

State-sponsored forced removals were among the most flagrant human rights violations of the apartheid era. Reflecting the political significance of this history, the Restitution of Land Rights Act was the first piece of "transformation" legislation passed by South Africa's newly constituted Parliament after democratic elections had ushered in the postapartheid era under President Mandela in April 1994. At the time there were high hopes that land restitution would not only redress the injustices experienced by black South Africans who had been dispossessed of land rights but also contribute to the objectives of tenure security, land redistribution, and rural development that underpinned the new democracy's wider land reform ambitions. In the event, these objectives have proven far more elusive than originally anticipated. Exploring why this has been so and what this means for assessing the program in all its variety are key aims of this book.

Now is a good time to take stock of this ambitious program of redress, reconciliation, and reconstruction.[2] For one thing, the full dimensions of

1

the official program are becoming clearer as the state pushes to meet its 2011 deadline (pushed back from earlier deadlines) for declaring finalization.³ It is now possible to undertake a far more comprehensive and informed assessment of the program's achievements than in earlier years, not only in relation to the scale of past forced population removals but also in relation to the promises of 1994 and the developmental challenges currently facing the country. For another, given that the state appears intent on finalizing the program as expeditiously as possible, it is important to reflect on what still remains to be done, not merely to settle all outstanding claims as quickly as possible—which often seems the state's overriding priority—but also to ensure that the settlements are durable.

Critics have consistently argued that restitution, as with land reform in general, has not been sufficiently prioritized by the African National Congress (ANC) government and that the state's record on postsettlement support for land-based restitution settlements is generally very poor. It is increasingly clear that restitution is best understood as a process, not a onetime event. The restoration of land as the formal settlement of a claim marks not the end of the restitution road but an early stage in an ongoing and often extremely complex process of community reconstruction. This process has proved to be challenging from a development perspective as well as socially and politically fraught. That the process has complex social, political, and developmental aspects is a major theme in this collection, cutting across urban and rural case studies (Aliber, Maluleke, Thagwana, and Manenzhe; Beyers; de Wet and Mgujulwa; Ellis; Kepe; Sato; and Wegerif).

Establishing the precise number of claims lodged with the agency entrusted with primary responsibility for processing claims, the Commission on Restitution of Land Rights (CRLR, also known as the Land Claims Commission or simply the commission) has proved a difficult research task (see Hall, chapter 1 in this volume). However, in April 2005 the acting director general of the Department of Land Affairs (DLA) reported to Parliament that the final count stood at 79,696 (DLA 2005), of which approximately 80 percent were urban claims and the balance rural. By March 2007 the commission was claiming that over 90 percent of all lodged claims—74,417—had been settled (CRLR 2007, 3). In contrast to its beleaguered status in earlier years, when claim settlements were few and far between, land restitution has come to enjoy the status of flagship in the state's larger land reform program, which also encompasses land redistribution and enhanced tenure security.

Introduction

Given the deeply conflictual nature of land reform in the southern African region, as well as the inherent difficulties of any state program aimed at restorative justice many years after the original acts of dispossession, the formal achievements of the program are noteworthy. However, as Hall's overview and other chapters in this volume make clear, what counts as success is open to debate. It is clear that the official national numbers are very poor indicators of what is actually happening in projects at the local level.

Although the restitution program is most commonly thought of as a core element of redistributive land reform, to date the bulk of land claim settlements have been in the form of financial compensation rather than restoration of land; urban rather than rural claims have predominated (CRLR 2007, 61). This situation is set to change as the outstanding claims are processed—all of them are reportedly rural, and many involve substantial tracts of land, especially in the northeast of the country. Nevertheless, formal ownership of restored land does not necessarily give claimants unrestricted rights of access to their land, as demonstrated by restitution settlements involving high-value agricultural enterprises and prime conservation areas (Derman, Lahiff, and Sjaastad; Kepe; Robins and van der Waal, all in this volume; see also Walker 2008). Claimants have also not always taken up the opportunity to settle on or use their land in accordance with state development plans (Aliber et al. in this volume). What these outcomes mean for agrarian reform more broadly are key issues for further analysis and policy debate.

Given the preponderance of urban claims, it is striking that to date most scholarly analyses of land restitution, as well as public political commentary, have focused on rural claims and rural land issues. The particular meanings of restitution in the urban context, including the extent to which urban financial settlements have contributed to a sense of closure on the past, have received relatively little in-depth analysis thus far (Bohlin 2004), although, as this collection reveals, this state of affairs is beginning to shift. A strength of this volume is its treatment of urban and rural claims as related elements of the same program rather than as discrete categories with very different requirements, trajectories, and assessment criteria.

Urban claims have brought out particularly clearly the difficulties of restoring land rights in contexts where land use and settlement patterns have changed substantially since the dispossessions driving the claims. The many constraints inhibiting the simple act of restoring land to those who were wronged are most apparent in the urban context, although similar complexities have begun to receive more attention in the rural context, in particular in relation to land claims on protected areas and on highly developed agricultural estates (see Kepe; Derman, Lahiff, and Sjaastad, this volume). Underestimated in the original policy framework for restitution was the likely impact of constituents who are not claimants making competing demands on land subject to restitution claims, as in Cato Manor, Durban (Walker, this volume), and, in a very different political context, District Six in Cape Town (Beyers, this volume).

In linking urban and rural land issues, the collection also highlights the complex meanings of land restitution beyond considerations of livelihoods and development. Several case studies explore the ambiguous ways in which ethnic and community identities are confirmed or reconstituted and also mobilized through the restitution process (Ellis; Robins and van der Waal; Sato; Walker). The volume also brings into focus the limitations of the official process in dealing with the symbolic dimensions of loss (Dhupelia-Mesthrie). South Africa's Truth and Reconciliation Commission (TRC) has received considerable attention internationally, but the land claims program has had a much lower profile as a program of reparations for human rights abuses and for dealing with the nonmaterial dimensions of land dispossession. Yet, given the number of beneficiaries the restitution program has reached and the significance of land for social identity, this is an issue crying out for attention. It is noteworthy that despite the undoubted political and symbolic significance of land restitution in national debate since the early 1990s, as well as the importance of land in the livelihood strategies of many of South Africa's rural poor, the policy debate on the restitution program has tended to fixate on the apparently tangible measurements of performance as represented by the total number of claims settled and hectares of land transferred. However, as the case studies in parts 2 and 3 of this volume underscore, this information opens only a small window on the significance of land restitution for claimants in postapartheid South Africa.

Another neglected dimension that this collection addresses is the extent to which South Africa's land laws have been challenged by judicial activism through the restitution program. Although there is an important tradition of legal scholarship on these issues, there has been relatively little cross-fertilization between legal research and general social science research until now, and even less public debate on the critical issues of jurisprudence and its reconfiguration of the country's land laws. Yet in recent years there have been significant developments in the area of property law as a result of judicial interpretation of key sections of the restitution legislation, not only by

Introduction

the Land Claims Court (LCC) but also by the Supreme Court of Appeal and the Constitutional Court. These judgments have challenged in potentially far-reaching ways hegemonic assumptions about the authority of the model of private landownership that until now has permeated South African law and dominated the political debate (Mostert, this volume). Furthermore, although the LCC has been criticized for making the settlement process unnecessarily legalistic even in noncontested claims, it has developed a set of judgments that, according to former LCC judge Alan Dodson (this volume), increases the onus on the state to take much greater responsibility than currently displayed for developmental support for claimants who have had their land restored to them.

The role of state institutions in land reform remains a controversial subject. Alongside a fierce debate on the relative merits of the market (see Hall, this volume), lack of state capacity and its overreliance on inappropriate models of agrarian reform are frequently cited problems. These concerns are well reflected in this volume, alongside some emerging alternative perspectives on possible solutions. Although most analysts criticize the state for failing to live up to its responsibilities, a couple of chapters question the authority accorded state-led development plans and foreground the importance of claimants taking control of their own futures, whether in developing independent food production models (Wegerif) or in making their own choices at the individual or household level about how or even whether to use the land rights that have been restored to them (Aliber et al.).

A related topic concerns the powerful role of civil society organizations, including NGOs and lawyers, in not only supporting claimant organizations but also shaping restitution outcomes according to their own preferred understandings. Although in general NGOs have played a valuable role in pressuring the state on behalf of claimants and providing claimant organizations with much-needed expertise and resources (Conway and Xipu; de Wet and Mgujulwa; Ellis, all in this volume), the client/patron relationships that develop are not innocent of power relations or without ambiguity.

CHAPTER OVERVIEW

The scale of black land dispossession in South Africa historically and the variety of tenure forms and land use that were affected at different times in different parts of the country have meant that the post-1994 restitution program has had to tackle an extraordinarily wide range of issues in terms of types of claims, levels of organization among claimants, possibilities for reconstruction, and local expectations of redress. Although it is not possible to treat the full range of issues in a single volume, the chapters in this collection achieve a wide thematic and geographical spread. They also showcase a variety of different perspectives. Although most contributors are academics, some are activists or have activist backgrounds; some were formerly located in the CRLR, the DLA, and the LCC.

The book is divided into four parts. Part 1, "Contextual, Comparative, and Legal Perspectives," comprises three general chapters that provide a broad overview for analyzing the program. Chapter 1, by Ruth Hall, provides a history of the restitution program as it has unfolded in South Africa since 1994. Beginning with a brief historical overview of land dispossession and the struggle to enshrine a land restitution program through the constitutional negotiations of the early 1990s, this chapter sets out the main features of the constitutional compromise on property rights that made the transition to democratic government possible in 1994, and then reviews the achievements, major policy challenges, and current debates on the significance of the program. Hall highlights the tension between restituting rights and enhancing livelihoods that has characterized the program in its implementation and concludes that, both materially and symbolically, land restitution's contribution to postapartheid reconstruction has been limited.

Chapter 2, by Derick Fay and Deborah James, provides a comparative overview of the experience of restitution as a state endeavor in South Africa and in other parts of the world. It thus helps locate the South African material within a larger literature and set of debates on the meaning, possibilities, and limitations of such an ambitious yet often circumscribed enterprise. The South African program, it emerges, carries a particularly weighty set of expectations as a result of the country's specific history of colonial and apartheid-era dispossession by a racialized minority; nevertheless, many of the challenges facing the program are not unique, including the ambiguities of demarcating claimants within the wider society as a distinct group with special claims on the state in terms of recognition and redress.

Chapter 3, by Hanri Mostert, brings an important legal perspective to the analysis, by tracing the way in which the courts have expanded the scope of the South African restitution program to include categories of claimants that a more conventional and narrow reading of the enabling legislation might have excluded. This has implications beyond the restitution program itself, as it has expanded the scope of South African land law in ways that,

Introduction

Mostert argues, have not been fully appreciated—not only by the wider public but possibly by lawmakers themselves.

Part 2, "Restitution Voices," shifts the focus from the large scale to the small scale. Through case studies based on in-depth fieldwork and research that weave together scholarly and activist concerns, part 2 brings to the fore the local, even individual, limits and possibilities in claimant experiences of the land claims process. Although the specific contexts discussed in this part differ, it is possible to trace certain continuities across them, most notably claimants' generally negative experience of bureaucratic inefficiency and the long delays they have faced in the processing of their claims. But although the frustrations engendered tend to undermine the symbolic value of restitution, the implications of the slow pace of restitution for the material outcomes of the program have not always been negative at project level.

Part 2 begins in chapter 4 with Uma Dhupelia-Mesthrie's deeply personalized account of the experience of former residents of Black River, Cape Town. Having first interviewed some respondents in the mid-1990s when they were just embarking on the land claims process, she is able to compare claimant hopes and concerns at the outset with their accounts of what has transpired since then. Unable to return to their former homes in what is today a well-developed, middle-class suburb, these claimants have opted for financial compensation. The chapter describes how they have deployed humor in the face of an often opaque officialdom and also how they have attempted to come to terms with the unsatisfactory nature of the compensation they have received. For some the cash awards were so small once the money had been divided among all family members that they signaled the failure of restitution, not its success. Yet for others the process of acknowledgment represented by the financial settlement did bring a measure of closure on the past.

Chapter 5, Marc Wegerif's account of a group of claimants from Mahlahluvani, in rural Limpopo, provides a striking contrast with that of Black River. Here, rather than endlessly waiting for the state bureaucracy to deliver a formal settlement, a group of subsistence farmers decided unilaterally to return to their former land and started producing crops on it, despite their claims still being under negotiation and their presence on the land regarded by officialdom as technically illegal. Wegerif highlights the productive and cooperative nature of this "illegal" production, which has been facilitated by an informal but efficient "production leadership" that contrasts sharply with the often conflict-ridden "political leadership" that the state has engaged as the proper representatives of claimants in the formal restitution process. For Wegerif the implications are clear: claimants should not rely on a fickle and misguided bureaucracy to regain their land but take control themselves of their land and livelihood needs.

The third chapter in this section, chapter 6, in which Anna Bohlin compares restitution in the two Western Cape urban communities of Kalk Bay and Knysna, echoes themes raised in Dhupelia-Mesthrie's chapter. Initially most claimants were committed to returning to their former land (in both cases situated in what are today classified as prime residential areas), but long waiting periods and frustrating encounters with the CRLR gradually eroded their belief that their land would be restored to them. This finally drove the majority to abandon hopes of land restoration and opt for financial compensation. In both places, then, the passage of time has undermined claimant cohesion, commitment, and sense of closure.

Chapter 7, by Angela Conway and Tim Xipu, the final chapter in part 2, provides a contrasting experience. It describes how claimants from the tiny community of Covie, on the southern Cape coast, assisted by an NGO, were able to use the long waiting period involved in the processing of their claim to their advantage. In this case they strategically delayed the transfer of land until they had ensured that various external parties had formally committed to concrete measures of support in the postsettlement phase. This account provides a useful corrective to the view that speed should necessarily be an overriding concern in the processing of claims. It also endorses the importance of securing developmental support in tandem with, rather than after, the negotiations to restore the land, and highlights the role of NGOs in supporting claimants around long-term goals.

Part 3, "Restituting Community," explores the many challenges involved in reconstituting communities through the restitution program. Although there are thematic continuities with part 2, the case studies in this part bring to the fore the contested nature of "development" among members of claimant communities as well as between claimants and outside groupings, including local authorities and other parties with an interest in the development of the claimed land. These chapters also examine the multilayered ways in which land claims can serve as a platform for the assertion of reformulated group identities that, although generally invoking the past, are firmly rooted in present-day struggles over power and resources.

Chapter 8, by Christiaan Beyers, focuses on the protracted battles around the redevelopment of Cape Town's District Six—one of the most enduring

Introduction

symbols of the ravages of apartheid. It examines the very different interests driving local government on the one hand and claimant representatives on the other in the redevelopment phase, once the formal parameters of a settlement framework that recognized the legitimacy of restitution claims had been negotiated. His discussion highlights the seemingly intractable nature of the conflicts that have dogged the process. Claimants fear that the City of Cape Town's call for broad stakeholder involvement and for commercial and housing development on "surplus" District Six land could weaken their own control over the land and the direction its redevelopment should take. Speaking in the name of community, the Beneficiary Trust has instead insisted on a claimant-centered approach, but it faces ongoing challenges from the city—on whose resources and legal authority it is dependent—as well as other potentially powerful actors in the battle over prime urban real estate.

Chapter 9, by Steven Robins and Kees van der Waal, reviews one of the best-known restitution cases involving a major conservation area, that of the Makuleke claim in the north of Kruger National Park. The authors discuss the ways in which the outcome of this case appears to embody the official objectives of reconciliation, nation-building, and economic development. The Makuleke's decision to maintain their land for conservation, as well as their apparent success in reconciling traditional and democratic governance institutions, positions them as a model tribe according to the authors. They argue that this claim's iconic status can be attributed to the Makuleke leadership's strategic deployment and creative assimilation of various development discourses. Here, notwithstanding the significant external resources that went into the settlement, claimant agency seems to have triumphed. However, lurking beneath the surface is a significant battle for authority involving traditional authority structures within and beyond the Makuleke, which threatens the progress made thus far.

Chapter 10, by William Ellis, explores another prominent claim on a conservation area, that of the ≠Khomani San on the Kgalagadi Transfrontier Park between South Africa and Botswana. This chapter focuses on the manner in which different groups of claimants deployed claims to an "authentic San identity," both before and after the land claim settlement, to try to maximize potential benefits for themselves. Ellis argues that the tensions and synergies among claimants have revolved around different interpretations of San identity, whereby San "authenticity" is required to gain membership in the claimant group and also used strategically to strengthen the legitimacy of the claim before external arbiters and brokers.

The following discussion of Chatha in the Eastern Cape in chapter 11, by Chris de Wet and Eric Mgujulwa, addresses one of the very few cases whereby people who were resettled through apartheid-era "betterment planning" in the bantustans, or former "native reserves," were compensated under the restitution program. "Betterment" refers to a land use management policy that involved the spatial reorganization of villages and consequent resettlement of people on a very large scale. At first CRLR officials argued that betterment claims could not be entertained under the restitution legislation. In the Chatha case, however, claimants were assisted by a local NGO to press their claim successfully, again highlighting the significance of external support networks for claimants. As in the ≠Khomani San and Makuleke cases, major challenges in the postsettlement phase were local politics centering on the legitimacy of governance structures and contestations over the content and control of the restitution award that was finally won from the state.

Chapter 12, by Chizuko Sato, the final chapter in part 3, explores the dynamics of land struggles and associated community politics in Roosboom, a previously black-owned farm in KwaZulu-Natal. Sato details how Roosboom claimants were prominent in the struggle for land restitution during the constitutional negotiations, leading to a settlement that predated the 1994 Restitution of Land Rights Act. However, like many other cases discussed in this book, the challenges of reconstituting a community that historically comprised both landowners and tenants, in addition to the lack of consensus on redevelopment priorities among claimants, make it very difficult to offer a simple verdict of success. Sato addresses the fraught relationship between former landowners and their tenants and the tensions surrounding who is a rightful beneficiary—a particularly thorny issue when restitution signifies not only reconnection with the land but also new, albeit often temporary, livelihoods through state development projects.

The chapters in part 4, "Restitution Policy," span urban and rural geographies and interrogate the competing mandates that postapartheid land restitution has had to confront on various fronts: to transform landscapes scarred by spatial apartheid and address deep inequities while protecting the environment, maintaining agricultural production, and acknowledging demands for economic development and social inclusion from more constituencies than claimants alone. A common thread running through these chapters is concern with the meaning of "development."

In chapter 13, a detailed case study of the Mkambati land claim on a protected area along the Wild Coast of the Eastern Cape, Thembela Kepe

Introduction

explores the tension between two constitutional imperatives: the first is to restore land to the dispossessed, and the second is to promote biodiversity conservation. He argues that the comanagement agreements entered into by claimant communities and conservation authorities have seen the reconfiguring, not the abandonment, of former exclusionary practices that privilege hegemonic conservation discourses over the land rights and livelihood activities of the poor. This forms the basis of a critique of the comanagement model in both its conception and its implementation in this claim.

In chapter 14 Cherryl Walker provides an account of the struggles surrounding the redevelopment of the suburb of Cato Manor, Durban. Here, as in District Six, the imperatives of land restitution have clashed with other demands for redevelopment and social inclusion, in this case by the residents of informal settlements that proliferated in the early 1990s on the land under claim. However, unlike in District Six, Cato Manor claimants never enjoyed a significant degree of local political legitimacy, and here the promise of restitution was ultimately compromised by the "default" presumptions of urban planners that favored low-cost housing for nonclaimants as the most pressing priority for the area. Drawing on this case study, Walker argues that the restitution framework was inadequate to handle both the volume and the particular political and developmental challenges posed by the deluge of urban claims that engulfed the CRLR at its outset, and that this has had major implications for how the program has unfolded overall.

Chapter 15, by Alan Dodson, a former judge of the Land Claims Court, reflects on the mandates that were given to the LCC and the CRLR respectively and how the developmental responsibilities of the restitution program could be better served through future institutional and legislative changes. In reviewing various LCC judgments relating to the restoration of land, he criticizes the view of the court as insufficiently pro-poor. He questions what is required to give restitution meaning through the implementation of settlement agreements, as well as where responsibility for achieving this should lie. He concludes that legislative change is needed to allocate specific responsibilities to a reconceptualized CRLR (or similar body) that will actively support claimants' use of restored land, in order to realize the program's underlying goal of supporting sustainable, dignified, and humane lives.

Chapter 16, by Michael Aliber, Themba Maluleke, Mpfariseni Thagwana, and Tshililo Manenzhe, offers a somewhat different slant on development. It highlights the tensions between restitution and rural development. The authors describe how, far from realizing the ANC's early vision of transforming what it regarded as the inefficient and environmentally destructive practices of white commercial farming in favor of smallholders, the restitution program came to regard the commercial farming sector as the model that rural restitution projects should emulate. Through an examination of four sets of claims in Limpopo province, the authors argue that the national debate on appropriate farming models echoes disputes at the project level. These generally divide claimants who favor settling on the land and possibly undertaking small-scale farming from those who prefer the land to be given over to unified commercial production. The important question is how to address the real-life heterogeneity that characterizes claimants and their interests in land-based settlements.

In response to the ostensible failures described by Aliber, Maluleke, Thagwana, and Manenzhe and fearful of what will happen when prime commercial farmland is restored to poor communities, the state is now proposing—even insisting on—deals between land claimants and commercial operators to ensure continuity in production. The emergence of the "strategic partnerships" model is described by Bill Derman, Edward Lahiff, and Espen Sjaastad in chapter 17, the final chapter, which looks at the early application of strategic partnerships in the lush, fruit-growing Levubu valley in Limpopo province. The authors interrogate how these partnerships were envisaged in terms of who makes the key decisions, who carries the risk, who gets the jobs, and, most fundamentally, how claimant communities (who are not allowed to live on or use their land themselves) may benefit from these deals, if at all. Although this experiment is still in its early stages, this chapter raises important concerns and provides a useful baseline from which to evaluate such deals and develop alternative, more claimant-centric models for restitution in the future.

The postapartheid state, driven by the desire to claim tangible results for land reform and yet also limit its responsibilities for land claims, has signaled its intention to wrap up the restitution program as speedily as possible. What the chapters in this volume collectively make clear is that the issues of community reconstruction and land redevelopment elude easy resolution in the unstable context of contemporary South Africa. The challenges of redress stubbornly extend beyond the parameters that the state has attempted to fix.

Introduction

NOTES

1. The collection is based on a selection of papers from an interdisciplinary conference held outside Cape Town, South Africa, in September 2006 that was cohosted by the Programme on Land and Agrarian Studies (PLAAS) at the University of the Western Cape, the Department of Sociology and Social Anthropology at the University of Stellenbosch, and the Human Sciences Research Council. The conference brought together researchers from South Africa and abroad, government officials, and representatives from NGOs and some claimant communities. The support of the Ford Foundation toward the conference and publication of this book is gratefully acknowledged.

2. Final updates to chapters were made in mid 2009.

3. In 2005 the ANC government set 2008 as its deadline for the finalization of the program. In early 2008 the date was shifted to 2011. In early 2010 government plans projected (rather more realistically) that the settlement of claims would extend to 2020.

REFERENCES

Bohlin, Anna. 2004. "A Price on the Past: Cash as Compensation in South African Land Restitution." *Canadian Journal of African Studies* 38 (3): 672–87.

CRLR (Commission on Restitution of Land Rights). 2007. *Annual Report 2006/07*. Pretoria: Commission on Restitution of Land Rights.

DLA (Department of Land Affairs). 2005. "Presentation to the Select Committee on the 2005 Strategic Plan by Mr. Glen Thomas, Acting Director General, 04.04.05." Pretoria: Department of Land Affairs.

Walker, Cherryl. 2008. *Landmarked: Land Restitution and Land Claims in South Africa*. Auckland Park, South Africa: Jacana Media; and Athens: Ohio University Press.

part one

Contextual, Comparative, and Legal Perspectives

one

Reconciling the Past, Present, and Future

The Parameters and Practices of Land Restitution in South Africa

RUTH HALL

Land restitution is intended to right the wrongs of the past: to redress unjust dispossession and to heal. In postapartheid South Africa, it is expected to help reverse racially skewed patterns of landownership in the countryside as well as in urban areas. As part of a wider land reform process, it must help dismantle racialized privilege in property rights. At the same time, restitution performs important symbolic work by acknowledging histories of injustice and their impacts on individuals, families, and communities.

Public ceremonies around the settlement of land claims have acquired iconic status in the democratic South Africa. They have brought into the public eye images of rural communities returning to their ancestral land, dispersed urban communities returning from the periphery to the site of their demolished homes—handshakes, speeches, singing, and dancing. This is part of a healing process. It is generally a happy but transitory moment that marks the culmination of the claiming process and the start of the work of reconstructing communities and livelihoods—and possibly signals reconciliation.

This chapter describes the parameters of land restitution in South Africa. It reviews the legislative and institutional frameworks that have governed the process from its inception in 1995. It also reflects on the scale and quality of the outcomes of a process that continues to be more complex than both those who designed it and those who hoped to gain from it ever anticipated.

THE HISTORICAL AND POLITICAL CONTEXT

The loss of black land rights in South Africa occurred through a protracted and complex process of direct coercion and indirect pressures spanning more than three centuries. Although conflict over land predated European colonialism, this long history of dispossession was shaped by the establishment of a Dutch settlement at the Cape in 1652, followed by the movement of both British and Boer settlers into the hinterland and an ensuing series of "frontier" wars.[1] Growing competition between white farmers and mineowners for cheap labor following the discovery of diamonds and gold in the late nineteenth century prompted measures to undermine the relatively successful and independent black peasantry (Bundy 1988). Most significant was the introduction of legal restrictions on black landownership through the Natives Land Act of 1913. This law designated land on a racial basis and prohibited black South Africans from acquiring, leasing, or transacting land outside small "native reserves," later formalized as ethnic "homelands" or "Bantustans," which were scattered across the country.

The displacement of the indigenous population exceeded that in any other colonial state in Africa. Through the twentieth century, black communities were forcibly removed from their land and independent farmers turned into tenants, who in turn either became landless laborers or were displaced. Many communities lost land in the name of conservation when large regions were proclaimed "protected areas" and residents removed to make way for national or provincial parks. Those who were not employed by the mines, farms, or factories were variously referred to as the "discarded" or "surplus" people (Desmond 1970; Platzky and Walker 1985) and, through a system of urban influx control, confined to the homelands. In towns and cities the Group Areas Act of 1950 etched deep divisions, segregating residential areas and prompting large-scale removals of black residents to townships on the urban periphery or in faraway homelands. The Surplus People Project, which investigated this legalized land theft, estimated that between 1960 and 1983 alone about 3.5 million people were forcibly removed from their land and homes (Platzky and Walker 1985, 9–12).

By 1990 South Africa was marked by a stark racial divide between the 13 percent of land reserved for black occupation and the remainder in so-called white South Africa, dominated by sixty thousand commercial farms covering 70 percent of the country's area. This divide had major political and symbolic significance within the struggle for national liberation. The Freedom Charter adopted in 1955 by the African National Congress (ANC) and its allies declared that: "The land shall be shared among those who work it" (quoted in Suttner and Cronin 1986, 263). Yet the ANC was deeply equivocal on the question of private property. Although nationalization of the land and mines formed part of its political platform in exile after 1960, this remained a point of internal contention and by the late 1980s, when talks paving the way for a negotiated political transition got under way, had been abandoned.

Meanwhile, inside the country, those who had resisted removals were connected through a growing network of nongovernmental organizations (NGOs) and residents' associations in defense of their rights. Localized resistance became linked to the growing mass democratic movement in the form of the United Democratic Front, and, through it, to the ANC in exile and its antiapartheid supporters. One of the exigencies, then, of the transition from apartheid to democratic rule was to respond to the popular demand that those removed from their land and homes be allowed to return. As later acknowledged in the ANC government's *White Paper on South African Land Policy*, "Forced removals in support of racial segregation have caused enormous suffering and hardship in South Africa and no settlement of land issues can be reached without addressing such historical injustices" (DLA 1997, 28).

However, restitution actually began under white rule. In its own preemptive reforms in the dying days of apartheid, the National Party repealed racist land laws through the Abolition of Racially Based Land Measures Act of 1991 and created an Advisory Commission on Land Allocation. Later formalized as the Commission on Land Allocation, this structure was assigned to oversee a limited process of restitution restricted to unimproved state land (Winkler 1994, 445; Steyn 1994, 453). Very few potential claims met this criterion since most dispossessed land was either privately owned by whites or had been developed by the state. These reforms were roundly rejected by the ANC, civil society organizations, and would-be claimants; treating the property rights of whites as sacrosanct would mean the denial of meaningful redress for those whose property rights had been so blatantly violated.

Following the unbanning of political parties in 1990, the ANC set out its demand for a specialist land court to adjudicate claims, restore land, or compensate those who had been dispossessed. Its Land Manifesto of 1992 conceived of restitution very broadly: "[S]uch a claims process must be based on a just set of criteria including productive use, traditional access, claims on the basis of birthright, title deeds, tenancy and usufruct rights (right to benefit from use and duty to maintain), historical dispossession and need" (ANC 1992, 2). During the constitutional negotiations, the ANC argued that, even though rights to personal property should be legally secured, an ANC-led government would not guarantee corporate property. Redressing the injustices of dispossession would of necessity confront the property rights of current owners. The National Party, bolstered by the powerful mining and financial sectors as well as the farming lobby, insisted on the constitutional protection of property rights (individual and corporate). The deadlock was resolved in late 1993 when the ANC discarded its insistence on confiscatory reform (ANC 1993). Following this compromise, the interim Constitution of 1993 confirmed the right to private property and to protection from deprivation of property (sec. 28). It also affirmed a right to restitution, limited to claims relating to dispossession *after* the promulgation of the 1913 Land Act (sec. 8 [3][b], sec. 121). Within these limits, the details of the restitution program were developed by a Land Claims Working Group in a process that was isolated from other agrarian reforms, including land redistribution and agricultural deregulation, which South African economists were framing in partnership with the World Bank (Hall 2004).

Restitution was, then, by definition a limited process, not a radical restructuring of property relations. The demand for restitution rested precisely on a foundation of private landownership: transferring ownership from current owners, including the state, to previous owners. Contrary to the vision of the Freedom Charter, the land would not be shared among those who worked it but would be redistributed through the market or, where feasible, restored to a limited category of those who had been unfairly dispossessed within a specific time frame. In this way, the constitutional compromise responded to the popular demand for redress but divided land claimants from the wider landless population.

Even so, restitution was envisaged as the central pillar in a wider thrust to deracialize landownership by redistributing at least 30 percent of white farmland to black South Africans (DLA 1997, 49). It was conceived as a form of restorative justice, but as the program progressed, questions emerged about whether it was possible to "turn back the clock" and reestablish scattered communities. Although historical claims to land carry strong political resonance within South Africa, they do not always coincide with current needs for development and livelihoods. As a result, the land claims process has highlighted tensions between addressing historical claims and responding to current priorities (Walker 2008). It has also brought into question the state's ability to respond effectively to claims and to link land restitution to a wider program of economic development.

THE FRAMEWORK FOR RESTITUTION: LEGISLATION AND INSTITUTIONS

The Restitution of Land Rights Act 22 of 1994 was the first law passed by the ANC-led Government of National Unity that set out to redress the legacy of apartheid rule. It affirmed the right to restitution and defined the process by which those who were deemed eligible could lodge their claims (sec. 10[1]). Restitution is a rights-based program in that the dispossessed or their descendants have an enforceable right, confirmed in the Constitution, to restoration of, or compensation for, property that was unfairly taken (sec. 25[7]).

The act established two institutions to drive the process: a Commission on Restitution of Land Rights (CRLR) and a Land Claims Court (LCC). The CRLR, established in 1995, was tasked with driving the process: assisting claimants, investigating the validity of claims, and preparing them for settlement or adjudication. Postsettlement support for claimants who got back their land was, initially, the responsibility of the Department of Land Affairs (DLA). The CRLR was placed under the authority of a national chief land claims commissioner, with regional land claims commissioners (RLCCs) responsible for its work in the provinces. Initially the process was highly centralized, but since 2006 RLCCs have exercised substantial authority over the process.

The LCC was established in 1996 as a specialist court to approve claims, grant restitution orders, and adjudicate disputes on the basis of the investigations presented to it; appeals against its judgments can be made to the Supreme Court of Appeal or, in specific circumstances, the Constitutional Court. The decision to separate the adjudicatory function from that of the commission was influenced by the experience of land tribunals in other postcolonial or postconflict situations, particularly Canada, Australia, and New Zealand. It reflected widespread distrust of the judiciary inherited from the apartheid era alongside the need for independent adjudication of land disputes.

The time frame for restitution set out in the 1997 *White Paper* was eighteen years in total from 1995. Initially three years were allowed for claims to be lodged; later the final deadline was extended to 31 December 1998. Five years were envisaged for the settlement of claims and a further ten years for the implementation of all court orders and settlement agreements (DLA 1997, 49). In recent years, however, political pressure has been brought to bear to close the commission and pass the work of finalizing outstanding claims and agreements to other state institutions.

THE CONTESTED PARAMETERS OF RESTITUTION

Three significant dimensions of restitution in South Africa concern who is eligible, what they should get, and who is to pay.

Who Is Eligible?

The Restitution of Land Rights Act clarified the criteria for eligibility as: a person or community who was dispossessed of property after 1913, as a result of racially discriminatory laws or practices, and was not adequately compensated; or the direct descendants or deceased estates of such people (sec. 2[1]). These criteria remain contentious.

Eligibility hinges on providing sufficient proof that property rights existed and were lost through racially discriminatory laws and practices. The jurisprudence around this has dealt with what constitutes a "community," what measures were racially discriminatory, and which rights to property can be restored (see Mostert in this volume). Most significant, perhaps, was the affirmation that restitution would not be limited to former freehold owners of land but would be extended to nonowners, since private titling had been very limited and most land held by blacks had been under forms of customary or informal tenure. Merely restoring land to black landowners would not redress the suffering experienced by those who, at the time of their dispossession, did not enjoy the market power of ownership rights. "Beneficial occupiers" were thus recognized as de facto owners by virtue of their uncontested occupation and use of land over time. Long-term tenants were also eligible to claim rights, as in the important cases of Cremin (a rural community in KwaZulu-Natal) and District Six (a suburb of the city of Cape Town) (see Walker 2008; Beyers, this volume).

The major limitations on eligibility, then, are the 1913 cutoff date and the 1998 deadline for claims to be lodged. Both have been energetically contested. The reason given by the minister of land affairs for not accepting claims predating 1913 is that this would open the way for claims on land already occupied by blacks, rather than focusing on white-owned land. In response to demands at a National Land Summit in 2005, the then minister, Thoko Didiza, pointed to the specter of interethnic conflict *among* black South Africans and with the neighboring states of Lesotho and Swaziland, arising from such claims (Didiza 2005). More fundamentally, this date, embedded in the Constitution, is the product of the political pacts that made the transition to democracy possible; it has proved useful for containing the obligations of the postapartheid ANC government.

Because colonial intrusion and dispossession started from Cape Town, heading eastward and northward during the eighteenth and nineteenth centuries, most black South Africans had lost independent access to land by 1913. Only in the far interior did black communities still retain independent access to large tracts of ancestral land under communal tenure. This explains why there are very few rural claims in the Western Cape and why large portions of Limpopo and Mpumalanga—estimated at between 50 and 70 percent of the farmland in those provinces—are subject to claims (*This Day,* "Up to 70 Percent of Farmland Being Claimed," 7 January 2004). These figures suggest that restitution in these provinces could, potentially, make a substantial contribution toward the state's target of redistributing 30 percent of commercial farmland through land reform (see Walker 2008, 215–16.)

Considering the scale of forced removals between 1913 and 1990, however, it appears that the vast majority of those affected never submitted claims for restitution. The CRLR's own estimate is that the claims it received reflect just 10 percent of those potentially eligible (CRLR 2007d), although Walker (2008, 220) suggests that the proportion may be somewhat higher overall. Certainly the claiming process has been uneven, with some regions and categories of claims better served than others. Some who missed the deadline in 1998—because they were unaware of the process or mistrusted it—have since called on the government to reopen the lodgment process, but campaigns around this demand have not found political traction.

The dates of 1913 and 1998 were confirmed at parliamentary hearings in May 2007. Here, the chief commissioner, Tozi Gwanya, reiterated the government's opposition to accepting new claims (which requires only ministerial approval rather than legislative amendment). Justifying this position, he told Parliament that late claimants were only pursuing their claims to get money, and this should not be entertained because "financial compensation has led to a lot of family disputes, fraudulent claims by wrongful claimants, abuse of the Restitution award on unproductive expenditures which do not prioritize sustainable livelihoods" (CRLR 2007d). However, more pragmatic considerations seem to explain the reluctance to open the floodgates to new claims. In 2005 the then RLCC for Gauteng and North West provinces, Blessing Mphela, outlined the implications rather frankly: "The financial burden on South Africa will be huge. . . . If just half of that 3.5 million [potential claimants] decided to reapply, the cost to the country would exceed the National Budget. . . . Would that be an intelligent way of investing in development when other areas . . . such as employment, are crying out for more funds?" (cited in Groenewald 2005).

What Should Claimants Get?

A second defining dimension of restitution concerns what is to be restored. Again, this is far from straightforward. Claimants are able to indicate their preference among having their land restored, obtaining alternative land, receiving financial compensation, or a combination. Restitution can also take a "developmental" form where compensatory funds are earmarked for investment in infrastructure or income-generating schemes for claimant communities, as has become the dominant form with "betterment" claims (see de Wet and Mgujulwa in this volume).

According to the DLA *White Paper,* restitution must be driven by "the just demands of claimants" and "solutions must not be forced on people" (DLA 1997, 49). However, claimants' choices are often constrained by the realities of poverty and old age. Bureaucratic delays have also driven many who originally aimed to return to their land to accept offers of cash compensation (Bohlin and Dhupelia-Mesthrie, both in this volume), despite the policy assertion that "wherever possible preference should be given to the restoration of land" (CRLR 2008). Many urban claimants who have rejected offers of cash have found their rights to restitution refracted through a web of alternative claims on the attention of the local authorities responsible for the redevelopment of their land (Beyers and Walker, both in this volume).

The notion of choice is also limited by the protection of property owners' rights and thus the availability and cost of the property under claim. Although the Constitution affirms the property rights of both owners and the dispossessed, in practice where these come into conflict—where claimants wish to return and current owners refuse to sell—current ownership has trumped historical claims. As of 2008, the government had used its constitutionally mandated powers of expropriation in just four cases, and in two of them the state revoked its expropriation notices to return to the negotiating table. Claimants, then, have an enforceable right to restitution but not an enforceable right to the restoration of their original property, and whether claimants return is in practice contingent on the willingness of current owners to sell at the prices offered by the commission. Lahiff (2007) has questioned whether adequate restitution is conceivable within such a framework, where the owners of claimed property have an effective veto on land restoration.

A second constraint is the limitation on *which* property is to be restored. Although restitution was initially defined narrowly as pertaining to "land" rather than the more expansive "property" stated in the Constitution, a number of landmark cases have challenged the range of property rights that can be restored. Most notable is the claim to the mineral-rich Richtersveld in the Northern Cape, in which residents successfully argued on appeal to the Constitutional Court that not only were their land rights *not* legally extinguished before 1913, but their rights extended to diamonds and other minerals. In this case a precedent-setting judgment ordered that claimants were entitled to restitution of the land as well as its minerals and precious stones (Constitutional Court 2003, 50–51; see also Mostert in this volume).

A third question is whether, as the CRLR claims, "compensation received at the time of removal . . . should be taken into account when determining redress to the claimant" (CRLR 2008). Such compensation, where it existed, was usually far from equivalent to the land lost, and generally claimants have not been required to sacrifice the compensatory land on which they may have spent years, if not decades, rebuilding their lives and communities. A further debate has centered on what constitutes just recompense and whether this should be limited to property or can extend to suffering and the loss of opportunities. In general, the CRLR and the LCC have restricted the ambit of restitution to land and housing; only in KwaZulu-Natal have orders for compensation for suffering—*solatium*—been granted in selected cases. There is no explicit aspiration in law or policy to restore people to the condition they would have enjoyed had they not been dispossessed of their property, although this was, at least initially, the widespread expectation among claimants (but on this see Dodson in this volume).

Who Pays?

A third dimension of restitution concerns who should carry the cost—those who benefited directly, those who own the land now, or society as a whole?

Unlike other postconflict contexts where it may be relatively clear who benefited from stolen property, the long duration of dispossession in South Africa presents a problem of intergenerational claims, compounded by the multiple transactions of property since the moment of dispossession. By the 1990s the owners of claimed land were often the indirect rather than the direct beneficiaries of dispossession. In this context, the property lobby at the constitutional negotiations argued that making current owners pay for past dispossession would be arbitrary and punitive.

By confirming existing property rights and providing for expropriation with "just and equitable compensation," the constitutional deal ensured that current property owners would *not* be expected to carry the cost of restitution. The political settlement confirmed that society as a whole, through the state and the fiscus, would carry the cost. Thus land claims are against the state, with the minister of land affairs the respondent. By placing the state at the center, South Africa's restitution process has limited the evidentiary burden on claimants. Compared to tribunal-type processes elsewhere, this responsibility has been shifted to the state itself, which, in the Restitution Act, is conceived of as the champion of claimants. This has the advantage of buffering conflict between owners and claimants, although the state-centric character of restitution has also meant that it is highly bureaucratized. The CRLR has, furthermore, found itself caught between its downward accountability to claimants and its upward accountability to defend the state's interests in containing costs.

A LEARNING CURVE: THE FIRST FIVE YEARS

The period 1995 to 1999 was a time of gearing up and learning some difficult lessons for the state. As well as setting up its central and regional offices, the CRLR had to solicit claims and set up systems to register and investigate them. By 1997, concerned that many people remained unaware of the process, it extended the deadline for lodging claims and launched a "Stake Your Claim" campaign with NGOs and church bodies to ensure that the public was aware of the opportunity to lodge claims. This mostly took the form of television, radio, and newspaper advertisements but also included public meetings in relocation areas, door-to-door visits in some regions, a national toll-free information line, and the distribution of posters, pamphlets, and claim forms (CRLR 2007d).

The settlement of claims started slowly. The challenges of establishing a new institution and the heavily legalistic framework were among the reasons given that only forty-one claims were settled in the CRLR's first five years. At this rate, settling claims would take a few *thousand* years. The Minister ordered a review in 1998, just three years after the inception of the program (du Toit et al., n.d.). This led to marked changes in the division of labor between the CRLR and the LCC: the CRLR's role was expanded and the settlement process streamlined. The Restitution of Land Rights Act was amended to give the CRLR delegated powers not only to investigate claims but also to negotiate and conclude settlement agreements (CRLR 1999, 31; Restitution Act, sec. 42D). Although previously all claims had to be referred to the LCC for finalization, under this approach "restitution claims will be resolved via agreements between the parties, with the court only intervening to decide on legal disputes or where there is a need for interpretation of the law" (CRLR 1999, 31). Since 1999 then, an administrative process has largely replaced the judicial approach to settling claims. The CRLR has also been integrated more tightly into the DLA, with commissioners accountable to the director general. This change has enhanced the potential to link restitution more closely to land reform as a whole, although in practice restitution has proceeded in a parallel "silo."

Also arising from the review, the CRLR's approach to financial compensation was standardized, especially in the urban context, leading to mass offers of cash compensation that did not require the separate valuation of each claim. Standard Settlement Offers (SSOs) were initially set at R40,000 for a residential property, with variations for major metropolitan centers (up to R50,000), and smaller amounts (R17,500) offered to claimants who were tenants at the time of dispossession (Hall 2003, 11).

Although cash compensation rapidly became the dominant form of settlement, the challenge of restoring land and ensuring its sustainable use also received attention. A 1998 amendment to the act allowed for the disbursement of (limited) funds to develop land after its restoration, marking the first recognition in law that restitution should be developmental. Although the CRLR has resisted expansion of its responsibilities for development after land is transferred and has a limited mandate in this regard, it has established specialized "settlement support" units in each regional office and attempted to coordinate the developmental contributions of other state agencies (Hall 2003, 18).

HOW FAR HAVE WE COME?

Government and public opinion have mainly measured the achievements of restitution quantitatively in terms of the number of claims settled and people who have benefited, and the extent of land restored to claimants. Relatively little is known about the quality of these outcomes, which remains the subject of much speculation and disagreement—although this volume begins to address these issues. In particular, not much attention has been given to the impact of restitution on social transformation or its contribution toward fostering national reconciliation, promoting gender equity, stimulating economic activities, and contributing to rural livelihoods. What can be reported with at least some degree of confidence are the quantitative measures.

Claims Lodged

A total of 63,455 claim forms were reported as lodged with the CRLR by the extended deadline of 31 December 1998, but it soon became apparent that the total was a shifting target (see table 1). When a number of claim forms were submitted by members of one community, they were consolidated into a single claim. More commonly, group claims were split up and

TABLE 1. Claims lodged by province

Province	Total claims as of December 1998	Total claims as of March 2002	Total claims as of February 2003	Total claims as of June 2007
Eastern Cape	9,615	9,469		
Free State		2,213		
Northern Cape	12,044	2,502		
Western Cape		11,938		
Gauteng	15,843	13,158		
North West		2,508		
KwaZulu-Natal	14,208	14,808		
Mpumalanga	11,745	6,473		
Limpopo		5,809		
Total	63,455	68,878	72,975	79,696

Sources: SAIRR 2000, 154; CRLR 2001, 11; CRLR 2002, 67; CRLR 2003, 10; and CRLR 2007a. (Provincial breakdowns for 2003 and 2007 are not available).

counted separately, for instance where land rights had vested in individuals or households, or where claimants were divided on the outcome (e.g., some wanting restoration and others opting for cash). The result is that even though no additional claims were accepted, the official total has been revised upward several times, rising to 79,696 by 2007.

Claims Settled

The pace of delivery accelerated dramatically from 1999, following the introduction of SSOs and the administrative approach. However, although the number of settled claims increased rapidly, the number of actual households benefiting and the amount of land being restored have risen more slowly. By the end of 2006, the CRLR reported a total of 73,433 claims settled, involving nearly a quarter of a million households.

In 2007, the minister announced that 74,417 claims had been settled and that only 5,279 rural claims remained, implying that all urban claims were settled (Xingwana 2007). However, the shifting definitions used by the CRLR make it difficult to establish with any certainty what has been achieved and what is yet to be done. In some provinces the number of settled claims has overtaken the total for claims originally reported as lodged, for instance in the Eastern Cape where settled claims now *exceed* by 70 percent the number of claims originally submitted (CRLR 2002, CRLR 2007a). Shifts in the

TABLE 2. Settled claims by province as of December 2006

Province	Claims	Households	Hectares	Land cost (in rands)	Total award (in rands)	Land cost as percent of total award[b]
Eastern Cape	16,081	47,742	72,075	216,811,427	1,218,659,673	18
Free State	2,582	4,601	44,464	9,845,559	109,152,504	9
Gauteng	13,146	14,262	7,557	89,633,196	772,414,448	12
KwaZulu-Natal	14,051	46,692	392,630	910,983,599	2,251,875,143	40
Limpopo	2,781	33,944	344,552	1,189,564,834	1,485,903,152	80
Mpumalanga	2,214	34,475	175,256	1,406,450,687	1,743,518,580	80
Northern Cape	3,620	11,649	296,108	201,731,769	505,083,172	40
North West	3,649	25,812	188,396	490,515,999	849,072,119	58
Western Cape	15,309	19,843	3,115	8,216,187	633,433,717	1
Total	73,433	239,020	1,524,153	4,523,753,257	9,569,112,508	47

[a] The figures have been rounded to the nearest rand.
[b] Author's calculations.

Source: CRLR 2007a.

CRLR's reporting format, from claims-as-lodged to claims-as-settled have served—perhaps unintentionally—to exaggerate progress and disguise the scale of the task still remaining, about which relatively little is known. What is clear is that as of the end of 2008 the majority of large rural claims were unaddressed. The commission estimated that about one-third of unsettled claims were "complex," involving disputes among claimants, disputes over the jurisdiction of traditional authorities, disputes on the part of landowners, or untraceable claimants (Xingwana 2007).

Amount and Cost of Land

In 2007 the CRLR reported that 1.5 million hectares of land had been restored through restitution—about a third of the land transferred through all aspects of land reform (CRLR 2007a). However, much of this land was merely earmarked for restoration, *not* transferred, and in some cases would not involve physical restoration to claimants, such as lands in protected areas. So the reported scale and cost of restored land refer to a mix of achievements and future commitments. They also differ widely across the provinces. Until recently, most restored land was in the more arid parts of the country, particularly the Northern Cape where several large restitution claims featured, including that of the ≠Khomani San (Ellis in this volume). However, since 2005 a focus on rural claims in the north has led to the settlement of claims on large tracts of valuable commercial farmland in Limpopo and Mpumalanga.

By the end of 2007, R4.5 billion (approximately US$562 million) had been spent on or earmarked for buying land, and slightly less, nearly R3.8 billion (about US$475 million) on compensating claimants in cash.[2] The proportion spent on land differs widely across the provinces. Where most claims are urban, as in Gauteng and the Western Cape, the bulk of restitution spending has been on cash compensation and grants. Conversely, provinces that have spent proportionately more on land are those, such as Limpopo and Mpumalanga, where large rural claims have been tackled—but where, for this reason, fewer claims in total have been settled. This inverse relation between the amount of land restored to claimants and the number of claims settled has posed a quandary for the RLCCs: with the political pressure to finalize claims mounting, their attention has understandably tended to focus on settling urban claims with cash rather than tackling rural claims, where a single claim may require years of negotiation.

Rural Claims Lodged and Settled

Rural claims account for less than 30 percent of all claims, but most entail groups of hundreds if not thousands of people, whereas urban claims are generally smaller, centered on individuals or extended families. For this reason, rural claims are widely considered to be the "backbone" of restitution. Provinces where rural claims predominate are Mpumalanga, Limpopo, and the Northern Cape. Elsewhere urban claims predominate, with over 90 percent of claims in the Free State and Western Cape being urban.

The cumulative statistics on settled claims that the CRLR publishes each year are not disaggregated to show how claims have been settled (land, cash, or other) or whether they are rural or urban. However, a CRLR database kindly made available for the purposes of this chapter allows for some unpacking of the numbers. According to this database, by March 2006 a total of 4,221 rural claims had been settled (about a quarter of lodged rural claims)—of which only 867 involved land restoration, which, because of multiple claims, constituted 233 projects nationally.

Funding Restitution

Contrary to expectations, money to buy back land has *not* proven to be the main impediment to speeding up restitution. From 2005 the budget allocation from the central government has grown sharply, but the CRLR's

TABLE 3. Settled rural claims involving land restoration as of 31 March 2006

	Rural projects involving land[a]	Rural claims settled[b]	Households	Beneficiaries	Hectares	Land cost (in rands)
Eastern Cape	23	162	17,347	72,871	67,248	28,194,616.00
Free State	6	7	1,655	8,121	44,094	7,213,850.00
Gauteng	3	0	2,028	12,168	3,444	19,392,497.00
KwaZulu-Natal	56	90	15,781	94,692	325,959	630,612,971.36
Limpopo	52	181	22,179	96,129	178,329	586,352,597.80
Mpumalanga	37	205	26,676	139,489	88,748	299,645,152.00
North West	41	64	12,630	68,796	86,781	124,203,005.41
Northern Cape	13	14	5,969	33,434	246,679	48,762,860.89
Western Cape	2	144	1,280	14,909	5,246	4,640,000.00
Total	233	867	105,545	540,609	1,046,528	1,749,017,550.46

[a] Author's calculations.
[b] Author's calculations.

Source: CRLR 2007b

inability to spend this budget—including underexpenditure of about R1 billion (US$100 million) in 2006/07—led to a reduced allocation at precisely the time that it was gearing up to finalize claims and was requesting more funds. Underspending is in large part the product of institutional weaknesses: although the capital funds for buying land, paying out grants, and compensating claimants have risen sharply, the proportion of the budget dedicated to commission staffing has shrunk over time. (See fig. 1.) Added to this has been a reluctance to expand commission offices in the face of the body's impending closure.

ASSESSMENT

Restitution in South Africa has been variously hailed as a great success and devastatingly critiqued as overly conservative, highly bureaucratic, and painfully slow. Among its achievements is the mass settlement of urban claims through cash payouts alongside a handful of alternative attempts to rebuild urban spaces. Progress toward unraveling the complex geography of rural claims has been much more modest; highlights have included the restoration of land to rural communities such as the ≠Khomani San in the Northern Cape (see Ellis in this volume), Elandskloof in the Western Cape, and Makhoba in the Eastern Cape. What follows is a brief review of the program's high and low points, with their attendant complexities and contradictions.

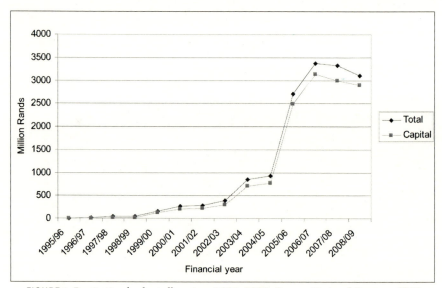

FIGURE 1. Restitution budget allocation, 1995–2008. *Source:* National Treasury 2008

Putting a Price on Restitution

Restitution cases involving the restoration and redevelopment of urban residential land are prominent precisely because they are exceptional. These include the Port Elizabeth Land and Community Restoration Association process in Port Elizabeth, Alexandra in Gauteng, and District Six in Cape Town (see Beyers in this volume). Less scrutinized are the great majority of urban claims that have been settled with cash. The relatively rapid settlement of urban claims with cash compensation is undoubtedly the major success story of restitution thus far. However, this has involved overwhelming pressure on urban claimants to accept standard cash payouts that bear no relation to the value of what was lost or its current market value. The result is that restitution has made few inroads into the tenacious geography of apartheid that continues to shape our cities.

Cash compensation has been derided as "checkbook" restitution, a quick fix solution to deep and intractable grievances. Yet although the bulk of claims have been settled this way (CRLR 2008), remarkably little attention has been given to what this money has meant to people's lives, how it has been spent, and the degree to which cash compensation has been experienced as redress. This onetime only windfall is often divided among large extended families and is generally too small to bring about lasting change in their lives; it is most often used to pay off debt and meet immediate expenses like school fees and consumer items (Bohlin 2004). As a result, available research suggests that those whose claims are settled in this way may *not* consider that justice has been done. As Bohlin (this volume) points out, it remains to be seen whether claimants, or the next generation, might reassert their claims in the future.

Restitution and Reparations

Another limitation is the disconnect between restitution and wider processes of reparation. This can be seen in the separation of restitution from the work of the Truth and Reconciliation Commission, also established in 1995, with a mandate to deal with gross human rights violations from the apartheid era. In this way a profound question has been elided: whether those who benefited from dispossession—white (and corporate) owners who obtained land cheaply from the previous government and may have developed it with public subsidies and cheap labor—have any responsibilities in the restitution process. As Dhupelia-Mesthrie (this volume) points out, this means South Africa's restitution program has missed the mark regarding reconciliation: it recognizes no *beneficiaries* of dispossession, only victims.

Competing Claims and Reconstituting Tradition

Rural restitution has opened up a layered world of overlapping land claims that raise fundamental questions about whose claims should assume primacy. Many rural communities were forcibly removed more than once, for instance, from land designated "white" to the reserves and then again into ethnically defined homelands under apartheid. Dispossession also took the form of reduced access to land, and it forced changes in land use where people remained in situ. Those living in communal areas were compromised, and their livelihoods disrupted both by "betterment" planning—forcing people into villages—and by the dumping of "surplus" people into the homelands, which led to overcrowding and widespread conversion of grazing and arable land into residential plots. Addressing this history poses the challenge of unraveling these pasts and dealing with competing claims. Traditional leaders have also used the restitution process to reassert or extend their jurisdiction, in some instances reigniting long-standing disputes over the status of various chiefs and headmen rooted in apartheid-era manipulation of the institution of traditional leadership (Ntsebeza 2006, Robins & van der Waal this volume).

New Dispossessions

In practice, restitution is also complicated by the sometimes arbitrary distinctions between those who have claimed and those who have not. Most fundamentally, it has privileged the claims of those who were dispossessed of land rights after 1913 over the rights of those who managed to remain on land designated as "white." This is most evident with regard to commercial farms, from which an estimated 1.5 million blacks were evicted between 1963 and 1980 alone (Platzky and Walker 1985). They can now claim restitution of their former rights and upgrade to ownership. Paradoxically, however, those who remained on these farms as workers cannot claim; furthermore, the claims by former farmworkers and labor tenants who were evicted during the twentieth century are being addressed at a time when present-day farm evictions seem to be gathering pace (Wegerif, Russell, and Grundling 2005). So even though restitution has affirmed rights for some, it has created divisions between land claimants and those who are currently threatened with land dispossession. It has also created opposing interests for claimants and farmworkers who may lose their jobs and homes if claims to the farms on which they reside are settled. It is not surprising, therefore, that, although restitution represents redress and closure for some, it is exacerbating feelings of marginality among others.

Reconstituting Community

Rural restitution outcomes have been shaped by the difficulties of reconstituting communities, as properties are restored in private ownership to communal property associations or trusts. Often these entities embrace large groups of people living in different places, with varied resources, assets, skills, and interests in the land they once owned. This has inevitably produced complex and often conflictual group dynamics, centering on how the land is to be used, who can settle on it and on what terms, how labor and capital will be mobilized for production, and how income will be either reinvested or distributed. Transactability of their restored property rights is crucial if claimants are to have real choices about whether they wish to invest in improving their livelihoods where they currently reside rather than returning to their restored land. Yet the community ownership model has prevented individual community members from liquidating their assets or directly deriving rents from the restored property that they are not using (Aliber et al. in this volume).

Rights and Development

Perhaps the most significant shortcoming has been the degree to which restitution has enabled beneficiaries to improve their livelihoods. Rights to land do not necessarily lead to development. The one major review of the program's developmental impact to date has found that the vast majority of projects (179 in the study) were dysfunctional in that little, if any, production was being pursued, with only one of the projects achieving its developmental goals (CASE 2006). Restitution has shown up the wider contradictions of land and agricultural policy. Poor communities are expected to emulate existing production systems in the capital-intensive farming sector and compete with established commercial farmers and the increasingly powerful and oligopolistic agribusiness sector (Hall 2004).

In contrast to the thrust of agricultural policy, which has been to withdraw state interventions, restitution has seen the state reentering land markets. Nowhere is the tension between the rights-based restitution program and wider economic policy more evident than in rural community claims where high-value agricultural land is claimed by large, sometimes amorphous and heterogeneous groups of people. As Aliber, Maluleke, Thagwana, and Manenzhe (this volume) point out, unlike the land redistribution program where self-selecting would-be farmers apply for land, restitution offers the state little scope to decide which people should benefit and which land should be targeted.

Strategic Partnerships

The poor track record of production on restored farms has prompted grave concerns, including in the top echelons of government, that to continue with the current approach to settling large rural claims will result in massive declines in agricultural production and lead to job losses in both primary and secondary agriculture. These concerns have combined with the complaints of landowners and investors about the uncertainty created by outstanding restitution claims, particularly where high-value farming and mining land is at stake. In response, the CRLR has put mounting pressure on claimants to agree to lease out their newly restored land via joint-venture agreements with strategic partners—and, thus, not to live on or use their land directly. Derman, Lahiff, and Sjaastad (this volume) draw attention to the uncritical way in which strategic partnerships have been embraced as the dominant model for the settlement of large community claims in the context of high-value commercial farming enterprises, and the degree to which these involve established companies sharing risk with poor rural communities who have little control over the farming and business decisions. The concentration of claims on commercial farmland in the northeast regions of the country seems likely to be resolved through the extension of this strategic partner model or other joint ventures. This is most marked where primary production is strongly linked through vertical integration into agro-processing, for instance in the forestry and sugar sectors where major milling companies have extended up and down the value-chain into input supply industries, milling, packaging, and transport. The undoubted priority being placed on continuity in production raises the question of whether restitution is being pursued in a way that maximizes its role in transforming unequal social relations and production systems in the countryside or involves as little change as possible, beyond transferring private title.

Wrapping Up Redress: Toward the Deadline

Because of slow progress in land reform generally, the CRLR's apparent success in settling claims encouraged the state to regard restitution as its flagship program. It attracted major budget increases from 2003 on and drew the attention of the president. In 2002 he set a deadline for the finalization of all restitution claims and the closure of the CRLR by 2005, later extended to 2008. In 2008 this deadline was pushed back further, to 2011, and again in 2009, to 2012, signaling the recognition that resolving claims will likely continue for some years to come. What this sense of urgency makes clear, however, is that the ANC government is anxious to limit further obligations in the future, finish off the frustrating unplannability of restitution, and move on to invest in a program that is more amenable to the state's vision of rational "development." These comments by the deputy minister of agriculture and land affairs epitomize this view: "Restitution is a priority in South Africa. We must finish it off. It's a matter of right. It's not a matter of pure economic development like you have in land reform as such. . . . It must be finished off so that we can go into systematic land reform, scientific land reform, to a far greater extent than we are capable of at the moment" (cited in Keet 2005).

Restitution in South Africa constitutes a major program of redress. In comparison with other countries, the process has been fairly rapid, with a substantial proportion of claims being settled in the first sixteen years of democracy. The cost has been substantial, but it is striking that public debate has focused on how to expedite the process and ensure lasting developmental benefits and has *not*, generally, called into question the merits or cost of the program. However, the available evidence suggests that the expectations of what can be achieved and the significance of restoring ownership of land on its own have been greatly overestimated.

As restitution turned from a political commitment to implementation, the process became massively depoliticized. Apart from periodic media reports on the settlement of particular claims, the institutions, procedures, and bureaucratic practices that have shaped restitution have by and large been beyond public scrutiny. The program has turned out to be immensely more complex and messy than anticipated by those—mostly lawyers—who designed it. As the attention of the ruling party turned from liberation to governance, restitution articulated with, and became circumscribed by, other priorities—keeping costs down, protecting the rights of owners, ensuring investor confidence, and promoting and controlling development. And as the scale of claims became apparent, it has been in government's interest to fast-track the process, limit future obligations, and get this work "off the table."

Restitution is a process at odds with two simultaneous processes of change: restructuring in the commercial farming sector (which is ever more hostile to poor people returning to their land and attempting to compete) and the attempts to reinterpret history and engage in public processes of reconciliation. The program has been limited on both counts—the material and the symbolic. In the process, the opportunity to use the land claims process to bring about *both* far-reaching economic transformation *and* reconciliation among the perpetrators, victims, and beneficiaries of the massive property theft that underpinned apartheid may have been missed.

NOTES

1. "Boer" [farmer] refers to the descendants of the first Dutch settlers.
2. Based on an exchange rate of 8 South African Rand to the U.S. dollar.

REFERENCES

ANC (African National Congress). 1992. "Land Manifesto for ANC Policy Conference." Unpublished paper. Johannesburg: African National Congress.

———. 1993. "A Bill of Rights for a New South Africa: Preliminary Revised Text." Unpublished document. Johannesburg: African National Congress.

Bohlin, Anna. 2004. "A Price on the Past: Cash as Compensation in South African Land Restitution." *Canadian Journal of African Studies* 38 (3): 672–87.

Bundy, Colin. 1988. *The Rise and Fall of the South African Peasantry.* 2nd ed. Cape Town: David Phillip; and London: James Currey.

CASE (Community Agency for Social Enquiry). 2006. *Assessment of the Status Quo of Settled Land Restitution Claims with a Developmental Component Nationally.* Pretoria: Department of Land Affairs.

CRLR (Commission on the Restitution of Land Rights). 1999. *Annual Report April 1998 to March 1999.* Pretoria: Government Printers.

———. 2001. *Annual Report April 2000 to March 2001.* Pretoria: Government Printers.

———. 2002. *Annual Report April 2001 to March 2002.* Pretoria: Government Printers.

———. 2003. "Validation Report." http://land.pwv.gov.za/land_reform/restitution.htm. Accessed 18 February 2003.

———. 2007a. "Statistics on Settled Restitution Claims: Cumulative Statistics: 1995–31 December 2006." Unpublished spreadsheet. Pretoria: Department of Land Affairs.

———. 2007b. "Report: Settled Restitution Claims." Unpublished spreadsheet. Pretoria: Department of Land Affairs.

———. 2007c. *Annual Report 2006/07: Year Ended 31 March 2007*. Pretoria: Department of Land Affairs.

———. 2007d. "Restitution Amendment Bill Proposal: Cut-off Dates 19 June 1913 and 31 December 1998." Powerpoint presentation. Pretoria: Department of Land Affairs.

———. 2008. "Background to Restitution." http://land.pwv.gov.za/land_reform/restitution.htm. Accessed 4 February 2008.

Desmond, Cosmos. 1970. *The Discarded People: An Account of African Resettlement in South Africa*. Harmondsworth, U.K.: Penguin.

Didiza, Thoko. 2005. "Address by Ms. Thoko Didiza, MP Minister of Agriculture and Land Affairs at the National Land Summit, Nasrec Johannesburg, Gauteng 27–30 July 2005." Pretoria: Ministry of Agriculture and Land Affairs.

DLA (Department of Land Affairs). 1997. *White Paper on South African Land Policy*. Pretoria: Government Printers.

———. 2007a. "Annual Report 2005/06. Presentation to the Select Committee on Land and Environmental Affairs. 19 June 2007." Powerpoint presentation. Pretoria: Department of Land Affairs.

———. 2007b. *Annual Report 2006/07*. Pretoria: Government Printers.

Du Toit, Andries, Peter Makhari, Heather Garner, and Alan Roberts. Undated. "Report: Ministerial Review of the Restitution Programme." Unpublished document. Pretoria: Ministry of Agriculture and Land Affairs.

Groenewald, Yolandi. 2005. "Late Land Claimants Want Another Chance." *Mail and Guardian*, 13 July 2005.

Hall, Ruth. 2003. *Rural Restitution*. Bellville, South Africa: Programme for Land and Agrarian Studies, University of the Western Cape (Evaluating Land and Agrarian Reform in South Africa series, no. 2).

———. 2004. "Land Restitution in South Africa: Rights, Development, and the Restrained State." *Canadian Journal of African Studies* 38 (3): 654–71.

Keet, Jacques. 2005. "Land Expropriation." *Mail and Guardian*, 8 November 2005.

Lahiff, Edward. 2007. *State, Market, or the Worst of Both? Experimenting with Market-based Land Reform in South Africa*. Bellville, South Africa: Programme for Land and Agrarian Studies, University of the Western Cape (Occasional Paper no. 30).

May, Julian, and Benjamin Roberts. 2000. *Monitoring and Evaluating the Quality of Life of Land Reform Beneficiaries, 1998/1999*. Summary Report prepared for the Department of Land Affairs. Pretoria: Department of Land Affairs.

National Treasury. 2008. *Estimates of National Expenditure*. Pretoria: Government Printers.

Ntsebeza, Lungisile. 2006. *Democracy Compromised: Chiefs and the Politics of Land in South Africa*. Cape Town: HSRC Press.

Platzky, Laurine, and Cherryl Walker. 1985. *The Surplus People: Forced Removals in South Africa*. Johannesburg: Ravan Press.

SAIRR (South African Institute of Race Relations). 2000. *Race Relations Survey, 1999/2000.* Braamfontein, South Africa: SAIRR.

Steyn, Lala. 1994. "1993 Land Legislation: Its Implications and Implementation." *Review of African Political Economy* 21 (61): 451–57.

Suttner, Raymond, and Jeremy Cronin. 1986. *Thirty Years of the Freedom Charter.* Johannesburg: Ravan Press.

Thomson, Alistair. 2004. "Dispossessed Want 20 Percent of SA's Farmland." *Reuters,* 7 January 2004.

Walker, Cherryl. 2008. *Landmarked: Land Claims and Land Restitution in South Africa.* Cape Town: Jacana Media; and Athens: Ohio University Press.

Wegerif, Marc, Bev Russell, and Irma Grundling. 2005. *Still Searching for Security: Farm Dweller Evictions in South Africa.* Pretoria: Nkuzi Development Association; and Johannesburg: Social Surveys Africa.

Williams, Rhodri. 2007. *The Contemporary Right to Restitution in the Context of Transitional Justice.* New York: International Center for Transitional Justice (Occasional Paper series).

Winkler, Harald. 1994. "Land Reform Strategy: New Methods of Control." *Review of African Political Economy* 21 (61): 445–58.

Xingwana, Lulama. 2007. "Speech for the Land Hand-over Celebration for the Hlabisa-Mpukunyoni Community Claim, Hluhluwe: KwaZulu-Natal." Delivered by the Minister of Agriculture and Land Affairs. Pretoria: Department of Land Affairs.

STATUTES

Constitution of the Republic of South Africa, Act 200 of 1993. Pretoria: Government Printers.

Constitution of the Republic of South Africa, Act 108 of 1996. Pretoria: Government Printers.

Restitution of Land Rights, Act 22 of 1994. Pretoria: Government Printers.

CASE LAW

Alexkor (Pty) Ltd and the Government of the Republic of South Africa v. Richtersveld Community and Others. 2003 19/03 (CC).

NEWSPAPER

This Day, Johannesburg, South Africa.

two

Giving Land Back or Righting Wrongs?

Comparative Issues in the Study of Land Restitution

DERICK FAY AND DEBORAH JAMES

Land dispossession is seen by some as the central political-economic issue of colonialism and central to the creation of modern capitalism. It has rested not only on force but on new forms of property and discipline; it has affirmed Lockean notions of property and civilization, and constructions of racial and ethnic difference. Land restitution promises the redress of such loss—and in so doing it brings the past into the present. It enables former landholders to reclaim spaces and territories that formed the basis of earlier identities and livelihoods. The loss and its later return, like land itself, bridge material and symbolic concerns. Drawing on histories of past loss, individual claimants and informal movements—and governments or nongovernmental organizations (NGOs) working on their behalf—have attempted not only to restore livelihoods but also to reclaim rights and rectify associated injustices and violations. Land restitution thus forces the moral principles of restoration and justice to confront the difficult practices of determining ownership, defining legitimate claimants, and establishing evidence for claims. It is an arena for state formation and nation-building, but also one where alternative forms of governance and counternational identities may emerge. Restitution may combine modernity's romantic aspect, nostalgia for the lost rootedness of landed identity, with its technicist aspect, as restitution is implemented through state bureaucracies and often tied to aspirations of "development."

Land restitution arises from and relies on key social relationships. Community belonging, often framed in terms of ethnicity or autochthony, may enhance the claims of certain dispossessed people but can exclude others. Restitution frequently involves brokerage, as NGO representatives and others mediate between land claimants, landowners, and the state. It also creates new relationships between states and their subjects: land-claiming communities may make claims on the state but also find the state making unexpected claims on their land and livelihoods. It may be a route to full citizenship or lead to new or neotraditional forms of subjection, for it invokes the two visions of nationhood and political order: "one based on a liberal ethos of universal human rights, of free, autonomous citizenship, of individual entitlement; the other assertive of group rights, of ethnic sovereignty, or primordial cultural connection" (Comaroff 1998, 346; cf. Mamdani 1996).

The study of restitution, then, ranges across a variety of intellectual and policy terrains. Although matters such as property, social transition, injustice and redress, citizenship and community, the state and the market are typically thought of as separate, the comparative study of land restitution requires us to think about points of convergence among them. It also prompts us to rethink each in turn. In this chapter we outline some central issues in the study of land restitution.[1]

THEORIZING RESTITUTION

Although scholars have recently questioned the "thingness," or materiality, of property (von Benda-Beckmann, von Benda-Beckmann, and Wiber 2006; Verdery and Humphrey 2004; Strathern 2005), land remains a particularly vexing and contested form of property. It is both material *and* symbolic, a factor of production and a site of belonging and identity (Shipton 1994). The return of spatial territory promises the freedom of autonomy and self-governance, but may be accompanied by the disadvantages of paternalism and even a second-class status in society. Landed property, in cases of restitution, offers the promise of citizenship in the modern state but is also a site where citizenship is fiercely contested.

The contexts of land restitution policies have some typical features worldwide. First, restitution appears in contexts of disjuncture and social change that provide space for demands to redress past injustices, often themselves the product of moments of social rupture. Those who have suffered the loss of a material, territorial basis of identity and livelihood now demand that past wrongs be set right. Second, restitution claims acquire a moral weight from the experience of being wronged and the gravity of things long past. They are based on both grievance and a shared memory of that grievance (Feuchtwang 2003; Rowlands 2004).

Restitution contexts are further defined by the role of the state: it is often a key actor, "both playing the game and making the rules" (Verdery 2003, 81). It may be important in making restitution possible, but it also intervenes to protect the beneficiaries of the process—at least temporarily—from the ravages of the market. Here, the study of restitution intersects with questions of state sovereignty in the transnational contexts of global capitalism (Hansen and Stepputat 2001; Trouillot 2001). In most settings, market-led models of development have supplanted older statist approaches, but returning land to its former owners is seen as a process that cannot be left to the market. The state is required to act as nursemaid, though it may be preparing eventually to set its charges loose in the world.

A further peculiarity is that the state, as part protagonist and part participant, does not aim to create a unified, national citizenry by laying out a single and homogenizing path to progress. Instead, restitution establishes the ground for a distinct kind of citizenship by constituting people as members of communities or groups, often in response to these groups' own insistence that they be seen in this way. The state may thus reinforce the idea of a community as native, indigenous, or autochthonous.

Restitution promises to restore land to specific groups who are understood as having earlier been unfairly dispossessed. It often represents a stage—but not necessarily the final stage—on a long-term set of struggles by such groups. The very fact that restitution is feasible reveals that a part of this intrasocial struggle has already been "won." But this may be only the first step on a long road, with the nature of property relations—and indeed of the social fabric in general—being contested at every point.

By promising to make concrete the past, to make viable what had become mere "history," restitution represents a poignant prospect: the installation of a new set of property relations, predicated on those that are said to have existed at some point in the past. Restitution may appear to offer boundless possibilities for social and political agency (Beyers 2005, 10; 2007). In making such promises it may also pose threats to those with a stake in the dominant order of property relations. Even if the particular pieces of land in question are not of great value in themselves, the symbolic weight attached to their return, and the extent to which property relationships and other sets of social linkages threaten to unravel in the process, are such as to generate fear. Perhaps because of the threats posed, restitution turns out in many cases to be either unachievable or so narrowly circumscribed that it fulfills only the most symbolic purposes.

A TEMPORAL PROCESS

Land issues are, of course, spatial. They are concerned with meaningful ties between people and places. Land restitution, however, focuses attention on the *temporal* aspects of land: the history of a piece of land over time is what defines it as suitable for restitution. Likewise, restitution itself is an extended social process through which property rights are contested and established (cf. Berry 1993).

Viewed comparatively, there are characteristic moments in the "restitution story." The first is dispossession itself, whether through conquest, treaty, expropriation, eviction, sale, or contested and misunderstood transactions. The means of dispossession matter in several ways. First, they affect the endurance of ties between dispossessed people and their land. In temperate regions of North America, dispossession often meant the removal of Native Americans to remote reservations. In southern Africa, in contrast, Europeans often acquired title over land that Africans continued to occupy; paper dispossession might take decades to translate into actual evictions. Second, they affect the kinds of evidence (titles, other archival records, physical traces of occupation, etc.) that will be available. Third, where treaties exist, these may provide a legal basis for future land claims, as in New Zealand and Canada (Bourassa and Strong 2002).

The interim period after dispossession is a second formative time. Again there are significant variations. Is the lost land the home of one's childhood or youth, imbued with nostalgia for a happier, better time? (Dhupelia-Mesthrie; Ellis; Walker, all in this volume). Or did it belong to some distant ancestors, with a connection that may have been forgotten—unimagined—prior to the land claim? Moreover, as time passes, land may be sold and bought in transactions where the cleansing magic of the market appears to wash away the guilt of dispossession; new owners may claim they bought land in a morally neutral transaction and argue that restitution will simply create new injustices (Blancke 2009).

The third formative moment is the creation of a restitution policy. Here one must inquire into the conditions of possibility of restitution: conditions that were clearly absent, for example, for the descendants of English peasants dispossessed of their land through enclosure. Where restitution programs are deemed possible, both the disjuncture experienced as a result of the original dispossession and the emergence of a new social order may facilitate their plausibility. Societies emerging after the end of the Cold War, such as those after apartheid and socialism, are the most obvious examples (see Comaroff and Comaroff 2000; Burawoy and Verdery 1999).

The programs themselves may claim to be comprehensive, even transformative. But in terms of who may claim and where restitution fits in national priorities, they are inevitably limited in scope. Creating a restitution policy entails identifying categories of potential claimants, whether on the basis of history, ethnicity, indigeneity, treaty status, or other markers. As Verdery (2003, 83) has shown, in Eastern Europe this meant asking "which precommunist property order should restitution recreate?" In South Africa, the 1913 cutoff date and the requirement of evident racial discrimination set limits. Creating criteria of legitimacy also creates significant exclusions: by defining those who are not eligible, policy may define those who could be vulnerable under restitution.

Regardless of the scope of policies, gaps may exist between restitution in principle and in practice. In the case of land claims in New York State, USA, and Western Ontario, Canada, the gap is evident in the lengthy negotiations between the federal government and white settler citizens who are reluctant to allow an Indian reservation in their "backyard" (Blancke 2009; Mackey 2005). In South Africa the gap appears in the contrast between the "constitutional priority" afforded land restitution and unrealistically small budgets (Westaway and Minkley 2006; Walker 2000). Without sufficient funds to settle the thousands of land claims, the "promise of the constitution" will remain unfulfilled, as high-minded principles of justice founder on the rocks of hard-nosed practicality.

The fourth formative moment is that of making particular land claims. Restitution policies define eligible categories, but actual land claims typically entail another round of boundary-drawing: concrete groups of people constitute themselves or are constituted as claimants through the brokerage of NGOs, activists, and benevolent—if paternalistic—state agencies. In effect, restitution requires the establishment of new forms of "imagined community" (Anderson 1983). As Ellis (this volume) describes, restitution may be a process through which an "authentic" identity is both required and acquired, whether based on geography, genealogy, language, ethnicity, culture, way of life, or race. Some grounds may prove more effective than others in securing land rights and mobilizing communities; other grounds may alienate potential claimants, who refuse to identify with previously stigmatized categories.

Claimant groups then enter into processes of negotiation and litigation. These may involve a range of "stakeholders," but typically the state is predominant—in institutionally diverse and sometimes contradictory roles as adjudicator, advocate, and opponent (Verdery 2003; cf. Sato; Walker, this volume). As a result, land claims may provide political opportunities but may also create new forms of dependency and opportunities for state control. In Mexico, land claims help constitute the state as a "hope-generating machine" (Nuijten 2003), whereas in Peru, restitution led to the transfer of land to a state-managed institution and resulted, decades later, in renewed demands for restitution (Nuijten and Lorenzo 2009). In South Africa the transfer of land to claimants triggered developmentalist state planning processes that had parallels to apartheid-era interventions (Van Leynseele and Hebinck 2009).

Negotiations may also reveal communities' weaknesses and de facto vulnerability. There was uncomfortable joking among negotiators when the unequal power relations between Canadian and Kluane First Nation negotiators came to the fore (Nadasdy 2009). Communities at Dwesa-Cwebe, South Africa, were dependent on state representatives to access archival evidence regarding their claim, leading to the mistaken perception that their claim might not succeed if pressed in court (Fay 2001). Ultimately, the need for fulfilling state-sanctioned definitions of community might exclude potentially valid claims. A land claim in Australia was rejected because the claimants failed to meet the legally sanctioned definition of a "local descent group," as defined—generations before—by anthropologists (Myers 1986, 147).

Claims processes also require establishing the basis on which *this* group of claimants has a right to *this* piece of land. Ways of proving entitlement can be of key importance where there is active opposition to a claim. In these contexts, social scientists' views of identity and community as fluid and contingent may undermine the conclusive proof required by the legal process, as when anthropologists failed to convince a Massachusetts court of the validity of a native land claim (Clifford 1988) or when a lawyer in the Richtersveld land claim in South Africa argued that anthropologist Suzanne Berzborn's description of the community as "constructed" destabilized its claim.[2]

In South Africa the expectation was that land claims would be "profoundly litigious and adversarial" but "the main problem . . . turned out to be . . . the practical problems that follow after that right has been assented to" (du Toit 2000, 80, 88). Here du Toit identifies the fifth formative moment in restitution: after the land claim has been "won," the hard work begins. Jacob Zuma told the audience at a handover ceremony in 2001, "prepare yourselves, people of Dwesa and Cwebe—development is coming your way!" (Palmer et al. 2002, 275). Such promises inevitably create the possibility of disappointment: a few years later, enmeshed in postsettlement struggles, some of these claimants questioned the decisions of their representatives in the negotiation process (Ntshona, Kraai, and Nomatyindyo 2006).

After the ceremonial transfers, when the politicians have gone home, claimants are confronted with the question of what to do with the land. This may engender "the loss of the loss" (du Toit 2000, 82), as the memory of dispossession loses its salience as a rallying point for unity, and the imagined past is confronted with the practical realities of the present. Unified "communities" may fracture, as in Cape Town's District Six, where fault lines emerged between owners and tenants, and between "coloured" and African claimants, about how (and whether) the past "community" should be reconstituted (Beyers 2009).

Despite the nominal transfer of ownership, there are many examples of how the demands of the state weigh heavily on the posttransfer process. In Peru (Nuijten and Lorenzo 2009), restitution transferred land to state-run institutions, effectively leaving demands for local ownership and control unanswered. In northeast Brazil, claimants were expected to use land communally as a condition for restitution, leading (with some difficulty) to collectivized production on land previously farmed by individual families (French 2009). In South Africa, a discourse of "tradition" and "custom" that was an asset in staking a claim became a liability when state planners demanded that claimants undertake "modern" activities on their newly acquired land (van Leynseele and Hebinck 2009). A key variable in the posttransfer studies in this volume is the degree to which claimants are able to deflect or control the state's interventions (see Conway and Xipu; de Wet and Mgujulwa, this volume).

The posttransfer phase of land restitution often entails resettlement, with all of the pitfalls that entails. Whether resettlement is desirable may depend on the past and present position of the claimants. For the African former residents of District Six (Beyers 2009), the prospect of returning to their former homes held little of the appeal anticipated by the framers of restitution policy; in the contrasting case of Black River, a few miles away, former residents' inability to return made their loss "even more real" (Dhupelia-Mesthrie, this volume). The decision may not be made by claimants: elsewhere in South Africa, state planners' concerns that resettlement will damage the environment or commercial viability of restituted land have led them to discourage resettlement in favor of lease agreements and joint ventures with commercial operators (Palmer, Timmermans, and Fay 2002; Derman, Lahiff, and Sjaastad, this volume).

The sixth and final temporality is the time "beyond restitution," when programs are phased out and claimants no longer receive privileged treatment from the state. Mexico in the 1990s ended a land restitution policy that had existed for most of the twentieth century (Tiedje 2009). Even as the country saw a growing movement for indigenous rights, the neoliberal state pushed for the privatization of *ejidos*: collective landholding structures that were created to allow communities to claim and receive land earlier in the century. With individual title comes the possibility that restitution itself may be "undone" and replaced by a new round of dispossession if newly titled land is sold under adverse circumstances.[3] Granting title that does not allow sale, however, may be perceived as paternalistic and a denial of full property rights (cf. James 2007; Ntsebeza 2005). If claimants lose their restituted land because of market forces, this loss is not typically designated as part of the restitution process.

Recognizing these defining moments in restitution—dispossession, policy formation, community formation, claim-staking, transfer, posttransfer, and postrestitution—allows for comparison across space and time. Case studies from widely differing contexts can be positioned in relation to the process overall, as a basis for comparative reflection.

PROPERTY, COMMUNITY, GOVERNMENT: CITIZEN OR SUBJECT?

The final phases of restitution may never occur. Not only may the process drag on because of bureaucratic delays or extended negotiations between contesting parties; other factors may create a sense of incompleteness. If property entails relations between people and things, restitution juxtaposes the most concrete of objects—land—with abstractions about past social relationships and vague promises about restoration in the future. It also conjoins pragmatic action in the present with invocations of justice.

But in the process of making the property promise come true, restitution often translates into a far narrower achievement. It may restore a hierarchical prior state or a segregated, not liberatory, landscape (Dorondel 2009; Walker, this volume), or give people an unwieldy asset that is more like a liability (Verdery 2004; Derman, Lahiff, and Sjaastad, this volume). Thus, even those to whom the state *has* delivered may feel they have been cheated and require a further, more complete form of restoration. Restitution charged with too burdensome a symbolic and material load may be unable to address the issues it aims to resolve.

The restitution of land is typically associated with certain assumptions. One is that those who have set themselves off from the broader social fabric by returning to this land require separate forms of governance. They are presumed to embody a particular—separate—approach to community living and collective property ownership. But at the same time these property relationships are being institutionalized through or integrated with the market forces permeating the rest of society. Definitions of the relationships between people and things are thus undergoing a transformation, in which claimants' views of property take shape in a complex dialogue between themselves and the broader legal discourse within the state. They assert, contest, or modify their ideas on their right to be recognized, hold property, and be governed, in interaction with the broader social world. In the process, limits to restitution become clear. At the same time, resentment may arise among those outside the process, who are made to "bear the burden" of whatever claims do materialize.

COMMUNITY AND GOVERNANCE:
"NO NATION WITHIN A NATION"

Contemporary restitution typically imposes expectations that people should lay claim to land as communities rather than as individuals. This discourse appears to be a recent phenomenon, a manifestation of what Kuper (2003) calls the "return of the native," with an emphasis on separation and cultural distinction that, in South Africa, may not sit well with the commitment to abolish apartheid's legacy.

Even where notions of "indigeneity" appear less problematic, not all claimants are willing to frame their expectations in these terms. Dissenters may disparage such discourses and the communal landholding that they imply or prefer to formulate claims based on a regionally distinct way of life rather than an indigenous one, as in the case of the Métis of Labrador (Plaice 2009). In South Africa, too, restitution communities have not necessarily been tied to collectivist, "traditional" claims. Some of the earliest cases involved so-called black spots, where mission-educated Africans had bought land under individual freehold title (James, Ngonini, and Nkadimeng 2005; Sato, this volume). Their claims to a privileged status as owners, distinct from tenants with no formal basis for the return of property, have produced contestations between different categories of the dispossessed.

Even where native or indigenous discourses are not readily embraced, expectations of community tend to remain. In South Africa, many misunderstandings over the nature of community identity and ownership have resulted. The state and its agents, basing their approach on a "communalist discourse," have imagined community to be egalitarian and inclusive—perhaps even a proxy for "nation" itself. Claimants, in contrast, often think of it as exclusive (James 2000). In the case of District Six, exclusivist and inclusivist versions of community coexisted and were in contention among claimants (Beyers 2009). State suppositions favored attempts to transfer ownership of farms to groups. One consequence was that communities were expected to take on the tasks of development, social services, and resolution of disputes. The rights and responsibilities for decisions about land use and dispute resolution among communal owners have remained unclear, causing many rural land restitution cases to founder (James 2006; Pienaar 2000).

Notions of community and separation come into tension with ideas about citizenship, sovereignty, nationhood, and "public interest" (Walker, this volume). If claimants, in partial collusion with the state, contend that they are members of a distinct group, their domains remain separate from the broader body politic. Exclusive ownership of land by a group may preclude its integration in matters of authority, law and order, and the provision of services. But autonomy may be accompanied by second-class status: claimants are assigned the character of subjects rather than citizens (Mamdani 1996).

Such claims to autonomy become more controversial when they strike against deeply held national values of political equality. This is evident in the dispute over the Cayuga Nation's land claim in New York: "[O]n reservations, Indian nations exercise their inherent sovereignty as 'domestic, dependent nations.' This struck many citizens and politicians as unfair. Why did Indians have 'special rights' when other Americans did not?" (Blancke 2009; see also Mackey 2005). Those opposed to the claim protested with billboards proclaiming "no nation within a nation." They made frequent reference to dimensions of their citizenship such as the "tax base" to show that *their* land ownership was not tied to "special rights" but reflected obligations incumbent upon all citizens. In this case special pleading generated new forms of special pleading in response. Opponents of restitution also used localist and antigovernmental discourses. They organized on a local basis (as residents of Seneca County rather than as citizens of the United States or of New York State), and their reference to the tax base asserted a local, Lockean claim to state parks—funded with *their* tax dollars—to oppose the equally parochial claims asserted by Indian nations. They claimed to have been politically disenfranchised by a federal legal process that marginalized the input of local residents.

In these and other cases, citizenship is claimed on the basis of being distinct from, rather than part of, the nation as a whole. One can find exceptions, where even as they constitute themselves as groups, claimants simultaneously assert national citizenship: claimants in the Brazilian Northeast flew the national flag while strategically "becoming Indian" (French 2009). But such a strategy of inclusivity may backfire: in Canada, the Labrador Métis claim conjoined regional and national identities but lost out to more compelling "indigenous" claims by Innu and Inuit (Plaice 2009).

THE INSTITUTIONALIZATION OF PROPERTY

Because the state acts as arbiter and implementer of land claims, land restitution is a site where both the authority of the state and the notion of property gain currency (Westaway and Minkley 2006). Participation in Canada's land claims process, for example, forced Kluane First Nation representatives to stake their claims in the language of property:

> Just to engage in land claim negotiations, [they] have had to learn a very different way of thinking about land and animals, a way of thinking that to this day many Kluane people continue to regard with disapproval. Despite this, many of them have put aside their

discomfort with the idea of "owning" land and animals, electing to participate in the land claim process because they see it as the only realistic chance they have to preserve their way of life against increasing encroachment by Euro-Canadians. (Nadasdy 2002, 258)

In Australia, similarly, says Myers (1986, 148), "Certain features of Aboriginal land tenure became 'fetishized' in the claims process. . . . [L]and claims are not indigenous processes, although they attempt to somehow reproduce traditional rights and claims."

Staking claims in the language of property does not mean, however, that property-holders are conceived as unmarked rights-holding individuals. An abstract "owner," devoid of personal or collective history, could not invoke the story of dispossession that restitution requires. Such stories not only lay down a record of claims; they also strengthen claimant "resolve as to the legitimacy of their claims" and may position the claimants strategically in a wider social discourse (Fortmann 1995, 1060–61). In the context of restitution, a successful claim requires compelling stories of loss that enlist the sympathy of powerful outsiders (du Toit 2000).

Such stories position claimants as eligible under a particular restitution policy. But stories of dispossession are not enough. Restitution processes, typically modeled on or taking place through courts, often require "evidence": documents such as title deeds and archival records. These documents are often produced and stored by those potentially opposed to claims. Occasionally, claimants may be able to introduce nontextual forms of evidence, such as grave sites and other physical markers. At Dwesa-Cwebe, South Africa, claimants led representatives of the Land Claims Commission to deep pits where their ancestors had stored maize. Braun (2002, 99) tells how land claimants and their NGO allies in British Columbia identified "culturally modified trees" and then "had to educate the court on how to properly read the forest."

Stories and documentation may not suffice where Lockean claims to property based on labor and "improvement" challenge claims based on prior occupation. Such arguments were commonplace justifications of European colonial land seizures worldwide (Verdery and Humphrey 2004, 4). In New York State opponents of a native land claim fought the transfer of a state park because they had contributed their tax dollars to the "improvement" of the area, creating a locally specific claim on a nominally state-owned public asset (Blancke 2009). Likewise, an opponent of a land claim in the

Brazilian Northeast "saw the land as representative of her father's hard work and ambition" (French 2009).

At the same time, the promise of "improvement" can make land claims more viable. Willingness to participate in "development" contributed to the eligibility of descendants of African slaves for land restitution in Brazil (French 2009). In South Africa, "improvement" has become a near-requirement. Land beneficiaries and policymakers face growing pressure to show that restitution is leading to "development" and "economically beneficial" land use, particularly in the light of declining productivity following the forcible takeover of commercial farms in neighboring Zimbabwe (van Leynseele and Hebinck 2009; see also Aliber et al. and Derman, Lahiff, and Sjaastad, both in this volume).

THE RIGHTS AND WRONGS OF RESTITUTION

Restitution is often thought of as a "right" to rectify earlier "wrongs." In South Africa, many thought of restitution as similar to the Truth and Reconciliation Commission, a way of setting right the record and achieving justice for the victims of apartheid. But the need for justice means that land alone was insufficient redress. Victims require a public acknowledgment of indignities suffered. Something beyond the mere restoration of land—which was their due—"was needed by way of redress for the terrible indignity of having their houses destroyed" (James 2007, 246).

Even in less clear-cut cases, a question lurks in the background: Who must be held responsible for whatever wrongs restitution is aiming to set right? If land is to be reclaimed, who will then lose it?

The state, again "both playing the game and making the rules" (Verdery 2003, 83), may take responsibility and negotiate its way out of the dilemma. In Canada the state appears to privilege restitution but in fact circumvents troublesome land claims in the broader national interest or in the interests of "development" (Nadasdy 2009; Plaice 2009; cf. Walker in this volume). Land claims, however morally weighty, have not precluded military and industrial projects on claimed land. Thus although lip service was paid to the importance of restitution in Canada, it was still judged secondary to matters of broader national interest.

Environmental discourse also enters into restitution, both for and against. Claimants can appeal to the discourses of the "environmentally noble savage" (Redford 1991; cf. Ellis, this volume) and to romantic notions of community resource management (Li 1996). But environmental arguments may benefit those opposed to claims. Writing of New Zealand, Dominy (1995, 365) describes "white settler assertions of native status," which included an environmental discourse and a claim to "a form of cultural and ecological adaptation that . . . enable[d] them to maintain the balance between agricultural production and environmental conservation on a particular property for generations." Even where land is restituted, concerns about conservation may severely restrict claimants' options for the development of their land, as in land claims on protected areas in South Africa (Ntshona, Kraai, and Nomatyindyo 2006; Palmer, Timmermans, and Fay 2002; Kepe, and Robins and van der Waal, both this volume).

Even as it rights some wrongs, restitution may re-create others. A policy may deliberately deny eligibility to some who have lost land. As Verdery explains, restitution in Czechoslovakia and Hungary set de facto limits on the categories of people who might claim land by setting the dates for eligibility at points that postdated the expropriation of land from Jews and Germans. Throughout Eastern Europe, "politicians in all countries . . . tried to select baseline dates that left out significant ethnonational others, who could be sacrificed because they had little electoral weight" (Verdery 2003, 84).

Specific groups of landowners may perceive that they, rather than the "nation," are being singled out to carry the costs of restitution. In response to the fears of the white majority, New Zealand excluded private land from restitution claims and resolved not to purchase private land for purposes of restitution (Bourassa and Strong 2002, 238–40).[4] In Zimbabwe white farmers have been singled out more violently; they have been "haunted by the specter of racialized dispossession" (Moore 2005, ix) and see themselves as being forced to bear the brunt of it. White South African farmers have made similar complaints but may hide this behind expressions of sympathy: "If you grow up with the land you also love it; I can understand their feelings," said one man whose farm had been sold to the state for restoration to its original owners. Such sentiments may, however, mask relief at finding a buyer for their land in a declining agricultural economy (James 2007, 215).

In these cases moral equivalence is asserted. One group of "chosen people" displaces another whose members may feel equally "chosen" and experience themselves as wronged if made to bear the cost of a broader project of social justice. These costs reflect the wider political and sociolegal context, which shapes how far restitution claims are allowed to occupy the moral high ground.

How then does the South African experience with restitution differ, if at all, from those others discussed here? In advanced capitalist economies where "first nation" descendants are now a tiny minority, successful restitution claims—for all their symbolic and political significance for those making them—are likely to have only minimal effects on prevailing systems of property rights and the economy. By contrast, in some European countries in the former Soviet bloc, the process of restitution concerns the transfer of landed property relatively recently seized by the state. South Africa is distinct from both in that, first, restitution affects not only state land but also threatens private property rights established through its long history of racialized dispossession; and second, restitution is associated with the redistribution of an asset that—perhaps too optimistically—is seen as making a potentially significant difference to the livelihood prospects of those (re)gaining the land, depending on its size, quality, and location.[5]

Everywhere the work of restitution remains unfinished, a reminder of histories of colonial and socialist dispossession. In Canada in 2003, 13 "comprehensive" land claims had been settled (encompassing about 40 percent of Canadian territory) whereas more than 70 remained under negotiation, alongside the settlement of 251 "specific" claims out of 1,185 submissions (Minister of Indian Affairs and Northern Development 2003, 8–11). New Zealand's Waitangi Tribunal had received 779 claims by 1999 and planned to entertain new claims through 2010 (Bourassa and Strong 2002, 243). Romania is perhaps the most extreme example. Following Law 18 of 1991, providing for liquidation of collective farms and restitution to prior owners, there were about 6,200,000 claims: "[I]n a 1998 interview, the Romanian Minister of Justice stated that Law 18 had produced the largest number of court cases in the history of Romanian jurisprudence" (Verdery 2003, 97).

Diverse experiences show that restitution is no panacea for rural poverty or underdevelopment; claimants are all too likely to face disappointment without other kinds of support to make land rights effective for production and livelihoods (Verdery 2003, 20). That restitution may disappoint seems almost inevitable, given the symbolic weight ascribed to it by claimants and activists alike. Nevertheless, it is also a persistent source of hope. This hope may entrench the state bureaucracy's "hope-generating machine" (Nuijten 2003), but it may also promise political and economic autonomy.

Legacies of dispossession persist: loss of land is not a onetime event, but an ongoing process that continues to shape the life chances of those affected and their descendants (Hart 2002, 39; Murray 1992). Likewise, demands for restitution seem unlikely to cease as states and citizens around the world confront legacies of colonialism and socialism. As claimants continue to organize, creating new forms of community and relationships with the state, restitution continues to offer a fruitful terrain for scholars seeking to understand the reworking of property and citizenship in contexts of political transformation; the politics of injustice and redress; the state and the market; and the place of memory in the present.

NOTES

1. This chapter draws upon a panel at the 2005 Annual Meeting of the American Anthropological Association and the introduction to Fay and James 2009.

2. "Identity of Richtersvelders under Scrutiny," *Sunday Times,* Johannesburg, 4 May 2005. http://www.suntimes.co.za/zones/sundaytimesnew/newsst/newsst1115212706.aspx.

3. In the United States in the late nineteenth century, sales of newly individually titled land among the Coeur d'Alene Indians led to "the irrevocable loss of approximately 84 percent of the tribal holdings, a total economic and political destruction of the tribal entity, and an almost complete loss of individual initiative" (Cotroneo and Dozier 1974, 405–6).

4. This had the unintended effect of making farmers who *lease* state-owned land particularly vulnerable to restitution claims (Dominy 1995).

5. We are grateful to Henry Bernstein for pointing out these key differences.

REFERENCES

Anderson, Benedict. 1983. *Imagined Communities: Reflections on the Origins and Spread of Nationalism.* London: Verso.

Berry, Sara. 1993. *No Condition Is Permanent: The Social Dynamics of Agrarian Change in Sub-Saharan Africa.* Madison: University of Wisconsin Press.

Beyers, Christiaan. 2005. "Land Restitution in District Six, Cape Town: Community, Citizenship and Social Exclusion." PhD diss., Sussex University.

———. 2007. "Land Restitution's 'Rights-Communities': The District Six Case." *Journal of Southern African Studies* 33 (2): 267–85.

———. 2009. "The Will-to-Community: Between Loss and Reclamation in Cape Town." In *The Rights and Wrongs of Land Restitution: "Restoring What Was Ours,"* ed. Derick Fay and Deborah James, 141–62. London: Routledge-Cavendish.

Blancke, Brian. 2009. "'We'll Never Give In to the Indians': Opposition to Restitution in New York State." In *The Rights and Wrongs of Land Restitution: "Restoring What Was Ours,"* ed. Derick Fay and Deborah James, 235–60. London: Routledge-Cavendish.

Bourassa, Steven, and Ann Louise Strong. 2002. "Restitution of Land to New Zealand Maori: The Role of Social Structure." *Pacific Affairs* 75 (2): 227–60.

Braun, Bruce. 2002. *The Intemperate Rainforest: Nature, Culture, and Power on Canada's West Coast.* Minneapolis: University of Minnesota Press.

Burawoy, Michael, and Katherine Verdery. 1999. Introduction to *Uncertain Transition: Ethnographies of Change in the Post-Socialist World,* ed. Michael Burawoy and Kathleen Verdery, 1–18. Oxford: Rowman and Littlefield.

Clifford, James. 1988. *The Predicament of Culture: Twentieth-Century Ethnography, Literature, and Art.* Cambridge, MA: Harvard University Press.

Comaroff, Jean, and John L. Comaroff. 2000. "Millennial Capitalism: First Thoughts on a Second Coming." *Public Culture* 12 (2): 291–343.

Comaroff, John L. 1998. "Reflections on the Colonial State in South Africa and Elsewhere: Fragments, Factions, Facts, and Fictions." *Social Identities* 4 (3): 321–61.

Cotroneo, R., and J. Dozier. 1974. "A Time of Disintegration: The Coeur D'Alene and the Dawes Act." *Western Historical Quarterly* 5 (4): 405–19.

Dominy, Michelle. 1995. "White Settler Assertions of Native Status." *American Ethnologist* 22 (2): 358–74.

Dorondel, Stefan. 2009. "'They Should Be Killed': Forest Restitution, Ethnic Groups, and Patronage in Postsocialist Romania." In *The Rights and Wrongs of Land Restitution: "Restoring What Was Ours,"* ed. Derick Fay and Deborah James, 43–66. London: Routledge-Cavendish.

du Toit, Andries. 2000. "The End of Restitution: Getting Real about Land Claims." In *At the Crossroads: Land and Agrarian Reform in South Africa into the 21st Century,* ed. Ben Cousins, 75–91. Cape Town and Johannesburg: University of the Western Cape and National Land Committee.

Fay, Derick. 2001. "Oral and Written Evidence in South Africa's Land Claims Process: The Case of Dwesa-Cwebe Nature Reserve." Unpublished paper presented at Oral History Association Annual Meeting, St Louis, October 2001.

Fay, Derick, and Deborah James, eds. 2009. *The Rights and Wrongs of Land Restitution: "Restoring What Was Ours."* London: Routledge-Cavendish.

Feuchtwang, Stephan. 2003. "Loss, Transmissions, Recognitions, Authorisations." In *Regimes of Memory,* ed. K. Hodgkin and S. Radstone, 76–90. London: Routledge.

Fortmann, Louise. 1995. "Talking Claims: Discursive Strategies in Contesting Property." *World Development* 23 (6): 1053–63.

French, Jan Hoffman. 2009. "Ethnoracial Land Restitution: Finding Indians and Fugitive Slave Descendants in the Brazilian Northeast." In *The Rights and Wrongs of Land Restitution: "Restoring What Was Ours,"* ed. Derick Fay and Deborah James, 123–40. London: Routledge-Cavendish.

Hansen, Thomas Blom, and Finn Stepputat. 2001. Introduction to *States of Imagination: Ethnographic Explorations of the Postcolonial State,* ed. Thomas Blom Hansen and Finn Stepputat, 1–40. Durham, NC: Duke University Press.

Hart, Gillian. 2002. *Disabling Globalization: Places of Power in Post-apartheid South Africa.* Berkeley: University of California Press.

James, Deborah. 2000. "'After Years in the Wilderness': Development and the Discourse of Land Claims in the New South Africa." *Journal of Peasant Studies* 27 (3): 142–61.

———. 2006. "The Tragedy of the Private: Owners, Communities and the State in South Africa." In *Changing Properties of Property,* ed. F. von Benda-Beckmann, K. von Benda-Beckmann, and M. Wiber, 243–68. Oxford: Berghahn.

———. 2007. *Gaining Ground? "Rights" and "Property" in South African Land Reform.* London: Glasshouse Press.

James, Deborah, Alex Xola Ngonini, and Geoffrey Mphahle Nkadimeng. 2005. "(Re)constituting Class?: Owners, Tenants, and the Politics of Land Reform in Mpumalanga." *Journal of Southern African Studies* 31 (4): 825–44.

Li, Tania Murray, 1996. "Images of Community: Discourse and Strategy in Property Relations." *Development and Change* 27 (3): 501–27.

Kuper, Adam. 2003. "The Return of the Native." *Current Anthropology* 44 (3): 389–95.

Mackey, Eva 2005. "Universal Rights in Conflict: 'Backlash' and 'Benevolent Resistance' to Indigenous Land Rights." *Anthropology Today* 21 (2):14–20.

Mamdani, Mahmood. 1996. *Citizen and Subject: Contemporary Africa and the Legacy of Late Colonialism.* Princeton, NJ: Princeton University Press.

Minister of Indian Affairs and Northern Development. 2003. "Resolving Aboriginal Claims: A Practical Guide to Canadian Experiences." Ottawa: Minister of Public Works and Government Services Canada.

Moore, Donald. 2005. *Suffering for Territory: Race, Place, and Power in Zimbabwe.* Durham, NC: Duke University Press.

Murray, Colin. 1992. *Black Mountain: Land, Class, and Power in the Eastern Orange Free State, 1880s–1980s.* Johannesburg: Witwatersrand University Press.

Myers, Fred. 1986. "The Politics of Representation: Anthropological Discourse and Australian Aborigines." *American Ethnologist* 13 (1): 138–53.

Nadasdy, Paul. 2002. "Property and Aboriginal Land Claims in the Canadian Subarctic: Some Theoretical Considerations." *American Anthropologist* 104 (1): 247–61.

———. 2009. "The Antithesis of Restitution? A Note on the Dynamics of Land Negotiations in the Yukon, Canada." In *The Rights and Wrongs of Land Restitution: "Restoring What Was Ours,"* ed. Derick Fay and Deborah James, 85–98. London: Routledge-Cavendish.

Ntsebeza, Lungisile. 2005. *Democracy Compromised: Chiefs and the Politics of the Land in South Africa.* Leiden: Brill.

Ntshona, Zolile, Mcebisi Kraai, Nandipa Nomatyindyo. 2006. "Rights Enshrined but Rights Denied? Post-Settlement Struggles in Dwesa-Cwebe in the Eastern Cape." Paper presented at the conference Land, Memory, Reconstruction, and Justice: Perspectives on Land Restitution in South Africa, Houw Hoek, September 2006.

Nuijten, Monique. 2003. *Power, Community, and the State: The Political Anthropology of Organisation in Mexico.* London: Pluto Press.

Nuijten, Monique, and David Lorenzo. 2009. "*Dueños de Todo y de Nada!* [Owners of All and Nothing]: Restitution of Indian Territories in the Central Andes of Peru." In *The Rights and Wrongs of Land Restitution: "Restoring What Was Ours,"* ed. Derick Fay and Deborah James, 185–209. London: Routledge-Cavendish.

Palmer, Robin, Derick Fay, Hermann Timmermans, and Christo Fabricius. 2002. "A Development Vision for Dwesa-Cwebe." In *From Confrontation to Negotiation on South Africa's Wild Coast: Conservation, Land Reform, and Tourism Development at Dwesa-Cwebe Nature Reserve,* ed. Robin Palmer, Hermann Timmermans, and Derick Fay, 272–305. Pretoria: Human Sciences Research Council.

Palmer, Robin, Hermann Timmermans, and Derick Fay, eds. 2002. *From Confrontation to Negotiation on South Africa's Wild Coast: Conservation, Land Reform, and Tourism Development at Dwesa-Cwebe Nature Reserve.* Pretoria: Human Sciences Research Council.

Pienaar, Kobus. 2000. "'Communal' Property Institutional Arrangements: A Second Bite." In *At the Crossroads: Land and Agrarian Reform in South Africa into the 21st Century,* ed. Ben Cousins, 322–39. Cape Town and Johannesburg: University of the Western Cape and National Land Committee.

Plaice, Evelyn. 2009. "The Lie of the Land: Identity Politics and the Canadian Land Claims Process in Labrador." In *The Rights and Wrongs of Land Restitution: "Restoring What Was Ours,"* ed. Derick Fay and Deborah James, 67–84. London: Routledge-Cavendish.

Povinelli, Elizabeth. 2004. "Cultural Recognition—At Home in the Violence of Recognition." In *Property in Question: Value Transformation in the Global Economy,* ed. Kathleen Verdery and Caroline Humphrey, 185–206. Oxford: Berg.

Redford, Kent. 1991. "The Ecologically Noble Savage." *Cultural Survival Quarterly* 15 (1): 46–48.

Rowlands, Michael. 2004. "Cultural Rights and Wrongs: Uses of the Concept of Property." In *Property in Question: Value Transformation in the Global Economy,* ed. Kathleen Verdery and Caroline Humphrey, 207–26. Oxford: Berg.

Shipton, Parker. 1994. "Land and Culture in Tropical Africa: Soils, Symbols, and the Metaphysics of the Mundane." *Annual Review of Anthropology* 23:347–77.

Strathern, Marilyn. 2005. "Land: Tangible or Intangible Property." Amnesty International lecture, Oxford.

Tiedje, Kristina. 2009. "Que Sucede Con *Procede?* The End of Land Restitution in Rural Mexico." In *The Rights and Wrongs of Land Restitution: "Restoring What Was Ours,"* ed. Derick Fay and Deborah James, 209–34. London: Routledge-Cavendish.

Trouillot, Michel-Rolph. 2001. "The Anthropology of the State in the Age of Globalization." *Current Anthropology* 42 (1): 125–38.

Van Leynseele, Yves, and Paul Hebinck. 2009. "Through the Prism: 'Shifting Articulations' and Local Reworking of Land Restitution Settlements in South Africa." In *The Rights and Wrongs of Land Restitution: "Restoring What Was Ours,"* ed. Derick Fay and Deborah James, 163–84. London: Routledge-Cavendish.

Verdery, Katherine. 1996. *What Was Socialism, and What Comes Next?* Princeton, NJ: Princeton University Press.

———. 1999. "Fuzzy Property: Rights, Power, and Identity in Transylvania's Decollectivization." In *Uncertain Transition: Ethnographies of Change in the Post-Socialist World,* ed. Michael Burawoy and Kathleen Verdery, 53–82. Oxford: Rowman and Littlefield.

———. 2003. *The Vanishing Hectare: Property and Value in Post-Socialist Romania.* Ithaca, NY: Cornell University Press.

———. 2004. "The Obligations of Ownership: Restoring Rights to Land in Postsocialist Transylvania." In *Property in Question: Value Transformation in the Global Economy,* ed. Kathleen Verdery and Caroline Humphrey, 139–60. Oxford: Berg.

Verdery, Katherine, and Caroline Humphrey. 2004. "Introduction: Raising Questions about Property." In *Property in Question: Value Transformation in the Global Economy,* ed. Kathleen Verdery and Caroline Humphrey, 1–28. Oxford: Berg.

von Benda-Beckmann, Franz, Keebet von Benda-Beckmann, and Melanie Wiber, eds. *Changing Properties of Property.* Oxford: Berghahn.

Walker, Cherryl. 2000. "Relocating Restitution." *Transformation* 44:1–16.

Westaway, Ashley, and Gary Minkley. 2006. "Rights versus Might: Betterment-related Restitution and the 'Constitutive Outside' of South Africa's New Capitalist Modernity." Paper presented at the conference Land, Memory, Reconstruction, and Justice: Perspectives on Land Restitution in South Africa, Houw Hoek, September 2006.

Yashar, Deborah. 2005. *Contesting Citizenship in Latin America: The Rise of Indigenous Movements and the Postliberal Challenge.* Cambridge: Cambridge University Press.

NEWSPAPER

Sunday Times, Johannesburg, South Africa.

three

Change through Jurisprudence

*The Role of the Courts in
Broadening the Scope of Restitution*

HANRI MOSTERT

South African land reform legislation has two major objectives: (1) to make good the injustices of past spatial discrimination based on race and (2) to address the massive underdevelopment resulting from such policies. The aim of restitution has been widely understood as falling squarely within the first objective. Essentially "backward-looking" (Gross 2004, 47), its primary goal is to redress the hardships caused by forced removals after 1913. Although part of the broader land reform program, its focus on past injustices makes it supposedly the most contained aspect of this program (Freedman 2003, 315). Yet restitution is popularly (even if mistakenly) often perceived as the "heartbeat" of land reform.

At the 2005 National Land Summit of the Department of Land Affairs (DLA), activists severely criticized the restricted scope and duration of the program. This event underscored popular expectation that restitution should contribute significantly to the transition in relationships to land from exclusionary and discriminatory to inclusive and accommodating. In the debate about reopening the restitution process, some delegates argued for legislative changes to render land expropriation a more effective instrument for speeding up the process. Delegates also stressed the need for alternatives to restitution-in-kind or in-cash (DLA 2005). The success of the restitution program was projected as increasingly dependent on partnerships between claimants, nongovernmental organizations (NGOs), government departments, and former landowners.

What is striking is how little attention was paid to the role of the judiciary. In this chapter I examine the judiciary as a powerful institution for addressing shortfalls in the restitution program. I argue that the judiciary's evolving understanding of the entry requirements for restitution has influenced the scope of the program and created new possibilities for the development of land law, possibilities that are not yet fully exploited. To illustrate this, I analyze a cross-section of decisions from the Land Claims Court (LCC), the Supreme Court of Appeal, and the Constitutional Court. I begin with a brief consideration of the constitutional background and statutory parameters for restitution. I then consider the judicial treatment of the entry requirements for restitution, focusing specifically on how links have been established between the concepts of "land" and "community" in selected community claims, in particular *Kranspoort, Richtersveld,* and *Ndebele-Ndzundza*. Thereafter I examine the judiciary's evolving treatment of the requirements around "discrimination" and "dispossession," in these and other cases, including *Slamdien* and restitution claims by white farmers. This suggests that the broadened understanding of restitution extends to individual as well as communal claims.

CONSTITUTIONAL BACKGROUND AND STATUTORY PARAMETERS

Activist dissatisfaction reflected at the 2005 Land Summit may be better understood against the backdrop of constitutional developments between 1990 and 1997. To appreciate the role of the judiciary since then, it is necessary to look briefly at the framework that was established for restitution, in particular the relationship between administrative and judicial structures.

Restitution was central to the land reform program envisaged by the Interim Constitution of 1993. During the drafting of the final Constitution of 1996, the negotiated compromise on restitution (see Hall, this volume) was retained and reinforced. A fundamental commitment to a broad land reform program, embracing restitution, redistribution, and tenure reform, now forms part of the property clause in the chapter on human rights. The constitutional right to restitution is incorporated in section 25(7) and forms part of what van der Walt (2005, 12–13) describes as the "reform purpose" of the property clause. In practice, however, the constitutional signal that land reform is a fundamental necessity was overshadowed by the challenges of land policy implementation after 1995 (Walker 2005, 816). The courts were left to spell out the implications of the right to restitution in the property clause.

The restitution process is now primarily administrative rather than adjudicatory. This was achieved by the insertion of section 42D into the Restitution Act in 1999. The amendment was promulgated because of concerns that the court-driven process was proving too antagonistic and slow. It gave the minister of land affairs powers to make restitution awards based on negotiated agreements and facilitated an exponential increase in the number of settled claims. However, the LCC still plays an important role in cases where the Commission on Restitution of Land Rights (CRLR) cannot achieve negotiated settlements. It also reviews decisions of the CRLR, considers appeals, and provides clarity on issues of interpretation. Direct access to the LCC is also possible in terms of section 38B(1) of the Restitution Act. If claimants elect this approach, it is not necessary for them to lodge a claim with the CRLR as well.

JUDICIAL TREATMENT OF THE ENTRY REQUIREMENTS

The main legislative instrument for determining the scope of the restitution program is the set of qualification criteria in section 2(1) of the Restitution Act, read with the definitions in section 1. For a claim to succeed, the claimant has to be either an individual (or a direct descendant) or a community (or part of a community) whose rights in land were "derived from shared rules determining access to land held in common by the group." The claimant has to have been dispossessed of "a right or rights in land" after 19 June 1913 because of "racially discriminatory laws or practices." Further, the claimants should not have received just and equitable compensation in respect of the original dispossession, and claims had to be lodged before 31 December 1998.

Van der Walt (2001, 283 ff.) has suggested that the restitution program's ability to navigate South Africa's biased land law system and promote a more diverse set of land relations is questionable, especially for communal land. Yet the approach of the Supreme Court of Appeal, in particular, and the Constitutional Court has significantly affected the transformation of core concepts in land law, for instance regarding the definition of claimants' "rights in land." Where courts have, additionally, given content to the concept of "community," the effect on existing property law is even more noticeable. Also significant is their interpretation of "dispossession" and "discrimination," and the way these are perceived, judicially, to influence each other.

THE INTERPRETATION OF "LAND" AND "COMMUNITY"

The South African legal system has always been biased toward westernized forms of ownership and land title (Freedman 2003). The primary conception of ownership is hierarchical, along the lines of civil law. It elevates ownership above other types of land control and, accordingly, affords it better protection (Mostert 2003; van der Walt 1999). Yet the Restitution Act acknowledges a broad range of rights in land, including the interest of a labor tenant, a customary interest, the interests of a beneficiary owner or a trust, and the "beneficial occupation" of the land. It can thus be used to transform ingrained ideas about land title.

The very nature of the injustices to be rectified through restitution reflects how many victims of dispossession never had more than tenuous occupation of land (Freedman 2003, 315). Communal land tenure especially suffered under the biased protective measures of South Africa's land law. The statistics of the restitution program underscore the importance of communal tenure for many South Africans. Rural claims represent only 28 percent of the total number of lodged claims, but they account for approximately 90 percent of all restitution beneficiaries; claims rooted in communal tenure involve large numbers of individuals (Portfolio Committee 2005).

The focus in the Restitution Act on the manner in which claimants used and controlled land establishes a link between the type of land rights that are eligible for restitution and the communal element of particular claims. In what follows, I trace the noticeable progression in the judicial treatment of the concept of "community" and "land" in the *Kranspoort, Richtersveld,* and *Ndebele-Ndzundza* claims.[1] The *Kranspoort* judgment (LCC 2000) demonstrated the need for some continued element of community cohesion for the successful implementation of a communal land claim. The decisions of the Supreme Court of Appeal and Constitutional Court in the *Richtersveld* case (SCA 2003; CC 2004) walked a tightrope between acknowledging the lack of a legislative requirement of communal cohesion and considering it anyway in this particular case. In the *Ndebele-Ndzundza* case (SCA 2005), the Supreme Court of Appeal engaged in a new way with communal and cultural attributes. (On the first two cases see also Dodson, this volume.)

Kranspoort

The decision of the LCC *In re Kranspoort Community* entailed a consideration of the concept of "community." The case involved an application for the restoration of land rights dispossessed under the Group Areas Act, under circumstances that caused major divisions within the community (see Freedman 2003). In considering whether the claimants indeed formed part of a "community," the court held that consideration of the identities of those making up the community was legitimate, even if not decisive, as it helped determine whether there was an element of commonality within the community at the time of dispossession (LCC [46]).

After the LCC had found that the only interest the claimants could rely on was that of beneficial occupation of the land for more than ten years and then decided to upgrade these rights to ownership in its restoration order, it dealt with various problems around the order. A major problem was that what remained of the original community was fragmented and poorly organized. The entry requirements in section 2 of the Restitution Act (read with the definitions) require no more than shared rules around land for a community claim to pass the threshold—the definition of "community" does not specify continued existence or any other definitive attribute. The LCC nevertheless assumed that some element of continued community cohesion was vital (LCC [34] ff.) and compelled claimants, through the restoration order, to form a communal property association (CPA) to ensure this. The decision thus demonstrates that although "sufficient cohesion" and "communality" do not qualify the definition of "community" at the entry level for claims, these qualifiers can affect the restitution order.

Richtersveld

In subsequent case law, the link between the communal element of particular claims and the rights to land that were reclaimed became even more pronounced. This judicial development is particularly evident in the dispute between the Richtersveld community and the state-controlled diamond-mining corporation Alexkor.

The Richtersveld is located to the south of the Garib (Orange) River. The people of the Richtersveld descend from various Khoi-San tribes that merged to become the Nama people. Britain annexed the land in 1847, thereby causing the Nama to lose sovereignty. However, the Richtersvelders were progressively denied access to their land only after the discovery of diamonds in the area in 1925. Prospecting and mining rights were awarded to a state-owned diamond-mining corporation, which eventually converted into a private stock company (Alexkor), with the state its largest shareholder. After 1994 Alexkor opposed the Richtersveld people's claim to restitution, leading to a protracted court battle that provided ample opportunity for the development of various aspects of land and restitution law, including the relationship between communal claims and land rights.

Various judicial decisions handed down in the course of this dispute provided evidence that some of the qualifying criteria of the Restitution Act were problematic. First, the date of the initial dispossession, 1847, fell well outside the cutoff date of 1913. It was also uncertain whether the Richtersveld people had any acknowledged "rights in land" under the act, even supposing these had survived annexation. It was also difficult to give content to these rights (LCC par [46]; SCA par [36]–[43]; CC par [70]–[82]). Further, the state argued that the dispossession after 1913 was in terms of the Precious Stones Act 44 of 1927 and thus not the result of racial discrimination (LCC par [83]–[92]; SCA par [97]). Although all these matters were addressed through the judicial process, the focus of this discussion is on the judiciary's treatment of the communal nature of the land rights and the link drawn between discrimination and dispossession.

The concept of landownership received judicial consideration at various levels, with comparative law playing an important part. In other commonwealth jurisdictions such as Canada, the United States, Australia, and New Zealand where disputes about the restoration of ancestral lands are adjudicated, solutions usually pivot on the doctrine of aboriginal title (see inter alia Lehmann 2004; Bennett and Powell 2005; Pienaar 2005a; Choudree 1994; Reilly 2000; Hocking 1999). The term "aboriginal title," or "native title," refers, broadly, to the proprietary, customary-law interests in land of indigenous communities and is used mainly in common-law jurisdictions (McNeil 1989; Ülgen 2002; Lehmann 2004). The doctrine recognizes that land was occupied by aboriginal or indigenous peoples before the advent of colonization and that these precolonial rights survived colonization, subject to their subsequent extinguishment by new governments (McNeil 1989). The doctrine applies, therefore, to lands occupied by indigenous people when the Crown acquired sovereignty, including rights to the subsurface and minerals. The doctrine has been invoked by various indigenous communities in postcolonial states, either to reclaim their ancestral lands or to assert cultural rights or rights to self-determination. However, even in perceived progressive judgments based on aboriginal title—such as the Australian case of *Mabo v. Queensland* (No. 2)—the doctrine appears to be more spectacular on paper than in practice (see Hoq 2002; Mostert and Fitzpatrick 2004; Anghie 1999; Reilly 2000).

Of major significance here is that in all the Richtersveld decisions the doctrine of aboriginal title was either ignored or even *rejected* as a means to resolve this particular dispute (LCC, [44]–[53]; SCA, [43]; CC, [34]–[37]). The judgments of the Appeal Court and the Constitutional Court show that a purposive reading of the Restitution Act, along with a progressive interpretation that emphasizes the role of customary law, renders reliance on aboriginal title unnecessary. Yet comparative aboriginal title literature played an integral part in the Appeal Court's identification of the Richtersveld community's right as a "customary-law interest in land" (Brink 2005, 181 ff.). However, the judiciary's indirect reliance on aboriginal title did not open a Pandora's box of claims by all those who lost land in the colonial era. To this extent, the Richtersveld judgments are in line with the original goals of the government's restitution policy, which excluded colonial dispossession from the scope of the act.

Yet the decisions do represent a major turn in South African jurisprudence on land rights. Whereas the LCC was unwilling to acknowledge anything beyond "beneficial occupation" as the basis of the Richtersveld community's claim (LCC [1], [4]), the Appeal Court described their "customary law interest" as something "akin" to common-law landownership and proceeded to deal with it on the basis of conventional principles of landownership (SCA [8], [29]). For its part, the Constitutional Court typified the community's right as one of "indigenous law ownership" (CC [49], [70]–[82], [87]), arguing that the time has come for South African courts to take legal pluralism seriously (CC [45]–[51]).

"Indigenous law ownership" as conceptualized by the Constitutional Court is essentially communal. It has its "own values and norms" and evolved according to the needs of the community (CC [53]–[58], [62]). In short, it is distinct from common-law ownership, which in South African law refers to the comprehensive nature of the real right bestowed upon the holder. It has been claimed that in principle ownership provides complete control over a thing, along with its exclusive enjoyment within the limits of the law (see van der Merwe 1989, 171). Some analysts have expressed unease with the definition and tried to provide alternatives that attribute more relativity to the concept of ownership and acknowledge its inherent restrictions (van der Walt and Pienaar 2006, 41) or refer to the relationship between ownership and its entitlements (Lewis 1985, 242). Nevertheless, the standard definition is deeply ingrained as a starting point in resolving issues about landownership.

However, the Constitutional Court's treatment of indigenous law ownership suggests that future attempts to give content to the concept of landownership will be imbued with other considerations than the current Eurocentric, civil-law view of ownership as unified and individualized, affording exclusive entitlements and absolute protection against interference. The Constitutional Court's typification of indigenous law ownership highlights the concept of "community" (see Pienaar 2005b, 61–70). In terms of the Restitution Act's definition of "community," which focuses on the manner in which the group uses and controls land, the Richtersveld people indisputably constituted a community. Nevertheless the Supreme Court of Appeal entertained evidence about their shared culture, language, religion, social and political structures, customs, and lifestyle to prove the existence of customary rules relating to land use (SCA, [17]–[18]). Furthermore, judicial consideration of the communal element of the claim influenced adjudication about the quality of the "indigenous" land rights at stake in this particular case. The subtle link drawn between the indigeneity of the community and the land rights of its members was informed largely by comparative law on aboriginal title (SCA [23]–[24]; (CC) [52]–[55]), even though the relevance of the latter was denied or downplayed. The way these precedents were used reinforced the encapsulation of Richtersveld society as static and custom-bound; this meant justice could be ensured for them without creating expectations of broad-based restitution for the many groups who were dispossessed in similar ways but are now dispersed and uncohesive (see Mostert and Fitzpatrick 2004).

Ndebele-Ndzundza

A challenge for restitution is that apartheid policies often resulted in the dispersal of communities. This affects claims by groups that were subjected to even more disruptive histories than the Richtersveld people. It was expected that the use of comparative aboriginal-title law would perpetuate the restrictive approach toward restitution (Mostert and Fitzpatrick 2004). Yet, paradoxically, the ethnicity of particular claimants seems to have encouraged more lenient judicial approaches and provided further opportunities for the development of land law and the extension of the scope of the restitution program. This is illustrated by the case of *Prinsloo & Another v. Ndebele-Ndzundza Community & Others* (SCA 2005).

The Ndebele-Ndzundza trace their history to a large tribal group that occupied land in present-day Mpumalanga in the precolonial era (SCA [1]–[7]) but was subsequently dispersed as a result of conflict with other groups and war with white settlers. Their ancestral lands were distributed among white settlers, and people scattered across white-owned farms as indentured laborers. The Ndzundza formed a specific subgroup that had remained longest on the farm subject to the restitution claim. They were eventually removed in terms of the Natives Land Act of 1913 and the Native Trust and Land Act of 1936. Although the land was registered as white-owned, it was never occupied by whites.

In some ways the community's claim for restoration fits under the ambit of the Restitution Act more easily than the *Richtersveld* case. It was, however, referred to the courts because of uncertainty about whether the requirement of communality was met and whether the Ndzundza continued to hold rights after the various tribal and settlers wars (LCC [18]; SCA [1], [11]). The Appeal Court's decision reinforced the link between the "communal" nature of restitution claims and the rights held: it found that the removal of the Ndzundza from their land did not fetter the communal nature of their land tenure arrangements (SCA [11]–[31]). Ironically, the racially derogatory name given the land under white ownership—that of *Kafferskraal*—was decisive in supporting a ruling that the land rights of the Ndzundza had not been extinguished by the earlier wars. Accordingly they still held interests in the land when racially discriminatory laws caused their relocation.

The Appeal Court then considered the content of the rights held by the Ndzundza by juxtaposing ethnological evidence about their occupation of the land against a particular brand of scholarship on the content of conventional (common-law) ownership, which regards ownership as a "bundle of rights" (SCA [32–40]). This approach, often used in Anglo-American jurisprudence, depicts ownership as a collection of rights that are severable and may be disposed of at will by the owner or someone with relevant authority (Honoré 1961; Lewis 1985, 1987; van der Walt 1995). Until now South African property law has shown more support for the idea of ownership as unified, hegemonic, and hierarchical, as developed in the civil-law jurisdictions of Europe (van der Walt 1999; Mostert 2003). This depicts ownership as a right elevated above other less comprehensive rights and stresses the residuality of ownership, even where the right is, substantively, without content. The court's opting for the "bundle-of-rights" scholarship enabled a finding that the Ndzundza's indigenous, communal ownership could coexist alongside the superimposed white individual title. There was, accordingly, no need for the court to look to the comparative literature on aboriginal title.

The *Ndebele-Ndzunza* case underscores the manner in which particular constructs of indigenous culture may affect the development of new forms of rights in South Africa. The Appeal Court's remark that "registered title is recognized as significant, but does not afford unblemished primacy" signifies a rejection of a hierarchical, civil-law system of property rights in favor of a more diversified model.

Assessment

The Ndebele-Ndzundza cases, as indeed the others discussed, cannot be taken to suggest that conceptions about the primacy of ownership based on registered title are fading. On the contrary, the judiciary still seems intent on ensuring that what is restored amounts to legally secure title. In the process of defining these rights, however, it has become necessary for the courts to move away from a *status quo ante* mind-set and to work creatively with other models of land control. They are fostering the emergence of a variety of forms of title, all on a par with ownership and potentially coexisting over the same land (see van der Walt 2001, 283 ff.). This is illustrated well by the order made in the *Kranspoort* case, where the "community" aspect of the claim was strictly interpreted and the mechanisms of the Communal Property Associations Act (Act 28 of 1996) were used to reestablish a more cohesive community.

It is undoubtedly difficult to restore land to people through a legal system relying on a status quo that is inherently discriminatory, especially where claimants have to rely on insecure relations to land or when overlapping claims exist. Communal claims are particularly problematic in this regard. At a policy level, the 1997 *White Paper* stated that restitution should be limited in terms of scope and time. At the same time, the legislature tried to be inclusive by defining "right in land" broadly, to cover a wide range of circumstances, even beneficial occupation for specified periods. This did not resolve the question as to *what* was to be restored in cases of so-called lesser rights, that is, rights that would not qualify for strong protection under South African common law.

The importance of this question becomes clear if the initial LCC decision in the Richtersveld case is compared with the eventual decision of the Constitutional Court. Had the community been successful before the LCC, the value of their acknowledged "beneficial occupation" would not have been nearly as high as that accorded by the Constitutional Court's typification of their rights as those of "indigenous law ownership." In the case of the *Ndebele-Ndzundza,* the Supreme Court of Appeal's description of the community's land rights was similarly beneficial. Accordingly, the judiciary's interpretation of the entry requirements for restitution, in particular the link between the "community" requirement for communal claims and the typification of such land rights, is giving new direction to land law, far beyond the original, pragmatic solution ventured in the *Kranspoort* case. This opens up new possibilities for expansive decisions about the interests to be restored and the kind of claims that may be entertained under the Restitution Act.

DISCRIMINATION AND DISPOSSESSION

The Restitution Act requires dispossession to have occurred as a result of racially discriminatory laws or practices. "Dispossession" is not defined in the Restitution Act or in the 1993 and 1996 Constitutions. Land measures that may be described as racially biased are also not enumerated. The courts thus have to find working definitions that could have been intended by the legislature. Here, too, there has been a move from cautionary and restrictive interpretations toward more open-ended definitions of dispossession and discrimination, and of the link between them.

Slamdien

This trend is illustrated by judicial developments since the early decision in *Minister of Land Affairs v. Slamdien* (1999 LCC) on whether the dispossession of land for the establishment of a "coloured" school constituted grounds for a restitution claim (see Pienaar 2005c, 198). The property was bought and registered in 1955, after which the area was declared a "coloured" group area under the Group Areas Act of 1950. In 1970 the property was purchased by the state, and a primary school was built on the land. The minister sought a declaratory order to the effect that the original owners were not dispossessed of a right in land as a result of past discriminatory laws or practices.

The LCC decision contextualized the reference to "racially based land measures" by a purposive interpretation that relied on the constitutional, historical, and statutory context of a particular provision (LCC [12–13],[21], [27]–[29]). Although the Group Areas Act was found to be well within the scope of the discriminatory measures envisaged by the Restitution Act, it was held that in this case discrimination as such was not a sufficient basis for restitution. Some link between the discrimination and the enjoyment of the land had to be sought for the dispossession to fall within the ambit of the Restitution Act, and this link had to relate both to the exercise of land rights and to the achievement of the purposes of racial zoning or spatial racial segregation (LCC [23–24]. It was accordingly found that in this case the dispossession was not "a result of" the Group Areas Act (LCC [41]).

Although this approach achieved certainty in the interpretation of an undefined requirement of the Restitution Act, it proved too exclusionary. For instance, dispossessions in terms of the Black Communities Development Act of 1984 would, arguably, not be deemed racially discriminatory, since that act was premised on urban renewal and clearing slums. Likewise, the Black Administration Act of 1927 arguably did not provide for racial zoning or the exercise of land rights as such. Yet these statutes lay at the heart of many dispossessive and inherently discriminatory practices. Nevertheless, the rather rigid approach in the *Slamdien* case was followed in quite a few restitution cases (Pienaar 2005c), until it was abandoned as "too restrictive" in the *Richtersveld* case.

Richtersveld

In the initial *Richtersveld* LCC decision, a *Slamdien*-type approach resulted in a finding that dispossession under a law or practice that was not designed to bring about spatial apartheid (in this case the Precious Stones Act) could not qualify as a dispossession for the purposes of the act. However, the Appeal Court focused on the presence of a motive or conscious failure to recognize the claimants' rights, which had the *effect* of racial discrimination, even if indirectly (SCA [105]). Since the government had bought into the patently biased colonial view that the community had no rights to start with, because they were "too uncivilized," the dispossession resulted from racially discriminatory practices (SCA [110]). The Constitutional Court's approach, albeit somewhat different, reached the same conclusion. This emphasized the impact or effect of seemingly racially neutral legislation such as the Precious Stones Act, which protected westernized land title rights and not customary law rights and thus had a racially discriminatory *result* (CC [99]). The consequence of the decisions of both the Appeal Court and Constitutional Court is that a law need not form part of racialized spatial legislation to fall within the ambit of the Restitution Act. Rather, the impact of the specific law is the most important consideration.

Khumalo; Allie

In this respect, too, the *Richtersveld* decision marked an important turn in South African restitution jurisprudence. A more generous understanding of the connection between dispossession and discrimination was generally followed in subsequent case law. Thus in *Khumalo v. Minister of Land Affairs* (LCC 2005), involving the effect of a commissioner's exercise of his powers under the Black Administration Act of 1927, the LCC confirmed that the *Slamdien* approach was too narrow and focused on the impact of the measure instead. Section 8 of the Black Administration Act had the effect of depriving registered owners of ownership "only if the registered owner was a Native" (LCC [19]). Because the same result could never have followed if the owner had been white, the act was found to be racially discriminatory and within the ambit of section 2 of the Restitution Act (LCC [21]).

Similarly, in *Abrams v. Allie* (2004 SCA) it was found that the underlying motive of the Black Communities Development Act of 1984 was not so much the professed cause of slum clearance as the facilitation of resettlement to further apartheid. In fact, the Black Communities Development Act, as sister legislation to the Group Areas Act, was intended to facilitate racial group areas (SCA [14]). If the focus was on the *impact* of the act, dispossession under this act would qualify as racially discriminatory and thereby meet the requirements of the Restitution Act.

Dulabh; Witz; Randall and Knott

The courts' understanding of "dispossession" followed a similar trajectory as its treatment of "rights in land." Initially it was thought that a particular moment must be pinpointed as the moment of dispossession, as in *In re Kranspoort Community* (1999 LCC) and *Jacobs v. Department of Land Affairs, In re The Farm UAP 28A* (2000 LCC [27]), where it was held that dispossession is not a gradual process. Since the Constitutional Court's decision on *Richtersveld*, however, the judiciary seems more willing to acknowledge the cumulative effect of various laws and practices in eroding the rights of claimants and, directly or indirectly, inducing them to vacate their land. South African courts are now willing to recognize that dispossession of rights may extend over time. Moreover, even where a removal did not take place forcefully, the dispossession requirement could still be met if the eventual disposal or loss of the land was involuntary. *In re Pillay* for instance, the LCC found that property in an area earmarked for a group area, which had been sold two years prior to such a declaration, could still form the subject of a restitution claim.

The common assumption that restitution would not cover white farmers who lost land to further the purposes of apartheid has also turned out to be mistaken. However, here it is worth noting that the threat of expropriation or loss of land would not automatically amount to a dispossession that qualified for restitution. In *Department of Land Affairs v. Witz, In re Various Portions of Grassy Park* (2006 LCC), the LCC had to consider whether the sale of properties subject to the Group Areas Act constituted a "dispossession." Here the white landowners were permitted to subdivide their property and sell it within one year. One particular owner, Witz, managed to sell off the properties over a period of eleven years, although he was not entitled to hold the land at all under the Group Areas Act 36 of 1966. The court emphasized the fact that the acquisition and subsequent sales of the properties were voluntary under a prescribed permit procedure and that Witz was a disqualified person during the process of acquisition and disposal (LCC [22], [24]). Accordingly it was found that no dispossession occurred.

This case may be distinguished from *Randall and Another v. Minister of Land Affairs* and *Knott and Another v. Minister of Land Affairs* (2006 LCC), where the LCC rejected the argument that privileged white persons could not qualify as being dispossessed under the Restitution Act, indicating that nothing of this kind was suggested by the act itself, or would be tolerated by the Constitution. These cases, which were decided jointly, involved the dispossession of white farmers in terms of legislation regulating the consolidation of the former homelands. It was clear that the owners were forced to sell off the relevant land. The manner in which the properties were acquired was problematic (LCC [9] ff.). The farms were acquired after they were earmarked for incorporation into the homeland of the Ciskei, in terms of the Development Trust and Land Act of 1936. This effectively excluded white ownership of the land or white farming activity on the land. The structure of the purchase prices was also suspect. In the *Randall* case, part of the purchase price was paid in the form of a registered stock certificate, with the balance paid in cash (LCC [30]). Not only did the owners not have a choice in how they were paid, but the government stock was effectively worth much less when it was finally realized (LCC [31]). In *Knott*'s case, almost half the purchase price was paid after transfer, over a period of twelve months, without any interest, after the owner accepted a nonnegotiable offer on a "take it or leave it" basis (LCC [41]). Under these circumstances, it was found that a dispossession had indeed occurred. There was no opportunity, as in the case of *Witz,* for the owner to dispose of the property at the best possible price.

Assessment

The ironies inherent in dealing with dispossessions resulting from discriminatory laws and practices are evident in the cases discussed above. In the case of *Randall* and *Knott,* as in the case of the *Ndebele-Ndzundza,* the measures giving rise to the dispossessions stemmed directly from the policy objectives of the apartheid regime and were obviously based on racial discrimination. Although the white victims in *Randall* and *Knott* were not "disadvantaged" in the sense probably contemplated by those who negotiated to incorporate restitution into the new constitutional order, yet the courts were prepared to include them within the ambit of the Restitution Act. Cases such as *Richtersveld, Allie,* and *Khumalo,* however, demonstrate that the spirit of apartheid pervaded the whole of South Africa's land law. Laws that at first glance appeared free from prejudice nevertheless had profoundly discriminatory impacts on people. Here, too, the courts' willingness to interpret the requirements of discrimination and dispossession broadly has extended the scope of the restitution program to cases not originally contemplated.

The South African restitution experience may be comparable to that in other jurisdictions, but there are important differences. It certainly is distinguishable from postsocialist programs inasmuch as it does not propose to address injustices brought about by the imposition of a socialist regime on private landowners. It also does not readily qualify as a postcolonial program, since it expressly excludes reparations for the colonial period. Instead, the South African restitution program was designed to redress the peculiar injustices of this country's recent political history. Yet in this respect, the company that it keeps with comparative law on aboriginal title continues to amaze. The idea of aboriginal title still frequents court decisions and academic literature, even beyond the point where its underlying principles were declared incompatible with South African law. The South African judiciary has only recently begun to rid itself, slowly, of the emotive force of this aspect of comparative law, as it realizes that the Restitution Act provides far more scope than originally perceived.

The redress afforded by the restitution program can never cancel out the physical, emotional, and psychological loss suffered by those who were dispossessed. Yet at all levels of the judiciary there is growing recognition that restitution represents an important mechanism for ensuring social justice and development as an integral part of the broader land reform program (see Dodson, this volume). The decisions of the Supreme Court of Appeal and the Constitutional Court in the *Richtersveld* dispute certainly mark a turning point in the interpretation of the entry requirements for restitution. Post-*Richtersveld* decisions at various levels of the judiciary indicate greater leniency in the interpretation of entry requirements such as "rights in land," "dispossession," and "discrimination."

Since then South African restitution jurisprudence has developed in ways that render a critical reconsideration of the goals of the restitution program necessary. Initially, policymakers intended to contain the scope of restitution in South Africa. Yet the matter is so politicized that the broadening of the program's focus was inevitable. Judicial interpretations have contributed to this but have also had a broader impact. The courts' treatment of the concept of landownership is influencing the design of a new land regime in South Africa. The judicial acceptance of the idea that restitution is not merely restorative but can be a meaningful agent for poverty alleviation and development has the potential for real transformation of South African law (see Dodson, this volume).

The case law discussed above indicates that judicial activism around the parameters of restitution can be more forceful than policy revision. This might not constitute a formal or even direct attempt to broaden the scope of the restitution program. Nevertheless, judicial extension of the scope of restitution has significantly affected the benefits bestowed through the restitution process. Thus the judiciary, through its restitution jurisprudence, has a significant hand in shaping the futures that the original proponents of restitution envisaged.

NOTES

1. References in the text are to the judiciary handing down the judgments—LCC for Land Claims Court, SCA for Supreme Court of Appeal, and CC for Constitutional Court—with the paragraph of the relevant judgment where applicable. Details are provided in the References and the Case Law section.

REFERENCES

Anghie, A. 1999. "Finding the Peripheries: Sovereignty and Colonialism in Nineteenth-century International Law." *Harvard International Law Journal* 40 (1): 1–80.

Asch, M., and C. Bell. 1994. "Definition and Interpretation of Fact in Canadian Aboriginal Title Litigation: An Analysis of *Delgamuukw*." *Queens Law Journal* 19 (2): 503–50.

Barry, M. 2004. "Now Another Thing Must Happen: Richtersveld and the Dilemmas of Land Reform in Post-Apartheid South Africa." *South African Journal of Human Rights* 20 (3): 355–82.

Bennett, G. 1978. "Aboriginal Title in the Common Law: A Stony Path through Feudal Doctrine." *Buffalo Law Review* 27 (Winter 1977/Spring 1978): 617–35.

Bennett, T. W. 1993. "Redistribution of Land and the Doctrine of Aboriginal Title in South Africa." *South African Journal on Human Rights* 9 (4): 443–76.

Bennett, T. W., and C. H. Powell. 2005. "Restoring Land: The Claims of Aboriginal Title, Customary Law and the Right to Culture." *Stellenbosch Law Review* 16 (3): 431–45.

Carey Miller, D. L., and A. Pope. 2000. *Land Title in South Africa*. Cape Town: Juta.

Choudree, R. B. G. 1994. "Mabo & Others v. The State of Queensland—A Pandora's Box?" *South African Law Journal* 111 (2): 431–38.

DLA (Department of Land Affairs). 2005. "Report of the National Land Summit 26–30 July 2005: A Partnership to Fast Track Land Reform: A New Trajectory to 2014." http://www.pmg.org.za/docs/2006/0608zznls.htm. Accessed 11 November 2006.

Du Plessis, W., N. J. J. Olivier, and J. M. Pienaar. 2001. "Evictions, Restitution, Spatial Information, the Right to Housing and Minerals: New Approaches from the Government and the Courts." *SA Publiekreg / Public Law* 16 (2): 181–216.

———. 2004a. "Land Matters: New Developments." *SA Publiekreg / Public Law* 19 (2): 458–70.

———. 2005. "Land Matters: New Developments 2005(1)." *SA Publiekreg / Public Law* 20 (1): 186–207.

Foster, H. 1992. "Forgotten Arguments: Aboriginal Title and Sovereignty in *Canada Jurisdiction Act* Cases." *Manitoba Law Journal* 21 (3): 343–89.

Freedman, W. 2003. "Restitution of Land Rights and the Recognition of Diverse forms of Land Tenure." *Obiter* 24 (2): 314–32.

Gross, A. M. 2004. "The Constitution, Reconciliation and Transitional Justice: Lessons from South Africa and Israel." *Stanford Journal of International Law* 40 (1): 47–104.

Hocking, B. A. 1999. "Australian Aboriginal Property Rights as Issues of Indigenous Sovereignty and Citizenship." *Ratio Juris* 12 (2): 196–225.

Honoré, A. M. 1961. "Ownership." In *Oxford Essays in Jurisprudence,* ed. A.G. Guest, 107–47. Oxford: Clarendon.

Hoq, L. A. 2002. "Land Restitution and the Doctrine of Aboriginal Title: *Richtersveld Community v. Alexkor Ltd and Another.*" *South African Journal on Human Rights* 18 (3): 421–43.

Lehmann, K. 2004. "Aboriginal Title, Indigenous Rights and the Right to Culture." *South African Journal on Human Rights* 20 (1): 86–118.

Lewis, C. 1985. "The Modern Concept of Ownership of Land." *Acta Juridica* 241–66. Cape Town: Juta.

———. 1987. "Real Rights in Land: A New Look at an Old Subject." *South African Law Journal* 104 (4): 599–615.

McNeil, K. 1989. *Common Law Aboriginal Title.* Oxford: Clarendon.

Minkley, G., and A. Westaway. 2005. "The Application of Rural Restitution to Betterment Cases in the Eastern Cape." *Social Dynamics* 31 (1): 104–28.

Mostert, H. 2000. "South African Constitutional Property Protection between Libertarianism and Liberationism: Challenges for the Judiciary." *Zeitschrift für ausländisches öffentliches Recht und Völkerrecht* 60 (2): 295–330.

———. 2003. "The Diversification of Land Rights and Its Implications for a New Land Law in South Africa." In *Modern Studies in Property Law II,* ed. E. J. Cooke, 3–25. Oxford: Hart.

Mostert, H., and P. Fitzpatrick. 2004. "Living in the Margins of History on the Edge of the Country—Legal Foundation and the Richtersveld Community's Title to Land." *Tydskrif vir die Suid-Afrikaanse Reg,* 2: 309–23 (part 1); 3: 498–510 (part 2).

Pienaar, G. J. 2005a. "Aboriginal Title or Indigenous Ownership—What's in a Name?" *Tydskrif vir Hedendaagse Romeins-Hollandse Reg* 68 (4): 533–45.

———. 2005b. "The Meaning of the Concept Community in South African Land Tenure Legislation." *Stellenbosch Law Review* 16 (1): 60–76.

———. 2005c. "'Racially Discriminatory Law or Practice' for the Purposes of the Restitution of Land Rights Act 22 of 1994: Recent Developments in Case Law." *De Jure* 38 (2): 195–208.

Portfolio Committee on Agriculture and Land Affairs. 2005. "Report of the Portfolio Committee on Agriculture and Land Affairs on Provincial Oversight Visit to Northern Cape, Free State and Eastern Cape, 25 October 2005." http://www.pmg.org.za/docs/2005/comreports/051101pcagricreport.2.htm. Accessed 15 September 2006.

Reilly, A. 2000. "The Australian Experience of Aboriginal Title: Lessons for South Africa." *South African Journal on Human Rights* 16 (3): 512–34.

Ülgen, Ö. 2002. "Developing the Doctrine of Aboriginal Title in South Africa: Source and Content." *Journal of African Law* 46 (2): 131–54.

van der Merwe, C. G. 1989. *Sakereg.* 2nd ed. Durban: Butterworths.

van der Walt, A. J. 1995. "Rights and Reforms in Property Theory: A Review of Property Theories and Debates in Recent Literature (part III)." *Tydskrif vir die Suid-Afrikaanse Reg* 3:493–526.

———. 1999. "Property Rights and Hierarchies of Power: A Critical Evaluation of Land Reform Policy in South Africa." *Koers* 64 (2) and (3): 259–94.

———. 2001. "Dancing with Codes—Protecting, Developing and Deconstructing Property Rights in a Constitutional State." *South African Law Journal* 118 (2): 258–311.

———. 2005. *Constitutional Property Law.* Cape Town: Juta.

van der Walt, A. J., and G. Pienaar. 2006. *Introduction to the Law of Property,* 5th ed. Cape Town: Juta.

Walker, C. 2005. "The Limits to Land Reform: Rethinking 'the Land Question.' " *Journal of Southern African Studies* 31 (4): 805–24.

STATUTES

Communal Property Associations Act 28 of 1996. Pretoria: Government Printers.

Constitution of the Republic of South Africa Act 200 of 1993. Pretoria: Government Printers.

Constitution of the Republic of South Africa Act 108 of 1996. Pretoria: Government Printers.

Precious Stones Act 44 of 1927. Pretoria: Government Printer.

Restitution of Land Rights Act 22 of 1994. Pretoria: Government Printers.

CASE LAW

Abrams v. Allie 2004 (4) SA 534 (SCA).

Alexkor (Pty) Ltd and Another v. Richtersveld Community and Others 2004 (5) SA 460 (CC).

Department of Land Affairs v. Witz, In re Various Portions of Grassy Park 2006 (1) SA 86 (LCC).

Dulabh v. Department of Land Affairs 1997 (4) SA 1108 (LCC) [29].

In Re Kranspoort Community 2000 (2) SA 124 (LCC).

In re Pillay and Others LCC 1/99 (unreported).

Jacobs v. Department of Land Affairs, In re The Farm UAP 28A [2000] JOL 6203 (LCC) (LCC 3/98).

Khumalo v. Minister of Land Affairs 2005 (2) SA 618 (LCC).

Minister of Land Affairs v. Slamdien 1999 (4) BCLR 413 (LCC).

Mphela and others v. Engelbrecht and Others [2005] 2 All SA 135 (LCC).

Ndebele-Ndzundza Community v. Farm Kafferskraal NO 181 JS 2003 (5) SA 375 (LCC).

Prinsloo & Another v. Ndebele-Ndzundza Community & Others 2005 (6) SA 144 (SCA).

Randall and Another v. Minister of Land Affairs; Knott and Another v. Minister of Land Affairs 2006 (3) SA 216 (LCC).

Richtersveld Community and Others v. Alexkor (Pty) Ltd and Another, 2001 (3) SA 1293 (LCC).

Richtersveld Community and Others v. Alexkor and Another 2003 (2) All SA 27 (SCA).

part two

Restitution

Voices

Memory,
Contestation,
Reconstruction

four

Urban Restitution Narratives

Black River, Cape Town

UMA DHUPELIA-MESTHRIE

THREE MEN AND A CLAIM

On 19 June 1996 about fifty people took their seats in a small hall in Rondebosch East, a suburb of Cape Town.[1] These individuals had a common history—they and their families had once lived in an area in Cape Town known as Black River (now a part of Rondebosch, see map 3). I was informed about the meeting by a few individuals whom I had interviewed a year earlier for a paper on the application of the Group Areas Act to Black River (see Dhupelia-Mesthrie 1995), and I attended the meeting. About three hundred families classified "coloured," Malay and Indian, totaling just under two thousand individuals, lived in Black River in 1966 when it was proclaimed a white group area. These included middle-class families (teachers, shopkeepers, and small-business persons); artisans (painters, plumbers, plasterers, bricklayers, carpenters, and tailors); and dressmakers, nurses, garment workers, cooks, washerwomen, shop assistants, cleaners, street sweepers, mail carriers, gardeners, messengers, and drivers. Most left between 1967 and 1971; the last two families moved in 1979. With the forced removals, traces of the Black River community have been erased from Cape Town's memory and geography. All we have is the suburb of Rondebosch, a Black River Parkway, and a canalized river that fails to evoke the past.

This meeting in 1996 had been convened to discuss restitution as provided by the Restitution of Land Rights Act of 1994. A member of the Commission on Restitution of Land Rights (CRLR) was on hand to make a brief presentation and answer questions. Three men, all in their sixties, had a leading role in the events leading up to the meeting: Ghamza Adams, Ebrahim Osman, and Abou Desai.

Ghamza, born in 1930, is the eldest son of Ebrahim and Hajira Adams, a family regarded by former residents as among the oldest of Black River. Ebrahim and his brother Mogamet Sallie ran a tailor's shop on Klipfontein Road and together with a third brother, Abdullah Adam, an imam at the mosque in Mowbray, they set up home in the 1920s on a substantial piece of land just off Strathallan Road. As the families expanded, Ebrahim Adams bought land in Roseland Road and built a house, "Mouhiba," in the 1950s. Ebrahim Osman, born in 1933, a son of Joseph (Yusef) and Gadija, dates his connection with Black River first through his maternal grandfather S. Harris, who owned property in Black River. Ebrahim's father, a builder (as is Ebrahim), built a home at 62 Loch Road in 1932. Like Ghamza, Black River is Ebrahim's place of birth. Abou Desai, born in 1931, a teacher, was a relative latecomer to Black River. Moving from Observatory, he bought a home called "Two Ways" in Roseland Road in 1957.

The inspiration to call a restitution meeting came from Ghamza and Ebrahim. They drew Desai in because he was known for his organizational ability and penchant for keeping records and because he was the professional among the three. Ebrahim describes why they called the meeting:

> The idea was because we felt, you know, that we actually started life, we started knowing ourselves in Black River. Right. We were a very close-knit community. We were a big family and that whole thing was shattered you know through the group areas. . . . You know we could take it . . . but what about our mothers and fathers that was still alive? How did they take it, you know, because they spent most of their time there all right. So we decided . . . that we're going to do something about this and that's where we came together. (Adams and Osman interview, 1997)

Ghamza had lodged his claim for his family home in October 1995. His file number A28 indicates he was among the earliest claimants at the Cape Town office. Reflecting a concern for the past Black River community, he personally informed people about the meeting and handed out claim forms (Adams and Osman interview, 1997). Desai saw himself as completing the duties he had assumed in the 1960s as the secretary of the Black River Ratepayers' and Residents' Association (BRRA). At that time they fought for people to safeguard their homes—now they would have to work for restitution (Desai interview, 2006).

Looking back at my notes of that meeting I am struck by the importance of the questions that people asked and how wrong some of the answers turned out to be. How serious was this business of claims? Was there enough money set aside for compensation? How much money did the commission actually have and did this include the staff's salaries? What happens to the process if the general elections in 1999 brought into power a new government? What compensation would be paid? Would it be determined by the current market value? How long would the process take? If land was vacant in Black River could they get this back? Behind all these questions was a central concern: if people were to invest time in a process to lodge claims, they wanted to be reassured that the outcome would be of significance. The official from the CRLR replied that by 2000 all claims would have to be settled, that there was a choice of restitution (financial, restoration, alternative land, consideration for quick access to housing). If land was in private hands they would have to negotiate, but if it was government or council land it would be easier. A formula had not yet been devised to calculate compensation. Useful information was provided about how to fill out the claim form.

In two papers I wrote subsequent to that meeting, I reflected on the fact that academic interest in the land restitution process was lacking compared to the interest in the Truth and Reconciliation Commission (TRC) ([Dhupelia-]Mesthrie 1998 and Dhupelia-Mesthrie 1999). Comparing the discourse of the two commissions, I highlighted the common vocabulary of reconciliation, healing, and justice. Critics such as Mayson (1996) and Levin (1998) pointed to the slowness of land restitution and its focus on negotiated settlement, the emphases on the legal process to the detriment of rural communities, and the limits to justice given the sanctification of private property rights and the cutoff date for claiming dispossession, namely 1913. Brown, Erasmus, Kingwill, Murray, and Roodt (1998) also provided a pessimistic account of the process because of bureaucratic wrangles and conflicts between the CRLR and the Department of Land Affairs. I argued, however, that the inadequacies of the commission had led to people taking the lead themselves—calling meetings and holding reunions. Reunions were a strategy of the people who lacked the public hearings of the TRC, and they were an important means of coming to terms with the past. The process of filling out forms led to a rediscovery of their city with the assertion of a new-found authority and citizenship of equality. Within families, old and young were drawn together in an effort to piece together the family history.

Both Ghamza Adams and Ebrahim Osman insisted in 1997 that the central reason for claiming restitution was to come to terms with "what was done to us" and especially to the elders. Financial rewards were not uppermost in their minds. When asked what he expected from restitution, Ghamza said, "Justice must be done." He then went on to tell me about how the Pirates Cricket Club was affected by removals. But what would be justice? Ghamza was unable at that stage to spell out the specifics. The government and CRLR, however, had a clear understanding that justice had to be reined in by reconciliation. As Derek Hanekom, the minister of land affairs in South Africa's first democratic government, made clear: "The Bill is not about taking away people's land again. It is not about confiscation and coercion. It is about justice and reconciliation."[2] Wallace Mgoqi, the first regional land claims commissioner in the Western Cape, assured whites in the elite suburbs of Cape Town that no awards would be made that would result in "social disruptions" (*Cape Argus,* 17 February 1996).

This chapter seeks to reassess the meanings of restitution for Black River residents, given that at the time of writing ten years had passed since that first restitution meeting. Have Ghamza Adams and other residents come to a better understanding of what justice is? Has healing taken place? Although residents may have met as a group, claims were submitted individually. This is so since there were many property owners involved; a return to the land was unlikely because of the changed landscape and also because they did not know enough about how to file a group claim (Osman interview, 2006). In the end, this became a personal family quest. The chapter thus tells individual stories of restitution, through which it hopes to provide a nuanced understanding of restitution.

This chapter also aims to get a better understanding of urban restitution. A national audit in 1999 revealed that 72 percent of claims were urban; in the Western Cape the percentage was 95 percent. A further audit in 2001 revealed that of 11,938 claims in the Western Cape, 595 were rural and 11,343 urban (Walker 2003, 5, 12). Statistics can be problematic, but the weight of the urban claims is not in dispute. It has been recognized that urban restitution will be limited in what it can achieve—it is only in exceptional cases that it will challenge the way in which apartheid has shaped our cities, partly because most of the claims will be settled by financial compensation. Walker (2003, 10) has argued further: "There has been a lack of attention by the state to the symbolic, cultural, and psychological elements of restitution. . . . [O]nly minimal attention has been given to the non-material issues around memory, public recognition and identity that inform many claims." My chapter points to how important these nonmaterial issues are. Yet it also tries to respond, in a small way, to Walker's call for assessments of the impact of financial settlements (2003, 10–11).

A STORY "FROM MY HEART"

> I said to my daughter: "Let's go to the bank. Did you take the day off?" She says "Yes." We said, "Let's go to the bank." We went to the bank. I took R10,000 from there and I blew it. I bought cake for the children and I came home and we had a celebration and all the grandchildren were sitting at the table. . . . I put money under their plates. "There's a party!" and I said, "Yes, look under your plates," and I gave them all as much money as I thought I could give them, and they had a whale of time with that money. (Dawood interview, 2006).

This is Mona Dawood's account of what she did that day in 2005 when she received her restitution check for R40,000. Since then most of the money has been spent on gifts for the family such as fridges, a decoder to access pay TV channels, a fan. Why did she do this? Her tale is an instructive one on the limits and failures of restitution.

Mona, born in 1920, is a very sprightly woman. Though eighty-six (at the time of the interview), she is busy—she teaches for three mornings of the week at her daughter-in-law's play school (she has been a teacher for most of her working life). I had not met her before, but through my research I had come across a news clipping where a Mrs. M. Dawood had defiantly told a reporter in 1961: "They will take this house away from us only over my dead body. Here we are, here we stay" (*Cape Times*, 6 April 1961). But they did get to take her house. When I met her at her home in Crawford I am struck by her appearance—this is no frail old lady. She is neatly dressed with a scarf covering her head. She wears glasses but is in good health. The interview reveals her robust personality, her belief in a strong work ethic, her generosity, and her happy family life. She is proud of her two daughters and son and speaks fondly about her six grandchildren and seven great-grandchildren. She and her family worked hard for what they have achieved, and she lives very comfortably.

Black River was well known to Mona in her childhood. There were many visits to the home of her maternal uncle on Strathallan Road. On her marriage to Ismail, a tailor (now deceased), her uncle helped them secure a plot on Balfour Road and helped build their home. Rashaad Adams, Ghamza's brother, explains how Black River residents built their homes: "You know how we built there. Say for instance, now you were a Black River citizen and you bought a plot there. Now you're owner-builder. Now the people in the area is plasterers, or carpenters or bricklayers. They will all come now on a Saturday and help you build your house. This is the way our house was built and many other people" (Rashaad Adams interview, 1995). How these homes were built is critical in understanding what people felt about the houses in Black River. Invested are many collective memories of hard work and fun on weekends. Each house had a name—the Dawoods' was "Ishmoo."

Removals brought sadness, grief, and a sense of hopelessness toward the government. Mona's story of restitution unfortunately reflects a parallel experience. She describes what restitution has meant for her in a way that the transcription of that interview cannot convey effectively. Much emotion lies behind the bare words: "From my heart it was sad. It was sad. Sad, sad, sad," she says.

Present at the restitution meeting in 1996, she subsequently lodged her claim with the help of her children. As a result of her age, her claim was eventually prioritized. She remembers asking the CRLR staff whether restitution would come "when I am ten feet under?" Mona's disappointment with restitution stems from the fact that after she had submitted her claim she saw her house advertised for sale. She and her daughters made a painful visit to the house, noting the alterations that had been made. They told the owner of the house they knew the house—this was their house. The owner was silent and uncomfortable.

Following this visit, and with the knowledge that the house could be bought, Mona made an urgent visit to the CRLR office. She informed them that she wanted her house back and she wanted help. The current owners wanted R500,000. Mona wanted help to bring the price down by negotiations and by a contribution towards the repurchase. She was within her rights—the law provided the option of securing the property back if feasible. The current price was an injustice given the pittance they had received when they had been forced to sell. In the 1960s and 1970s, in the climate of forced sales, residents disposed of their Black River homes for between R5,000 and R12,000.

Mona describes the reaction of the CRLR staff:

> And guess what they told me? "We can't put those people out." I said, "I didn't tell you to put the people out. I want to buy the place but not at that price." So they said "No, but we can't do anything about it. We can't tell the people to lower the price for you." So I said, "Yes but you [government] could throw us out. Wasn't that a nasty thing to do?" . . . So they said either you can get another piece of land or you can take the money. . . . So I said . . . "I don't want another piece of land. Where you going to give me land? There's no land there." . . . He said, "Then the alternative is you will have to take the money." So cold and callous.

Mona's sadness comes from not getting her house: "I didn't want the money. I wanted *my house*," she stresses. "It would have satisfied my heart. That is mine. . . . Ja and I got it back." I ask her if she considered getting legal help. "Why?" she says. "I had an experience of lawyers, man. We all contributed there in Black River. We got nothing." Her response refers to the ineffectiveness of lawyers to prevent their removal from Black River, as the BRRA hired L. Dison in 1964 to prevent the area from being declared white.

Mona says she "brought the roof down" at the commission's offices trying to get her view across but failed. Her final conclusion about restitution is: "They failed me. Yes. Big." She explains why she spent the money in the way she did: "They didn't want to give me my heart's desire so I am giving the children their heart's desire. I don't think they have ever seen so much money before." And from this giving, Mona gets some happiness. But her story of restitution is accompanied by a retelling of the story of removals—the hardship of finding a new home and starting all over again. In the context of the failure of restitution the one narrative has to be accompanied by the other and is retold with intensity.

A SMALL DONATION

Baboo Mohamed, born in 1943, was nine years old when his parents moved from Grassy Park to Black River. They took over the Park Estate Lucky Store on Strathallan Road and occupied the house behind it. In 1960 Baboo's father, Hassan, bought the shop and house from Hassan Mathews. Mohamed was classified Indian and Mathews Malay so a transaction could not legally take place between two "races." Pending the declaration of group areas, land transactions between races had been frozen since 1951. The Mohameds did what many Indians in Cape Town did—they used a nominee to purchase the house. The nominee, a relative, was by their account an "Indian through and through" but had managed to get classified Malay. In this way, the Mohameds secured what they thought was a safe home. Three years after Black River was proclaimed white, Hassan Mohamed died. Through the nominee the house was sold in 1969 but Hassan's wife and children continued to live there as tenants until 1979. With much difficulty they finally found a home in Rylands, the Indian group area.

Baboo, sixty-three years of age (at the time of the interview), is semi-retired. He keeps busy. He runs a small carpool taking children to school and until recently offered a service to students wanting to travel to the University of the Western Cape. Constant increases in the price of gasoline have not made this a profitable business. When Baboo lived in Black River, cars were his passion; he worked as a part-time panel beater (autobody repairer) and serviced cars. His sister, Fatima, born in 1947, is an accountant. She had shared the house with him in Black River and still lives with Baboo, his sons, and grandchildren in Rylands. The brother and sister are very close, and this determined how they worked on their restitution claim. Dividing the work, Baboo worked on the Black River claim while Fatima focused on her father's extensive properties in Windermere. Just a few weeks before my interview with him, Baboo had been in to sign what the CRLR calls his vouchers. His claim was about to be settled, and he knows what he will receive for the two properties on Strathallan Road though he would rather not disclose the sum publicly. He need not be so wary—the amount is what tenants receive all over Cape Town according to a Standard Settlement Offer. The final resolution and knowledge of the sum to be received influence their tale of restitution.

Although the Mohameds were owners, they made their claims as tenants. Baboo is resigned to this. They had no proof that they were the owners. He was reluctant to visit the nominee's family—they might claim the properties for themselves. However, the Mohameds are not going to grumble. Fatima explains:

> My take is . . . we lost it, na, whatever reason. The government of the day took it from us. Virtually took it from us. . . . Whichever way. . . . You

> know, it was a whole moan and groan affair going on there in the offices [the commission's]. And you come here, you phone. . . . I was one of them, OK. So they don't answer you. They say they going to phone you back and they never do. You got to make ten calls. You know. But afterwards I also gave it a thought you know. Forty years or thirty years ago my father lost what he lost you know for a pittance, and here I never in my mind or nobody, none of them, even thought you would get come back to this where we could claim that.

And to what use will the settlement be put? They will pool what they get, settle their debts and if anything is left over then each one will decide. Baboo thought only fleetingly about taking land as an alternative. "I was thinking about it but then you must have excess money if you want to build. Say, you going to get the land . . . then what you going to do if you haven't got money? . . . So I just left it. I didn't worry with that because the money is more important to me."

I ask Baboo what restitution has meant to him—does it finally lay the past to rest? I have to press him about four times over almost thirty minutes to get a definite answer. The first time he notes that they sold each of their properties for R7,000 in 1969. He then launches into a long story that he had also told me in 1995 about how impossible it was to get a property in Rylands. Officials needed to be bribed, and honest people like him without much money were unable to secure land. The second time he talks about the friends he had in Black River, the youth who came to his garage and the games they played—a life without apartheid. I didn't quite hear him preface this with a soft answer that the settlement cannot really settle the past so I press him for a third time. "The answer to the question is that I miss that. I miss that." A fourth time I prod him further—perhaps too relentlessly. He finally says:

> This means—what can I now say. This is a little part of the settlement. That can't buy me . . . money can't buy happiness. Peoples is gone. Living here, there and you can't go to each and every one. . . . That whole community there. Whatever religion, whatever culture was one big happy family. One person gets sick, everybody's there to come and help. One person dies, everybody's there to help. That's how that community was. It was fantastic. This [he points to the letter of settlement] is just a small donation [he laughs]. . . . I am grateful for that. . . . I can pay whatever I can pay—finish now. Right. Whatever little bit that's left

then I can get something through it and then we can just start all over again. But the memories of Black River will always remain.

In the course of the interview he tells a story of his youth. He and his friends would gather weekly at the bottom of Strathallan Road and weave their way through each of the streets making their way to the Rondebosch Common. Then, after a run around the Common, they would weave their way back down each street until they reached Strathallan. This is a tale of belonging, a tale of what was taken away. Each time Baboo drives down Klipfontein Road near the Common his wife has to ask him to "'Look in front of you.' My head is turned to the left looking over."

THE MONEY OR THE BOX

Emily Eager, born in 1930, is seventy-six years old (when I meet her). She lives alone in Pinati but manages to get around to do some small chores. Her link to Black River dates to the early years of the twentieth century when her grandfather, reputedly an African American, stepped off a ship in Cape Town never to reboard. He married in 1902 and bought several properties in Loch Road, eventually retaining one house with four plots of adjoining land. He operated a horse-driven cabby service for residents of Rondebosch till his death in 1926; his wife worked as a cleaning woman. Over the years, children were born and grandchildren too, and soon other homes were built on the properties. Emily Eager is the daughter of William, one of the sons. William was a furniture polisher, and Emily's mother, Caroline, was a cleaning woman. Emily, on finishing school, worked at a clothing factory. She remained in Black River after her marriage to Tommy Eager, a plasterer, whose parents had bought a home in 1928 in Loch Road.

When I visit Emily Eager I am struck by the very cooperative way the family has worked on their claim. Emily has knowledge of two claims—one is for her grandfather's property, which she filled in for her deceased father and his siblings. The other was lodged by her husband for his parents' home. Emily regards it as an Eager matter though she was already a member of her husband's household when they moved. Emily herself did the research for her family claim, but she soon handed the work over to her sixty-eight-year-old cousin, Jerry Kannemeyer (son of Annie, sister to William). They work well together sharing all their information, with Emily giving advice about getting all the identity documents together in time.

The story they tell is of the long "waiting period," of faxes that were sent to the CRLR but never reached the person they were intended for, of poor communication, and more seriously of lost files. The commission lost her first file—she had to go and get affidavits to say that she had handed it in and re-research and resubmit the claim. The Eager claim will bring in R60,000. This will be divided between the five children of the original owners. Tommy has passed away, and his share of R12,000 will be divided among his two daughters. Emily's family claim covers two plots so it will bring in much more (R53,000 plus R68,000). It will have to be divided several times over. Two of the original siblings had five children, all of whom are deceased, and each share of R24,200 will be subdivided among the next generation. Since William and Caroline had six children, Emily herself will get R4,033—one sixth of William's share. Jerry will get his mother Annie's full share since he is an only child.

Neither Emily nor Jerry was interested in land at their age. As Jerry says, "You got to take land where they want to give you land and you can't resell it" (according to the commission, when land is granted it cannot be resold within ten years). Referring to the popular radio show of years gone when contestants were offered the money or a box with uncertain contents Emily has a good sense of humor: "I said some day I will have to take the box—at the moment I want the money." She laughs, yes, she is talking about "the big box" [her coffin]. "I want the money now. Because the box I will have to take eventually. I don't want the box." The delay in receiving the money is frustrating—they are getting on in age. Emily hopes to use her share to visit her children in Canada though she realizes it will cover just part of the fare. Jerry hopes to do some home improvements. Emily thinks of her elders and what restitution would have meant for them: "It would have meant a lot to . . . our parents. . . . But . . . the parents are all dead now . . . It would have been so nice if this had happened in their lifetime." Emily has since passed away, and what restitution ultimately meant to her is taken to her grave.

A CEILING, MANDELA'S GIFT, AND TWO JOKES

And what of the three men who took a leadership role? Ghamza, when I interviewed him again in 2006, was seventy-six years old. In 1999 he suffered a stroke but began a slow period of recovery. I was expecting the worst when I went to see him. It had been impossible to see him for several days because he was always sleeping. When I see him at his son's home in Ottery, he looks good and is still the humorous man I had got to know well. Ghamza has all his documents in a file, including the plans of their home in Roseland Road. Two letters dated 2001 in the file point to him trying to get a response to his then six-year-old claim from the CRLR. He presses them for "a good answer," "an amicable reply." No reply came. In 2005, his claim was finally settled.

Ghamza tells me how he and his siblings went to collect their checks from the CRLR office: R40,000 divided among the eight siblings, with each receiving R5,000. One share of R5,000 was divided among the children of a deceased brother—each got about R800.

> We went straight from the office of the Land Claim there in Strand Street. They gave us the cheque and said you can go and cash our money now by Absa Bank—Adderley Street. From there we went to the District Six Museum. So they had a corner there . . . Black River was a corner [an exhibition in the museum]. So we said to the people there, "We got our money today." So this girl there took a photo of us. Now my one brother—I don't know if it is the first time he had R5,000 in his hand . . . [he] was so excited now. "Ja I got my money." So they said to him "open up the R5,000 like a fan" . . . There was a photo of me [on display] standing with a horse . . . I saw yes but it's me here.

The Black River exhibit that Ghamza went to see had been created after I had donated the Black River photographs I had collected from residents to the museum. Ghamza's brother had given me many of the Adams family photographs—thus he came to see himself there that day. His reaction speaks to the importance of the District Six Museum in the lives of the once dispossessed people of Cape Town. It provides validation—the space becomes symbolic of lost homes and lives.

This seemed like a happy day, but I now ask Ghamza: Has justice been done? He explains that when he first made his claim he had some hope of getting the house back but soon realized that this would be "a long story." His brothers thought they should take money, but the sum per sibling is small. Ghamza tells how his brother cracked a joke with commission staff that he was going to buy a Mercedes that day. He points out that they got R11,000 for their home in the 1960s—today, the houses are going for

R800,000 to R900,000. He says with no hesitation, "I think justice wasn't done." He recalls how he and his brother dug out the trenches to lay the foundation for their home, pulling out rocks and stones with their bare hands. But Ghamza is understanding: "You can't grumble grumble about that because at least the ANC gave us—I mean—made some of it right." The ceiling of his son's newly constructed house now reflects the history of the Adams family's life in Black River—for that is how he used his R5,000. We both laugh as I say, "So Black River is now in your ceiling." But as I gather my tape recorder and file to leave, he shows me a photograph of the Pirates Cricket Club—the Adams family are well represented and this image of the past is clearly treasured. Just over a month after this interview, Ghamza passed away.

Ebrahim Osman is a soft-spoken gentleman who is well informed about land matters in the city, not surprising since he has been a builder all his life. Unlike the others, he has opted for alternative land. He explains his choice: "At least you know our President Mandela who gave us something. . . . [L]et's make it worth it what he's giving us." At the end of 2008, the CRLR and the city council have still not provided him with land, and now seventy-five years old he is determined to wait this through.

Abou Desai's claim should have been a fairly simple one to settle. He was the owner of the house at the time of the removals, and he is the sole claimant. He is frustrated that other people's claims have been settled but not his, and also that these people are younger than he is (he was seventy-five at the time of the interview). He fails to discern the logic of the commission's workings. He is D180, but another claimant, D179, has been settled. I had previously analyzed Desai's story of removals and had concluded that he tended to tell jokes about officialdom as a way of maintaining his dignity in a situation that carried humiliation (Dhupelia-Mesthrie 2000). Once again he tells jokes:

> I spoke to one to one of the operatives one day and he said to me very nicely. He said, "Mr. Desai, let me just explain to you how this thing works," and halfway through his explaining he just burst out in laughter because the whole thing was so ridiculous, and the two of us had a jolly good laugh over it. And I had said to him, "At the time while I have you I want to give you a change of address," and he said to me, "Are you moving?" "No, I'm not moving, but you take this change of address," I said. " . . . Plot No. So and So, Vygekraal Cemetery." (He laughs.)

He has sympathy for the young staff—one of them was in grade seven when he lodged his claim. They are good to him on the whole. He explains why he has been able to maintain a sense of balance: "So, oh, it's hilarious, and why I've been able to survive because of the attitude of the clerks in the department. This fellow said to me 'You know, Mr. Desai, what'll happen is your forms will go to Pretoria. That will go into the in-tray. And then three months later somebody's else's forms will come in and they will go on top of yours.'" (Desai laughs.) "He says, 'And a month later somebody else's forms will come in and will go on top of that.'"

Behind these stories is a lot of frustration, and he admits "some anger." Three months after that interview an elated Desai phones me to say he has received his money. The money is not as important as is the process of restitution begun and completed with success.

THE SCOPE AND LIMITS OF RESTITUTION

The stories in this chapter are drawn from owners (albeit some had to claim as tenants). This is not by design but is a reflection of the fact that it is predominantly the owners in Black River who have lodged claims. An explanation for this lies in the history of the community at the time of removals. Leadership then emerged from the owners, and a strategy of the BRRA was to emphasize the middle-class, property-owning residents. Only a small percentage of tenants attended the BRRA meetings. One important reason for the apathy was that many tenants along Klipfontein Road were affected not only by the Group Areas Act but by the city council's road widening plan. Had leadership emerged from the tenants, then they would have been prominent in restitution. Ghamza Adams and Ebrahim Adams did to their credit try to publicize the restitution meeting in 1996 as widely as possible, but few of those living in poverty in Manenberg on the Cape Flats attended. Although the CRLR did publish a guide for ex-tenants, restitution has failed those who may have needed it the most. The process requires some level of literacy, and if the lower and middle classes have expended so much time, energy, and money traveling to the CRLR offices, those on the economic margins cannot afford such luxury. Andries du Toit has warned that restitution carries the danger of rewarding elites (2000, 76, 79). Restitution in the case of Black River has indeed not been about poverty alleviation. It has, however, helped an embattled lower middle class improve their lives in the short term.

In a study of the impact of cash compensation in Knysna and Riebeek-Kasteel, Anna Bohlin concludes that "money, as a relatively empty signifier, is invested with meanings in creative and open-ended ways, often becoming about 'home' and 'belonging'" (Bohlin 2004, 683). In Knysna claimants invested their money upgrading poor homes. In one case, in Riebeek-Kasteel, a cupboard is given meaning, and history is attached to it: "There is the money" (Bohlin 2004, 677). However, the Black River examples show that with the division of money into such small amounts, money will carry but a temporary and relatively insignificant meaning. "Mandela's gift" would also have been more valued had it come sooner. For some, like Mona Dawood, the money is a sign of the failure of restitution.

Although the government intended it to promote the healing of the nation, in fact restitution has had all the potential for a negative and disruptive impact on families. The families featured here fortunately worked harmoniously together during the restitution process, but this is not the case for many others. Black River claimants know now that justice cannot be done. Some have reconciled themselves to that, others not. Lodging a claim entailed, for many, an almost romantic engagement with the CRLR. It served to acknowledge that the past had been unkind, that rights had been violated. Restitution, as one claimant argued, entailed "making a statement" about that ([Dhupelia-]Mesthrie 1998, 256). As time passed, restitution came to be very specifically about the end result—in the urban case, money. The inability of the CRLR to present itself as an efficient agent has seriously lessened the impact that restitution could have had. Its office in Strand Street, Cape Town, represents the face of bureaucracy, and several interviewees use humor to deal with their frustrations. Finally, it is significant that in almost every interview, the restitution narrative has been accompanied by the removals narrative.

Du Toit has argued that "to lodge a claim is . . . to re-awaken . . . old ghosts and open half-healed wounds" (2000, 81). Black River interviews reveal that at the time of lodging their claims, the past was recalled in a fairly happy way—their lives, homes, activities. This happiness was not long-lasting. Du Toit accurately predicted that old wounds would become exposed, but he also anticipated that a new feeling would emerge when land was restored. This was the "loss of the loss," a phrase adopted from Slavoj Žižek. Once returned to their land, du Toit argued, people may find that "we never had what we thought we had lost" (du Toit 2000, 82). Black River narratives, however, reveal that the loss has become more real. Restitution characterized by delays and limited financial settlements has left an aching gap.

NOTES

1. I was among the five women in the group. I dedicate this chapter to the Black River people I have got to know and appreciate over the last decade and more. All names have been used with their express permission. I also want to acknowledge *Kronos* for permission to use this article, which was originally published in a fuller version in 2006 as "Tales of Urban Restitution, Black River, Rondebosch," *Kronos, Journal of Cape History* 32 (November): 216–43.

2. Debates in the National Assembly of the Republic of South Africa (*Hansard*), 1994, no. 14, 3991–2, 3995.

REFERENCES

Bohlin, Anna. 2004. "A Price on the Past: Cash as Compensation in South African Land Restitution." *Canadian Journal of African Studies* 38 (3): 672–87.

Brown, Marj, Justin Erasmus, Rosalie Kingwill, Colin Murray, and Monty Roodt. 1998. *Land Restitution in South Africa: A Long Way Home*. Cape Town: Idasa.

[Dhupelia-]Mesthrie, Uma. 1995. "Swallowing the Gnat after the Camel: The Fraserdale/Black River Group Areas Proclamation of 1966 in Rondebosch." Unpublished paper presented at the South African Historical Society Conference, Rhodes University, July 1995.

———. 1998. "Land Restitution in Cape Town: Public Displays and Private Meanings." *Kronos* 25: 239–58.

Dhupelia-Mesthrie, Uma. 1999. "The Truth and Reconciliation Commission and the Commission on Restitution of Land Rights: Some Comparative Thoughts." Paper presented to Conference on the Truth and Reconciliation Commission, History Workshop, University of the Witwatersrand, 11–14 June 1999.

———. 2000. "Dispossession and Memory: The Black River Community of Cape Town." *Oral History* 28 (2): 35–43.

du Toit, Andries. 2000. "The End of Restitution: Getting Real About Land Claims." In *At the Crossroads: Land and Agrarian Reform in South Africa into the 21st Century*, ed. Ben Cousins. Bellville and Johannesburg: Programme for Land and Agrarian Studies, University of the Western Cape, and National Land Committee.

Levin, Richard M. 1998. "Politics and Land Reform in the Northern Province: A Case Study of the Mojapelo Land Claim." In *Land, Labour and Livelihoods in Rural South Africa: Vol. 2*, ed. M. Lipton, F. Ellis, and M. Lipton. Pietermaritzburg: Indicator Press.

Mayson, David. 1996. "Land Restitution in the New South Africa." Unpublished report. Cape Town: Surplus People Project (SPP).
Walker, Cherryl. 2003. "Urban Restitution." Unpublished paper presented at Seminar on Urban Land Challenges in South Africa, 3 April 2003. Pretoria: DFID.

INTERVIEWS

Adams, Ghamza. Cape Town, 23 August 2006.
Adams, Ghamza, and Ebrahim Osman. Cape Town, 10 March 1997.
Adams, Rashaad. Cape Town, 2 May 1995.
Dawood, Mona. Cape Town, 16 August 2006.
Desai, Abou. Cape Town, 11 August 2006.
Eager Emily. Cape Town, 8 May 1995.
Eager, Emily, and Kannemeyer, Jerry. Cape Town, 13 August 2006.
Mohamed, Baboo. Cape Town, 19 August 2006.
Mohamed, Fatima. Cape Town, 16 August 2006.
Mohamed, Baboo and Fatima. Cape Town, 16 November 1995.
Osman, Ebrahim. Cape Town, 8 August 2006.
Pangarker, Aziza. Cape Town, 1 May 1995.

NEWSPAPERS

Cape Argus, Cape Town, South Africa.
Cape Times, Cape Town, South Africa.

five

The Right to Land Restitution as Inspiration for Mobilization

MARC WEGERIF

This chapter is an initial exploration and sharing of experiences and ideas based on a case study of a group of small farmers who have occupied and are producing on land to which they believe they have a historical right. The group, called Mahlahluvani (although they include people from other communities and claimant groups), is part of a not-yet settled land claim that has been lodged on the land they now occupy. I open with an account of a day with one of these farmers and then give an overview of the occupation and the nature of their production at Mahlahluvani. Reference to other cases (Davhana and the Vukeyas) shows that the Mahlahluvani experience is not a unique phenomenon. I then explore lessons from these cases for five key issues in land reform: the nature of production, leadership, conflict and ethnicity, people-driven land reform, and debates on the property clause in the Constitution.

In the context of a failing land reform and land restitution program in South Africa, one that is neither returning sufficient amounts of land to people nor facilitating the effective use of the little land returned (Hall 2004; Wegerif 2004; Ministry of Agriculture and Land Affairs 2005), I believe the people of Mahlahluvani and other land occupations are showing a potential way forward. They deserve support, provided that support does not undermine the initiatives they have taken. Land reform debates could also benefit from more empirical and in-depth research on such cases; with this chapter, I hope to stimulate debate and interest in such research.

The material presented here is based on my own fieldwork in 2006, when I was privileged to spend a little time with some of the farmers, and on the fieldwork notes and interviews of Themba Maluleke and Tshililo Manenzhe.[1] The research also involved a participatory rural appraisal mapping exercise with the farmers, informal conversations, site visits, and observation. It is part of a project sponsored by the Institute for Poverty, Land and Agrarian Studies (PLAAS) that focuses on the impact of land redistribution on poverty reduction and livelihoods.[2]

MAHLAHLUVANI: A DAY ON THE FARM

It was just before six on an April morning—the sun had not yet risen—as we set out from the three *rondavels* [dwellings] that make up the homestead of Xikalamazula Sithole,[3] his wife Johanna, and their family in the village of Nwaxinyamani, Limpopo. Xikalamazula led the way, followed by his eight-year-old grandson, Godsave, who was on school holiday, and Johanna. I stayed close to Xikalamazula, chatting to him as we walked briskly in the dawn light along a bumpy mud road between further homesteads all crowded onto small plots, around 30 by 30 meters in size.

We were setting out for a day's work in the fields that Xikalamazula has illegally cleared and planted on land he believes is rightfully his. His parents were removed from the land in the late 1950s while he was a boy. Despite the land claims process mandated by the Restitution Act, Xikalamazula and other members of the Mahlahluvani community have not yet had their land returned, but a group of nearly forty families has decided not to wait any longer and has occupied the state-owned land. They have been threatened with eviction but continue farming; Xikalamazula says his family has to eat.

Xikalamazula and his wife had been farming the land for five years when I met them in 2006. He said he started plowing there because he was hungry and was going to their *marumbini* [the place where they used to live]. He only got to standard two (grade four) in school, and his wife has less education; neither of them speaks English. Xikalamazula has found it difficult to get work, something he attributes partly to the disability he has in one foot that causes him to limp but is not sufficient for him to get the state disability pension. Some time ago he lived in Alexandra, Johannesburg, and worked for a white person in the garden of their large house in the wealthy suburb of Sandton. He has not had a regular job for a long time and is too young to get an old-age pension. He has survived by doing some temporary "piece jobs" and sometimes cutting and selling firewood. One day he was at a meeting at the local traditional leader's house and heard that people could get back their land. When he saw others were plowing at their marumbini he decided to join them.

Xikalamazula has three children, one still at school and the others out of school but unemployed. Two live at home and the third in Makhado, formerly Louis Trichardt (the nearest town, about forty kilometers away). He also has two grandchildren living at home. One receives a child support grant of R190 per month, which is the only source of income aside from what the family sells from what they produce and gather on the land. Almost all they produce is used for home consumption, although some firewood that they bring back is sold to get the cash needed for such things as school fees and seeds.

The path we were following went through open land used for cattle grazing and then worked its way between fields planted with maize and other crops. Xikalamazula looked with disdain at the withered maize stalks visible in the fields we passed. "This soil has nothing; you are wasting your time to try and grow crops here," he said. The path became narrower and started to rise until we were climbing a steep slope surrounded by thick bush. As we got higher we found ourselves soaked by a morning mist. Eventually we reached blue gum trees that form part of a commercial plantation and then, on the top of the ridge, joined a track used by forestry vehicles, which we followed toward the valley where Xikalamazula and others are farming.

An hour and ten minutes after leaving Nwaxinyamani we arrived at a rough gate in a fence made from sticks and thorn bushes. Looking over the gate one could suddenly see a whole valley that had been cleared and planted with maize and other crops, as well as a few small huts in the different fields that covered the slopes of the valley and the hills on the opposite side.

Before starting work Xikalamazula called out to his neighbors to see who was around. A few voices answered from across the valley. With the mist it was hard to see anyone, but there was smoke rising from a hut some distance away, indicating someone was already cooking or just getting warm. It was a Tuesday morning after the long Easter weekend and it seemed that the

The Right to Land Restitution as Inspiration for Mobilization

other farmers were slower than usual in arriving to work in their fields. The misty morning and rain may also have encouraged some to linger at home. As the day wore on more farmers passed by and could be seen working in their fields. One neighbor came over and discussed plans for the funeral of a farmer who had passed away a few days before. Xikalamazula suggested the farmers should each contribute R5 to assist with funeral expenses. The person who had passed away was a man in his late fifties who had been working for a few years on the land. I asked what would happen to his land, and Xikalamazula explained that the man's wife who had been working with him on the land would continue, as they were now her fields.

There was also a discussion with a few neighbors about cattle getting into the fields and eating maize. A farmer said she had found cattle in the fields the day before and chased them out but had not been able to find where they had got through the fence. The crudely constructed perimeter fence that they all assist in maintaining surrounds Xikalamazula's and a dozen or so other fields in that valley. Between each plot are smaller fences made of sticks that mark the boundaries, but in most cases these would not deter cattle or other animals.

The main task for the day was harvesting maize. We collected the maize cobs, putting them into cloths tied around our shoulders and then transferring them into sacks when the cloth was full. Xikalamazula wanted to collect the maize that was close to a beehive while it was still cold and misty, as he knew the bees would not be active in those conditions. He gave Godsave an old *atchar*[4] bucket and got him to start collecting small tomatoes growing among the maize stalks. After a while Johanna went to another part of the field to harvest peanuts. She came back with a small sack of peanuts and was also chewing on sugarcane.

While we were working, Sarah, a widow living near Xikalamazula in Nwaxinyamani, arrived and started harvesting maize in her field. Her husband passed away about five years previously, and, as she had no work, Xikalamazula suggested she join them in farming. After about an hour the mist turned to light rain that we endured for a while before taking refuge in the hut. The round thatched hut of about three and a half meters' diameter was used for storing produce from the fields and items such as old buckets and sacks used for collecting crops. More valuable tools such as axes and hoes are carried home or hidden in the bush to avoid theft. Half the floor of the hut was covered in a mound of maize cobs harvested by Xikalamazula; a smaller pile belonged to Sarah. There were a number of pumpkins in a pile, some firewood, and pots used for cooking lunch. On a previous visit I drank *Mcomboti* (home-brewed beer made from maize and sorghum) that Xikalamazula stored in a five-liter container; this time there was no sign of the beer.

When the rain stopped we went back to the fields. Xikalamazula now worked on the land that had been plowed by Sarah, and I joined him there. Sarah's plot is within the field fenced by Xikalamazula and no boundary was visible to me between their fields. Despite this, and the assistance we gave with harvesting, she and Xikalamazula were very clear on what was her crop and what was his. At one point as I reached to pull a maize cob from its stalk, Xikalamazula, who I thought was absorbed in his own work, stopped me, and said, "That is mine." I left the stalk and moved further to the side plowed by Sarah, taking care to check where Xikalamazula stopped harvesting. All the maize we picked in her field went into a separate sack and was stored separately although in the same hut.

Johanna worked in a different part of the fields, collecting pumpkin leaves and flowers. The work proceeded at a steady pace, and hours passed. We were not overstraining ourselves and chatted now and again as we worked and with other farmers who passed by. The maize cobs varied in quality; many were a bit eaten by some worms, and others were clearly small, but nevertheless a substantial crop was being harvested. It is hard to estimate the total amount of maize the family would have got that season. By the time I was there they had hired a *bakkie* (pick-up-truck with a one-ton load capacity) to take two loads to the village, in addition to the sacks they carried back themselves; at least two more *bakkie* loads were taken to the village that season. Certainly they had considerably more than they could eat that year and planned either to store it for the following year or sell a portion. Also of great importance is the fresh maize that is picked and eaten on a daily basis when ripe. When asked to estimate how much maize is eaten in that way before the harvest, Xikalamazula explained that for about two months they had eaten at least two cobs each while working in the fields. They roast these on the open fire and then carry twelve to fifteen cobs home with them every day for the family.

Thomas Ndlovu, Johanna's brother, stopped and took shelter with us during the rain on his way to his fields. Later we saw him returning, and Xikalamazula asked him if it would be possible to use some of his land, which is next to a small river, for planting vegetables such as cabbage and spinach. Xikalamazula's plot is quite high up the hill and not close to any water; if he can plant next to the river on the land of his brother-in-law he will water by hand and be able to grow vegetables throughout the dry winter. Xikalamazula suggested clearing the land to be used and, after getting the crop, leaving this cleared land for Thomas to use in the future. He emphasized that the land belonged to Thomas, as it had been Ndlovu fields before they were removed. The discussion did not finish with any clear agreement; Thomas seemed to agree but was also a little cautious.

The total land area fenced by Xikalamazula could be around three hectares, including the land currently used by Sarah. It is hard to measure because of the contours of the land and the uneven shape of the plot. Xikalamazula and his wife plowed the whole area with hand hoes and have also cleared the bush themselves. A few areas of bush remain within the fenced fields that could still be cleared. A few shade trees have also been left in place. There are graves of Xikalamazula's grandparents on the plot, adding weight to his historical claim to that area. As well as the field crops there are a number of pawpaw trees and lemon trees.

Early in the afternoon I went with one of the neighboring farmers, Daniel Khumalo, to look for Pushy Hlongwane, the first man to return to Mahlahluvani to farm. He had begun farming in 1998 on land previously occupied by his parents near a stream at the bottom of the valley. Others had apparently followed his example. I was interested to find out more about this man who had reportedly started the land occupation that led to large amounts of previously unused land being plowed. We walked through several fields. At the bottom of the valley, alongside a small stream was a line of sugarcane. One of the huts we passed had neat rows of maize cobs tied by their stalks and suspended upside down from the ceiling. On another plot neat rows had been shaped in steps along the contour of the hillside, and the farmer was preparing to plant an early winter crop of vegetables.

Daniel gave the same reasons as Xikalamazula for settling on the land, saying it was his family's marumbini and his family had been hungry. He added that he had seen people coming back with maize and other produce from the land and had asked where they were coming from. One day he joined them and started clearing his own piece of land.

When we got to Pushy's fields no one was to be found, only a dog to frighten away intruders, monkeys, and bush pigs. The rectangular hut, incorporating a *toolu*[5] full of maize, was locked with a padlock. There were numerous avocado and mango trees on the plot, as well as pawpaw, lemons, and sugarcane. A large number of pumpkins could be seen through cracks in the hut door and maize, peanuts, beans, and sweet potatoes were visible in the fields. When I did get to interview Pushy Hlongwani later, he said he had begun farming in the area "after hearing that people must get their land back if they were removed" and because of hunger (interview 13 March 2006). He only reached standard two at school and used to work in a steelworks outside Pretoria. He lost this job in about 1981 and then survived doing "piece jobs" around Makhado until he started farming. He says the plowing he does now is much better than the work he did in the past.

Walking back from Pushy's farm, we took a different route going past Daniel's fields, where we found his wife and a friend sitting by a fire in their hut. Daniel took his hoe and dug up some sweet potatoes that he gave to me. He said he sells sweet potatoes in the village at R10 per four-kilogram atchar bucket. When I got back, I found Xikalamazula collecting thin poles for building a toolu at his place in Nwaxinyamani. He had also chopped up some old blue gum poles that he bound together to carry back to the village for firewood.

As we worked we ate a few of the raw peanuts that Johanna had collected, and I got a piece of sugarcane. Xikalamazula decided, I think out of sympathy for me, to leave earlier than usual (he said they normally stay until four or five in the afternoon). Another reason was they had not brought maize-meal to cook that day. So at about two-thirty, after seven and a half hours in the fields, we started gathering all we would take with us on the journey home.

The walk back was mostly down hill, but this time we were carrying heavy loads, with everyone assisting. We were carrying fresh maize cobs from late-planted maize that would be eaten that day, tomatoes, pumpkin leaves and flowers, a large pumpkin, peanuts, sweet potatoes, sugarcane, and two different types of wood, one for cooking the meal and one for building. We also had a sack of dry maize cobs that were being moved bit by bit down the hill to take for grinding at the mill in the next village. I realized we were carrying everything the family needed to eat and cook that evening, aside from water and the maize-meal that they still had at home from the previous year's crop.

About ten hours after arriving I said goodbye to the Sithole family and drove away carrying gifts of sweet potatoes and sugarcane. I had also gained a renewed belief in the need for and potential of land reform if it can be truly driven and shaped by those who want to produce.

OVERVIEW OF THE OCCUPATION

The people of Mahlahluvani were removed from the land east of Ribolla Mountain over a number of years, mostly in the 1950s, as the land was taken over by different white farmers and Tsapekoe Estates (a large commercial farming enterprise that produced tea and other crops, originally owned by the state). The land is on an escarpment about forty kilometers to the east of Makhado in a border area between the former bantustans of Venda and Gazankulu. Whereas most of the Xitsonga speakers were moved to the village of Nwaxinyamani to the south, the Venda speakers, who had been living in the same area, were moved to the village of Mashau to the east.

The area has fertile soil, a temperate climate with no frost, and good rainfall due largely to the escarpment conditions. The terrain includes steep slopes and valleys and several perennial streams. A plantation of eucalyptus trees covers most of the state-owned land, with some indigenous bush and forest left on the steeper slopes.

In the mid-1990s four different land claims were lodged for the same land. The claimant groups/communities are Mahlahluvani, Mashau, Piet Booi, and Davhana. At the time of writing, none of these claims had been formally settled, and the negotiations around them were filled with conflict and riddled with ethnicity-based tensions.

Yet although there had been no progress in the formal settlement of the claims, a number of families from across the different claimant groups, such as the Sitholes, started to clear the land and start production. These farmers have cleared the bush and occupied unused pockets of land, largely leaving the eucalyptus plantation alone as the forestry company would not tolerate their chopping down the trees.[6] The leadership of the land claim committees recognized by the Commission on Restitution of Land Rights (CRLR) has tried to discourage these claimants. The CRLR and the Department of Public Works also initiated legal actions against the land occupants, but these actions came to a halt partly because of negotiations led by the NGO Nkuzi. Some occupiers were discouraged, but others continued to produce and clear more land.

During my fieldwork, a number of farmers reported starting to plow in the area after seeing Pushy Hlongwani and, later, other farmers plowing there and returning with crops. Almost all said they were occupying the land because of hunger and had returned to their marumbini. This was not a planned or dramatic land occupation but the gradual encroachment of individuals acting quietly to improve their lives, akin to the "everyday forms of peasant resistance" described by Scott (1985).

The results of structured household interviews carried out by Themba Maluleke give an indication of the significance of farming for the families producing at Mahlahluvani. Thirty-seven families were covered through the interviews, 19 headed by men and 18 by women, 11 of them widows. These families comprised 140 adults (71 women and 69 men) and 59 children under 16 years of age. Seventy of the adults were unemployed, 22 received old-age pensions, and 4 were disabled, although not all 4 got disability pensions. Only 11 of the 140 adults had formal jobs, mostly as builders and shop assistants, with a few in white-collar or professional jobs such as teaching. The rest were housewives, still attending school, doing "piece jobs," or self-employed (for instance, running a *spaza* shop).[7] Excluding the production on the occupied land, 20 of the 37 households interviewed lived below the internationally recognized poverty line of $1 per person per day, and a further seven households lived on less than $2 per day per person.[8] The average income per person per month across all the families was R354.

All 37 respondents said that their lives had improved since becoming part of the land occupation. This compares favorably with two redistribution projects studied as part of the same research—at the Monyomane redistribution project just 6 out of 12 respondents said their lives had improved, and at the Dikgale redistribution project 10 out of 13 reported this, with the rest saying it was the same or worse. The Mahlahluvani families plowed around 130 hectares of land in total. Eighteen would like to plow more land if they could get it, most asking for just one or two hectares more. Those not wanting more land said they were too old or did not have the resources to use it at the time. The main crops were maize, peanuts, beans, pumpkins (grown as much for the nutritious leaves and flowers as for the pumpkin itself), onions, and sweet potatoes. Farmers close to the streams were growing spinach, cabbages, and other vegetables. Most had some fruit trees, including avocados, mangoes, bananas, and pawpaw. There were also considerable amounts of sugarcane and small amounts of other crops such as tomatoes and chillies interspersed with the main crops.

Most of the produce was used by families for their own consumption, with some local sales. Many of the people interviewed did not sell on a regular basis, but rather when they needed cash. For example some reported selling bags of maize to pay for school fees, and others reported small sales driven by cash needs, such as selling sugarcane to a neighbor in order to buy bread. A few of the wealthier farmers were more actively marketing and selling produce for cash, but mostly locally in the villages where they live. Cutting and selling firewood from the occupied land and surrounding forests, for their own use and for sale, was also an important part of most livelihood strategies.

The farmers at Mahlahluvani have developed an informal organization that involves coming together occasionally in meetings to share information and discuss matters. They assist each other with activities such as funeral arrangements and fencing. The demarcation of family land seems to be done by individuals in interaction with their immediate neighbors and is loosely informed by where each family used to live and plow before the forced removals. It is not possible for everyone to go back to exactly where his or her family were before due to the forestry plantation. Although respondents said there was no conflict, some said if difficulties arose, they would be resolved by Pushy or Xikalamazula calling people together to find a solution. Xikalamazula seemed to be one of the most active members whereas Pushy appeared quiet and reserved; he did not stand out as a leader at group meetings, but he was clearly respected.

MAHLAHLUVANI IS NOT UNIQUE

The Mahlahluvani land occupation is not an isolated case. Without seeking them out, I came across two other occupations in the area. A few kilometers west of Mahlahluvani Chief Davhana had occupied an old government house, allocated plots of land to fifty families, and started farming on the surrounding land. He had planted six thousand tomato plants and fifteen hundred macadamia nut-tree seedlings and was supplying butternuts, cabbages, and other crops to a supermarket in Makhado. Davhana saw the land as his and his people's, on which he had a right to settle, although he was aware that the land claim was not yet settled (interview).

About twenty-five kilometers southeast of Makhado land was returned to the Shimange claimants in 2001. As is typical of many settled land claims, the communal property association (CPA) that owns the farm is absorbed by conflict, and there is no effective management of the land. Although a few individuals have been involved in small-scale production, much of the land is underused, and the tractor donated by the government has broken down and not been used for some time. In contrast, a group of six interrelated families, the Vukeyas, are involved in intensive production on an adjacent piece of land. They are part of the Shimange land claim, but their land has not been returned, apparently due to an error in the investigation by the CRLR. On hearing the claim was settled, the Vukeyas returned to what they believed should be their land; technically they are illegal land occupiers. The result is that they are not subject to any government-run business planning and not involved in the conflicts within the CPA. The Vukeyas have started plowing the fields that their families used to use and building houses. Their plots are between four and eight hectares each and are used for crops including maize, peanuts, beans, pumpkins, and chilies. They are also planting fruit trees such as mangoes. One of the families is selling produce in the neighboring villages and to shops in town.

IMPLICATIONS FOR LAND REFORM

Nature of Production

At Mahlahluvani we see poor people making their own choices—without government, NGO, or consultant intervention—about the type of production they want and can engage in. What can be learned from this is much more valuable than any response to a theoretical question about what people would like to do should they get land, since here we see people acting in real circumstances, making decisions informed by what they would like as well as by the conditions that constrain them. They have managed to go forward with production with no assistance from the government or anyone else. The outcomes are very different from scenarios where government officials and consultants are involved in advising and drawing up business plans that are almost always commercially focused and in many cases never implemented (Lahiff 1998; Wegerif 2004). Although further analysis is required, the level of production in the Mahlahluvani, Vukeyas, and Davhana cases appears to be very good compared to the majority of settled restitution and redistribution projects, especially considering the low input costs.

Leadership

At Mahlahluvani we see an interesting example of effective informal organization. The group is clearly deriving confidence from their shared struggles to get land and produce. There seems to be an important social dimension to their interactions, with practical assistance during harvesting and joint responsibility for things such as fencing. People also share ideas and information and copy and learn production techniques from each other.

Leaders such as Xikalamazula and Pushy have emerged from among the group. There is no indication that either of these men derives authority from traditional leadership connections, wealth, or education. Xikalamazula plays a facilitative role in bringing people together, and Pushy is turned to for advice if needed. Importantly, each family runs its own production on its land, making its own decisions and coming together with the others when it suits everyone. In contrast, the leaders of the formal land claims committee (such as the chairperson and deputy chairperson) are not plowing the land. They are wealthier and more educated. They have cell phones, cars, and speak English. They are easier for the CRLR staff to deal with and appear to derive power from the recognition that the CRLR gives them. These leaders have tried to tell those plowing to stop, and in turn they have been threatened and told to stay away from the land.

I would characterize these different types of leadership as a "production leadership" emerging from among those actually producing, based on the respect of fellow producers, and a "political leadership" that gains power from its ability to interact with and be recognized by external authorities such as government officials. The "production leadership" derives authority from its initiative and skills in production. The "political leadership" wins support through being articulate in the language of government officials and, because of resources such as transport, phones, and education, being able to maneuver through the organizational politics required of people who wish to benefit from government programs.

The administrative and legal complexity of government land reform programs (whether restitution, redistribution, or tenure reform), along with a lack of specific support to assist the less educated and less wealthy to access these programs, seems to be systematically drawing out "the political leadership" at the expense of the producers who have the interest and ability to use the land.

Conflict and Ethnicity

The government frequently complains that conflicts within and between communities are delaying the settlement of land claims in Limpopo (Didiza 2003; Gwanya 2003), and the situation around Ribolla Mountain is a worst-case scenario with four competing claims, ethnic divisions, and leadership disputes. This is certainly a difficult situation to resolve, yet the farmers at Mahlahluvani have overcome these divisions and conflicts and got on with production. In their meetings there is frequent switching between Xitsonga and Tshivenda, and farmers from settlements in former Venda and Gazankulu work alongside and assist each other.

In discussions some of the farmers have said that they always lived together as one community. There has also been intermarriage that has helped cement bonds across what some see as ethnic divides. It appears to be at the level of the land claims committees and the "political leadership" that ethnic and other divisions come to the fore, as leaders try to use whatever advantage they can to bolster their power through control of land, people, and access to officials.

One example of the farmers' ability to deal with what could easily be a recipe for conflict came up in discussions with Pushy, who is Xitsonga-speaking and stays in Nwaxinyamani. His parents' graves are on a piece of land now being plowed by Mr. Masindi, who is Tshivenda-speaking and lives in Mashau. Despite Masindi's plowing around another family's graves, there is no conflict. Although Pushy started plowing in a fertile part of his parents' former land that is close to water, Masindi started at the graves, because the land his parents used to plow is now within the eucalyptus plantation. Pushy says that since he knows him and he was living in the area before they were all removed, there is no cause for conflict. The farmers at Mahlahluvani have found ways to accommodate each other regardless of ethnic origin or other such factors. Thus they have in practice overcome divides that the CRLR still finds insurmountable.

PEOPLE-DRIVEN LAND REFORM AND THE PROPERTY CLAUSE

There has been much talk of the need for people-driven and demand-led land reform, as well as for the related concept of community-driven development (Binswanger and Aiyar 2003; DLA 1997; Gupta, Grandvoinnet, and Romani 2003; Lahiff 2005). No effective strategies are being implemented, however, to make this a reality in South Africa. At Mahlahluvani we see a truly people-driven process, with outcomes that respond to people's needs and are quite different from those of official land claim settlements and redistribution projects.

Current government procedures for dealing with land claims and redistribution projects tend to disempower the beneficiaries, especially the poor and those with little education. Furthermore, the current paradigm sees the CRLR and DLA pushing people into large-scale commercial farming. People such as those at Mahlahluvani have little interest in this form of production and few of the skills necessary for it. It is only the more educated and wealthy who will have a voice and space in such a paradigm. Given the dominant view and the snail's pace of official land reform, the occupation of unused land offers the poor a way whereby they can shape their own land reform initiatives and meet their livelihood needs.

Many who want a far-reaching land reform program not limited by the protection of existing property rights have criticized the property clause (sec. 25) in the Constitution for its protection of private property (Ntsebeza 2007). More progress might have been made, however, if people such as the farmers at Mahlahluvani had been told how the Constitution asserts "that South Africa belongs to all who live in it" (Preamble to the Constitution of South Africa, Act 108 of 1996). Landless people's feeling that they have a right to land could be reinforced by emphasizing that the Constitution gives those who had land taken away a right to their land back (sec. 25[7]) and that land can be taken from landowners for land reform (sec. 25[2] and [4]).

The discourse of the right to land restitution provides the perfect vehicle for mobilizing the direct actions of the poor through which they can lead and shape land reform. Hundreds of thousands of people have expressed a demand for land by lodging land claims as individuals or as members of communities and groups. Many of us in NGOs have been too clever in explaining to them the complexity of the Constitution and the law. We have been too good at convincing people of technicalities, such as there being a difference between the restitution of a right to land and restoration of the land itself. We can continue to subvert people's desire for their land into the bureaucratic malaise of the complex restitution of land rights procedures or channel it into campaigns and direct actions to get land.

There are, however, risks attached to such an approach. Widespread land occupations, especially if driven by political motives, as seen in Zimbabwe since 2000, can lead to the loss of production, conflicts, instability, and other negative outcomes. The addition to the South African Constitution of a social obligations clause similar to that of the Brazilian Constitution offers a potential way for dealing with the risks while giving real constitutional support to the notion of people's right to occupy and use unused land. Chapter 3 of the Brazilian Constitution creates the concept of a "social function" for rural land that requires land to be adequately used in a way that preserves the environment, respects labor laws, and benefits the owner and the laborers. The same chapter gives the government powers to expropriate land not performing its "social function" and, further, gives land ownership to a landless person (a person not owning any other rural or urban property) who for a period of five years occupies and makes productive use of rural land, up to a maximum size of fifty hectares.

This clause has been important in the land occupation strategies of movements such as the MST (Landless Rural Workers Movement) that has settled hundreds of thousands of families on close to five million hectares of previously unused rural land in Brazil (Branford and Rocha, 2002). Such a clause in the South African Constitution could give poor and landless people, and those who were dispossessed in the past, the right to occupy and use unused or underused land, thereby affirming that land is a national resource that is there for those who can work it. This could give enormous impetus to a truly people-driven land reform, not so much because of the legal mechanisms it would open up, but because of the message it would send to people such as the farmers at Mahlahluvani and others who may want to follow their example.

NOTES

1. Both Themba Maluleke and Tshililo Manenzhe were formerly with Nkuzi Development Association (Nkuzi), a Limpopo-based land NGO; they are also co-authors of chapter 16, this volume.
2. I am grateful to PLAAS, Nkuzi, and the researchers involved for allowing me to use the material. The views expressed here are my own and not necessarily those of any other organization with which the project or I may be associated.
3. Xikalamazula, a bracelet made of goat's skin, is the nickname Morgan Sithole was given as a boy.
4. *Atchar* is a type of mango pickle.
5. A *toolu* is a traditional structure used for storage that keeps the maize off the ground.
6. There have been conflicts with the forestry company over the land.
7. A *spaza* shop is a small local shop with a limited range of basic items for sale.
8. Financial calculations are based on an exchange rate of $1 to R7.

REFERENCES

Binswanger, Hans P., and Swaminathan S. Aiyar. 2003. *Scaling up Community-Driven Development: Theoretical Underpinnings and Program Design Implications.* Washington: World Bank.

Branford, Sue, and Jan Rocha. 2002. *Cutting the Wire: The Story of the Landless Movement in Brazil.* London: Latin American Bureau.
Constitution of the Republic of South Africa, Act 108 of 1996. Pretoria: Government Printers.
DLA (Department of Land Affairs). 1997. *White Paper on South African Land Policy.* Pretoria: Government Printers.
Didiza, Thoko. 2003. "Address by the Minister for Agriculture and Land Affairs, Ms. Thoko Didiza, at the Budget Vote of the Department of Land Affairs, 1 April 2003." Pretoria: Government Printer.
Hall, Ruth. 2004. "Land and Agrarian Reform in South Africa: A Status Report 2004." Bellville: Programme for Land and Agrarian Studies, University of the Western Cape (Research Report no. 20).
Gupta Das, Monica, Helene Grandvoinnet, and Mattia Romani. 2003. *Fostering Community-Driven Development: What Role for the State?* Washington, D.C.: World Bank Development Research Group.
Gwanya, Tozi. 2003. "Land Restitution in South Africa: Our Achievements and Challenges." Pretoria: Office of the Chief Land Claims Commissioner.
Lahiff, Edward. 1998. "Northern Province District Study." Polokwane: Nkuzi Development Association.
———. 2005. "From 'Willing Seller, Willing Buyer' to a People-Driven Land Reform." Cape Town: Programme for Land and Agrarian Studies, University of the Western Cape (PLAAS Policy Brief no. 17).
Ministry of Agriculture and Land Affairs. 2005. "Delivery of Land and Agrarian Reform." Report to the National Land Summit (July 2005). Pretoria: Ministry of Agriculture and Land Affairs.
Ntsebeza, Lungisile. 2007. "Land Redistribution in South Africa: The Property Clause Revisited." In *The Land Question in South Africa: The Challenge of Redistribution and Transformation,* ed. Lungisile Ntsebeza and Ruth Hall, 107–31. Cape Town: HSRC Press.
Scott, James C. 1985. *Weapons of the Weak.* New Haven: Yale University Press.
Wegerif, Marc. 2004. "A Critical Appraisal of South Africa's Market-Based Land Reform Policy: The Case of the Land Redistribution for Agricultural Development (LRAD) Programme in Limpopo." Bellville: Programme for Land and Agrarian Studies, University of the Western Cape (Research Report no. 19).

six

Choosing Cash over Land in Kalk Bay and Knysna

The Time Factor in Urban Land Claims

ANNA BOHLIN

A common scenario in restitution cases around South Africa has been that early on in the process significant numbers of land claimants wish to have land restored to them.[1] As time passes, however, this number decreases, and by the time the claim reaches the settlement stage, only a small core group of individuals, if any, still opt for land, whereas most choose cash compensation. Given that a key goal of the restitution program has been to promote desegregation and transfer land to previously disadvantaged groups, a pertinent question is: What is it about the passage of time that has led so many land claimants to change their minds and opt for financial compensation?

This chapter addresses this issue through an analysis of two restitution cases in the Western Cape: Kalk Bay, a fishing community and suburb of Cape Town (see map 3), and Knysna, a town on the Garden Route.[2] Both involve urban claims in attractive coastal areas where the demand for and value of property is high. Apart from all other forms of value—social, cultural, and emotional—the houses and plots that were lost represent significant economic assets: one house under claim in Kalk Bay was sold in 1995 for close to R500,000 (about US$70,000) and would be worth much more today. Furthermore, in both cases there were possibilities for land restoration or alternative land. Thus compared to cases where the land under claim is either unavailable or economically unattractive, these cases offer compelling economic arguments why claimants would pursue the option of land restoration—which, initially, many claimants did.

The chapter begins with an outline of the history of displacement and land claims in each place and then analyzes how claimants' preferences changed as circumstances shifted. An exhaustive analysis of claimants' reasons for choosing financial compensation—including economic, psychological, and social reasons—is beyond the scope of the chapter; it focuses, rather, on some dimensions of temporality that are relevant for understanding the dynamics involved in claimants' change of mind.

CLAIMING LAND IN KNYSNA

When around a thousand individuals in Knysna lodged a land claim with the Commission on Restitution of Land Rights (CRLR) satellite office in the town of George in 1996, the initial idea was that land would be restored to them. The claim had come about after public meetings in Knysna arranged by the Southern Cape Land Committee (SCLC), a local nongovernmental organization that was informing the public in the region about the recently introduced land restitution program. Although the claim was initially submitted as a community claim, in actual fact it involved individual households from all over Knysna,[3] for neighborhoods where the application of the Group Areas Act and other policies had resulted in racially motivated forced relocation from the 1950s through the 1980s: Salt River, Welbedacht, Vlenters, Wit Lokasie, Ouplaas, and Hunter's Home, to mention a few.

Although each place had its own character in terms of demography and tenancy arrangements, there were some commonalities around tenure before removals. More than 70 percent of the people classified as "coloured" in Knysna, in total some 750 families, lived in the areas of Ouplaas (Heidevallei) and Eastford (later known as Salt River) (CRLR 1999). They leased plots that varied from 0.4 to 3.3 hectares from white farmers and the Anglican Church. Some fifty white and twenty African families were also listed as living in these two areas. Most of the tenants had built their own homes, the majority out of wood and zinc. About 10 percent lived in brick houses. Most had well-established gardens where they grew vegetables, and many kept livestock on communal grazing areas. Both areas were affected by proclamations in terms of the Group Areas Act in 1966, and from 1969 to 1978 tenants classified as "coloured" were relocated to Hornlee, an area east of town with electricity and water, and those classified as black to plots without such basic services around Knysna. The church-owned ground of Salt River was sold to Knysna municipality and subsequently subdivided and sold to white buyers (CRLR 1999). Most houses were demolished or abandoned, but some of the brick houses still remain. The Heidevallei land, situated next to the N2 highway, was bought and is still owned by the municipality. Although part of it has been used for residential development, a large area has remained undeveloped, with a few scattered house foundations and old paths still visible.

In the early stages of negotiations around the land claims, in 1996/97, claimants discussed various pieces of land in Knysna as potential candidates for land restoration. In order to make the claim more effective, they decided to focus their efforts on Salt River and Heidevallei, the two areas from which most claimants had been displaced. During the first few years of the land claims process, the vast majority of claimants wanted land restored to them. According to Aurick Swartbooi, a former official at the CRLR office in George, "[I]nitially the only option discussed was land. That was the basis of negotiation" (Swartbooi interview, 2003). In interviews with the author in 2002 and 2003, claimants estimated that in 1998 90 percent of the group had wanted land.

What did they want the land for? One claimant, a shop assistant in his fifties, recalled in 2006 that "at that time [in 1997–98], we didn't concentrate so much on what we wanted to do with the land. The main thing was to get hold of it, and after that we would make plans" (Rhode interview, 2006). However, a contingent of claimants specifically wanted to re-create a smallholding environment where they could engage in small-scale agriculture. They were mainly older claimants who remembered their days as small-scale farmers. They formed a committee devoted to exploring how land restoration could provide agricultural opportunities. Henry Rhode, who chaired this committee, remembered how their early plan was to obtain some of the original land in Salt River, "suited for agriculture because it's a river valley," and complement farming activities with residential development on the steeper parts of the land (Rhode interview, 2002). They also discussed lodges for tourists as a possibility, given the scenic nature of the Salt River land and Knysna's significance as a tourist destination.

A proposal based on this idea was drawn up, and negotiations began between the claimants, CRLR staff, the landowner—who was willing to sell, but at what was considered a high price—and a developer (Swartbooi interview, 2003). Simultaneously, the agricultural committee explored the possibility of obtaining and then selling land in other parts of Knysna, such as Heidevallei, in order to purchase additional agricultural land outside Knysna. Kathleen Schulz, a former staff member of the CRLR George office, remembered in an interview in 2007 how members of this committee "would even be prepared to take over farmland thirty kilometers from Knysna, that's how motivated they were." Claimants who were not interested in farming presented different reasons during interviews for wanting land restored to them: to achieve a sense of healing and compensation for past suffering, to improve their and their children's living situation, and to contribute to a more equitable pattern of ownership in the highly segregated and overwhelmingly white-owned Knysna region.

Some simply missed their former living places and hoped to return for this reason. One such individual was Enid Fredericks, a nurse assistant in her fifties. Before evictions, she had lived in a brick house built by her father, a bricklayer, in Salt River. The house had a kitchen, a pantry, a living room, a dining room, two bedrooms, a bathroom, and a spare bedroom. It had a well-kept garden in front and electricity generated by a wind charger. In an interview in 2007 she remembered: "You know, my dolly house, it was also built out of bricks. I just remember it in my mind. Sitting on the *stoep* of the house, we could see the ships coming in through the Heads [cliffs marking the mouth of Knysna Lagoon]. It was far away, but we could see it." At the time of this interview, she believed the house was still standing but had refrained from going to see it as it would make her "heartsore." She had joined the land claims process in the hope that it would enable her to return to live somewhere in Salt River, and belonged to a group of claimants committed to exploring options for land restoration.

However, negotiations around the land claim were slow. By 1999, three years after it was lodged, not only were claimants getting impatient with the perceived lack of progress but so were commission staff, Schulz remembered (Schulz interview, 2002). She said that Knysna municipality regarded the land claim as an "obstruction" to the housing problem in the area, since the land identified as potentially available for restoration was situated on the urban fringe, where urban expansion plans were heading. Meetings with the regional land claims commissioner (Wallace Mgoqi at the time), councillors, and municipal officials from Knysna yielded little progress; neither did meetings between facilitators appointed by Mgoqi, who traveled from Cape Town once a month, and municipal officials. According to Schulz, "All the municipality wanted to know was when the claim would be settled and what was required [of] them, and how the claim would affect their IDP [integrated development plan]. All the commission could say was that no one was able to develop on the land under claim. . . . Clear policy within the national ranks of the DLA [Department of Land Affairs] on how to deal with tenancy claims had not been established" (Schulz interview, 2002).

The lack of policy affected all aspects of the process. Schulz remembers identifying land parcels and submitting property descriptions and telephone numbers of private landowners in Salt River to appropriate DLA personnel, only to hear that they were unable to facilitate purchasing until the monetary value of the claim had been established. Meanwhile, the CRLR was waiting for national directives on how to settle tenancy claims, and, according to Schulz, for the Land Claims Court to set legal precedents on monetary value in other tenancy claims. (For further discussion on the absence of policy on how to settle urban claims see Walker, this volume.)

A local teacher from Hornlee, who had been active in the Knysna land claims process from the beginning and assisted the CRLR with verifying lists of claimants, remembered claimants' growing frustration: "People had to wait. I can't say the process *was* too long—the first time [restitution] happens there will be mistakes, stuff like that. But people were still impatient: 'The government are only promising us things; it won't happen. Why waste your time?' Maybe the process was too long, for most of the people" (Bouw interview, 2003).

At around this time the newly elected chair of the claimant committee began telling claimants that they would be better off choosing financial compensation. Claimants describe him as a powerful, charismatic speaker with a booming voice, to whom people listened. Enid Fredericks recalled: "He said: 'If you take land, you will end up with rates and taxes, you will owe the municipality.' We [those pursuing the land option] could not explain to them [why they should choose land]; what he said was more sensible to them. He talked the people's language. We talked about what you *can* get, you know. We see empowerment, betterment, that's why we opted for land. But you know how long this thing had been dragging on by then" (Fredericks interview, 2002).

Several claimants, as well as staff at the CRLR George office, said in interviews that a reason why the new chairperson lobbied for financial compensation was that he was trying to use the land claim to leverage political support for his newly established political party, the Knysna Community Forum, a contender in the municipal elections of 2000. One claimant remembered: "He used to sort of say: 'Vote for me, then I will make sure you get your money.' But never in the open, so we couldn't confront him." Whatever the truth of this characterization, most individuals involved in the land claim agree that the chairperson's influence was profound. Some claimants had recently bought their existing houses from the municipality and had to pay municipal rates (property-related taxes) for the first time. They feared that if land were returned to them, it might become a liability and could even be forfeited if they failed to pay rates. One claimant in the group committed to land restoration remembered: "For them land became a problem. A deficit, not an asset. We said to them, 'Let's get the land first, we will find a solution.'"[4]

When the claim was formally settled, on 15 February 2001, 1,079 claimants[5] (822 "coloured" and 257 African) chose financial compensation of R16,495 per claimant.[6] Around 30 claimants, calling themselves the "Restonia Trust," decided to wait for land restoration. At the time of writing, this group was officially down to 24, including one claimant who had applied to the CRLR for financial compensation instead of land as she had become a pensioner and needed the money. The overwhelming preference for financial compensation meant that the Salt River option eventually had to be abandoned, since the CRLR considered the market price of the land for sale there as not justifiable, given the now reduced number of claimants (Waring interview, 2007). Instead, this group intensified its efforts to acquire the municipal land at Heidevallei identified for restoration in the 2001 settlement agreement.

After protracted negotiations, on 31 January 2006 the 24 claimants, Knysna municipality, and the CRLR signed a statement of intent in which the municipality agreed to make land in Heidevallei—an area from which some of the claimants had been removed—available to the Restonia Trust. Although the media hailed the agreement as a breakthrough ("Ten-year land struggle will see residents get homes," *Herald,* 23 January 2006; "New homes for families after successful land claim," SABC News website, 31 January 2006), nearly two years later, no agreement had been reached on the size of land to be returned to the claimants or the time frame for such a handover. The Restonia Trust claims that after other claimants were paid out, an area of 76 hectares of land in Heidevallei was identified as viable for land restoration by a task team comprising the town manager, town councillors, CRLR staff, and the claimants (Restonia Development Trust 2003). This understanding formed the basis for a business plan the Restonia Trust subsequently drew up. Aurick Swartbooi, formerly of the CRLR George office, verified that this was claimants' understanding at the time, although the precise size of the land was "a grey area that needed to be clarified" (Swartbooi interview, 2003). However, Lauren Waring, director of community service, Knysna municipality, suggested in 2007 that claimants would be eligible for a total area of 1.69 hectares—the amount of land that can be bought with the combined cash awards of R16,495 per claimant plus a planning grant, and interest on the original settlement amount (Waring interview, 2007). In 2008 claimants agreed to this figure and will receive land to this extent in an integrated housing development.

In Knysna claimants realized that it would be highly impractical to lobby for a return of all, or even most, of the pockets of land from which people had been displaced. In addition, far from all claimants wanted to move back to the places from which they had been evicted; as described above, there were other reasons for lodging the land claim. In contrast, the land claims submitted by people from Kalk Bay were strongly motivated by the hope of being able to return.

FROM LAND TO MONEY IN KALK BAY

When Kalk Bay was declared a white group area in 1967, around 120 individuals, about one quarter of the fishing community there, were forced to leave. Most of them were classified as "coloured," some as Indian. From this group some twenty households submitted sixteen claim forms in December 1998. In the months leading up to the lodging of the claims, the claimants—former owners and tenants—met on a number of occasions, a process I facilitated as a consequence of fieldwork that I had conducted for my doctoral dissertation (Bohlin 2007). A recurrent theme in these meetings, as well as in my interviews with former residents during 1997/98, was the longing to return to live in Kalk Bay. The reasons were rooted in the particular history of Kalk Bay and, more specifically, the unusual manner in which the Group Areas Act proclamation had been implemented.

Situated on the shores of False Bay, Kalk Bay is known for its beautiful scenery, quaint architecture, and authentic "village" feel. During apartheid, Kalk Bay, like the suburb of District Six, was known as a "grey zone" or a "colour-blind place" in otherwise increasingly segregated greater Cape Town, suggesting "dangerous potentials for mixing and melding, glimpses of an alternative reality" (Shepherd 2001, 353). The presence of the fishing community was a crucial reason for this perception, as was the fact that Kalk Bay had one of the few beaches open to people classified as nonwhite.

The Group Areas proclamation of 1967 triggered intense protests by local residents, liberal organizations, and newspapers. The Anglican Archbishop of Cape Town wrote that "even the most ardent supporter of separate development must feel a qualm of conscience" (*Cape Argus*, 31 July 1967), while Ms. Price from Muizenberg asked, "Have we gone stark, staring mad?" (*Cape Argus*, 15 July 1967). Because of the protests, the government, in a highly unusual action, decided to exempt those living in city council flats (built for the fishing community in the 1940s) and gave them a fifteen-year period of respite from the proclamation. Those living outside this exempted area were informed that they were occupying their homes illegally and had to leave. They were resettled mainly in the group area suburbs of Steenberg and Retreat, but also in other areas in the Cape Flats, a low-lying area outside Cape Town. Subsequently, in 1982, the government decided to rescind the proclamation and allowed the remaining fishing families to stay (Bohlin 2007).

The fact that the majority of the community managed to stay has had particular implications for those who were forced to leave. Nearly all of those who left have family members and friends in Kalk Bay. Besides feeling attached to their former places of living because of its intimate atmosphere, natural beauty, and quietness compared to the violence and crime of the Cape Flats, most of those who left have continued to visit Kalk Bay on a regular basis for social reasons, such as attending Sunday family lunches, weddings, birthday parties, and funerals. As in other cases of dispossession, they have also continued to worship in Kalk Bay, in churches and the mosque. Furthermore, many fishermen have continued to fish out of Kalk Bay harbor, commuting at night in order to catch the boats before they leave in the morning (Bohlin 2007). Continuing to identify socially and culturally with Kalk Bay, with some depending on their connection to Kalk Bay for their livelihood, many claimants saw the land restitution program as an opportunity to fulfill their long-standing wish of returning.

However, not everyone was interested in moving back to Kalk Bay. Some claimants, particularly the elderly, said they had moved too many times already, and that the steep hills and steps of Kalk Bay would be difficult to manage at their age. In the thirty years since they had moved, they had built up new networks in their current areas of living and had no wish to leave their present homes (Bohlin 2006). At a meeting in October 1997, therefore, claimants decided to submit claim forms separately and let each claimant household decide which form of compensation they would prefer. Those who wished to return to Kalk Bay included in their claim forms documentation showing vacant plots in Kalk Bay owned by the state or the city council, which might be used for the development of new accommodation. Alternative land was identified even though most of the original properties still stood, since the state was reluctant to expropriate property for restitution purposes, and claimants were strongly against the idea of displacing current owners or tenants.

Between the lodging of the claims in 1998 and their settlement in 2005–2007, I stayed in contact with some of the claimants, visiting their homes, meeting up in Kalk Bay, and speaking to them on the telephone. By 2003 the sense of positive achievement and hope that they had expressed in the early stages of the process had been replaced by frustration and disillusionment. They had been informed by the CRLR that their documents had been misplaced, and they needed to submit new copies of certain documents. This caused one claimant to say that the CRLR "made her sick," and she felt "very disheartened." Elaine Herman, another claimant and former property owner in her fifties, described the same incident: "We all received letters saying that the files had gone astray and that we needed to submit the information again. We had to go to Woodstock [suburb of Cape Town]; they gave us an appointment. . . . When the guy came, I asked him, 'How could the documents go astray?' He said, 'Wait, let me have a look.' And then he came with the file. Honestly!" (Herman interview, 2006). The claimants were also deeply discouraged by the amount of time that had passed since they had lodged their forms; they participated in two public marches, arranged by claimants from other parts of Cape Town, to draw attention to the slow pace of land restitution.

Claimants were also frustrated by the difficulty of finding suitable land in Kalk Bay for restitution purposes. They had investigated a vacant plot of state-owned land but were told that this was to be used by a nearby school. They had also inquired about a row of properties that had been demolished in the 1970s for the building of a tunnel, a project later canceled. The land belonged to the city council and was leased to South African National Parks because it was on the border of the Table Mountain National

Park. However, they were met with vague and evasive answers from the CRLR. Although they had submitted maps of these plots along with their application forms in 1998, they discovered in 2003 that the CRLR staff was unaware of both the maps and the vacant land. Instead claimants were offered alternative land near Prince George's Drive on the Cape Flats, an area about which one claimant commented: "I wouldn't even live there for free" (Boltman interview, 2003).

The cumulative effect of the delays, the lost files, and the difficulties in identifying alternative land was that claimants began to doubt whether the restitution process would be successful and, particularly, whether they would ever get land. In April 2003 I offered to facilitate a meeting to explore possibilities for alternative land in Kalk Bay, but by that time most claimants had been contacted by the CRLR and had filled out forms indicating that they would prefer monetary compensation. The account given by one of the claimants I interviewed illustrates the reasons behind this change of heart. This woman, Marie Boltman, had originally wanted land mainly because her brothers and her son were fishermen and would benefit from having a base in Kalk Bay. However, since she was already in her sixties and her mother, who had also been evicted from Kalk Bay, was in her eighties, she said that holding out for land no longer seemed a realistic option.

The claims were finally settled between 2005 and 2007. Claimants were paid the Standard Settlement Offers, around R40,000 for former owners and R20,000 for tenants. The only claimant who opted for alternative land was still waiting at the time of writing in late 2008.

SHIFTING PRIORITIES IN KNYSNA AND KALK BAY

The cases outlined above differ in several respects. Yet in both cases the initial commitment to land restoration was replaced by a desire for financial compensation, and in both places claimants cited the long waiting period as a crucial reason for this shift. How, more precisely, did the passing of time affect claimant preferences?

An obvious impact of temporality on claimants' choices was that of aging. Although initially many of the elderly claimants in both Knysna and Kalk Bay were willing to wait for land to be restored, as months became years they realized that they might be too old to make meaningful use of the land or, worse, that they might pass away before this happened. In some cases, even though the claimants were young, they switched from land to financial compensation for the sake of their older relatives. A more complex dimension of temporality concerns the relationship between the passing of time and claimants' faith in the restitution process as well as the broader political system. During the early stages of the discussions in Kalk Bay in 1998 many claimants expressed ambivalence regarding the new democratic government led by the African National Congress (ANC). Although nearly all expressed immense admiration for then President Nelson Mandela and some had voted for the ANC, many simultaneously spoke about the dominance of African interests in national politics and their fears that they, previously classified as "coloured," would be marginalized (Bohlin 2007). Their views of the land restitution program echoed this ambivalence: although they welcomed the opportunity to address what they perceived as the morally wrong and deeply unjust actions of the apartheid government, claimants were nevertheless unconvinced that the new political dispensation would be willing, or able, to right those wrongs. Their faith in a positive outcome from the process was thus already fragile at the time of lodging their claims. When years went by with seemingly no progress, and with frustrating experiences with the CRLR, their faith in the possibility of a successful outcome diminished still further.

In my fieldwork in Knysna from 2002, I came across sentiments that were similar to those expressed by former residents of Kalk Bay, particularly among those previously classified as "coloured." In interviews the group holding out for land (all "coloured" except for one African woman) spoke about their growing fears that the issue of "race" might compromise their cause. One claimant said that the ANC-governed Knysna municipality "seem[s] to think we are a group of coloured people making trouble." In contrast, African claimants generally viewed both the local and national government more positively. Yet even within this group many expressed a profound sense of alienation from officialdom in general and were skeptical that authorities of any color would effect improvements in their lives. This was reflected in the immense surprise and even disbelief claimants felt when their land claim actually resulted in payments, something described in several interviews.

Thus in both places claimants' trust in the restitution process was fragile from the outset. Trust was further undermined by long waiting periods, frustrating meetings, and negative encounters with the CRLR. The issue of diminishing trust is significant in the light of the uncertainty surrounding the option of land restoration. Speaking about the Knysna claim, Andile Shoko from the CRLR George office made a comment that is also applicable to the situation in

Kalk Bay: "It wasn't an informed choice between 'A: here is the cash' and 'B: there is the land,' a specific piece of land. It was, 'here is the cash, you can get it now, or the government can try to identify *some* land for you.' Claimants *knew* much more about cash than land" (Shoko interview, 2007).

Anthropological studies of risk and uncertainty have shown that when stakes and probabilities are conceived as highly uncertain, one way of coping is by means of high trust in decision makers or other governing forces or principles (Boholm 2003). If, however, "trust is low, or there is only weak faith, the remaining options are precaution or avoidance" (Boholm 2003, 171). With faith in the restitution process diminishing over time, the uncertainty surrounding the idea of land restoration is thus likely to have assumed an increasingly important role when claimants weighed their options. Even though restoration of highly sought-after coastal land could potentially result in a more valuable asset, it was unclear to claimants when, if ever, this possibility would be realized, and cash appeared a less unknown and therefore safer option.

The passing of time also affected claimants' shifting perceptions in other ways. Borrowing from Geertz (1983), Boholm speaks of risks that are "experience-near," embedded in practices of everyday life and personally experienceable, and those that are "experience-far," which "emerge as abstract, distant calculations" and are beyond the sphere of normal experience (2003, 172). For many claimants in Knysna and Kalk Bay, who had had personal experience of evictions and forced displacement, the risks associated with attachment to land can be described as experience-near. In contrast, the idea of successfully owning and managing high-value property represented an experience-far, relatively abstract possibility. Such experience-far scenarios are typically understood, mediated, and communicated via various collective narratives (2003, 173), something illustrated in both Knysna and Kalk Bay where the delays in the process allowed claimants to reassess their initial impressions of the restitution options by drawing on information from local leaders and the mass media. In Knysna many claimants changed their minds because of the warnings of land becoming an economic liability, issued by an influential local political figure. In Kalk Bay claimants took part in public marches, where they exchanged experiences with claimants from other regions, most of whom had negative experiences with the wait for land restoration. In both communities claimants also said they were influenced by newspaper articles and television reports that described how other communities in the country had struggled to get their land back.

Significantly, claimants from both places said in interviews that they did not feel they had actively chosen money over land. Instead they spoke about the decision to choose cash as one that for various reasons they "had" to make: because of the inability of the CRLR to offer acceptable alternative land, the risk management described above, and because of their urgent need for financial resources given their general poverty. Many spoke of the impossibility of making a "correct" choice, and described the personal and even moral dilemma this entailed.[7] Although not everyone felt this way—some were confident that they had made the right decision—it is noteworthy that the formal alternatives available in the restitution program were not always experienced as offering a real choice between comparable options.

Finally, an important aspect of temporality concerns how these choices will be viewed in the future. When land claims are settled with monetary compensation there is a particular elasticity inherent in the interpretation of the process, since, unlike land, cash does not reflect what was lost in any immediate or tangible manner (Bohlin 2004). Given that the experience of the loss of a home or land is a dynamic process, often intensifying with the passing of time (Bohlin 2007; Stites 1999; see also Fay and James in this volume), the question of the amounts paid out and their perceived fairness is likely to be revisited, first by claimants themselves. In Knysna, for example, some said in interviews that they regretted taking cash after seeing "huge mansions" being built on the land on which they used to live. Second, descendants of claimants may well question whether cash accepted by their parents has adequately settled the "moral accounts" of the dispossession, since they would have been more likely to benefit from property (see Irwin-Zarecka 1994, 76).

This chapter has identified three dimensions of temporality significant for understanding claimants' shift in Knysna and Kalk Bay from preferring land restoration to choosing financial compensation. First, in both places claimants' age became an increasingly important factor as time passed, and claimants realized that waiting for land restoration might be in vain. Second, claimants' faith in the restitution process, fragile to begin with, diminished as time went by and encounters with the CRLR seemed to yield little result. Waning confidence in the restitution process made claimants increasingly unwilling to pursue the comparatively unknown and uncertain option of land restoration, even though it could potentially result in an asset of far greater value than the compensation that they ultimately accepted. Third, for most claimants the idea of successfully owning property represented an "experience-far" possibility communicated and understood through various public narratives. In both communities the passing of time intensified this process of mediation, exposing claimants to public information that highlighted negative consequences of choosing land restoration.

The chapter has also raised the issue of how financial compensation will be viewed as time passes. Loss of land rights is a temporal process that has ramifications into the future, and what counts as fair compensation takes on a particular elasticity when land claims are settled with cash. Despite the assumption that lost land rights can be compensated and settled in a one-off transaction, it is unlikely that all claimants and their descendants will view the issue in this manner in the future.

NOTES

1. I am grateful to claimants in Kalk Bay and Knysna who generously shared their time and information with me. Thanks to Ruth Hall and Cherryl Walker for comments on previous versions of this chapter, and to the Swedish International Development Cooperation Agency (Sida) for financial support.

2. Fieldwork involved semistructured interviews and participant observation in Kalk Bay 1997–99 and intermittently in the period 2000–2006, and in Knysna intermittently in the period 2002–2007.

3. SCLC was uncertain whether it would qualify as a community claim and subsequently submitted individual claim forms to the CRLR (interview with Kathleen Schulz, 2007).

4. See Fay and James, this volume, for a discussion of the liabilities and risks associated with the ownership of property.

5. The number of claimants receiving financial compensation later rose to around 1,400 as the verification process was reopened through an intervention of the minister of land affairs (Bohlin 2004).

6. The figure is based on the value of the land at the time of dispossession and escalated according to current values (CRLR 2000).

7. Compare Hohnen's study of poor consumers in Denmark (2004/2005, 94–95).

REFERENCES

Bohlin, Anna. 2004. "A Price on the Past: Cash as Compensation in South African Land Restitution." *Canadian Journal of African Studies* 38 (3): 672–87.

———. 2006. "Claiming Land and Making Memory: Engaging with the Past in Land Restitution." In *History Making and Present Day Politics: The Meaning of*

Collective Memory in South Africa, ed. H. E. Stolten. Uppsala: Nordic Africa Institute.

———. 2007. *In the Eyes of the Sea: Memories of Place and Displacement in a South African Fishing Town.* Göteborg: Acta Gothoburgensis Universitatis.

Boholm, Åsa. 2003. "The Cultural Nature of Risk: Can There Be an Anthropology of Uncertainty?" *Ethnos* 68 (2), 159–78.

CRLR (Commission on Restitution of Land Rights). 1999. "Summary of Research Report" by Sylvia Hoch, Directorate of Restitution Research, 19 May 1999. File belonging to the office in George.

———. 2000. "Request for Ratification of Negotiations Framework; Amendment." KRK/6/2/3/A/14/162/1145/7 A 351.

Geertz, Clifford. 1983. *Local Knowledge.* New York: Basic Books.

Hohnen, Pernille. 2004/2005. "Pengeformer Blandt Fattige Forbrugere i Danmark" [Money among poor consumers in Denmark]. *Tidsskriftet Antropologi* 49:85–96.

Irwin-Zarecka, Iwona. 1994. *Frames of Remembrance: The Dynamics of Collective Memory.* New Brunswick, NJ: Transaction Publishers.

Restonia Development Trust. 2003. "Business Plan to Acquire Post Restitution Settlement Funding." Unpublished report submitted to National Development Agency.

Shepherd, Nick. 2001. "Comments on Part II: Far from Home." In *Contested Landscapes: Movement, Exile and Place,* ed. B. Bender and M. Winer, 349–57. Oxford: Berg.

Stites, Elizabeth. 1999. "Spirit of the Land: Politics, Memory and the Sacred in South African Land Claims." Master's thesis. University of Cape Town.

INTERVIEWS

Boltman, Marie. Telephone interview, 8 April 2003.

Bouw, Joyce. Knysna, 22 February 2003.

Fredericks, Enid. Knysna, 20 October 2002; telephone interview, 7 September 2006.

Herman, Elaine. Telephone interview, 5 September 2006.

Rhode, Henry. Knysna, 20 October 2002.

Schulz, Kathleen, former CRLR official. George, 21 October 2002; telephone interview, 5 September 2007.

Shoko, Andile, CRLR official. George, 27 July 2007.

Swartbooi, Aurick, former CRLR official. George, 20 February 2003.

Waring, Lauren, director of community services. Knysna municipality. Telephone interview, 28 June 2007.

NEWSPAPERS

Cape Argus, Cape Town, South Africa.
Herald, Port Elizabeth, South Africa.

seven

Securing Postsettlement Support toward Sustainable Restitution

Lessons from Covie

ANGELA CONWAY AND TIM XIPU

Travel down the world-famous Garden Route and you will be struck by the beauty: majestic coastlines on one side and the Outeniqua Mountains on the other, with lakes, forests, and *fynbos* (indigenous vegetation) in between. This is indeed a piece of heaven, a place abundant in natural resources, with potential for sustainable lifestyles.

Drag your eyes off the natural splendor, and you will be struck by the opulence around you: huge houses on the coastline, cutting off access to the beaches and standing empty for most of the year; fences and walls, behind which live enclaves of the wealthy, secure in their own piece of paradise; golf estates gobbling up vast tracts of land and enormous amounts of water; hotels and holiday resorts—a playground for the rich.

Go off the beaten track and look over the hills of Sedgefield or the mountains of Hoekwil and you will be struck by the contrast. Poor people hidden away in overcrowded townships with limited access to land, forcing dependency on state grants. There is little sign of the so-called trickle-down effect of development. Patterns of apartheid spatial planning and development remain unchanged or compounded as land becomes ever scarcer and people are squeezed into diminishing spaces. The divide between rich and poor grows.

Many of the families in the overcrowded townships suffered the effects of forced removals: people who lived on the banks of the lakes, fishing and farming, were moved over the mountain as if they were a "threat to the environment"; people who lived along the coastline, fishing and celebrating high days and holidays at the beach, were moved into townships far from the coast. These are people unable to afford land, even within the land reform program, as the mismatch between the escalating price of land and land reform grants grows. These are people dispossessed and impoverished by apartheid and now by "development."

Covie is one such community. It enjoyed land rights in one of the most beautiful parts of the Garden Route. Now it is a community discarded, poverty-stricken, and scattered, yet united in its vision of restoration of land, culture, and livelihoods. As it involves prime coastal land, the restoration and development of Covie into a sustainable rural settlement has strategic significance: it will begin to challenge the current development paradigm and foster social and economic transformation.

This chapter is based on work undertaken by the Southern Cape Land Committee (SCLC) with the Covie claimants in their struggle for restoration. It is a reflection on some of the strengths and challenges of this case.

BACKGROUND TO COVIE: A "FORCED REMOVAL" OR NOT?

Established in 1884 as a woodcutters' location, Covie is situated approximately fifteen kilometers east of Plettenberg Bay on highly valuable land adjacent to the sea. One enters it by driving through a tunnel of lush indigenous forest that ends with open skies and breathtaking sea views. Before removals, this "mixed" community of white and "coloured" families—the majority classified as "coloured"—were mainly woodcutters in the surrounding indigenous forests. The colonial government had granted them rights to the commonage on a perpetual quitrent basis of ten shillings. Some residents applied for title, resulting in the allocation of thirty arable plots to white and "coloured" owners, but those who were not woodcutters were refused title. By the time of their dispossession in the 1970s most residents were employed by the Department of Water Affairs and Forestry (DWAF).

In the early 1930s the indigenous forests were closed for harvesting for two hundred years, which resulted in loss of employment for many Covie residents. As a consequence, residents turned increasingly to agriculture and fishing. Sharecropping opportunities on white-owned farms were also plentiful but began to decline in the 1960s as commercial agriculture expanded. However, work in the commercial forest plantations remained an important source of employment. Thus Covie was a rural community of landowners and tenants, enjoying land rights, practicing subsistence farming, or working for DWAF in the plantations, with access to the sea to supplement the food they bought or cultivated. Former residents remember it as a place where people lived in harmony. According to Irene Barnardo (known as Auntie Rene), a trusted pillar of the community, there were many community bazaars, strong bonds between neighbors, and well-cultivated living spaces. At that time Covie "wasn't so full of trees. People were living everywhere" (Barnardo interview, 2007).

The dispossession of the community was incremental throughout the 1960s and 1970s. From the late 1960s Covie began to be affected by DWAF provisions for a segregated workforce. Ironically, the first dispossession was of the white residents. This took place after the adoption of the National Forest Act, which legislated that white employees should live separately from "coloured" employees. With the adoption of this act the "coloured" residents, fearing the forced removals that had begun in other forestry settlements and given that "coloured" families were the majority, requested the government to declare Covie a "coloured settlement." On 29 September 1978 the government granted this request and Covie was declared a Coloured Group Area. White residents were expropriated and granted compensation for the land they owned. The majority accepted the compensation and left, with the exception of five families who retained title.

After the white residents were expropriated, services to Covie were cut off, resulting in a drastic decline in living standards. So began a slow process of "strangulation" that forced many people to leave the community "voluntarily," some to a township built to accommodate Covie residents and some further afield. Two years later, the remaining residents were asked to relinquish rights to the commonage because the parastatal South African Forestry Company Limited (Safcol) wanted to plant trees on the land. This was in accordance with the contents of the title deed, in terms of which the state could take the land at any time for public use. However, the conditions spelled out in the deed, that any dispossession would be by negotiation and mutually agreed upon, were not fulfilled, and the Covie community was merely informed by letter that their rights to the commonage were to be expropriated. Thus, the community was dispossessed of its rights to negotiate as well as its rights to land. Commonage users were compensated with checks of R50 per household. A group of landowners refused to cash the checks and threatened civil disobedience by pulling out any trees planted on the land. They also sought legal support to continue grazing their livestock on the land but were unsuccessful.

The Covie committee chairperson, John Pedro (Oom John), recalls that the threats were more than idle: "Safcol was planting trees on the community ground. We had a meeting, and I tell the people, 'Safcol is planting trees: we must pull the trees up and then put them in the fire.' We did this and they have never planted more trees" (Pedro interview, 2007).

Further pressure to relocate was then exerted on the residents, particularly those still employed by DWAF. They were threatened with loss of employment and criminal prosecution if they did not relocate to Coldstream, a forestry settlement some ten kilometers inland. Eventually the police, health inspectors, and DWAF officials were called in and began removing DWAF workers (seventeen households). That left behind about thirty people, either not employed by DWAF or classified white; these survived primarily through small-scale agriculture and fishing.

Auntie Rene, one of those who remained in Covie, remembers this period well. Community life broke down, and the former gatherings of people ceased: "It wasn't a nice time when the people left Covie because there [had been] lots of people in Covie. . . . Those that had to move to Coldstream lost all their cattle. They couldn't even take a cat or a dog. It was a very sad, sad story" (Barnardo interview, 2007).

Other losses occurred because of the 1974 proclamation by the South African National Parks Board (SANParks) of the Tsitsikamma National Park along the coastline. This park traverses the Covie commonage, and thus the remaining residents were cut off from the sea. As the community had supplemented their food by fishing for generations, this was a great loss. Nonetheless, no consultation with the community took place, nor was any compensation paid out.

It was this struggling group of people who first approached SCLC for help regarding their lost land rights. One of the objectives of SCLC at the time was to support claimants of the southern Cape in lodging claims before the cutoff date on 31 December 1998. Many of the removals in the area had taken place under an environmental pretext but were executed by the Community Development Board, the state organ responsible for implementing the Group Areas Act. One of SCLC's strategies was to collect oral and archival evidence of racial ideologies and see how these underpinned the so-called environmental concerns. The experiences of Covie seemed to make this a suitable case for SCLC's involvement.

Beauty Sampo, the SCLC fieldworker who first worked with the community, began by meeting not only the claimants who had lost access to land but also those who had been dispossessed. She recounts that despite residing elsewhere, former residents said, "We are living *here* [in Covie]," thereby taking the first symbolic step on the long, hard road to restitution (Sampo interview, 2007).

In 1998 Auntie Rene lodged a land claim on behalf of the Covie community for seventeen plots and 733 hectares of public land, as well as for compensation for the coastal strip incorporated into the Tsitsikamma National Park. However, as with most cases in the region, Covie was not a straightforward case of evictions but rather an example of the slow strangulation of a once-vibrant community. Thus the first challenge facing Covie was to convince the Commission on Restitution of Land Rights (CRLR) that they had rights to compensation within the restitution program. This required diligent collection of oral evidence and supporting documentation. To strengthen their voices Covie claimants also became part of a regional forum of claimant communities, the Southern Cape and Karoo Land Restitution Forum (SKKLRF). SKKLRF consisted of thirty-two claimant communities who organized themselves into a forum to strengthen their lobbying and mobilization strategies.

Covie claimants were united in their choice for land restoration, as opposed to other compensation options offered within the restitution program. As Oom John says, "The land is more important than money. If you take money, after five months, it's gone. With land, you have land to leave for your children. We tell [the government] that they took our land, and now they must pay for it. Let them help to bring Covie up, because it's down" (Pedro interview, 2007).

SCLC and the Covie Claimant Committee organized a number of mass meetings to secure a mandate for land restoration, which was unanimous. The broader claimant group met on two occasions, facilitated by SCLC, to develop and refine a vision of sustainable rural settlement, where people practice small-scale agriculture and the environment is preserved. Central to this vision was a wish to preserve the character and beauty of the place, including the fynbos, views, and forests. This vision has been the basis of all subsequent development discussions and plans. Committee member Norman Roman explains: "The environment is very important because as the community of Covie, we just can't live without the fields. Without nature, the birds will go away, the wildflowers, the bucks, the bush pigs, and then the tourism. That's why we need SANParks to help with conservation. We don't want to spoil everything" (Roman interview, 2007).

TO SETTLE OR NOT TO SETTLE

With the formal validation of the claim complete, and as a buildup to the national elections later in the year, in March 2004 the Land Claims Commission offered to "settle" the Covie claim and suggested a public signing of a section 42D agreement, thereby handing over the land before verification of claimants or institutional arrangements had been clarified. However, through their involvement in SKKLRF, claimants were aware of how claimants from Dysselsdorp, a semirural settlement in the region, had struggled to realize the benefits of their so-called settlement. Shortly before the national elections of 2000, the Dysselsdorp claim was "settled" when a check of R25 million was handed over to the community at a public ceremony. This took place before verification of the claimants had occurred and institutional arrangements established, resulting in conflict, which, at the time of writing in 2008, has left Dysselsdorp claimants unable to implement the settlement agreement. Because of the negative experience at Dysseldorp, SCLC, together with the Covie committee, recognized that it would be a mistake to settle the claim immediately, establish a communal property association (CPA), and take the land. Thus, the claimants resisted signing the section 42D agreement, instead opting to ensure that a development plan was in place before any transfer, to lay out appropriate institutional arrangements and the necessary implementation funds and skills.

At a public ceremony on 22 March 2004, the various stakeholders signed a memorandum of understanding (MOU) binding them to a process toward signing the section 42D agreement and the land transfer; the parties included the claimants, the CRLR, the local municipality, the Department of Housing (as landowner and to support the future development of the township section of Covie), Department of Public Works (as the commonage landowner), DWAF (to support livelihood options and as owner of possible "alternative land" to be restored in lieu of the land lost to the national park), and the Department of Environmental Affairs and Tourism (DEAT) (to support livelihoods building on the tourism potential of Covie). The signatories then constituted the Covie Steering Committee (Steering Com), which was given the task of "ensuring the co-ordination of the activities of the parties for the purpose of achieving the objectives of the MOU."

"We had a feast when the MOU was signed," Auntie Rene recalls. "Covie has never had such a big feast as we had that day. Lots of people from all over came. The commissioner and two ministers, SANParks, and the municipality." Oom John echoes these feelings: "It felt *great!*" (Barnardo and Pedro interviews, 2007).

APPROPRIATE PLANS AND APPROPRIATE ARRANGEMENTS

The next step was to translate the MOU into practice. The CRLR supplied a planning grant, used to employ a service provider to compile the Covie Development Plan. One of the roles of the Steering Com was to draw up terms of reference for this plan and to monitor the service provider. This was useful in that the Covie committee, as part of the Steering Com, was also part of the monitoring process. A challenge, however, was that the meetings were predominantly in English, whereas the claimants are mostly Afrikaans-speaking and could feel somewhat overwhelmed. Further challenges included the fact that many of the Steering Com members had little experience in development planning and that continuity of representation was not secure (many departments continually changed the representatives whom they sent).

Through the Steering Com various resources for development and post-settlement livelihoods were secured, including grants from the CRLR and DEAT. An important advantage of binding various stakeholders together in one forum was that it allowed for the generation of creative and integrated ideas, and facilitated the sourcing of resources. The local municipality supported the process and included Covie in their integrated and spatial development plans, and DWAF agreed to release alternative land.

The Covie claimants' vision has remained central to the development plan. As members of the Steering Com, they have been able to ensure that the plan fulfills their needs and does not become some consultant's unimplementable idea. As the process has become increasingly technical and bureaucratic, so the challenge for the Claimant Committee to remain abreast has become greater. This has required preparation and debriefing, undertaken by SCLC, before and after all Steering Com meetings. Advisers have therefore played an important role, both from SCLC and from the Legal Resources Centre (LRC).

One of the biggest challenges in any land reform program is to find appropriate institutional arrangements. The Covie Claimant Committee, which had clearly defined roles, rights, and responsibilities, was established at the beginning of the Steering Com process as an interim committee until a permanent legal entity would be agreed upon. The Steering Com agreed that SCLC, with the support of the LRC, be responsible for advising the claimants about appropriate legal entity structures. The community opted for a CPA, which provides some mechanisms for support through the Department of Land Affairs. The constitution of this CPA, which was adopted in December 2007 along with the election of an interim CPA, has detailed rules for asset management and use that will support its mandate to protect Covie's valuable assets. SCLC, LRC, and the Covie committee thus resisted pressure from the Steering Com to establish the CPA prematurely, and insisted that the institutional design of the CPA was informed by the needs and interests identified in the development plan. At the time of writing in 2008, the local municipality had agreed to take responsibility for service provision. Still to be negotiated was whether it would also manage the communal land, thereby relieving the CPA of the sole responsibility of controlling land use.

As with most community restitution claims, Covie was challenged to identify what exactly this "community" is. Ex-residents have spread throughout the country. The committee undertook a planning exercise and generated criteria for membership, agreed upon in community and family meetings, according to which membership does not bring any automatic rights to restitution. Instead, all rights will be applied for within the development process. The various categories of members include current landowners, original owners or tenants, and people who presently live in Covie. The committee has taken the lead in drawing family trees for each of these categories, and the final verified list of original members will be adopted along with the CPA constitution. The challenge is to convince the CRLR that in the case of a community claim, membership must be defined as people who have real links with Covie and not strangers who have no interest and may prevent future decisions being made. Future members will be over eighteen years of age and must reside in Covie.

LESSONS FROM COVIE

What lessons can be learned from the case of Covie? A crucial factor shaping the claim is the *unity* demonstrated among claimants from the outset. This unity can be understood in the light of many factors: a relatively small population; a continued interrelatedness and sense of family (many of the members stem from a few original families who have continued to return and take an interest in Covie over the years), and a close-knit but diverse leadership, which minimizes conflict and promotes cooperation. This unity has enabled the claimants to speak with one voice in terms of choosing land as the settlement option and crafting a vision for Covie (Zoanni 2007).

Another important factor has been support from nongovernmental organizations (NGOs) such as SCLC and LRC. The bureaucratic nature of the claim process does not facilitate people-centered development. If claimants are truly to benefit and improve the quality of their lives, it appears necessary to have outside support to strengthen struggles, interpret documents and procedures, share experiences of other claimants, and enable community and committee members to gather regularly—the latter being perhaps the most important. As recounted above, SCLC has tried to provide such support for the Covie claimants. One of the challenges of this involvement has been to delineate the role of the NGO versus that of the various government departments and service providers and, most importantly, to cut the fine line between creating dependency and providing a resource for people to grow their own skills and become the leaders of their own development.

Another lesson concerns the advantages of ensuring that the land claim is not hastily settled, thereby avoiding the failures and disappointment of cases such as Dysselsdorp. It is of central importance to ensure that all the pieces of the development puzzle are in place before the transfer of land, and SCLC and LRC, together with the claimants, are trying to make sure this occurs in Covie. Rather than rushing the community into making decisions, the rights and responsibilities of beneficiaries were carefully discussed and clarified, as was the question of suitable institutional arrangements. Bringing all stakeholders into a common forum, the Steering Com, enabled them to fulfill their various mandates in an efficient manner. Furthermore, state departments were involved in order to identify budgets, technical expertise, alternative land and other resources, thus easing the burden on cash-strapped and struggling local authorities.

However, the restitution process is long, laborious, and bureaucratic, often creating frustration and conflict. By insisting that institutional arrangements and postsettlement support is secured before land transfer, there is a danger that this process will be protracted even further. There is a need to look for creative ways of shortening the process while retaining full participation from the claimants, who need to see some tangible benefits from the years of struggle. A further challenge is that the CRLR needs to demonstrate delivery and therefore places pressure on claimants to sign a settlement agreement even though the contents of the MOU are not fulfilled. Lately the CRLR has begun to sideline SCLC and to work with individual members of the interim CPA in an effort to convince them to sign a settlement agreement. It is crucial that all claimants are fully aware of the vision and contents of the MOU to prevent being steamrollered into premature settlement.

A further challenge still facing Covie is to constitute and run the currently interim CPA in a manner that is informed by real development needs. In Covie the technical and complex nature of the implementation phase sometimes deters people from engaging. The challenge is how to make this process more people-friendly, enabling claimants to own and actively participate in the process. This requires enhancing technical capacity and understanding within the leadership and ideally also within the wider group of claimants.

Although not finally settled at the time of writing, the Covie restitution process has the potential to serve as an example for future restitution settlements. From the community's strong and effective mobilization and passion for land restoration to its resisting hasty settlement, and from the integrated manner of securing postsettlement support and appropriate institutional arrangements, the case of Covie shows innovative ways of meeting the challenges of land restitution that could inspire others.

REFERENCES

Zoanni, Tyler. 2007. "Settlement as Development: Current Warnings, Insights, and Suggestions for this Moment in the Covie Claim." Unpublished report. George: Southern Cape Land Committee.

INTERVIEWS

Barnardo, Irene. Covie, 27 June 2007.
Pedro, John. Covie, 26 June 2007.
Roman, Norman. Covie, 9 July 2007.
Sampo, Beauty. Covie, 29 June 2007.

part three

Restituting Community

Politics, Identity, Development

eight

Acrimonious Stakeholder Politics

Reconciliation and Redevelopment in District Six

CHRISTIAAN BEYERS

The protracted and difficult process of land restitution has to be understood not just in terms of the various legal and institutional complications of the program but also in terms of the political dynamics among key local-level stakeholders, including local government, representatives of claimants, and the office of the regional land claims commissioner (RLCC). These dynamics become especially relevant in the case of development projects once claims have been finalized. Local stakeholders have different political interests, face different institutional and organizational imperatives, and make use of different sets of material and symbolic resources in the struggle for position. How these dynamics are entrenched within and constrain the overall process of restitution and redevelopment is thus an important area for analysis.[1]

Stakeholder conflict is likely to be particularly high in restitution cases involving the redevelopment of substantial tracts of well-located and valuable urban land, which are typically subject to intense pressure for allocation to developers and other government programs. This chapter explores these dynamics in the high-profile case of District Six in Cape Town, historically a high-density, ethnically diverse, and largely working-class neighborhood adjacent to the central business district, which was proclaimed a "whites-only" group area in 1966. Over the years, approximately sixty thousand residents, the majority of them classified as "coloured" under apartheid, were relocated to new townships on the barren Cape Flats (see Western 1981).

After 1995 a total of 2,293 individual restitution claims were lodged in this case (CRLR 1999).[2] After a contentious process of litigation and negotiation, a broad development agreement was reached that envisaged that over half the claimants would resettle in new homes to be built in District Six. The area represents tremendous, untapped economic and social potential for a city still attempting to reinvent itself in the postapartheid era (Dewar 2001, 55). However, by early 2007, twelve years after the restitution program was launched, only 24 of a projected total of 4,000 housing units had been built and occupied, with building planned for the next 125 units (Voice of the Cape [VOC], 7 February 2007). Today this largely demolished neighborhood in the heart of Cape Town still stands as a painful testament to the injustices of the past.

Why—despite the obvious urgency of restitution and development—has the process been so prone to stalling? In good part the answer is to be found in local political dynamics. In District Six the contest for control over the redevelopment of the area has been particularly intense between two of the key stakeholders: the District Six Beneficiary and Redevelopment Trust (hereafter the Trust), which formally represents claimants, and the City of Cape Town (hereafter the City). By examining their different planning and development priorities and how these differences translated into institutional and procedural constraints, this chapter shows how the dynamics of stakeholder politics can encumber the urban restitution process. (The third stakeholder, the Commission on Restitution of Land Rights (CRLR), provides less of a focus here because its function at the redevelopment stage is mainly facilitative.)

The discussion begins with an overview of the relationship between land restitution and local governance and then contextualizes the District Six case within broader local and regional political dynamics. The next section outlines the restitution process in District Six in the early years of the land reform program, when the City as well as the provincial government attempted to use the Restitution Act to preclude an individual claims process in favor of an integrated, state-controlled development project. A hard-fought campaign by organizations representing ex-residents ultimately culminated in the defeat of this initiative and the formation of the Trust as the authoritative representative of claimants. This set the stage for a new phase of negotiations after 1998; the different approaches of the City and the Trust to "integrated development" in this period provide the central focus of the discussion. The chapter concludes with an overview of developments since 2004, when the process has shifted from the broad terrain of urban planning toward a narrower and more local level of development planning focused on eventual implementation. In this phase previously underlying tensions came to a head, resulting in a second decisive breakdown of relations between claimant representatives and local government. By the end of 2006, the cutoff point for this discussion, these acrimonious stakeholder negotiations had given way to a new phase in which the central challenge is how to accommodate fundamental tensions between land restitution, local economic development, and broader housing delivery in the Cape Town region.

RESTITUTION AND LOCAL GOVERNMENT IN CAPE TOWN

It is useful to begin by examining the interface between land restitution and local governance. The architects of the 1993 Constitution envisioned land restitution as a nationally legislated and centrally administered program—restitution was not included in schedule 6, which listed the major competencies of provincial and local government. The failure to define the role of local government meant that restitution was not integrated into local spatial planning and development processes (see Roodt 2003). This was recognized by the 1998 ministerial review of the commission that, among its various recommendations, called for "building . . . a shared understanding of the role of local government in the restitution process," particularly in urban areas where there was "a need for a greater emphasis on synergistic and collaborative work with local and metropolitan authorities" (cited in Roodt 2003, 269). However, as the District Six case demonstrates, ensuring more effective integration with local government processes has continued to be a major challenge.

The success of restitution-related urban development requires establishing restitution as a priority vis-à-vis other kinds of urban development and land-use initiatives, and this depends on the ability of claimant groups and the CRLR to gain leverage with respect to both local government and business. Restitution projects have to fit into provincial growth and development strategies, local government integrated development plans (IDPs) and other spatial development frameworks, as well as municipal and district level plans for service delivery (Ramballi and Maharaj 2002, 39). Since 1995 this has been rendered still more complicated by far-reaching restructuring of municipal government and the gradual transformation of apartheid-era bureaucracies at the local level. Although a comprehensive system of planning and development policies has been put in place in most metropolitan areas, many local government programs have been plagued by inadequate delivery and a chronic lack of continuity in personnel due to ongoing institutional restructuring. In Cape Town these problems were compounded by heightened political instability in both local and provincial government.

The politics of Cape Town and the Western Cape are remarkably distinct from the rest of the country, as the following overview of the turbulent succession of governments in the region since 1994 makes clear. The Western Cape was the only province where the National Party (NP), the ruling party under apartheid, was voted into office in 1994. The NP's success had much to do with its ability to court favor among the Western Cape's majority "coloured" population, thus extending a particular history of paternalism and selective accommodation into the postapartheid era (see Giliomee 1995). However, electoral support for the NP faltered significantly in the 1999 elections, in spite of the party's attempts to shed its apartheid past by refashioning itself as the New National Party (NNP). In the 1996 local elections the African National Congress (ANC) won Cape Town (although the NP took the other five municipalities then making up the metropolitan region) and in 1999 won the greatest number of votes in the province—only to be deprived of office by the Democratic Alliance (DA), a composite of the NNP and the former Democratic Party (DP). The DA went on to win the 2000 local government elections but, following a 2001 scandal about street renaming, the NNP decided to leave the party. In 2002 twenty-seven DA councillors took advantage of new "floor-crossing" legislation to move to the NNP while the NNP opportunistically entered into a coalition with the ANC. This coalition eventually gained control of the Cape Town metropolitan government, and in 2004 NNP legislators moved to the ANC to give it control of the province. However, in the 2006 local elections the NNP was dissolved, and, by means of a coalition with five small parties, the DA narrowly wrested control of Cape Town from the ANC and the newly formed Independent Democrats (see Zolobe 2007). Throughout this period "coloured" identity continued to be a flashpoint for politics in the region.

It is difficult to trace ideological influences at party level either on municipal policies and administration or on development projects such as District

Six. Moreover, most local civil servants have continued to operate within a relatively consistent set of parameters (see McDonald and Smith 2002), thus often maintaining a certain coherence of approach, despite the political volatility. However, political instability has had an effect on District Six because it offers politicians an expedient opportunity to capitalize on its symbolic value in the process of political gerrymandering. As one of the most notorious symbols of the legacy of apartheid, District Six has a national and international appeal that is disproportionate to the material, social, and economic space that it occupies. Ex–District Sixers also constitute a significant voting constituency; since 1994 the balance of power in Cape Town has lain in the "coloured" voting population residing largely on the Cape Flats, among whom District Sixers are widely dispersed (Nagia interview, 2002). The District Six population thus represents a critical mass for political entrepreneurs. However, more or less overt calls for a return of District Six as a "coloured homeland" are potentially highly divisive, as the various reincarnations of apartheid-era political parties have continued to make use of the so-called *swart gevaar* (black danger) politics of old to incite popular fears that the historic character of the Western Cape as a "preferential area" for "coloured" and "white" people under apartheid is threatened by an advancing army of "African" migrants previously excluded from the area.

ESTABLISHING THE PRIMARY "PUBLIC":
THE BATTLE OVER SECTION 34

The stage for current stakeholder conflict was set by the 1996 application made by the City and the provincial government—then still in the hands of the NP—in terms of section 34 of the Restitution Act. This application sought to manage the restitution process through a state-controlled development project.[3] The application was advanced by the Cape Town Community Land Trust (CTCLT), an overarching body with broad organizational representation, which had been created by the City to hold the land and drive development. As in Cato Manor (Walker, this volume), the District Six section 34 application proved highly controversial. However, unlike in Cato Manor, here restitution claimants were accepted as primary beneficiaries of the City's redevelopment agenda.

Many elements of the CTCLT's vision of 1996 continue to inform the City's approach to development (CCT-P&E 2003, ii, 4, 34). The CTCLT extended the concept of "community" toward a broader understanding of "public" by defining the target recipients of redevelopment as "the working class"—by which it evidently meant anyone of relatively low income in the city, including people with no direct historical relation to District Six. The CTCLT envisioned an "integrated development" project consisting of large apartment blocks in which various categories of beneficiaries would be accommodated, including the city's homeless (CCT-P&E 2003, 2, 33–34). At the same time, and complicit with the views of white ratepayer associations in neighboring areas (Nagia interview, 2002), the first democratically elected city council asserted, "Property owners should be consulted with regard to any development affecting their property especially if it is development on adjacent property. It is important to recognize all property owners as legitimate stakeholders and it is imperative that they be brought aboard with the inception of the process" (SU-CTPB 1996, 41).

This vision contrasted with that of the most influential and widely representative organizations of claimants, in particular the District Six Civic Association and the District Six Ex-Residents and Traders Association. They framed justice in terms of restitution specifically for former residents and rejected their assimilation into other categories of beneficiaries. They argued that the CTCLT—contrary to its rhetoric—did not effectively represent them, and that its application was in fact being used to limit involvement by District Sixers and channel their participation (Fredericks interview, 2006). The majority of ex-residents and claimants insisted that restoring District Six land to ex-residents was nonnegotiable and should occur irrespective of current use of that or surrounding land (see, for example, *Cape Argus,* 7 October 1996). Opponents of the CTCLT further criticized the city council as largely constituted by apartheid-era administrators who had found that a liberal interpretation of central government directives was conducive to establishing local distributive regimes that perpetuated the status quo.

The section 34 application was defeated in August 1997, thus setting the stage for the current framework of dealing with individual land claims according to a rights-based approach. Opposition to the application had the effect of consolidating prospective land claimants as an organized political entity, as various disparate ex-resident organizations and sectors were brought together under what was known as the District Six Land Restitution Front, led by Anwah Nagia (*Cape Times,* 17 September 1996). The Front brought together former owners and tenants, and worked to bring marginalized African ex-residents into the claims process as well.

Following the defeat of the application, the LCC mandated that a facilitation process be conducted for several months to inform potential claimants of their rights, and to gauge popular opinion on how restitution and redevelopment should proceed (*Cape Argus,* 20 March 1997). This process expanded the number of claimants, particularly tenants. The facilitators recommended that a beneficiary trust be formed to act as a vehicle to represent all claimants (Clarke and Alexander n.d.), and in August 1998 a large meeting was held in the District Six Museum at which the constitution for the Trust was adopted (Nagia interview, 2002). On 13 September 1998 the three principal stakeholders—Trust, City, and CRLR—signed the District Six Record of Understanding. It represented a "peace treaty" between the parties previously in litigation (Ally interview, 2006) and endorsed the following vision: "To provide restitution for those forcibly removed from District Six, through an integrated redevelopment which will result in a vibrant multi-cultural community and whose dignity has been restored in a developmental environment, grounded in, and meeting the social and economic needs of the claimants and broader community that will contribute towards the building of a new nation" (District Six Beneficiary Restitution Trust, Department of Land Affairs, and City of Cape Town. [D6BRT et al.] 1998). The agreement provided for a Steering Committee drawn from the Trust, the City, and the RLCC's office to oversee the development of a series of implementation agreements—most significantly, a development agreement. In contrast to Cato Manor, the redevelopment of the area would henceforth center on the claimants, for the most part to the exclusion of other possible categories of beneficiaries.

NEGOTIATIONS AND PLANNING AFTER 1998

Whereas the RLCC's office played a major role during the pre-agreement phase, the approach of the other stakeholders to questions of justice came into play most strongly around the issue of redevelopment. The Trust was able to gain leverage early in the process, because of its formation as an outcome of the section 34 battle. This was resented by City officials, who complained that they were being sidelined (de Tolly interview, 2002; Wessels interview 2001). The Trust has also been astute in using its status as the legal representative of claimants, backed by the moral prerogative of "the community," to harness public attention to its advantage, particularly through the media.

It would, however, be a mistake to underestimate the considerable leverage that the City enjoys in terms of capacity and resources to shape the development process. Although responsible mainly for negotiating the transfer of land, it has used this narrowly defined mandate to maximum effect in exercising influence over the process. In District Six the City is the "main approving authority" (CCT-P&E 2003, 24) as well as the legal landholding body until the claims have been settled. By strategically deploying their greater access to capital resources and local professional expertise, City officials have attempted to direct state funds into processes over which they have the greatest amount of control. In the words of Peter de Tolly, then the City's director of special projects and head urban planner for District Six, in 2002: "I would imagine that the Beneficiary Trust . . . has the major clout in terms of [the] development vehicle [that will need to be formed], but even that's a tricky one given who owns the land" (de Tolly interview, 2002).

The City's trump card has been its control over the decision about when it is appropriate to transfer the land. Moreover, City officials insist on sound planning as a prerequisite for any development and deploy their resources and expertise toward shaping these plans in their interest. The required package of plans for the area will, when complete, take in the City's general contextual framework, a more specific development framework, as well as more detailed precinct and other implementation plans. City officials have tried to insist that these prerequisites cannot be completed and a development vehicle formed until all land claims have been settled and comprehensive information about the future client body is available (Planning Portfolio Committee [PPC] 2001), thus shifting responsibility for delays onto the RLCC. For its part, the RLCC's office has maintained that many of the planning processes do not require the prior validation of all the restitution claims (Waring interview, 2002).

Formal planning aside, what is critically needed before building can begin is the provision of bulk services infrastructure such as roads, electricity, sewerage, and water supply. This is, in fact, the City's major financial responsibility and prospective contribution. In recent years there has been a realization that the old bulk services infrastructure is largely unusable and needs a major overhaul. The City has made piecemeal contributions of R1.6 million and R4.5 million toward this (Ally 2006), provoking complaints from the Trust that it hands out a bit at a time when it is expedient but has failed to come through on its full commitment, thus seriously impeding progress (Ally interview, 2005).

Notwithstanding repeated public pronouncements by local politicians of their commitment to District Six, why has the City continued to stall? To begin with, the City is principally liable for the project in the long run and needs to ensure that it is economically viable and in the best interest of its broader constituency. Furthermore, from the standpoint of the City restitution is not profitable but costs. The RLCC has called upon the City to transfer the land to the community at no or minimal cost, but the City has asserted that it cannot responsibly "give public land away" (Murison interview, 1 July 2005) and has, in turn, called upon the RLCC to make a viable offer for the land. The RLCC and Trust have insisted that this ought to be less than market price, given the council's historical role in the removals and the fact that it acquired the land for "next to nothing" (Ally interview, 2006).

However, according to Isgak Murison, acting manager for land restitution at the City in 2005, this is not viable because of shrinking budgets and the need to maximize the City's assets in order to obtain bank loans for development (Murison interview, 2005). Indeed, from a City budgeting perspective, settling claims through monetary compensation may be preferable, as the money comes from elsewhere, that is, from the Department of Land Affairs, and this form of restitution would free up land that the City could otherwise be compelled to sell below market value. In practical terms the City has also to consider the possibility of litigation by former landowners for handing over to the Trust what they consider to be their land (Ally interview, 2005). Thus in several respects the City's practical interests are directly opposed to those of both the RLCC and the Trust, and this is reflected in the discrepancy between its general policy commitments and its lack of political will around effective implementation of the District Six agreement.

The City's capacity to implement the agreement has also been seriously compromised by the ongoing restructuring of local government. This involved the amalgamation of twenty-eight small municipalities into the Cape Town Unicity in December 2000, which coincided with the City's first integrated development plan (IDP). A major challenge has been how to effect the institutional coordination, rational spatial planning, and broad public consultation that the IDP prescribes in the light of human resource constraints, including staff turnover and reallocation of functions (see Turok 2001; Wilkinson 2004). Navigating the maze of policies governing restitution and development requires a substantial amount of expertise, and new staff members have to acquire an extensive knowledge base for each restitution case. There is, after all, a limit to what can be learned from files, and the nuances of understanding built up over time escape new officials, no matter how competent (Murison interview, 1 July 2005).

CONFLICTING PRIORITIES, 1998–2004

At least in rhetoric, both the City and the Trust recognize the need to promote both economic viability and social redress. However, although both want the redeveloped District Six to be, in the words of the City, "safe, secure, vibrant, multi-cultural" (CCT-P&E 2003, 10), they have disagreed sharply on how this is to be done.

The City: Compaction in Line with Market Principles

The City has committed itself to "meet the needs and aspirations of the land claimants" (CCT-P&E 2003, 1). However, it has also insisted that since "legitimate claimants" opting for resettlement will occupy only a fraction of the available land in District Six, if resettled at appropriate densities, "a unique opportunity [exists] for appropriate forms of inner city development as envisaged in the Metropolitan Spatial Development Framework," namely, a compact, high-density, mixed-use development (CCT-P&E 2003, 38). Officials tend to emphasize the priority of the market and underscore the need for economic and institutional compatibility between the District Six project and existing development, especially in the immediately adjacent central business district. In line with the original draft document prepared by the CTCLT and the City's IDP, the contextual framework stipulates that the role of the City is to "ensure that the redevelopment of District Six and the growth of economic activities reinforce the inner city as a whole, complementing and supporting redevelopment initiatives in surrounding areas"; it must also enable "higher residential densities to increase the opportunities for people of different income levels to live in the area" in order "to support increased commercial and institutional uses" (CCT-P&E 2003, v).

An important area of disagreement with the Trust has been the socioeconomic profile of prospective beneficiaries. City officials have advocated that claimants should assume a higher proportion of land and building costs than the Trust accepts. The extent of City officials' commitment to accommodating low-income groups in District Six—apart from an undetermined number of people from its housing list—is therefore uncertain. The City has placed a premium on "stability" and "security" as prerequisites for expanding existing investment and buttressing the socioeconomic profile of current residents in the adjoining city center, so as to avert their out-migration to the suburbs (de Tolly interview, 2002). To deal with the shortfall of funds and the issue of affordability, de Tolly has also advocated a market-oriented solution of cross-subsidization. In this schema, houses further up the mountain slope, which would be more expensive to develop but would also fetch higher prices, could subsidize low-income housing (de Tolly interview, 2002). The Trust, however, has opposed cross-subsidization because it means accommodating wealthy outsiders (Nagia interview, 2002).

City officials have also advocated a professionally planned and management-based approach to development, based on technical expertise. De Tolly recommended that a development vehicle should be formed on which representation would be extensive, "given the complexity of the area" (de Tolly interview, 2002), including from the Trust, the City, central government, and the province. This again raises the question of what control claimants would have over the redevelopment process. According to de Tolly:

> From the point of view of the people living in District Six . . . they should be looking to the City as something that will be of benefit to them. . . . Do they need to set up a development vehicle for District Six . . . or should it go further into developing some kind of management vehicle for District Six—analogous to the CID [central improvement district][4] by the way? So that you work cooperatively with the City: you have a service agreement or a set of service agreements with the City; the City provides certain levels of service. Then you might provide other levels of service, or you take over some of those responsibilities from the City. And you have a much more active role to play in the management of your area than is normally the case. (de Tolly interview, 2002)

Such rhetoric appears consistent with a neoliberal shift within the City, where public participation is encouraged in order to compensate for local government's retreat from service provision. Participation is conceptualized as institutionalized incorporation into a system of local management, where service delivery occurs on a contractual basis.

The Trust: Social Redress for the Dispossessed

In contrast to the City's concern with economics, the Trust's primary point of departure is social redress for the victims of removals. The Trust works closely with the District Six Museum, which was founded in 1989 to memorialize the history of District Six, and although a discussion of the museum is beyond the scope of this chapter, its importance for promoting popular participation in the restitution case needs noting (see Rassool and Prosalendis 2001; Beyers 2008).

As a grassroots organization, the Trust has tended to speak first in the language of social activism, before engaging with legal and planning discourses. According to the chairperson of the Trust in 2002, "We believe that integration would mean bringing together those people who have been separated in various townships and locations, in various economic positions and dispositions. . . . So integration basically bottom line is, we are going to reside and occupy District Six with rich and poor living side by side—black, white, Indian, and coloured, living side by side, that's the bottom line" (Nagia interview, 2002).

Despite the reality of class differentiation, the new District Six is thus imagined as infused with the egalitarian, nonracial, and cosmopolitan ethos of the old District Six. Integration is understood primarily as the survival of a particular social form that is presumed to have existed before. In this sense, the Trust's active promotion of the resettlement option for claimants ties into a voluntaristic political ethics: choosing to return is seen as vindicating the nonracial social experiment that District Six is thought to have represented (see Soudien 2001). "Integrated development," then, is about community building. In contrast to the City, the Trust is more sanguine about the issue of affordability. It has proposed various activities to supplement earmarked state funds, including soliciting international state funding and arranging cheaper interest rates with well-disposed banks (Nagia interview, 2002).

The Trust has also advocated greater and, at least in rhetoric, more politicized participation of the ex-resident community—particularly claimants who have opted for land—and casts itself as the "voice of the community" to preempt the City when it opposes its agenda. The success of such a value-committed stance requires a strong popular support base, a base that has, however, been diminishing as the process has lagged. Although the Trust was able to play a highly politicized role as an oppositional popular front during the section 34 application, it has since been drawn increasingly into the technocratic business of managing development. During this period it has persistently tried to force the hand of the City on implementation, but its oppositional role has often been lost on claimants, who increasingly have blamed it directly for the failure of "delivery."

The chairperson of the Trust has, in turn, blamed the City and business sector for delays, condemning their "political chicanery around the social delivery of the District Six area" (Nagia interview, 2002) and their ulterior political and economic agendas. Rather than wait for all planning and development prerequisites to be fulfilled for the whole project, the Trust advocated a pilot phase of development, during which an initial set of model houses would be built. The head of the RLCC's District Six Team until 2002 also favored engaging the City on this possibility (Waring interview, 2002). However, speaking in a manner reminiscent of the section 34 application, a city planner cautioned against haphazard and unplanned development: "It wouldn't be right for us to start planning for certain sections; we must look at it holistically and in an integrated manner" (Wessels interview, 2001). Eventually the Trust began construction of a twenty-four-unit pilot phase in 2002, without the legal consent of the City. The City then rushed their plans and approved the project in time for the handover of the keys in February 2004 (Ally interview, 2005).

The Trust frames its role in the redevelopment of District Six not just in developmental terms, but in sociocultural terms. It requires that all claimants moving into their new homes sign a "social compact"—something that has raised concerns about continuities with social engineering practices under apartheid (Soudien interview, 2004). The compact stipulates that property sold within the first five years of occupancy will revert to the Trust and pledges that claimants will not use their homes for *shebeens* [informal taverns], prostitution, rent exploitation, or gambling, and will be tolerant toward all religions.

The Housing Question

Whereas the City promotes a functionally diverse socioeconomic community, with plenty of endogenous commercial activity to equip residents for participating in the consumer market of the city center, the Trust invokes the spirit of the old District Six in support of a socially dynamic community with a strong egalitarian ethos. The Trust is committed to a neighborly, interactive design that, in the words of its chairperson, is "going to force the rubbing of shoulders of people" (Nagia interview, 2002) and serve as a vanguard for revitalizing the city. Participating in the project of reconstruction thus implies buying into a particular social contract and even a political project, one that does not apply to those who in effect opt out by choosing monetary compensation.

The redevelopment of District Six has thus come to be defined in terms of competing priorities of the market or of redress. As the next section shows, compromises between the City and the Trust have come to be framed in terms of mediating these poles, thus to a certain extent precluding a broader discussion on the relationship between social justice and development. In particular, the possibility of incorporating non–District Sixers from the City's housing list—something first raised by the CTCLT, albeit probably for strategic rather than ideological reasons—was largely overshadowed. Although acknowledging the seriousness of the housing crisis, the chairperson of the Trust nevertheless argued in 2002 that "[l]ocal government and other players [are] saying that . . . we must really try to resolve the housing question via restitution—you can't do that. Restitution [is] a direct result [of] the whole question of the laws of conquest and the laws of dispossession in this country. It had nothing to do with accommodating the state's problem of creating affordable homes. . . . [Y]ou were forcibly removed from an area irrespective of what the housing crisis in the country [was]" (Nagia interview, 2002). Although, as discussed below, the Trust has softened this position recently, it continues to insist on prioritizing restitution claimants over housing-list beneficiaries.

Trustees (and some City officials) often construe restitution as politically progressive because it aims to restore a formerly working-class neighborhood, and this is reflected in the commission's prioritizing former tenants over former owners in the processing of claims and the roughly equal value of their respective resettlement packages. Operating primarily within a register of restorative justice, the public discourse on restitution in District Six has subverted a broader discussion about the imperative of redistributive justice, in part by incorporating the latter under the rubric of restitution.

However, many District Sixers have achieved substantial upward social mobility since their removals. Furthermore, the majority of claimants who are inclined to and can afford to come back tend to have attained a measure of relative material comfort, at least in comparison to nonclaimants in the City's housing queue (see Beyers 2007a). Given public perceptions of District Six as historically a "coloured space" (Soudien 2001, 117), as well as the identity of most claimants as "coloured," in contrast to the assumed "African" identity of most would-be housing beneficiaries, the issue is potentially politically volatile. The Trust is constantly engaged in a balancing act of championing the restoration of District Six's putatively unique character while attempting to redefine it in nonracial terms. Since its formation in 1998, it has actively promoted the participation of African District Sixers and often consciously foregrounded African claimants in public gatherings and ceremonies.

ONGOING ARGUMENTS, 2004–2006

Housing delivery was brought back into the negotiations after the announcement in 2003 of the N2 Gateway project—a massive new housing project targeting informal settlements along the N2 freeway from the Cape Town airport to the city center. In spite of persistent disagreements, initially the Trust and the City both appeared optimistic over the prospect of linking District Six to this project. Plans included building some five hundred new houses in District Six for people currently living in informal settlements, with no personal history with District Six. The N2 Gateway Project quickly became a primary component of the City's IDP, and the housing minister Lindiwe Sisulu promised R15 million for houses in District Six (*Cape Times*, 8 February 2006). For the City this was not only an opportunity to use District Six to promote its housing efforts but also a way to gain access to some vacant land not earmarked for restitution-related redevelopment.

For the Trust the N2 Gateway Project held out prospects for kick-starting the stalled redevelopment process in District Six. Moreover, as development slowly became a reality and it became clear how much surplus land and housing would be available, the case became stronger for accommodating non–District Sixers or commercial properties on surplus land. Talk of joining the N2 Gateway Project did not, however, represent a deviation from the Trust's claimant-centered approach. Prospective N2 Gateway beneficiaries were placed last on its list of priority beneficiaries, behind: (1) District Six claimants; (2) former residents who had not submitted claims by the official deadline but had subsequently come forward;[5] and (3) claimants in other restitution cases seeking alternative land. The Trust hopes to incorporate about two thousand District Six "latecomers" and thus ensure that most of the planned four thousand units are used for restitution purposes (Ally interview, 2006). Using a claimant-centered but pro-poor rhetoric, trustee Nadeem Hendricks has argued: "We cannot forget that there is a total of 52 acres of land meant for restitution in District Six and these 1,500 claims will still leave a portion of the land—some 20 to 30 acres—free. The last thing we want to allow is for that valuable land to be made available for commercial purposes because that is not the intention of land restitution and we will go on fighting against it. If we don't, poor people will never win the right to return to District Six" (VOC, 30 October 2006). The apparent progress made by the City and the Trust on the District Six component of the Gateway project came to naught when the latter was transferred to the national government in mid-2006, following broader political conflict over its management (*Cape Times,* 13 June 2006).

Despite persistent areas of disagreement between the City and the Trust, by mid-2006 they appeared to have reached a compromise on many issues of prior disagreement. The major general-level planning requirements were met after a few rounds of public consultations, and the City appeared keen to push the project ahead. In late 2006 the new DA mayor, Helen Zille—ostensibly speaking on behalf of claimants—remonstrated with the Trust and the RLCC that "it is absolutely critical that we speed up the process at all costs" (VOC, 2 November 2006). The sense of urgency was perhaps in part because the City feared losing the project to the national government but more generally because District Six is a significant hindrance to further development in the city center and especially the East City precinct—a dilemma accentuated by the prospect of hosting the 2010 Soccer World Cup (Molapo and Sasman interview, 2006). The Trust also appeared more receptive to a cross-subsidization scheme, given the serious lack of funding for its own building construction (Ally interview, 2005; Nagia cited in VOC, 7 February 2007).

However, there continued to be fundamental disagreements over the locus of decision making and responsibility for development costs. In addition to the accumulated mistrust, the Trust is ideologically opposed to the DA administration, which it sees as an apartheid-era remnant (Fredericks interview, 2006). The Trust has continued to insist on being the exclusive developer, but its legitimacy has been challenged by some claimants as well as by City and RLCC officials who charge that the Trust has banked on its reputation as a grassroots organization for too long while neglecting communication with claimants (Molapo and Sasman interview, 2006; Nero interview, 2006). This impasse was resolved toward the end of 2006 when the CLCC decided to assume direct responsibility for District Six, transferring leadership of the project from the local to the national level while retaining a structure of joint responsibility among local stakeholders.[6] As a result, the redevelopment of District Six has been reintegrated into the now nationally controlled N2 Gateway Project (*Cape Times,* 3 November 2006).

Delays in the land restitution process are attributable not only to the slow process of finalizing claims but also to political conflict over land development priorities. In District Six this has been intensified by ongoing mistrust and antagonism between claimants and the local authority, dating back to the section 34 drama. Subsequently, both the newly established District Six Beneficiary and Redevelopment Trust and the City of Cape Town became increasingly rigid around their respective positions in the formal stakeholder negotiations. The Trust used its legal and moral authority as representative of the claimants to cast "integrated development" in the language of restorative justice and political activism. For its part, City officials pursued a market-oriented and utilitarian approach, using public management and planning discourses to try to broaden the basis for political representation and reconfigure the basis for authority. They have thus promoted a managerial forum in which the City would have a supervisory role, with its planning and management expertise deployed to maximum effect to shape the terms of reference for development. City officials have continued to advocate accommodating nonclaimants on surplus land once all "legitimate claimants" have been resettled (CCT-P&E 2003, 38). The Trust, in turn, has seen the call for broad stakeholder involvement as a ruse for wresting control from claimants and is adamant that most of the land should be used for restitution—including for latecomers.

Whereas the section 34 application in Cato Manor was used to eclipse restitution, in District Six its defeat led to claimants taking center stage. However, the effect has been to draw out the restitution and development process and make space for a protracted quarrel between the Trust and the City. Claimants are indeed dying before their claims are settled, as is often stated in political rhetoric, and the prospect of return is growing dimmer for others who cannot afford the ever-rising costs of resettlement. Of more far-reaching significance, the Trust's claimant-centered approach has also tended to reify District Six and the legacy of its "spirit," and precluded wider deliberation on how to strike a fair balance between restorative and redistributive justice. The reincorporation of District Six into the N2 Gateway project in 2006 presents an opportunity to reopen the question of accommodating poor nonclaimants in need of land and housing. However, it has been overshadowed by a recent legal challenge to the legitimacy of the Trust by a group of former owners who reject integrated development in favor of claimants' developing individual plots on their own. This has further delayed housing construction and may have strengthened the City's hand (VOC, 4 January 2008; *Mail and Guardian*, 13 March 2008).

NOTES

1. I thank Cherryl Walker for comments on an earlier draft and the Centre for African Studies at the University of Cape Town for institutional support. The research for this chapter was supported by a Doctoral SSHRC Scholarship and Trent University Internal SSHRC funding. Another version of this article appears as "The Contentious Politics of Integrated Urban Development in District Six," *Social Dynamics* 34 (1) (March 2008): 86–100.

2. This represents not only the lion's share of claims in Cape Town but also a large portion of the 13,108 claims lodged in the two provinces of the Western and Northern Cape (Mgoqi 2001).

3. For a detailed account of this phase see Beyers 2007b.

4. District Six borders the Central City CID, which incorporates the East City CID. Long-term plans include the incorporation of a significant portion of District Six in this CID (CCT-P&E 2003, 7). According to McDonald and Smith (2002) the designation of certain districts as CIDs is a prominent feature of the City's neoliberal agenda.

5. It was agreed that former residents of District Six who had not filed a claim by the deadline would be entitled to the same resettlement package as claimants but without the state subsidy to which the latter are entitled.

6. This opens the way for the national government to bring its own agenda directly to bear, thus further complicating the process.

REFERENCES

Ally, Nas. 2006. "Answer Booklet." May 2006. Unpublished document for distribution to claimants.
Beyers, Christiaan. 2007a. "Land Restitution's 'Rights-Communities': The District Six Case." *Journal of Southern African Studies* 33 (2): 267–85.
———. 2007b. "Mobilizing 'Community' for Justice in District Six: Stakeholder Politics Early in the Land Restitution Process." *South African Historical Journal* 58 (1): 253–76.
———. 2008. "The Cultural Politics of 'Community' and Citizenship in the District Six Museum, Cape Town." *Anthropologica, Special Issue: Citizenship, Politics and Locality: Anthropological Perspectives*, ed. Catherine Neveu 50 (2): 359–73.
Clarke, Elaine, and Neville Alexander. N.d. "The Final Report of Facilitators in the District Six Restitution Case." Cape Town: Office of the RLCC.
CCT-P&E (City of Cape Town, Planning and Environment). 2003. "District Six: Draft Contextual Framework. March 2003." Cape Town: City of Cape Town.
CRLR. 1999. *Newsletter.* February. Cape Town: Office of the RLCC.
Dewar, Neil. 2001. "Seeking Closure: Conflict Resolution, Land Restitution, and Inner City Redevelopments in 'District Six' Cape Town." *South African Geographical Journal* 83 (1): 48–55.

District Six Beneficiary Restitution Trust, Department of Land Affairs, and City of Cape Town. 1998. "District Six Record of Understanding." 13 September 1998. Cape Town: Office of the RLCC.

Giliomee, Hermann. 1995. "The Non-Racial Franchise and Afrikaner and Coloured Identities: 1910–1994." *African Affairs* 94 (375): 199–225.

McDonald, David A., and Laïla Smith. 2002. *Privatizing Cape Town: Service Delivery and Policy Reforms Since 1996*. Municipal Services Project Occasional Papers Series, Number 7, February.

Mgoqi, Wallace. 2001. "Briefing Document on Land Restitution in South Africa." In *Putting Land Rights in the Right Hands*. Pretoria: Commission on Restitution of Land Rights.

PPC (Planning Portfolio Committee). 2001. "Land Restitution Claims: District Six." Cape Town: Office of the RLCC.

Ramballi, K., B. Maharaj, U. Bob, and I. Kwaw. 2002. "Land Reform and Restitution in South Africa: A Critical Review." In *Transforming Rural and Urban Spaces in South Africa during the 1990s: Reform, Restitution, Restructuring*, ed. R. Donaldson and L. Marais, 29–52. Pretoria: Africa Institute of South Africa.

Rassool, Ciraj, and Sandra Prosalendis, eds. 2001. *Recalling Community in Cape Town*. Cape Town: District Six Museum.

Roodt, Monty J. 2003. "Land Restitution in South Africa." In *Returning Home: Housing and Property Restitution Rights of Refugees and Displaced Persons*, ed. Scott Leckie, 243–71. Ardsley, NY: Transnational.

Soudien, Crain. 2001. "District Six and Its Uses in the Discussion about Non-racialism." In *Coloured by History, Shaped by Place: New Perspectives on Coloured Identities in Cape Town*, ed. Zimitri Erasmus, 114–30. Cape Town: Kwela Books.

SU-CTPB (Shelter Unit, Cape Town Planning Branch). 1996. "Redevelopment of District Six, Site Analysis: Draft." Document AF.1997–339. Cape Town: South African National Library Archives.

Turok, Ivan. 2001. "Persistent Polarisation Post-Apartheid? Progress towards Urban Integration in Cape Town." *Urban Studies* 38 (13): 2349–77.

Western, John. 1981. *Outcast Cape Town*. London: George Allen and Unwin.

Wilkinson, Peter. 2004. "Renegotiating Local Governance in a Post-Apartheid City: The Case of Cape Town." *Urban Forum* 15 (3): 213–30.

Zolobe, Zwelethu. 2007. "Things Fall Apart, Can the Centre Hold? The State of Coalition Politics in the Cape Metropolitan Council." In *State of the Nation: South Africa 2007*, ed. Sakhela Buhlungu, John Daniel, Roger Southall, and Jessica Lutchman, 78–94. Cape Town: HSRC Press.

INTERVIEWS

Ally, Nas, CEO of District Six Development Initiative. Cape Town, 7 July 2005; 17 April 2006.

de Tolly, Peter, director of special projects, Cape Town City Council. Cape Town, 11 June 2002.

Fredericks, Terrence, District Six Museum and District Six Beneficiary and Redevelopment Trust trustee. Cape Town, 1 September 2006.
Molapo, Pogiso, and Nicky Sasman, Human Settlements Department, Cape Town City Council. Cape Town, 24 August 2006
Murison, Isgak, acting manager for land restitution, Cape Town City Council. Cape Town, 1 and 15 July 2005.
Nagia, Anwah, chairperson of the District Six Beneficiary and Redevelopment Trust. Cape Town, 4 June 2002.
Nero, Willem, project manager for District Six, RLCC's office, Cape Town. Cape Town, 11 September 2006.
Soudien, Crain, professor at the University of Cape Town. Cape Town, 25 July 2004.
Waring, Lauren, head of District Six Team, RLCC's office, Cape Town. Cape Town, 17 June 2002.
Wessels, Nadia, planner, Cape Town City Council. Cape Town, 28 August 2001.

NEWSPAPERS AND MEDIA

Cape Argus, Cape Town, South Africa.
Cape Times, Cape Town, South Africa.
Mail and Guardian, Johannesburg, South Africa.
Voice of the Cape (community radio station), Cape Town, South Africa.

nine

"Model Tribes" and Iconic Conservationists?

Tracking the Makuleke Restitution Case in Kruger National Park

STEVEN ROBINS AND KEES VAN DER WAAL

On a recent visit to Makuleke village on the western border of the Kruger National Park (KNP), we went to greet formally the Makuleke chief Phahlela Joas Mugakula, who asked us, somewhat playfully, why we were so interested in Makuleke. The chief's question prompted us to reflect critically on why we, like so many others, were drawn to the Makuleke land restitution case. This is probably one of the best-known restitution cases in South Africa. What is it about this land claim that makes it stand out?

During our visit to Makuleke a large delegation of big business leaders and African environmental ministers were converging on the Makuleke's two extremely upmarket game lodges in their contract park located inside the KNP. These visitors included the British business tycoon Sir Richard Branson, Cheryl Carolus, the former South African Ambassador to the UK and currently a big player in the South African tourist industry, and numerous representatives from African governments and multinational companies such as De Beers, Goldfields, and Mittal (SANParks 2006a). Only a few days earlier Thabo Mbeki, then South African president, together with his counterparts from Zimbabwe and Mozambique, had officially opened a border gate entry point into the Mozambican side of the Great Limpopo

Transfrontier Park (GLTP). According to Mbeki, ecotourism in the GLTP offered enormous tourism and development opportunities, especially in the light of the 2010 Soccer World Cup (Kruger2Canyons.com 2006). Big business and governments were meeting in the Makuleke Region of the KNP to explore these investment opportunities. However, Lamson Maluleke, a key community leader, was not invited to this meeting in the bush. Although he and members of the Makuleke royal family and local leadership were not present at this high-profile business indaba, members of a Makuleke theater group were invited to entertain delegates by performing a play based on the community's forced relocation from the KNP in 1969.

To understand the iconic status of the Makuleke, it is necessary to situate this land-claimant community within the broader restitution discourse. It would seem that, like South Africa's Truth and Reconciliation Commission, official land restitution discourses focus on reconciliation, nation-building, and economic development rather than retributive justice (see Rijke-Epstein 2006). The Makuleke appear to embody these official restitution objectives through their development-oriented approach to environmentally sustainable ecotourism. Rather than opting to move back to the land in the KNP and exploit it for agricultural purposes or for diamond mining or trophy-hunting revenue, they chose instead to enter into a partnership with park management and commercial tourist operators and establish a contract park on their restituted land. The Makuleke case came to represent "the solution" to the dilemmas of how to manage relationships between communities and conservationists, people and parks. They seemed to be a "model tribe," who, as victims of apartheid forced removals, had opted for the goals of national reconciliation, conservation, and sustainable development, thus underwriting what is widely celebrated as the new model for people-nature interaction, namely community-based natural resources management (CBNRM).

In addition, the Makuleke case has also been celebrated as an exemplar of the possibility of wedding traditional leadership to the principles of constitutional democracy, including gender equity. Land, gender, and legal activists within organizations such as the Legal Resources Centre (LRC) and the Institute for Poverty, Land and Agrarian Studies at the University of the Western Cape (PLAAS) have identified the Makuleke as an example of a rural community that has succeeded in reconciling "modern" and "traditional" institutions. Whereas many land-claimant communities have witnessed fierce competition and conflict between traditional authorities and democratically elected communal property associations (CPAs), the Makuleke appear to have averted these clashes. The case has been lauded as "one of the most advanced programmes of community involvement in conservation and wildlife anywhere in the world" (Steenkamp and Uhr 2000, 2). Another possible reason why the Makuleke restitution settlement has been received so positively is that the government desperately needs a land reform success story. In addition, the GLTP was implemented at the time of the Makuleke agreement, and a "cooperative community" exemplified the win-win relationship that was needed by the advocates of CBNRM and the social ecology approach (Friedman 2005, 51–52).

It was for similar reasons that land activists and scholars associated with PLAAS and the LRC included the Makuleke case in their high court challenge against the 2004 Communal Land Rights Act (CLRA) (see Claassens 2003, 2005; Cousins and Claassens 2004; Cousins 2007).[1] For a variety of reasons the Makuleke have become the key applicants in this legal challenge to this act.

This chapter investigates how the Makuleke's iconic status has come to play such a key role in land reform discourses in South Africa and beyond. It raises questions that complicate the ways in which the Makuleke story has been deployed by various actors, including nongovernmental organizations (NGOs), activists, academics, conservationists, the state, and business. We question the way in which the Makuleke narrative has entered into discourses on land restitution and conservation. We do this by pointing out the continuities as well as the ruptures and adaptations that are part of the Makuleke historical experience. We also highlight the controversies and different positions taken in the course of this remarkable case.

We first present historical material highlighting the link between the local politics of the land claim and the perceived need to promote and project an image of a strong and cohesive tribal identity. We discuss this response against the backdrop of the community's experiences of living in the borderland Pafuri region of the KNP before their forced removal. We then investigate the specific ways in which the chieftaincy and its relation to tribal land have been strengthened as a result of local mobilizations against threats to its existence emanating from the neighboring Mhinga Tribal Authority. We also show how ongoing conflicts with Chief Mhinga have affected Makuleke claims to land and independent tribal status. Looking at the role of the royal family in these processes, we suggest that one of the central social tensions in the Makuleke saga is the contradiction between the democratic principles governing the legal entity controlling the land (the CPA) and the traditionalist patriarchal principles of the tribal authority. We show how these restitution-linked processes have become implicated in the establishment in 2002 of the GLTP. Finally, we show how the idea of the Makuleke as a "model tribe" is both a product of changing historical circumstances and a contributor to contemporary discourses on land restitution and conservation.

MAKULEKE REVISITED: BACKGROUND TO THE CASE STUDY

In an account of the Makuleke community's removal from the KNP, David Bunn (2001, 18) writes that "the idea of Shangaan identity is closely associated in Kruger Park with notions of loyalty, of people who have given up external political rights for the [paternalistic culture of] citizenship of the Park." Bunn distinguishes between parks board notions of the "loyal Shangaan" trackers, "police boys," and gate guards who worked in the KNP, and the board's suspicion, if not outright hostility, toward the independent Makuleke of Pafuri, whose territory straddled the relatively permeable South African, Mozambican, and Zimbabwean borders. Bunn notes that beginning in 1947, the parks board argued that the Makuleke were neither citizens with property rights nor did they constitute a "proper" chieftaincy. Instead, the board claimed that historically they were vassals of neighboring Chief Mhinga, who lived to the west of the KNP. Bunn cites Sandenbergh, then the warden of the KNP, who regarded the Makuleke with deep suspicion because of their "unstable" identity, which he associated with their transfrontier allegiances and historical experiences: "As the years went by the Makuleka [sic] natives started repudiating [their allegiance to Chief Mhinga] and as they were situated in a remote part became increasingly independent and a law unto themselves. They married women from Mozambique and Southern Rhodesia and natives from both these territories trekked in and settled there. It became a lawless sanctuary for fugitives" (cited in Bunn 2001, 18). Whereas the Department of Native Affairs wished to modernize the Makuleke tribe through the establishment of an irrigation scheme, the board persistently argued for their removal from the KNP and their relocation to Chief Mhinga's tribal area. Forced removal was justified on the grounds that the Makuleke were no longer subject to customary rule and had become "a law unto themselves." In other words, the warden's warning was that they were becoming autonomous and ungovernable agents rather than the disciplined tribal subjects the authorities desired.

It was not only the Makuleke who were perceived by the authorities as "a law unto themselves" in the Pafuri area. T. V. Bulpin's *The Ivory Trail* (1954) is an account of the life of the white ivory poacher Cecil S. Barnard, also known by Shangaan-speakers as *Bvekenya* [The-one-who-swaggers-as-he-walks]. The book is an adventure narrative about the elephant hunter, who lived in the Pafuri area of the Makuleke Region known as Crook's Corner. Bulpin portrays Bvekenya as a colorful and enigmatic character who lived on the margins of colonial and African society. Drawing on Bulpin's writings, William Wolmer (2007, 24–25) refers to the "Wild West image" of Crooks Corner as "a lawless frontier zone harbouring an assortment of white petty criminals, desperados, outcasts and fugitives who, as well as illicit labour recruiting, depended on gunrunning, extortion and poaching for their living." Bulpin describes *Bvekenya* as an outlaw and "adventurer of the wilds who defied the police of three countries and fought a one-man war with complete success against all control and authority."

This adventure narrative also reveals that the Makuleke lived in scattered villages throughout the Pafuri region. In drought years most of the men migrated to the Transvaal mines and factories and returned to their fields once the rains came. This relatively autonomous existence came to an abrupt end in 1969 when the Makuleke people were forcibly removed from the Pafuri region and unceremoniously dumped along the western border of the KNP, in the then Gazankulu bantustan, in an area about a quarter of the size of their lost land and without compensation. A song recorded by Patrick Harries expresses the feelings of loss and anger that the people felt when they were moved by the government:

> Go into the wilderness
> They take us into the wild country
> We have left our figs and our *mafura* and *lala* beer
> We have left our graves behind us at this place
> We are being overcome at the wild place
> We have left our wild fruits
> And there is no more relish in this place
> Malnutrition is destroying us.
> (quoted in Friedman 2005, 19)

At this new site the Makuleke did not have many of the rich resources they were used to. Sufficient water was not provided when they arrived, and this suffering was aggravated by serious droughts in the first years of settlement. Friedman (2005, 51) writes that despite the eventual restitution of their land, the Makuleke permanently lost their traditional methods of subsistence, family organization, political structures, and concept of home.

In 1998 the Makuleke successfully won back their land through a celebrated restitution case and, after complex negotiations with the Department of Land Affairs and South African National Parks (SANParks), signed a historic legal agreement whereby they would comanage the land with SANParks and thereby derive substantial benefits from ecotourism.[2] Whereas Bulpin had portrayed *Bvekenya* in the mold of the colonial image of the heroic white hunter, at the start of the twenty-first century it was the Makuleke's commitment to nature conservation, rather than elephant hunting, that made them a model tribe in conservationist and ecotourism circles.

In response to the successful restitution claim, Chief Mhinga lodged a counterclaim seeking to nullify this claim on the grounds that Chief Makuleke was not a chief but merely a headman. As Chief Mhinga's subordinate, so the argument went, the Makuleke could not submit an independent land claim. Chief Mhinga commissioned a University of South Africa anthropologist, Dr. Chris J. Van Vuuren, to compile a report that was submitted to the Northern Province (later Limpopo) RLCC. This 1998 report drew extensively on classical ethnographies by Henri Junod and N. J. Van Warmelo to argue that "Headman Makuleke" was indeed Chief Mhinga's subordinate and that Mhinga was the rightful claimant. Similarly, a memorandum submitted to the CRLR in 1997 by Chief Mhinga cited Van Warmelo's (1935) *A Preliminary Survey of the Bantu Tribes of South Africa* to argue that the chief of the Makuleke was a subordinate of Chief Mhinga and that "by the 1930s the Mhinga Tribe consisted of six areas each headed by a headman [including Headman Makuleke]."[3] Meanwhile, in an attempt to counteract Mhinga's claims, the Makuleke submitted an application to the national government's Ralushai Commission on Traditional Leadership, and later the Nhlapo Commission (established to investigate the legitimacy of various claims to traditional leadership status) for official recognition of their chieftaincy.

These tensions have a tumultuous history, going back to at least 1950 when Mhinga first tried to gain control over the Makuleke people (Friedman 2005, 15). When visiting Makuleke village one is struck by the sign "Makuleke Tribal Authority," an indication that the legacy of the tribal authorities established by the architects of apartheid is far from dead and buried. Both the Makuleke and Mhinga communities have sought to strengthen and reposition their respective traditional authorities within the new political landscape of postapartheid South Africa. Yet Van Vuuren's detailed ethnohistorical accounts of the Mhinga tribal structure were deemed "irrelevant" by the RLCC, who argued that in terms of the Restitution Act it was the people's forced removal of 1969 through racially based legislation that mattered.

The Mhinga leadership, and its anthropologist consultant, appeared to misread the CRLR's brief by persistently producing historical accounts of Mhinga tribal structures in order to reinforce their point that "Headman" Makuleke had no legal standing to submit the land claim. Both sides had to engage ideas about tribes, chiefs, and ethnic groups that had been "invented" and sanctioned by apartheid's architects (see Robins 2001, 2003). However, these strategies are by no means signs of a return to a pristine traditionalism but, rather, attempts to synthesize claims based on land, tradition, and cultural rights alongside demands for land restitution through the modern legal system. Access to the state resources that could flow from constituting an officially sanctioned Makuleke Tribal Authority, or a strengthened Mhinga Tribal Authority, could also contribute toward establishing greater connectivity between these bodies and the nerve centers of economic and state power.

When we visited Makuleke village in 2006 it appeared that much had changed since the mid-1990s, when the land claim submissions were being prepared. Yet some things remained the same. Chief Mhinga and his claim of control over the traditional authority was still perceived as a threat by the Makuleke people whose traditional leader was still awaiting the outcome of his submission to the Nhlapo Commission. The earlier Ralushai Commission had confirmed the independence of the Makuleke chieftaincy, but this recommendation had not led to official recognition. Meanwhile, together with the LRC, the Makuleke leadership was in the process of challenging the constitutionality of the CLRA. This act was perceived to strengthen Chief Mhinga's claims over the Makuleke CPA resources, including revenue from its tourist lodges and land inside the KNP as well as the irrigation scheme in the Makuleke area.

The provision made for the control over land by traditional authorities in CLRA appears to be the result of a deal between the ANC government and the traditional leader lobby, just before the elections of 2004. For many activists this represented a step away from the democratic transition of

1994, as this legislation would strengthen traditional authorities, to the disadvantage of the population living on communal land and of gender equity. In areas where the claims of one recognized tribal authority over another community was contested, as in Makuleke, this also implied that local control over land might be lost. The act is therefore being challenged in the High Court in Pretoria by representatives of three communities whose affidavits have been prepared by the LRC. The central grounds for challenging CLRA are, first, "that tribal authorities, entrenched by colonialism and apartheid, are not the proper land-holding entities, as it is argued that families and neighborhoods are the real land-holders and allocators of rights in land in subtle systems of shared and nested rights that exist in rural areas"; second, "that gender equity and security of tenure for land-users will not be served by the patriarchal system of traditional authorities controlling land"; and, third, that communities, such as the Makuleke, were "put under the wrong tribal authority during apartheid" (LRC 2006).

Although from the Makuleke perspective the opposition to CLRA is perfectly understandable in terms of the threat posed by Chief Mhinga's claims, the issues of land and chieftaincy and the relationship between them are more complex than that. Our research in Makuleke suggests that they were not fundamentally opposed to having a recognized traditional authority that would be in control of their land. To understand this, it is useful to look at the historical antecedents of the present forms of "tribal entrepreneurship" and traditional leadership among the Makuleke.

"BORDERLAND ENTREPRENEURS" AND THE CULTURE OF IMPROVISATION

The Makuleke have a long history of living in a transfrontier zone. Their geographical position was not one of isolation, but rather of intense interaction with traders and neighboring communities. These interactions have been shaped by a variety of factors, including war, drought, refugee movements, trade, and tourism. Centuries ago, the Limpopo valley served as an important trade route for ivory, gold, and slaves between the interior and the coast. This was especially the case at the trade centers of Mapungubwe and Thulamela. When organized labor migrancy developed toward the end of the nineteenth century, chiefs and headmen benefited from the fees paid for the supply of labor to the offices of the Witwatersrand Native Labour Association or from the illegal trade in workers. As in many other tribal areas, the Makuleke area was attractive as a base for migrant laborers of various origins, many of whom in recent decades were refugees from the Mozambican civil war.

As the Makuleke tribal leadership no doubt recognized, absorbing migrant workers and refugees could be advantageous. Attracting more people to settle on tribal land could enhance their status, and the resulting population pressure on services could be used to strengthen claims for better provision of schools, clinics, roads, and other forms of infrastructure and services. In Makuleke there continue to be strong ties with relatives in Mozambique and Zimbabwe. Due to the recently rapidly deteriorating economic conditions in Zimbabwe, many recent immigrants have come from there to settle amongst relatives, adding to the number of people already moving into the area from Mozambique. Because of their kinship linkages, these immigrants are often welcomed and their contribution to the local economy is valued, even if they are, strictly speaking, illegal. They are provided with a residential stand and can apply for a South African Identity Document after a few years; after five years they qualify for South African citizenship. Clearly, the Makuleke have a long history of adapting to the exigencies of life in a transfrontier zone. These historical experiences have also shaped their responses to recent initiatives to develop the GLTP into a transfrontier conservation area (see Spierenburg, Steenkamp, and Wels 2006; Spierenburg and Wels 2006).

A SPECIAL KIND OF CHIEFTAINCY AND A SPECIAL KIND OF LAND?

Two directly related issues are part of the Makuleke historical experience and continue to shape their present condition: a contested chieftaincy and a contested land struggle. After the forced removal of 1969, the Gazankulu bantustan authorities regarded the Makuleke as falling under Chief Mhinga. In 1976 the father of the current Makuleke chief, Chief Mugakula, was installed as a headman under Chief Mhinga, despite the former's attempts to become officially recognized as an independent chief. Given the ongoing conflict with the Mhinga chieftaincy, the Makuleke traditional authority continues to attract strong local community support.

Although the struggle for the recognition of a Makuleke chieftaincy has been ongoing since the mid-twentieth century, a new opportunity presented itself with the enactment of the Restitution Act of 1994. The Makuleke's land claim was successful and became the focus of a series of development interventions. As a result, the Makuleke came to be seen by outsiders as a model for reconciling (tribal) community and conservation needs. One of the effects of these developments, which were actively supported by donors, NGOs, and a Friends of Makuleke support network, was that the chieftaincy was "democratized" while being strengthened in relation to its quest for official recognition.

In the new South Africa, tribal authorities are once again being resurrected in the service of the state. Despite the prior animosity between the national liberation movement and traditional leaders, a stronger sense of strategic collaboration has surfaced since 2000. It would seem that the government is seeking to accommodate traditional leaders through measures such as CLRA. There is also evidence of the "retraditionalization" of the South African countryside, largely as a result of the collapse of the civic movement and the need to overcome gridlock between democratic local government structures and traditional authorities in their areas of jurisdiction (see also Derman, Lahiff, and Sjaastad, this volume).

Another aspect of the ongoing Makuleke land struggle is the perceived need by the leadership to portray the people as belonging to a coherent and bounded community. This view is shared by many academic, donor, and journalist commentators. For instance, Steenkamp and Uhr (2005, 5) note that "The Makuleke are an exceptionally cohesive 'community.' Their internal organisation further displays a marked degree of institutional 'hardness' and is able to cope well with the classic internal community tensions and frictions. In the course of the land claim these were practically always subordinated to the need to show a 'united face' to the outside." This conception is overstated, downplaying the contestations and differentiation found within any social grouping. However, both the previous and the present government, as well as NGOs, land activists and development agencies, have tended to reinforce these ideas of community and tribal coherence. These representations, which are reproduced by both insiders and outsiders, have also contributed toward portrayals of the Makuleke as having successfully reconciled traditional and modern democratic institutions, as well as their livelihood and conservation needs. A number of internal lines of social division are usually underemphasized in relation to the ongoing tensions between Mhinga and Makuleke. These include gender, age, and generation differences, as well as tensions between those who are part of the core group that came from the old Makuleke land and settlers that have come recently from Mozambique and Zimbabwe. In addition, divisions between royal family members and commoners occasionally surface.

The Makuleke Tribal Authority is based on strong patriarchal principles, and this has triggered some calls for more institutional participation by women in terms of the constitutional principle of gender equity (Claassens 2005). The Women's Rural Movement, for instance, has criticized the tribal authority because its composition does not reflect equal gender representation, as required by the Traditional Leadership and Governance Framework Act (see Claassens 2003). Women of the Makuleke royal family are said to be involved in decisions made in the inner circle of the chieftaincy, yet no women have as yet been elected to the council of the traditional authority. Men are seen as so powerful that women have found it difficult to become community leaders or influence decisions made by the traditional authority. Even the possibility of a woman president for the country, as proposed by former President Mbeki, was considered highly unlikely, and possibly unwarranted, by men and women whom we spoke to. Although there may be more room for gender equity in national politics, women we spoke to in Makuleke village responded that "here it is more traditional." The low status of women is evident in the fact that women are still called to do unpaid work for the chief.

These observations about women's experiences question the claims made by some commentators that the Makuleke community has successfully and seamlessly combined traditional and democratic principles of governance. The following section focuses on the changing circumstances within which the royal family is operating. These changes include the impact of CLRA, the CPA, and the GLTP.

RECONCILING CHIEFTAINCY, DEMOCRACY, AND CONSERVATISM

The Makuleke CPA was established as the formal landholding body under the restitution settlement. It is a constantly evolving entity that is based on democratic principles: executive members are elected and all residents in the tribal area eighteen years of age or older are members. It seems that initially the membership of the executive was restricted to those who had originally lived on the old Makuleke land, as indicated by the operation of two lists of members of the tribe, differentiated by origin and thereby excluding a large portion of the population (Friedman 2005, 46). A close association between the CPA and the tribal authority is reflected in the overlapping membership of their executives, the exercise of chiefly duties by the CPA (such as land allocation and deciding on economic opportunities), and the fact that the chief is routinely elected as the CPA chairperson. Even though the constitution of the CPA prescribes gender equity for the executive, only three of the nine executive committee members were women. Participation by women in decision making tends to be confined to being recipients of the benefits of CPA resources such as access to jobs in the projects that the CPA runs.

In mid-2006 the CPA executive was reconstituted, as prescribed by its constitution. Before the election, some teachers lobbied for stronger representation of well-educated professionals on the executive. There was a general feeling that it was no longer tenable to have only members of the royal family and their closest allies as the members of the executive committee of the CPA. The new executive has more representation of teachers, though the chief is still the chair; he pointed out that he had submitted himself to a democratic election. The election, of course, only concerned the CPA, not the traditional leadership structure itself.

The emergence of the CPA as a local institution more than ten years ago was the result of a series of discussions with, among others, the environmental activist and journalist Eddie Koch. With the help of the Friends of Makuleke and the LRC, the Makuleke land claim was eventually submitted to the CRLR in 1996. It took another two years before the historic out-of-court settlement between the Makuleke and SANParks, then still known as the National Parks Board, was reached (Steenkamp and Uhr 2000, 1). Initially the conservation authorities opposed the land claim, urging that the Pafuri region of the KNP should remain a highly protected area without communal or private ownership. A leadership change within SANParks and political pressure on the organization eventually led to the settlement, which was hailed as a "'world class' agreement that had established a new 'harmony of interests' between the park and the people" (Steenkamp and Grossman 2001; Steenkamp and Uhr 2000, 14, 15). SANParks had apparently moved from a protectionist position toward a "social ecology" approach that claims to integrate the concerns of wildlife conservation with the socioeconomic needs of communities (Tapela and Omara-Ojungu 1999, 148).

Although the land was restored to the Makuleke CPA, restrictions on land use prohibited access to the livelihood resources that were available before 1969 (Friedman 2005, 43). Meanwhile, the Makuleke's relationship with SANParks has remained ambivalent: on the one hand, the park authorities are an important partner in terms of the conservation activities and expertise that is needed, but, on the other hand, they are also viewed with suspicion and are sometimes seen as opposed to the Makuleke Contract Park model (see Steenkamp and Grossman 2001).

The ambivalence on the part of SANParks toward the "Makuleke model" of CBNRM has emerged in the context of a proliferation of about forty land claims by various communities in recent years, covering about a quarter of the area of the KNP. SANParks has opposed many of these claims and sought new guidelines for handling them, arguing that the Makuleke model of public-private ecotourism is not financially sustainable (Groenewald and Macleod 2005). In other words, notwithstanding the iconic status of the model, SANParks has increasingly demonstrated deep reservations about its replication elsewhere.

Provision was made in the settlement agreement for a joint management board where SANParks and the Makuleke would both be represented on equal footing. What frustrates members of the Makuleke leadership is that they are not always treated as the landlords by SANParks but are often positioned as simply one of many "neighboring communities." Being perceived to be the "landlords of Pafuri" is of great importance to the Makuleke—and-ownership of the Pafuri heartland of the GLTP symbolizes ultimate control over highly valued resources as this region contains particularly high levels of biodiversity. Yet for the Makuleke it appears that power continues to reside with SANParks, largely due to its technical expertise and state-given mandate to protect the natural resources in the KNP. It is therefore hardly surprising that community participation is often perceived to be largely rhetorical (Friedman 2005, 36, 47). From the perspective of many members of the Makuleke community, the social ecology approach of SANParks has not contributed significantly toward their empowerment. The 52 percent of household heads at Makuleke who work for SANParks are generally in unskilled and low-wage jobs (Tapela and Omara-Ojungu 1999, 154).

The idea of a Transfrontier Park, as "an exemplary process of partnerships between governments and the private sector" (SANParks 2006b), features prominently in the plans and policy documents of conservation-oriented organizations such as the Peace Parks Foundation, donors, big business, and governments. Yet at the village level there is little direct evidence of the benefits of these grand plans (see Hughes 2005; Spierenburg, Steenkamp, and Wels 2006). Neither was the idea of the GLTP well understood by the community members to whom we spoke. The chief and other core CPA members have been to conferences about transfrontier parks in Zimbabwe and KwaZulu-Natal, but it remains unclear to them how this will actually affect them at the local level. The Makuleke land has featured centrally in the planning of the GLTP; it is sometimes portrayed as its heart. Moreover, the Makuleke land settlement is portrayed as a shining example of a working transfrontier park arrangement, in stark contrast to the problematic political and economic situation in Zimbabwe and the underdeveloped conditions in Mozambique. Nevertheless, the feeling of some of the leadership at Makuleke is that they have been sidelined by the GLTP planners and are not treated as the true landlords that they consider themselves to be.

Yet, it is also clear that there have been significant developments in the Makuleke village and park. The land claim settlement brought government grants of about R7.5 million that were used for different development projects in Nthlaveni (Hollemans 2004). Furthermore, the CPA was the recipient of resources and interventions from a range of NGOs who identified the importance of strengthening this institution so that it could fulfill its democratic and conservation purposes. The Ford Foundation, the German GTZ, the Endangered Wildlife Trust, Goldfields, the African Wildlife Foundation, and Resources Africa have all been involved since 1996 in training the leadership, advising them on strategic action, and facilitating development projects (Marnewick 2005). The advisory group Friends of Makuleke has been especially influential.

As already noted, unlike many land-claimant communities, the Makuleke community is widely perceived by academics, NGOs, and donors to be a relatively cohesive and consensual community. The perception of continuity and cohesiveness, is, we argue, not simply the product of pure fiction. It can perhaps be partly attributed to the fact that the Makuleke have lived in the same place and under the same traditional leadership structures since their eviction from the KNP in 1969. This state of relative stability is probably also due to the community's successful rallying strategies in its ongoing conflicts with neighboring Chief Mhinga, the son of the traditional leader who colluded with the apartheid government in the forced removal of the Makuleke people.

Another aspect of the Makuleke success story is the perception among NGOs and donors that the community is receptive to engaging with outside actors and expertise as well as entrepreneurial activities. For instance, NGOs and ecoactivists from the Friends of Makuleke group were intimately involved in the early mobilizations around the land claim. Similarly, in the postsettlement phase a number of NGOs and donors have provided training to CPA members to "professionalize" the CPA and transform it into a democratic and modern bureaucracy, distinct from the tribal authority, while the tourism-based income generated by the CPA has been used to fund electricity connections and to build classrooms and a clinic. A large agricultural irrigation project has also been established with the assistance of the Development Bank of South Africa. However, despite efforts to separate the functions of the two bodies, in practice there remains ambiguity and tension about their roles and responsibilities. Funds generated by the CPA have been used to strengthen the tribal authority and fund its many expenses, leading to tensions about the independence of the CPA. So, although the apparent creative meshing of modern and traditional institutional cultures has contributed to the widespread appeal of the Makuleke model, everyday practices of those involved in these institutions are more complex and messy.

The apparent capacity of the Makuleke to reconcile traditional and democratic governance structures and practices was likely made possible by virtue of the fact that the Makuleke leadership was never fully incorporated into the political culture and formal institutions and structures of bantustan rule. This was a direct result of Chief Makuleke's resistance to forced removal, which meant that the Makuleke traditional leadership was never officially recognized as a chieftaincy. This apartheid past of political marginalization meant the Makuleke tribal leadership was able to retain legitimacy and develop relatively democratic and decentralized forms of traditional leadership and land allocation. The history of collaboration of neighboring Chief Mhinga with the bantustan system has probably also contributed to strengthening the political legitimacy of the Makuleke claim for a traditional authority independent of Mhinga. However, by the end of 2008, the Makuleke were still waiting to hear whether the government commission on traditional leadership had decided to recognize their chieftaincy claim.

The Makuleke land claim continues to animate discussions on how to reconcile conservation and community development. Their historical engagement with restitution and struggles for recognition as an independent traditional authority have also contributed to their status as a "model tribe," a tribe that is simultaneously traditionalist, democratic, and environmentally conscious. However, this iconic status should not blind us to the complexities involved in ongoing struggles for land and livelihoods in the Makuleke area. Local control over land has continued to be perceived as precarious, even in a postapartheid constitutional democracy that is meant to provide security of tenure. The ongoing uncertainty with regard to the formal recognition of the chieftaincy has necessitated concerted action on the part of the Makuleke leadership. This has involved strengthening the CPA and its landowning and development functions. It has also involved becoming part of the legal challenge to the CLRA.

The Makuleke contestation over land and traditional authority is framed by the recent developments in South African legislation: the Constitution, restitution legislation, the legislation on traditional authorities, and the legislation on communal land rights. Contradictions and ambiguities in the principles underlying this legislation are used strategically by local communities and their legal representatives. These strategies include arguments about historical and "tribal" continuity that are used to buttress claims to traditional authority and land. At the same time, discourses on democratic governance also underpin the strategies of the Makuleke community and their opposition to the CLRA.

Although the Makuleke continue to retain their iconic status among donors and NGOs, the situation is considerably more complex and precarious than most of their admirers acknowledge. There are, for instance, indications of ongoing challenges to the traditional leadership as well as the CPA as a result of gender, lineage, and generational differences. Discourses on traditional authority, community participation, public-private partnerships, and democratic governance coexist and contradict each other in complicated and changing ways. Yet it is also clear that both the CPA and the traditional leadership are responding in creative ways to these challenges, and that considerable adaptation, reinvention, and fluidity are involved in these processes. The iconic status of the Makuleke may itself be largely the outcome of their strategic deployment and creative assimilation of these mobile development discourses.

NOTES

An earlier version of this chapter was published in 2008 as "'Model Tribes' and Traveling Models: Tracking the Makuleke Restitution Case in Kruger National Park," *Development and Change* 39 (1): 53–72.

1. Our account of local perspectives on the Makuleke traditional authority and the act was informed by discussions we had with the Makuleke leadership and villagers. However, it is possible that there are alternative perspectives that we did not access due to fear of the repercussions of disclosing views that are critical of the current Makuleke traditional authority.

2. Members of the tribe contributed R20 per household to help pay for the legal costs incurred by the tribal leadership. One reason the tribal members were mobilized was the danger posed by the old dispute with a neighboring chief.

3. Memorandum of a land claim by Chief Shilungwa Cydrick Mhinga on behalf of the Mhinga Tribe in Terms of the Restitution of Land Rights Act, Act no. 22 of 1994. Fax submission dated 4 February 1997.

REFERENCES

Bulpin, T. V. 1967. *The Ivory Trail.* Cape Town: Books of Africa.

Bunn, D. 2001. "Comaroff Country." *Interventions* 3 (1): 5–23.

Claassens, A. 2003. *Community Views on the Communal Land Rights Bill.* Bellville: Programme for Land and Agrarian Studies, University of the Western Cape (Research Report No. 15).

———. 2005. *The Communal Land Rights Act and Women: Does the Act Remedy or Entrench Discrimination and the Distortion of the Customary?* Bellville: Programme for Land and Agrarian Studies, University of the Western Cape (Occasional Paper 28).

Cousins, B., and A. Claassens. 2004. "Communal Land Rights, Democracy, and Traditional Leaders in Post-apartheid South Africa." In *Securing Land and Resource Rights in Africa: Pan-African Perspectives,* ed. M. Saruchera, 139–54. Bellville: Programme for Land and Agrarian Studies, University of the Western Cape.

Cousins, B. 2007. "More Than Socially Embedded: The Distinctive Character of Communal Tenure Regimes in South Africa and its Implications for Land Policy." *Journal of Agrarian Change* 7 (3): 281–315.

Friedman, J. 2005. *Winning Isn't Everything: What the Makuleke Lost in the Process of Land Restitution.* BA thesis, University of Chicago.

Groenewald, Y., and F. Macleod. 2005. "Land Claims Could Kill Kruger." *Mail and Guardian,* 18 February 2005.

Hollemans, E. 2004. "Paradise Regained." *Mail and Guardian,* 14 December 2004.

Hughes, D. M. 2005. "Third Nature: Making Space and Time in the Great Limpopo Conservation Area." *Cultural Anthropology* 20 (2): 157–84.

Junod, H. A. 1927 [1962]. *The Life of A South African Tribe.* New Hyde Park, NY: University Books.

Kruger2Canyons.com 2006. *Presidents Open Kruger Border Crossing.* Online: http://www.kruger2canyons.com/news/2006_08_01_archive.html. Accessed 17 November 2007.

LRC (Legal Resources Centre). 2006. *Press Statement (20/04/06).*

Mahony, K., and J. Van Zyl. 2002. "The Impacts of Tourism Investment on Rural Communities: Three Case Studies in South Africa." *Development Southern Africa* 19 (1): 83–103.

Marnewick, M. D. 2005. "Conservation and Development: The Makuleke Training Project." BA honors thesis, University of the Witwatersrand.

Rijke-Epstein, T. 2006. "Official Discourse(s) of Land Restitution in Post-Apartheid South Africa: A Case Study of Makhoba." MPhil diss., University of Cape Town.

Robins, S. 2001. "NGOs, 'Bushmen' and Double Vision: The ≠Khomani San Land Claim and the Cultural Politics of 'Community,' and 'Development' in the Kalahari." *Journal of Southern African Studies* 27 (4): 833–53.

———. 2003. "Whose Modernity? Indigenous Modernities and Land Claims after Apartheid." *Development and Change* 34 (2): 1–21.

SANParks 2006a. "SANParks Launches the Leadership for Conservation in Africa Initiative." http://www.parks-sa.co.za/about/news/2006/august/lcm.php?PHPSESSID=hmicdliabuke52ai7rpiq32pk4. Accessed 12 September 2006.

———. 2006b. "Great Limpopo Transfrontier Park." http://www.sanparks.org/conservation/transfrontier/great_limpopo.php. Accessed 12 September 2006.

Spierenburg, M., C. Steenkamp, and H. Wels. 2006. "Resistance against the Marginalization of Communities in the Great Limpopo Transfrontier Conservation Area." *Focaal: European Journal of Anthropology* 2006 (47): 18–31.

Spierenburg, M., and H. Wels. 2006. "'Securing Space': Mapping and Fencing in Transfrontier Conservation in Southern Africa." *Space and Culture* 6 (3): 294–312.

Steenkamp, C., and D. Grossman. 2000. *People and Parks: Cracks in the Paradigm.* IUCN, http://www.cbnrm.net/pdf/iucn_001_ptt0101.pdf. Accessed 12 September 2006.

Steenkamp, C., and J. Uhr 2001. *The Makuleke Land Claim: Power Relations and Community-based Natural Resource Management.* Evaluating Eden Series, IIED (Discussion Paper no. 18).

Tapela, B. N., and P. H. Omara-Ojungu. 1999. "Towards Bridging the Gap between Wildlife Conservation and Rural Development in Post-Apartheid South Africa: The Case of the Makuleke Community and the Kruger National Park." *South African Geographical Journal* 81 (3): 148–55.

Van Warmelo, N. J. 1935. *A Preliminary Survey of the Bantu Tribes of South Africa.* Pretoria: Government Printer.

Wolmer, W. 2007. *From Wilderness Vision to Farm Invasions: Conservation and Development in Zimbabwe's Southeast Lowveld.* Oxford: James Currey.

ten

The ≠Khomani San Land Claim against the Kalahari Gemsbok National Park

Requiring and Acquiring Authenticity

WILLIAM ELLIS

This chapter tracks the progression of the ≠Khomani San land restitution case affecting the Kalahari Gemsbok National Park, beginning with the initiation of the claim, to the present postsettlement activities of some of the claimants.[1] The chapter examines the manner in which "authentic San identity" was deployed before and after the settlement in order to capture benefits. The land restitution package resulted in the return of a total of 68,000 hectares of land, including 25,000 hectares inside the Kalahari Gemsbok National Park and the remainder outside the park. The ≠Khomani San were also given cash to purchase more land, as well as grants to cover the cost of their relocation to the restituted land.

Through the analysis of the activities of the claimants, the chapter explores the tensions, synergies, and power plays that existed and how those involved interpreted the unfolding events. As is shown later, at the core of the different interpretations lay an interpretation and reinterpretation of San identity, whereby San authenticity was either required or acquired in the process. The chapter discusses how this controversy influenced or was influenced by the restitution package, local livelihoods, outsiders working with the local people, and local politics.

William Ellis

BACKGROUND TO THE ≠KHOMANI SAN LAND CLAIM
Conceptualization and Framing of the Claim

During the early 1990s Regopstaan and her son, Dawid Kruiper, approached Roger Chennels, a lawyer for the South African San Institute (SASI), about lodging a land claim on behalf of "the San of the Kalahari" for land lost in the Kalahari Gemsbok National Park (hereinafter KGNP or the park). Late in 1994 the Southern Kalahari Land Claim Committee was formed and comprised former residents living on a Northern Cape farm by the name of Kagga Kamma, along with several of the remaining speakers of the supposedly extinct N/u language and their relatives.

The San claimants and their lawyers chose to focus on the establishment of the KGNP in 1931, whereby the San of the southern Kalahari were confined to certain sections of the park, denied access to other areas they needed for livelihoods, and not allowed to hunt with guns or dogs (Cleary 1989). The proclamation of the park in 1931 initiated a process of dispossession that would culminate in the removal and relocation of the last San residents from the area, to the town of Welkom, eight kilometers south of the park, in 1976 (Wildschut and Steyn 1990). Not only were the San confined to an ever-smaller territory before physical removal from the park, but they were also prevented from engaging in their traditional foraging practices. Therefore, the claim of the ≠Khomani San was not solely for "ownership of land" but for "traditional '*use*' (hunting and gathering) rights" (Chennels 1998).

Initial Resistance to and the Resolution of the Claim

The submission of the land claim in 1995 brought the ≠Khomani San into conflict with several other stakeholders, including the "coloured" residents of the Mier rural area, the Mier local government officials and the South African National Parks (SANParks). At the time SANParks opposed land claims against national parks (Poonan 2002). The Mier local government wanted to defend their interests as current owners of part of the land under claim—land that is located directly south of the KGNP within the Mier rural reserve. They thus saw the land claim as a threat to the existing land use in Mier, especially the game camps, which are a major source of revenue for the Mier local government.

With the support of the Bastervolk Organisasie and Mier Residents Association, the Mier local government decided to lodge a land claim in direct contest to the ≠Khomani San claim. The Mier claim was based on several instances of dispossession, two of which are related to land inside the boundaries of the park and the others to Mier communal lands that were dispossessed by the state under war measures during World War I as well as land that was privatized between 1960 and 1990. Mier wanted restitution for the removal of "*Basters*" (literally "bastards") from farms in the southern part of the park after its proclamation in the 1930s (Kloppers 1970). Further rights to other tracts of land in the south of the park were lost in the 1960s when the park's southern border was fenced and land that had been used by Mier communal farmers was no longer available to them (Bosch 2002a). Land adjacent to the then German South West African border was dispossessed by the state for strategic purposes during World War I (DLA 2002). The last instance of dispossession occurred through the implementation of "economic units laws" (e.g., Coloured Rural Areas Act no. 24 of 1963, Rural Areas Act no. 1 of 1979, and the controversial Mier Rural Area Bill of 1990) in Mier. Under these programs land was divided into portions and sold off or rented to private individuals, thus reducing the land available for communal use. The Mier community argued that many were indirectly dispossessed through this process (Wildschut and Steyn 1990).

A note here on the evolution of land tenure in the region is necessary. Autochthony in this region belongs to the San. The ancestors of the "basters" settled in the region in the late 1860s, and it is only after the First World War that Europeans settled the region in significant numbers. It follows that the rights in land that the Mier community could claim through the restitution program are rights that they held as part of a nested set of rights or, in other words, rights that nest and overlap with those that the San claim.

Two key developments helped the parties involved reach a settlement and develop restitution packages that satisfied both the ≠Khomani San and the Mier group. First, through their interaction with the Mier group, the Commission on Restitution of Land Rights (CRLR) realized that there were several unresolved land disputes and an acute land shortage in the Mier region, and therefore proposed some form of relief by finding additional land for them. Second, SANParks radically changed its approach to land reform in conservation areas and accepted the outcomes of land claims so long as the goals of conservation would not be compromised (Wynberg and Kepe 1999; Magome 2002; Poonan 2002).

THE RESTITUTION PACKAGE

Although the Park was central to the ≠Khomani San claim, the land offered by the government as part of the settlement inside the park did not meet the various land use needs by different groups of the San. These included hunting, game farming, and livestock farming. Even though full title to land inside the park was offered to the ≠Khomani San, the area identified by SANParks for use by the San was only a small percentage of the land they claimed and excluded many of the sites that have cultural and symbolic significance for the ≠Khomani San. Further, no agricultural, mining, or residential activities were to be allowed on the land inside the park.

Considering all these conditions, including limitations on land use, the CRLR developed a multifaceted package intended to satisfy the ≠Khomani San's diverse needs. The package offered to the ≠Khomani San included the following:

- Freehold title to 25,000 hectares of land within the boundaries of the park;
- Symbolic rights (such as access to grave sites, former residential sites, and any other sites of cultural significance) and commercial rights (such as income from any commercial venture or other commercial revenues) on land inside the park;
- 36,000 hectares of farmland outside the park for grazing and game farming;
- 7,000 hectares of land donated by the Mier community as restitution for land rights that the ≠Khomani San had lost to the Mier community in the past,
- R517,000 for the purchase of commonage around the town of Welkom,
- Purchase of game animals to stock the farms, and
- The allocation of discretionary grants to all those who moved onto the new farms in the amount of R3,000 per household.

However, despite these seemingly positive aspects of the land-claim settlement, as well as the sorting out of certain conflicts, the persistence of deeper issues concerning identity and who had rights to benefit from the San land claim, remained a major challenge. These issues are discussed next.

GROUP FORMATION AND AUTHENTICITY

Pinning Down the ≠Khomani

Before moving into the discussion about group formation within the land-claiming communities, it is necessary to give some sense of the institutional framework within which it takes place. Before lodging the land claim, there was no organized structure that represented the southern Kalahari San. Evidence points out that even the referent "≠Khomani" is a term that is completely bound up in academic ascription and only appeared for the first time as a supposed ethnic referent in the work of Dorothea Bleek in 1911. She divided the San of the region geographically into an eastern group, the N//n, and a western group, the ≠Khomani. Later the "Wits expedition" in the 1930s would use and thus inscribe the term ≠Khomani into popular use (Rheinhalt-Jones and Doke 1937). ≠Khomani has emerged as the dominant self-referent in the process of identity formation that is intricately bound up in the land claim against the park (Crawhall n.d). Before the land claim the San were dispersed and mainly consisted of scattered family groups. Many of the people who participated in the land claim did not even refer to themselves as San. In other words, there was no grouping that referred to itself as "the ≠Khomani San."

Ethnographic work points to the southern Kalahari as being the home of several ethnolinguistic communities of San people (Duggan-Cronin 1942; Crawhall 1998). Several distinct San groups are identified, including the N/amani (!Xo speakers), the /Auni-≠Khomani (N/u speakers), and the Vaalpens (Khattea speakers) (Rheinhalt-Jones and Doke 1937; Lee 1979). Early on in the land-claim process a number of these ethnic terms were used to apply to the claimant group, including the N/a-mani, /Auni, and ≠Khomani. The initial choice of a general geographic term—southern Kalahari San—to describe the group reflects the difficulties of finding a single ethnic categorization to describe the collective claimants.

With the decision to lodge the land claim, the process of group formation also began. First, the claimants were all drawn together as the Southern Kalahari Land Claim Committee, which grew over time, but as the claim was about to be settled, the ≠Khomani San Communal Property Association (CPA) was formed. The formation of the CPA was necessary to effect transfer of ownership of the land to the claimant group.

Gaining Membership in the Claiming San Community

The definition of claimant community changed many times during the claim process. First, there is the group of "original claimants," that is, those who initiated the ≠Khomani San claims process. They resided on the game farm, Kagga Kamma. This group then sought its relatives to inform them of the intention to submit a land claim. The members of the group based their claim on their removal from the park during the 1970s, after which they were dispersed to various locations in the Northern Cape. Second, there is another group of "original claimants" that is made up of three family groups who linked their membership in the claimant group to the removals that took place in the 1930s. These families, sometimes referred to as "Bain's Bushmen," are well documented in the ethnographic work by scholars from the University of the Witwatersrand in 1936–37 (Rheinhalt-Jones and Doke 1937).

All applicants to be considered as claimants could be screened using genealogical research as a reference point, and if an individual or family were not recorded in the genealogical charts, their membership and claim to San-ness could be assumed to be spurious. The system of validating claimants through the genealogical studies was thought to lessen the possibility of opportunistic claims to San identity. Several speakers of the N/u language had been traced, and it was realized that many of them did not necessarily have links to the chosen moment of dispossession, which is the proclamation of the park in 1931. It was conceded, however, that to exclude these people simply because they had never lived, worked, or had any historical links to the park would mean an insufficient restitution benefit for the San of the southern Kalahari. A third group emerged, therefore, between 1995 and 1998, when determination of membership was broadened to include those who spoke N/u. The Southern Kalahari Land Claims Committee received applications from individuals in the Mier region for membership. Many of those who applied had no clear legal basis for participation in the restitution case. Ethnic identity thus became the key criterion for membership in the claimant group.

Fourth, an addition to the claimant community resulted from an advice in 1998, by officials from the Department of Land Affairs (DLA), who advised the existing claimants that it would strengthen their claim, and ensure that more resources would be made available, if they included all other San from the Northern Cape. A common sentiment shared by many of the ≠Khomani San is that as a result of this suggestion of soliciting new members, many individuals who were "not really San" joined the claimant group. Additionally, the people who were invited did not meet the criteria of membership set out in the constitution of the CPA (Notes, 2001; Bosch

2002b). Thus a new debate about San authenticity emerged. Those who joined the claimant group later were seen by the original claimant group as culturally less pure. People from the original claimant group (also known as traditional San) readily referred to them as the "western San" in this case because they speak no Khoesan languages and because they have adopted various other "western," that is, westernized, ways.

POSTSETTLEMENT DYNAMICS AROUND THE LAND CLAIM

In addition to the questions about the identity of the various claimant community members, the claimant community could be divided into three groupings in terms of livelihood goals. They had different reasons for participating in the land claim and therefore different views of the appropriate direction for "San" development. Their experiences and interpretations highlighted the fragility of the group cohesion that was assumed to exist.

The first group, comprising about fifty individuals under the leadership of Dawid Kruiper, which I will call the Kagga Kamma group, wanted to make a living from harvesting natural resources and from performing for tourists. The second group, including three elderly sisters and their extended families from Swartkops near Upington, thought that the return of land meant they would be able to access certain benefits, such as housing, electricity, and running water. For the third group, three livestock farmers from Mier, the land offered them the opportunity to raise domestic animals, a privilege they never had enjoyed in Mier. These varying and sometimes opposing expectations would lead to several conflicts between the groups on the farms and with the CPA executive.

Subsistence as Authentically San and Disparities in Use of Resources

The members of the Kagga Kamma group are mostly from the Kruiper family, plus relatives from local farms and settlements in the Mier region. High levels of unemployment, low levels of education, dependence on state pensions, alcoholism, domestic violence, and associated social problems—all characterized this group. The Kagga Kamma group was involved in hunting, gathering medicinal plants, harvesting of thatching grass, collection of fuel wood, and gathering of other plant material for the manufacture of crafts that they sold to tourists. Not only were they the most directly dependent on natural resources, but they also used the widest variety of natural resources. This is in contrast to the livestock owners who were dependent only on grazing lands and had other off-farm means of making a living. The use of natural resources by the Kagga Kamma group and its attempts to exclude others from using them led to conflicts between it and the CPA executive, as well as with other members of the CPA. The CPA executive claimed that the hunting by the members of the Kagga Kamma group was illegal because they did not have hunting licenses and much of the hunting took place outside the hunting season (generally between May and August).

Early in 2001 the CPA executive, with the assistance of some of the local farmers, undertook a series of game captures on the farm Witdraai. A large number of springbok were captured and sold to cover the day-to-day running costs of the organization, such as transportation, salaries for the CPA administration officers, rental of office space, and fees for the executive members to travel to and attend meetings. The sale of springbok initiated a protracted debate about who has the right to manage and make decisions about the game and other resources on the farms. At the same time it highlighted the contestations about the strategies and uses of the resources available to the CPA. The question was whether the resources should be used by the organization (CPA), with benefits going to it, or whether individual households should be allowed to benefit directly from the natural resources through consumptive activities such as hunting. This episode, and others like it, supported the view held by many of the ≠Khomani San that the CPA should no longer be responsible for the management of the game on the farms.

The important distinction between the two opposing groups is that the Witdraai residents engaged in low-intensity hunting of game for subsistence whereas the CPA executive used vehicles and hired labor to capture and sell off large numbers of the springbok for high financial returns. Thus the members of the Kagga Kamma group harvested animals to supplement their other livelihood strategies, whereas the CPA executive needed large amounts of cash.

In defining San-ness, the Kagga Kamma group used its particular mode of harvesting natural resources as one of the markers of authenticity. Following the intensive hunting and sale of game by the CPA, all those who benefited from the resources for reasons other than household use were taken to be less authentically San. The plans that the Kagga Kamma group had, which were for the revival of San culture through the use and control of the natural resources on the farms, did not come to fruition. The perceived control that the Kagga Kamma group thought it held over resources on Witdraai was never realized. All around them others (CPA executive, woodcutters, and neighbors) made decisions about the resources this group thought it owned. The Kagga Kamma group placed its hopes for the control of and access to natural resources such as game, medicinal plants, and wild plant foods (and through this a revival of a San lifestyle) on the park. This was before the park land had been officially handed over as part of the restitution settlement. Their hopes were shattered when learned that the land in the park had serious land use limits. Dawid Kruiper also started talking about splitting the land into farms and the park, and added that Vaalie (the CPA chairperson at that time and considered *western* San) could have the farms and his group would take the park, which is seen as the home of the "traditional San," or the area for its exclusive use. The battle lines had been drawn, and the cracks in community cohesion were starting to show.

Restitution as the Delivery of Social Services

The Swartkops sisters and their families moved from the settlement Swartkops, outside Upington, to the farm, hoping to get away from the violence of "the location," where periodically they would be robbed of their pension money. For them the move to the farms meant a life without the dangers of urban life and a new beginning, where their dignity would be restored and their culture, especially the language, would be transmitted to the youth. The members of this group were largely dependent on their pensions and crafts sold to the occasional visitor. They claimed that when they moved to the farms the leadership of the CPA promised them that they would receive houses and other services, including transport to the pension pay points. So for them the land restitution deal was additionally attractive due to the possibility that it would make it easier to access government assistance and other services. However, when no houses were built, the sisters and their relatives, numbering about twenty individuals, took possession of the farmhouse on the farm Andriesvale. In response to their occupation of this house, other CPA members decided also to occupy the houses on the remaining farms. By November 2001 CPA members had occupied all of the farmhouses.

Livestock Farmers' Authenticity and Antithetical Livelihoods

The livestock farmers moved to the ≠Khomani San's farms because the grazing they had access to in Mier was either insufficient or under dispute. Hans Tieties came from Groot Mier where the commons were overgrazed and overcrowded; his mixed herd of just over a hundred animals that he had purchased after his retirement was also too big for the commons, where occupants are limited to fifty small livestock units. Hendrik Vaalbooi had been involved in a dispute over water rights at the Mier game camp, Geisamap, with eleven other occupants and was violently forced off the grazing land by the other occupants. He was a member of the CPA and made a request that they be temporarily accommodated as an emergency measure on the farm Witdraai. After they had moved onto the farms, they depended largely on the grazing available and did not make use of any other natural resources. They kept mixed herds of cattle, goats, sheep, and horses, sheep being the most abundant species.

Jan van der Westhuisen moved to the farm in 2000. He did not have a large herd and kept a few donkeys for transport and a few goats, subsisting further from hunting with his dogs plus some income earned from the crafts he sold. His livelihood strategies had several aspects in common with those of the Kagga Kamma group and the Swartkops sisters. He was involved in craft production, tourist performances (including for the production of films), and harvesting of natural resources; like the traditional group, he was poorer than the other stock farmers. The other livestock farmers tried to get him off the land by claiming that he was not a real farmer and that he was there only to scavenge and steal.

In general, the livestock farmers were, in some sense, villainized by the Kagga Kamma group and the nongovernmental organizations (NGOs) because their livelihood was seen as the antithesis of San culture. Ironically, although the Swartkops sisters were eventually involved in livestock farming, they were never labeled westernized San, largely because their legitimacy as San was based on their linguistic and biographical authenticity. Another inconsistency concerns Jan van der Westhuisen, who enjoys legitimacy as a traditional San because his livelihood mirrors that of the other traditional San, although his biographical and linguistic authenticity is questionable. Other people on the farm, such as Hendrik Vaalbooi and Hans Tieties, had no such grounds for claiming authenticity and had to legitimate their presence on the farms through internalizing the "westernized San" identity, by describing themselves as "San farmers."

After about two years on the farms, very little had been done to promote economic growth and the implementation of development plans. Rather, what happened was a scramble for houses, the questioning of the stock presence of stock farmers by traditionalists, and disputes about the right to manage natural resources. These conflicts were interpreted by many CPA members and NGO workers as competition between "western pursuits" (such as stock farming, large-scale hunting, and wood sales) and "traditional livelihoods" (such as hunting strictly for household consumption, performing for tourism, and medicinal and food plant harvests for personal consumption). In essence the disputes were seen as a competition between "traditional" San who wanted to lead a "genuine San way of life," and supported a revival of that lifestyle, and those who were interested in the economic gains to be had from landownership in a "western" manner.

However, this interpretation falls short of the mark and masks a range of other factors that have led to dissatisfaction among many of the ≠Khomani San CPA members. Two aspects are important in the analysis of the dissatisfaction after the settlement of the claim: (1) the economic and power relations between the two "groupings" (traditional and western) and other dynamics, masked by the simplistic interpretation of the conflicts, and (2) the expectations that members have of the restitution process.

THE "TRADITIONAL" AND "WESTERN" SPLIT: CRACKS IN COMMUNITY COHESION AND THE DEFINITION OF AUTHENTICITY

The distinction between "western" and "traditional" San is not purely one of cultural loss or authenticity. There are wealth aspects to the division. The so-called western San are generally the wealthier group in a number of respects, including ownership of formal housing in the towns of Mier or Upington, access to alternative income from jobs and self employment, ownership of vehicles, and ownership of significant numbers of livestock; in addition they have some education and significant political ties. In contrast, the traditional group does not have, or has not had in the past, access to such an array of resources.

Besides wealth differences among members of the claimant community, the "traditional/western" split masks the common geographic origin and family membership of those labeled in these terms. Almost all those in the Kagga Kamma group are from the park and were at Kagga Kamma at the time the claim was lodged. The members of the so-called western group are from the settlements in Mier and have no association with the park, and many, but not all, are related to the Vaalboois, either as consanguine relatives or affines. The division corresponds with the first two sets of members who joined the claimant community—Dawid Kruiper and the traditionalists are basically the original set of claimants that initiated the land claim, whereas the westerners are by and large those extralegal San claimants who joined the claimant group afterward. The CPA executive is understood by many members to be representative of western interests. Common geographic origin came to the fore strongly with the membership drive that took place before the last CPA election. The executive committee that was elected in that particular election had campaigned heavily in the settlements where their relatives lived and where they could capture a greater number of votes.

Additionally, San society has been defined by its livelihood strategies more than anything else. They are understood to be foragers and not cultivators, hunters not herders. Many writers have, however, shown the difficulty of trying to apply this seemingly obvious defining criterion to San groups (Boonzaier et al., 1996; Schrire 1980). According to Robins (2001) the endorsing of primordialist notions of the San as hunter-gatherers has led to the devaluation and marginalization of alternate livelihood strategies. This can be seen in the distinction made between stock farmers in the group resident at Witdraai and those who have a different set of livelihood strategies, such as natural resources harvesting, tourism, and acting in films. For those who belong to the traditional group, there are markers that can override their livelihood strategies. The most important of these is their knowledge of the N/u language (as in the case of the Swartkops sisters). Kinship also acts as an overriding factor. For instance, the members of the Kruiper family are almost automatically counted as representing the interest of the traditional San.

But is the distinction between the two groups and the various factors it masks, such as livelihoods and wealth, solely responsible for the problems experienced by the ≠Khomani San? The answer is no. There is another underlying cause of the conflicts of which these are but symptoms. Restitution has created, through no fault of any one person or organization, various expectations among members.

"RETURN TO THE OLD WAYS":
GROUP EXPECTATIONS AND THE MEANING OF RESTITUTION

In line with other writers, I argue that the narratives surrounding restitution may be what are at fault. The ≠Khomani San claim is not the only claim where one finds a narrative of a "return to the old ways." In many land claims the narratives have been about the loss of more than the land. It has been about nostalgia for the almost mythical idealized and romanticized "community that was lost" (James 2000; Walker 2000). For the "traditional" southern Kalahari claimants the return to the land was to mean a return to a way of life and an authentic San identity of which they had been deprived.

There were other expectations as well, and herein lies one of the shortcomings. The claimants expected the restitution process to set in motion a range of other revival, reconciliation, reconstruction, and rediscovery processes. But the restitution program is only a land and rights acquisition program, and there was to be no land-based TRC (Truth and Reconciliation Commission) for the victims.

The community members in the ≠Khomani San CPA continue to deploy the narrative of dispossession linked to the land, and this has continued long after the land claim has been settled. Quite recently I was struck by the talk circulating about how people would be able to hunt again. Many seemed to entertain the belief that they would live as their ancestors did, by hunting and gathering. For others the "return" meant that the children would learn the language of the ≠Khomani San people. The survival skills of the San, so the belief went, would once again be passed from elders to the younger, skills such as tracking, use of *veld* (herbal) medicine, and other survival tactics. And above all, life would be better for them. The initial euphoria of having some of the land back and the plans for the revival of the old ways soon dissipated. A realization dawned on many of the claimants that there would be no return and that the restitution of land did not mean the magical re-creation of a former lifestyle.

As time passed the nostalgia shifted; the revival plans were now located in a different piece of land. Although it was part of the restitution package, the land in the park was not open for access, and people did not feel that it was in their possession. Possibly because they were not physically present on the land, many felt that their rights and land in the park would still come. Often one would hear people talk about "when we get the park, things will happen." So, once the realization of "no return to the old days" had come, people projected their nostalgia onto the park. Through what they voiced, it seemed they felt that their return would be delayed until they had taken possession of the "park." The farms became a place that was corrupted by the influence of the westerners, and many blamed the westerners for the supposedly ruinous state of the farmland. The inability of a portion of the Witdraai residents to engage in livelihoods (specifically hunting) that they foresaw as possible was also laid at the door of the western San and their activities on the farms. The NGO (SASI) personnel unfortunately reinforced the romanticism felt by many of the ≠Khomani San people. Many of the early proposals for economic activities on the land were based on a perceived notion of what San people are supposed to have done in the past. To residents on the farms it seemed that since their dreams had not come true on the farms, the parkland would nullify the losses when they took possession of it.

The individual stories of loss cover more than the loss of land and livelihoods. Many of the tales of personal loss focus on a specific episode of loss or items that were lost, as well as stories of culture loss and impoverishment. It follows that for many of the CPA members the restitution of land rights remains an inadequate conclusion to the story. Many demands are being made for other forms of restitution and redress. But it is important to note that the return of land was not meant to heal all the scars and return all goods lost; it was only the return of land. The land in the park has become the focus of calls for restitution beyond the return of the land. The demands and dissatisfaction have become greater since it has become clear to many that their rights in the park are limited, with no residence or unorganized hunting allowed in the parklands. So the ≠Khomani San people cannot stay there, and there is to be no revival of a hunter-gatherer existence.

It can be argued that the land claim itself—its conceptualization, implementation, and eventual conclusion, as well as the activities of the claimants afterward—was driven by the narratives of authenticity held by the actors involved. These narratives define what some perceive to be a "San norm": a prescriptive tool that sets out appropriate San behavior. The Kagga Kamma group has tried to exclude those who do not conform to this "San norm," but no one is able to enforce the "norm," and attempts at exclusion have not been successful.

The ≠Khomani San land claim and the postsettlement activities of claimants are driven by narratives of authenticity. The manner in which the land claim was conceptualized suggested that the claimants were and would be involved in hunting and gathering, activities generally accepted by laypersons and academics as definitive of the San. When Chennels undertook the agreement with Regopstaan and Dawid Kruiper that they would ensure the return of the southern Kalahari San to their ancestral lands, it was with the added provision that they would be able to hunt again. The research done by Steyn (1984) underwrites this perception. His work took the amount of land needed for hunting as a measure of the extent of the land that was lost. When the CRLR looked for land, they sought out specifically game farms and also stocked some of the land with game.

The definition of San-ness was linked to a specific resource—wild game—and a specific livelihood—hunting. The use of the game had to be of a specific type to be considered genuine; it must be for household subsistence because use for profit was seen as westernized and less authentically San. Certain livelihoods strategies of CPA members were viewed as antithetical, and the proponents of authentic San livelihoods attempted to exclude those who engaged in these other livelihoods; hence the call for the livestock herders to be moved to other farms.

The vying for resources that took place after the settlement of the claim was similarly driven by a contestation over authenticity. The different groups resident on the farms were assigned different degrees of authenticity by their fellow CPA members. The members of the Kagga Kamma group, the most vocal architects of authenticity in the contestation, thought that they would be able to exclude those they viewed as less authentic. They reasoned that the people who were not practicing an authentic San way of life—in other words those who did not conform to a supposed "San norm"—had less claim to resources, especially to the game animals. However, I argue that their pursuit of authenticity and appeal to "San norms" led to their eventual exclusion from and loss of control over the use of resources. Thus the claim to authenticity backfired. While they were trying to advance their cause by calling for a revival of an authentic way of life, others in the CPA were doing things the "western way."

NOTES

1. In 2000, the Kalahari Gemsbok National Park merged with the Gemsbok National Park on the Botswanian side to form the Kgalagadi Transfrontier Park.

REFERENCES

Boonzaier, E., C. Malherbe, P. Berens, and A. Smith. 1996. *The Cape Herders: History of the Khoikhoi of Southern Africa*. Cape Town: David Phillip; Athens: Ohio University Press.

Bosch, D. 2002a. "Finale Konsep : !Ae Kalahari Erfenispark-ooreenkomspark waardeur die grondeise van die ≠Khomani San en die Mier gemeenskap gefinaliseer word." 21 February 2002. Unpublished. Copy in possession of author.

———. 2002b. "Finale Konsep : !Ae Kalahari Erfenispark-ooreenkomspark waardeur die grondeise van die ≠Khomani San en die Mier gemeenskap gefinaliseer word." 15 March 2002. Unpublished. Copy in possession of author.

Chennels, R. 1998. "The San-Kalahari Restitution Case." Appendix E to an IUCN report on a Workshop on Land Claims on Conservation Land. Johannesburg: South Africa.

Cleary, S. 1989. *Renewing the Earth: Development for a Sustainable Future*. London: CAFOD.

Crawhall, N. 1998. "Reclaiming Rights, Resources, and Identity: The Power of an Ancient San Language." In *Voices, Values and Identities,* ed. Y. Dladla. Pretoria: South African National Parks.

———. n.d. "Too Good to Leave Behind: The N/u Language and the ≠Khomani People of Gordonia District." Unpublished manuscript. Cape Town: South African San Institute.

Department of Land Affairs (DLA). 2002. "Evaluation of the Mier and Khomani San Projects." Pretoria: Department of Land Affairs.

Duggan-Cronin, A. M. 1942. "The Bushman Ttribes of Ssouthern Africa." Kimberley, South Africa: Alexander Macgregor Museum.

James, D. 2000. "'After Years in the Wilderness': The Discourse of Land Claims in South Africa." *Journal of Peasant Studies* 27 (3): 142–62.

Kloppers, H. 1970. *Gee my 'n man*. Johannesburg: Afrikaanse Boekhandel.

Lee, R. B. 1979. *The !Kung San: Men, Women and Work in Foraging Society*. Cambridge: Cambridge University Press.

Magome, H. 2002. "Sharing South African National Parks: Community Land and Conservation in a Democratic South Africa." Paper presented at Pan African Programme for Land and Resource Rights Inaugural Workshop, Cairo.

Notes. 2001. Notes of constitutional crisis meeting, 19–20 November 2001, held at farm Uitkoms, Andriesvale, Northern Cape, in possession of author.

Poonan, U. 2002. "An Overview of Land Claims in Protected Areas in South Africa." Paper presented at the Ford Foundation EDAG conference, Cape Town, South Africa, 21–25 January 2002.

Rheinhalt-Jones, J. D., and C. M. Doke, eds. 1937. *Bushmen of the Southern Kalahari*. Johannesburg: University of Witwatersrand Press.

Robins, S. 2001. "NGO's, 'Bushmen' and Double Vision: The ≠Khomani San Land Claim and the Cultural Politics of 'Community' and 'Development' in the Kalahari." *Journal of Southern African Studies* 27 (4): 833–53.

Schrire, C. 1980. "An Inquiry into the Evolutionary Status and Apparent Identity of San Hunter and Gatherers." *Human Ecology* 8(1): 9–31.

Steyn, H. P. 1984. "Southern Kalahari Subsistence Ecology: A Reconstruction." *The South African Archeological Bulletin* 39 (140): 117–24.

Walker, C. 2000. "Relocating Restitution." *Transformation* 44: 1–16.

Wildschut, A., and L. Steyn. 1990. "'If One Can Live, All Must Live': A Report on the Past, Present and Alternative Land Use in the Mier Rural Reserve in the Northern Cape. Athlone, Cape Town: Surplus People Project.

Wynberg, R., and T. Kepe. 1999. "Land Reform and Conservation Areas in South Africa: Towards a Mutually Beneficial Approach." Pretoria: IUCN.

eleven

The Ambiguities of Using Betterment Restitution as a Vehicle for Development

An Eastern Cape Case Study

CHRIS DE WET AND ERIC MGUJULWA

"Betterment" planning, or "rehabilitation," has given rise to the most widespread form of resettlement in rural South Africa. It differs from other forms of forced resettlement in that it took place entirely within the former bantustans (homelands). Officially portrayed as an attempt to combat erosion, conserve the environment, and improve agricultural production, betterment planning was unable to achieve these goals because these areas were already overcrowded. What resulted was a rearranging of the land-use system by dividing each locality into arable, residential, and grazing areas, with everybody having to move to the new residential areas. Although betterment took place in all ten bantustans of South Africa, it did not affect them the same way. Daniel (1981) estimates that betterment planning occurred in about 80 percent of the former Ciskei homeland, whereas it was less in other areas. Westaway and Minkley (2005, 108) quote recent research estimating that "375 villages in the [former] Ciskei and 900 villages in [former] Transkei were dispossessed of land rights through the implementation of betterment."

Some of the undesirable aspects of betterment planning included reduction or loss of arable land; longer distances from resources such as wood,

The Ambiguities of Using Betterment Restitution for Development

water, and crop fields; and poor compensation (if at all) for loss of any resources or assets. Additionally, the move to the new residential areas had a significant impact—often negative—on patterns of social relationships, with patterns of conflict in postbetterment situations being related to the way in which betterment rearranged social groupings and resources, or reinforced existing divisions, within "communities" (de Wet 1995). It is these losses and indignities that are now being broached by the provision of land restitution.

In this chapter we sketch the case of the first betterment restitution award in South Africa. Building on extensive prerestitution fieldwork on the impact of betterment planning in Chatha (de Wet 1985, 1995), this chapter is based on postrestitution research in 2001, 2006, and 2007. The chapter briefly provides the historical context within which betterment occurred and considers the impacts of betterment as the necessary background to restitution. It then discusses the negotiations around the restitution award and monitors reactions and resistance to the terms of the restitution award since the award in 2000. In conclusion, it considers the strategy of using betterment restitution to catalyze development more widely at a provincial level.

BETTERMENT PLANNING IN CHATHA, KEISKAMMAHOEK

Chatha is a rural village in the Keiskammahoek magisterial district of the former Ciskei homeland in the Eastern Cape Province. Established in the 1850s by the British colonial authorities, it is one of six villages in which extensive research was conducted as part of the Keiskammahoek Rural Survey from 1948 to 1950. This research provides preapartheid and prebetterment baseline data on Chatha (see Houghton and Walton 1952; Mills and Wilson 1952; Wilson et al. 1952).

The betterment planning document for Chatha and two neighboring villages (Gxulu and Mnyameni) appeared in October 1958 (Department of Native Affairs 1958). Land judged unsuitable was to be taken out of cultivation (to avoid further land deterioration)—but without decreasing the number of people on the land. The total amount of land under cultivation in Chatha thus dropped from 495 morgen (424 hectares) to 193 morgen (165 ha) when betterment was implemented in the mid-1960s. Most new holdings were half a morgen (0.4 ha) in size, with twenty-four irrigation settlers each receiving arable allotments of 1.3 ha. Some twenty-six people lost all their arable land as a result of betterment. In 1958, 10 percent of homesteads were landless (Department of Native Affairs 1958). Due to an increase in population and new households being set up, now more than 50 percent of households in Chatha are landless.

Life in Chatha before betterment was to a considerable extent organized along territorial lines, with several residential hamlets forming a village section, which constituted the basis of social interaction in terms of agricultural cooperation, political mobilization (particularly around competition for the headmanship and for land allocation), and ceremonial celebration. In a sense, people were constituted by their relationship to the land (de Wet 1995). This relationship was undercut and transformed by the way betterment rearranged residential and land use patterns. The sense of outside imposition and loss of autonomy at the time of the actual move comes most strongly from the local people's accounts of betterment and is central to any understanding of loss of land arising out of forced relocation. The way in which people in Chatha adjusted to the relocation and the other changes in their setting brought about by betterment, as well as their reaction in the postbetterment era, including land restitution, was critically influenced by the way in which the new residential settlements were laid out during betterment.

Before betterment, village politics centered on the headmanship of the village, including competition for the position. The significant internal political unit in the village was the village section made up of several neighboring residential hamlets. Since the establishment of Chatha, the Dlamini (pseudonym) lineage has played a prominent and controversial role in the headmanship of Chatha, with the village being settled under Dlamini in the 1850s. The headmanship has been hotly contested in Chatha from at least the 1880s (de Wet 1987). It was lost by the Dlamini lineage as early as 1912, due to the intervention of the state, who favored three successive (non-Dlamini) candidates from the other side of the settlement, in spite of, or perhaps because of, ongoing attempts by Dlamini candidates and their supporters to reinstall a Dlamini headman. We suggest that in order to understand the conflict around land restitution in Chatha, one has to appreciate that, over time, the idea of Dlamini headmanship has for many people in the Nyanga-based grouping of village sections come to represent Chatha's resistance to the imposition of outside authority, the right to choose their own leader, and to run their own affairs. That is why there have been so many attempts to reinstate the Dlamini headmanship—and

The Ambiguities of Using Betterment Restitution for Development

why it reemerged in 1980 when the (non-Dlamini) incumbent retired and a suitable Dlamini candidate was elected unopposed.

With betterment, the numerous hamlets were rearranged into two large new residential areas, New Nyanga and New Skafu, with a small new irrigation scheme, which for most purposes aligned with Nyanga. New Nyanga was formed by people from the other village sections moving into the old Nyanga area. People from old Nyanga either stayed where they were or had to move slightly. The same applied to New Skafu. Because of the topography of the land, including the steep slope between the two new areas, it is not possible to build new infrastructure, such as a school or a clinic, between these areas. Whereas New Nyanga has twice as many sites as New Skafu, Skafu is more accessibly located on the road out of the settlement for other villages needing to use resources such as the clinic or the school.

The topography along with the layout lends itself to a binary factionalism—which builds directly on the previous political history of Chatha. The 1980s were characterized by bitter struggles between Nyanga and Skafu about the location of infrastructure and resources. Nyanga mobilized around its key resource of the headmanship (which after 1980 had again been restored to the Dlaminis), whereas Skafu mobilized around its resources of leadership in the areas of education, the church, and village enterprise.

From the mid-1990s, with the end of apartheid and the introduction of a new local government system, the nature of the divisions in the village has taken a new turn. Following the new political dispensation in 1994, the headmanship ceased to exist on an official level in the former Ciskei. The South African National Civic Organization (SANCO) replaced the headmanship as the agent of local government at the village level, allocating residential sites and (in coordination with the recently constituted communal property association [CPA]) dealing with officialdom and development agencies at a wider level. The nature of the division in the village has become charged along party political lines. Supporters of SANCO—their protestations notwithstanding—for the most part are, and are seen as, supporters of the ruling party, the African National Congress (ANC); those who do not regard the SANCO system as representative and legitimate, but as an imposition by an ANC interest group, tend to support the United Democratic Movement (UDM), mobilizing around the former headman.

Development projects never come into an empty context. The cumulative history we have briefly outlined was waiting to influence restitution as it unfolded in Chatha, and we suggest that the tensions around restitution have served to resuscitate some of those historical and territorially based alignments.

RESTITUTION IN CHATHA

Betterment planning had originally been excluded from the provisions of the Restitution Act of 1994. However, various land nongovernmental organizations (NGOs) began to campaign for a restitution that accommodates betterment planning cases. Thus in early 1998 the Border Rural Committee (BRC) undertook to challenge the exclusion of betterment dispossession from the restitution program. The Keiskammahoek area of the former Ciskei became the test case for this campaign (Westaway and Minkley 2005).

Chatha was used as a pilot claim in this regard, partly because it was the best documented case of betterment on record (see de Wet 1985, 1995). One of the authors (de Wet) was also asked to submit an affidavit to the Land Claims Court (LCC) on the situation in Chatha and the damaging consequences of forced resettlement, as well as a list of all the heads of household, the average number of huts per homestead, and the distance between homesteads before betterment resettlement in the mid-1960s. This was to help the surveyor assess the loss incurred as a result of the move. The BRC worked closely with the community of Chatha and coordinated the claim, which was submitted to the LCC in 1999.

In 2000, the government acknowledged that some betterment claims might satisfy the criteria set out in the Restitution Act (Westaway and Minkley 2005). The Chatha claim was the first betterment claim to be settled in terms of land restitution. The agreement was signed in October 2000. The Department of Land Affairs (DLA) and the Chatha community agreed to R31,697.50 monetary compensation per claimant family, calculated from loss of arable land, dwellings, and residential land (Chatha Settlement Agreement 2000). It was also agreed that each duly verified claimant family should receive only half of the compensation amount (i.e., R15,848.75) and that the remaining half should be used for development projects for the whole community. The then minister of land affairs, Thoko Didiza, presided over the paying out of the checks to the 334 claimants in Chatha amid great celebration in December 2000 (see Lahiff 2002). People used their money for building or improving houses, educating their children, buying appliances, and on rituals for their ancestors. For a while everybody seemed happy.

The Ambiguities of Using Betterment Restitution for Development

THE AMBIVALENCE AND MOBILIZATION AGAINST THE TERMS OF RESTITUTION, 2001

On 14 May 2000, that is, before the 50/50 dispensation had been finalized (i.e., half of each claimant's award being paid out in cash and half going into a community development fund), a key meeting was held at Chatha.

> There was discussion on whether it is constitutional for the DLA to take [a] unilateral decision by enforcing 50% of the financial compensation to be used for the development of Chatha . . . the community was very concerned [by] the lack of consultation on such [an] important matter . . . at the ultimate end [the] issue was accepted. The beneficiary list was then put on the table and Mr [X.Y] recommended that the list be closed. The meeting unanimously agreed on closure of the list registration. (Chatha General Meeting, Minutes, 14 May 2000)

However, a significant portion of the community, especially the youth, clearly had problems with the DLA ruling. By late 2001, the concerns raised at the 2000 meeting had become articulated. A group had formed, mobilizing under the former (Dlamini) headman around two issues: first, that not everybody who was entitled to claim for the restitution payment had in fact been included and, second, that the process in terms of which the decision to divide the restitution award into two parts had been arrived at was suspect, and the people of Chatha did not want the development projects that had been imposed on them but wanted their restitution payments in full. Support for this position was expressed at meetings held at the former headman's place during 2001, marches he led against the members of the Restitution Committee, and in a report/petition to the minister of land affairs about the way the land restitution process had been handled in Chatha. Concern also surfaced strongly in 140 interviews that one of the authors conducted across Chatha in late 2001.[1]

Part of the logic for the campaign to increase claimants was to paint the Restitution Committee as ANC and to suggest that it was favoring ANC members in the claims process. The former headman has been the leader of the anti-ANC grouping in Chatha. However, there is not any noticeable difference in the way pro-ANC/SANCO and pro-UDM informants recalled events in 2001. The majority of Chatha seemed to support the ANC and be behind SANCO, with the majority of those interviewed holding the view that it was made clear that the award was to be divided 50/50. However, a number of respondents—and again, not only from Nyanga (the historical seat of the headmanship)—stressed what they perceived as coercion, particularly by the Restitution Committee, to get them to agree to the 50/50 deal, claiming they were not told the full story right from the start.

Because the committee was the immediate face of the restitution process in Chatha and consisted of local people, it became the scapegoat for the unpopular aspects of restitution. That Chatha actually had no choice in the 50/50 matter is acknowledged across all constituencies in the restitution controversy. The committee was caught in between the government and the people—not unlike the headman with the implementation of betterment in the 1960s. The committee was seen in some quarters as unconsultative and not responsive to the wishes and needs of the people, who, not surprisingly, were blurring the line between the DLA and their own elected committee, as well as between what restitution was about and how they perceived it as being implemented. Again, the parallels with betterment are too obvious to overlook. A cynical interpretation of the 50/50 dispensation held that, as one person commented: "We were told that government does not have the money for projects, so it is going to use our money."

Although some were positive about what restitution projects—which had not yet been initiated—might bring to Chatha, others were skeptical, feeling that taxes, rather than their restitution awards, should be paying for development projects and doubting whether the benefits of these projects would be equitably distributed within the settlement. In late 2001, many people were thus morally confused and even conflicted as to what to make of the development aspect of restitution.

POLARIZATION AND CONFLICT, 2002 TO 2006

In 2006, the authors undertook detailed fieldwork in Chatha and found that the restitution issue was very much alive. Legal proceedings relating to developments in the village around restitution were in process and due to come to a head. Some people felt that, because the research of one of the authors (de Wet) had contributed to the restitution claim's being successful, he might have some influence in helping resolve what they saw as the burning issues at stake. However, he took care not to be seen to choose sides in the restitution-related disputes.

In 2006 it was the common belief that the terms of the 50/50 deal had been imposed on Chatha, with some people well placed to know stating that had

The Ambiguities of Using Betterment Restitution for Development

Chatha not accepted these terms, the government would have taken its money and gone elsewhere. For some people, the fact that the 2000 meeting agreed to the proposal seemed to give it legitimacy and to bind the community to go along with it. For others, that they were presented with a decision over which they effectively had no say was in itself problematic, if not illegitimate.

During interviews a number of very positive views were expressed about the 50/50 dispensation and on attitudes toward the projects. These comments were predominantly from people in CPA-related committees and projects:

> Development is the right way to go because it helps us and all the young people; I like this development way of doing things—if we were given the money fully, there would be no money for development.

> You cannot see the forestry project now—but it is a light to the future.

Other people supporting the project approach argued that the total award should in fact have been given to development, because some people had spent their money unwisely and had nothing to show for it.

In contrast, others, who wanted the restitution awards to be paid out in full, emphasized the fact that the 50/50 decision was imposed, linking this clearly to the way they perceived their own welfare. They had this to say:

> We say we want all our money because we built our houses when we moved [i.e., with betterment]—that is the money we used—you cannot now say that it is to be used for ploughing the land or planting the forest plantation.

> It was not a right agreement—we were forced to reach agreement. . . . I have no child—nobody from my house can benefit from projects.

The moral ambiguities in which the 50/50 dispensation seemed to involve people are aptly evoked by two quotes, the first from a person who was serving as a political official involved in the restitution process of Chatha at the time (and sympathetic to the ANC and the process) and the second from an "antidevelopment," pro-UDM supporter:

> Yes, it's is a fact that it is government's responsibility to pay for development—but if you are instructed by government, you cannot refuse. . . . We did not know where this money was coming from . . . so,

> we had no option: We were going to get something and government was going to take something.
>
> If you have no water, and are thirsty, and somebody gives you dirty water and tells you that if you don't take that water, you won't get even that dirty water. Then, the only solution is to drink that dirty water instead of dying of thirst. So we had no option but to accept the terms.

Almost everybody we spoke to was at the very least uncomfortable with the fact that, in their perception, the 50/50 dispensation had been imposed upon the community. Why then did people adopt such very different responses?

As mentioned earlier, the former headman led a group seeking to extend the number of restitution claimants. This may relate to the fact that the committee had modified the criteria for qualifying as a claimant during the process to include men married at the time of the move, thereby opening up room for contestation. In the process of pushing the claims process, the headman led various marches, demanding the full payment of restitution awards. This resulted in a restraining order being placed on him and several of his followers (Magistrate, Keiskammahoek, 17 July 2002).

Since then the group in favor of full payment has taken the line that any development initiative in Chatha paid for out of restitution funds is problematic because it diminishes the amount of money that will be left over to be paid out to the people in cash if and when they win the right to have the restitution award paid out in full. They have initiated court proceedings to this effect, with the matter not yet heard in court as of 2008. Their vision of restitution and the 50/50 approach that includes development are thus mutually exclusive—and they have thus sought to hinder development on a number of occasions.

A major event, with legal consequences and significant implications for some twenty-two individuals and their families in the village occurred in late October and early November 2003. According to the legal affidavit subsequently submitted against the former headman and his supporters, a group setting off to work on a restitution forestry project was prevented by a group of other Chatha residents from moving along the road up to the forest. In the affidavit it is claimed that the respondents (the former headman and twenty-two others) "intimidated and threatened the work group." The former headman allegedly wanted "his own people represented on the project." This blocking of the workers happened on two successive days, with the police being called in to sort matters out. After various meetings and continued blockades, several of the former headman's group were arrested. Violence also broke out between the factions, leading to some people ending up in the hospital.

At a subsequent meeting on 21 November 2003, the group demanded full payment of their restitution awards, saying that they were not interested in projects. When they were told that they had signed acceptance of the 50/50 dispensation and if they wanted to change that, they would have to use the appropriate legal channels, they walked out of the meeting (Affidavit 25 November 2003). As a result of these events, legal papers were served on the former headman and twenty-two others (Affidavit 25 November 2003). These legal proceedings came to a crisis in 2006 when the respondents found themselves unable to pay the court costs and legal charges, and the sheriff of the court arrived in Chatha to repossess some of their goods. This led to various meetings and to a regional UDM politician temporarily standing good for the costs.

Why has the 50/50 dispensation issue raised such passions in Chatha? At least part of what seems to be going on is that the former headman and the group that he represents have been cultivating a sense of identity that is predicated in significant measure on a nostalgic reconstruction of their prebetterment identity—which is intimately bound up with the history of the headmanship and the tradition of resistance to authority in his family. This has given rise to a series of tensions within the settlement, including the following:

> 1. The 50/50 dispensation emphasizes the residents' association (SANCO) instead of the now officially defunct headmanship system of village administration. CPA and SANCO meetings now take place in the Daliwonga Mbangamthi Hall, a restitution project, which is seen as SANCO-controlled, as opposed to the headman's residence. A number of the former headman's group refuse to collect their pensions or do other business at the hall, "until we know whose money built that hall."
>
> 2. The emphasis on development and on centralized control and allocation of land through the CPA challenges ideas of village section identity, which still has some significance in the postbetterment situation, particularly of Nyanga as the hereditary seat of the headmanship in

Chatha. The only way to hold on to that is to push for the individualized, total grant, which is also a way of resisting authority imposed from above. This is directly related to the history of the Dlamini family struggle around the headmanship from the 1890s onward. Here again the association between resisting authority and resisting restitution becomes apparent.

3. The 50/50 dispensation also changes the role of both gender and generation in village affairs, as the younger generation and women are significantly represented in a number of the CPA committees. The *inkundla* (literally the headman's court, although in Chatha, it is now technically the former headman's court) tends to be frequented mainly by older people and is run by men.

4. Besides these very local territorial and historical-political considerations—which are always central to local disputes—there are also important moral issues behind the 50/50 dispensation, which were raised in the May 2000 meeting and again in the 2001 interviews, as well as by people representing the different constituencies to whom we spoke in 2006. The full payment lobby taps powerfully into these moral issues.

Restitution, as a new source of resources in the settlement, has inevitably become politicized. What seems to have happened is an alignment of three developing sets of tensions, which serve to reinforce each other: SANCO versus inkundla, with their respective gender and generational dynamics; ANC versus UDM; and the pro–50/50 dispensation versus pro–full payment, and thus pro- and antidevelopment views of restitution.

Some people are rationalizing what has been happening in Chatha along party political lines. The full payment lobby charges that restitution problems are squarely the fault of the ANC. The UDM holds meetings in private homes because the Daliwonga Hall is seen as ANC territory. More tellingly, some of the full payment/UDM camp saw restitution as an ANC exercise and did not initially submit their claims. In 2006 leaders in both camps held out for meetings in their territorial bases and on their terms, with both claiming exclusive legitimacy. Some people saw no simple way forward. One informant, who sits astride the political divide and supports the 50/50 dispensation, put it like this: "The way forward is to pull together to make our projects work. It is very difficult to find another way—because all of these things involve politics. After a while, it became about organizations—now some talk about SANCO, and some talk about UDM. If we could sit down and talk; if we could do away with organizations." Some UDM meetings that have been mobilized around the restitution issue have evidently been well attended. "If it were not for this money issue, there would not have been so many people at the meeting." In the words of a member of the (former) headman's court: "This is why we decided to go back to the headmanship and to the chief. We had to go back to square one because a lot of councillors are misusing our money. So, we could not turn to them, so we decided to go back to the old system."

Our understanding is that this is not a "nativistic" resurgence of the headmanship, but people temporarily turning to wherever they think might get their problems resolved. Although many people are supportive of the idea of development—particularly those who got the few restitution jobs available—in 2006 "this money issue" seemed to be compromising some of the legitimacy of SANCO. However, by nailing his and his supporters' colors to the UDM mast, the former headman and leader of the full-payment, antidevelopment group made a strategic error, as it seems to have alienated a pro-ANC grouping of people who might otherwise have supported the cause. The ultimate credibility of their cause will of course finally hinge on what happens (if and) when their challenge to the 50/50 dispensation has its day in court.

In 2006 there was considerable tension within Chatha, although apparently nothing like the violence of a few years earlier. As one informant poignantly put matters: "We were supposed to be happy but instead we are fighting—never mind that some of us have misused the money—because it was the first time to have such money."

ADDING INSULT TO INJURY:
HIGHER RESTITUTION AWARDS TO OTHER VILLAGES

Against the background of the successful claim of Chatha, the BRC managed to facilitate successful land restitution claims for nine other villages that had also undergone betterment in the Keiskammahoek district. However, these villages received substantially higher awards, approximately R54,000 per household, as against the R31,697 of Chatha. The difference seems to lie in the way in which the losses and, particularly, the value of huts lost during the move at the time of betterment were evaluated in the case of the other villages.

Thereupon Chatha, with the assistance of the BRC, called in a second evaluator, who examined a set of old ruins to get an idea of the size of pre-betterment huts and used 1950 aerial maps. According to informants, the second evaluator came up with a figure much closer to that of the other villages. Chatha has since put in a request that their restitution award be retrospectively increased to be on a par with that of the other villages and as of 2008 was still waiting to hear the outcome.

Although many people are anxious to do this in the proper manner, by appealing to the good will of the officials concerned and not resorting to litigation, it is an issue on which people across the board feel strongly. That people are angry and upset about being awarded less than people in other villages is apparent in the fact that it is an ongoing topic of conversation. People ask how differentiated awards could have arisen when, as one well-placed informant claims, they had been told in 2000 that there would be a uniform award across villages. It is seen as a matter of Chatha's having been done an injustice. It has the potential to sour Chatha's relationship with the authorities and to create negative attitudes toward the restitution initiative generally. Some people are conflating the emotionally charged issues around the 50/50 dispensation and the campaign for full payment with that of the award vis-à-vis other villages. The former headman's group has taken this issue on board as part of its platform.

DELIVERING DEVELOPMENT AND REALIGNING
THE POLITICS OF RESTITUTION, MID-2007

When we enquired into attitudes to restitution in 2001, no projects had started. By 2006 the community hall and classrooms had already been built out of restitution money, and there had been intermittent work on the roads in Chatha. The revival of the irrigation scheme was under way, and the forestry project was already two years old. The CPA has followed the policy of providing short-term employment contracts of several months, so as to spread the income more widely. Since 2000, close to three hundred short-term jobs have been made available in Chatha, paying out over R1.2 million in wages (*Chatha Communal Property Association Newsletter*, March 2008). However, by 2006, many of the projects providing these jobs had come to an end. People on the irrigation scheme were not being paid,

The Ambiguities of Using Betterment Restitution for Development

receiving income only from sales of produce, and the only jobs available were the twenty or so in the forest. It was in this context that a number of people were still doubtful whether development was going to take off or not, and were still prepared to consider supporting the former headman's antidevelopment, pro–full payment stance.

However, by mid-2007 the development and job scenario had changed dramatically. Upgrading of roads had started again; work on the internal roads was being paid for out of restitution funds; and work on the main access roads into Nyanga and Skafu (which got all-weather surfaces) was carried out by the Department of Works. This work employed fourteen people, plus a subcontractor in Chatha with a few of his workers. The forestry project was on schedule to begin sales in the next few years, although no firm marketing agreement had yet been finalized. Some forty hectares had been cleared and pine trees planted; twenty-one people were employed. The irrigation scheme had fundamentally restructured itself, with its workforce now "permanently" employed (on one-year contracts): fifteen were paid with restitution money, and the senior manager was paid by the BRC. Restitution thus provided some sixty jobs in Chatha, paying between R40 and R60 per day. A "toposcope" had also been constructed, with the names and details of all the households that were moved through betterment. This was to be part of a heritage trail in Chatha, to commemorate the forced move and to attract more tourists. The toposcope was funded by money raised externally by the BRC, but its construction, which lasted several months, employed some fifteen local people.

By mid-2008 the picture was more mixed. A key development from late 2007 had been the construction of several tourist chalets overlooking the Nyanga area. The construction contractor was from outside Chatha, but the project provided employment for some twenty-five people from Chatha. It was not without problems, as (according to a CPA member) the workers were not sufficiently skilled or hardworking, and as of mid-2008, the project was behind schedule. By that time the wattle-planting project in the forest and the roads project were no longer operational. Apart from the chalet work, which was completed early in 2009, with several tourism jobs resulting, this left the forty or so jobs on the irrigation scheme and the pine forestry project, which by then appeared to be effectively no longer rotational but to provide, in the words of a CPA official, "permanent" jobs.

In addition to these jobs, people in Chatha have also benefited from cheap vegetables from the irrigation scheme. When crops are not suitable for sale, they are made available to the community free of charge. An informant wryly remarked that even leading members of the antidevelopment faction have been seen getting vegetables from the irrigation scheme.

As of early 2009 development's limited but visible takeoff seemed to have swung feelings the way of the prodevelopment lobby. This may swing the other way if jobs do not increase markedly and are not seen to circulate. The antidevelopment, pro–full payment group had by no means given up. They were adopting a new strategy, trying to bypass the CPA and SANCO. An inkundla meeting in July 2007, for example, was attended by various senior ANC politicians. Those present complained that the CPA was not employing people associated with the inkundla (which, according to employment records at the hall, is not the case) or informing inkundla people about jobs at the hall. People from the antirestitution group have also been complaining that they are unable to go back to their old sites to perform rituals because the forest project now covers the area: the appeal to traditional ideas of territory is thus being raised in opposition to the project-associated ideas of territory. The former headman's grouping, even with declining attendance at inkundla meetings, was evidently still pressing on with attempts to bring the 50/50 division down in court. The impact of his death, in late 2009, remains to be seen.

Restitution-based development is starting to take off in Chatha, but questions need to be asked about its sustainability. Much of the success is directly the result of the sustained (although potentially narrowly focused) training, administrative and financial input of the BRC—something that is openly acknowledged by the CPA—with an element of dependence in the way some of the key players speak of the NGO. The BRC has initiated and steered the restitution process, driven the developmental planning process, raised funding from overseas, and has been intimately involved in the entire process, including legal proceedings against the former headman and his supporters. It has effectively funded the entire resuscitation of the irrigation scheme, including hiring a consulting manager, leasing a tractor, and purchasing other equipment. As of 2008 it was paying the new manager's salary.

The BRC has made it clear (as it should) that it will be withdrawing from Chatha in time. This raises significant succession issues. The current CPA leadership is very capable indeed, and is preparing for the transition in tandem with the BRC, but it expresses concern about difficulties in recruiting satisfactory successors, as the most capable people are employed in town and in government. It will also have to learn to negotiate the fundraising world, because the R5.5 million set aside for development can employ sixty people at R60 per day for only five to six years, without taking increases in wages or any production or maintenance costs into account. Without funds, restitution will become just another level in the archaeology of failed development projects and accumulated resentment in Chatha.

Chatha is a special case but one that has potentially wider implications. The BRC has stated (Westaway 2007) that Chatha has to be seen to work so as to make a case for people-driven development, to leverage funds and development assistance from the government. The BRC is in the process of trying to facilitate the Vula Masango Singene [Open the gates and let us go in] campaign, whereby all settlements in the former Ciskei and Transkei that underwent betterment should receive restitution awards (Westaway and Minkley 2006). This could potentially lead to the release of R12 billion for rural development. Although Vula Masango Singene's idea of using the right to development and community capacity to leverage development from the government has potential, it needs to proceed with caution and be clear about what is replicable and what is not. Chatha is a special case, given the combination of a dynamic NGO with a wider agenda, a highly capable and shrewd CPA leadership, *and* a political opposition with significant support and some compelling arguments, which unintentionally pushed the CPA to drive development in order to neutralize that opposition. It also has been the focus of a detailed research process over time, which has promoted a sense of history and empirical knowledge of itself as a community.

It would, furthermore, be surprising if the government did not want to exercise tight control over an amount as large as R12 billion or if the tensions that have emerged around restitution in Chatha did not also surface in other communal tenure villages with similar territorial histories and experiences of betterment. Vula Masango Singene may well open the gates to more than just resources. We argue that a significant part of the lesson that the Chatha case provides is that it *is* in many ways a special case and that development *is* a slow process that *has* to be built up in situation-specific circumstances. Resources by themselves do not deliver development, let alone the local capacity necessary to do so. We are speaking as observers of the "community" over time, rather than as activists who get things done. Development delivers intended as well as unintended outcomes. Our intuition is that for it to be institutionally, politically, socially, and economically sustainable, we should rather be thinking of development on a *vula isango* by *isango* [open gate by gate] basis—lest development repeats, unintentionally, the very mistakes of betterment that it is trying to make good.

NOTE

1. In order to respect informants' confidentiality in a volatile political context, interviews are not individually referenced in this article.

REFERENCES

Affidavit. 25 November 2003. Contained in legal papers served on the former headman of Chatha and twenty-two others.
Chatha Communal Property Association Newsletter 2, no. 1 (March 2008).
Chatha General Meeting. Minutes of meeting of 14 May 2000.
Chatha Settlement Agreement. October 2000. Commission on Restitution of Land Rights.
Daniel, J. B. 1981. "Agricultural Trends in the Ciskei." *South African Geographical Journal* 63 (1): 3–23.
Department of Native Affairs. 1958. Report on the Rehabilitation and Settlement of Gxulu, Mnyameni and Cata Locations, Keiskammahoek District. October 1958.
de Wet, C. J. 1985. "An Analysis of the Social and Economic Consequences of Residential Relocation Arising out of the Implementation of an Agricultural Development Scheme in a Rural Ciskei Village." Unpublished PhD diss., Rhodes University, Grahamstown.
———. 1987. "The Dynamics of Political Factionalism in a Rural Ciskei Village from 1880 to 1950." *African Studies,* 46 (1): 57–78.
———. 1995. *Moving Together, Drifting Apart—Betterment Planning and Villagisation in a South African Homeland.* Johannesburg: Witwatersrand University Press.
Houghton, D. H. C., and E. Walton. 1952. *The Economy of a Native Reserve.* Pietermaritzburg: Shuter and Shooter.
Lahiff, E., ed. 2002. *Land Reform and Sustainable Development in the Eastern Cape Province.* Bellville: Programme for Land and Agricultural Studies, University of the Western Cape (Research Report No 14).
Magistrate, Keiskammahoek, 17 July 2002. Letter contained in legal papers served on the former headman of Chatha and twenty-two others on 25 November 2003.
Mills, M. E., and M. Wilson. 1952. *Land Tenure.* Pietermaritzburg: Shuter and Shooter.
Westaway, A. 2007. Personal communication, e-mail.
Westaway, A., and G. Minkley. 2005. "The Application of Rural Restitution to Betterment Cases in the Eastern Cape." *Social Dynamics* 31 (1): 104–28.
———. 2006. "Right versus Might: Betterment-Related Restitution and the 'Constitutive Outside' of South Africa's New Capitalist Modernity." Unpublished paper. Conference on Land, Memory, Reconstruction and Justice: Perspectives on Land Restitution in South Africa. Houw Hoek, September 2006.
Wilson, M., S. Kaplan, T. Maki, and E. Walton. 1952. *Social Structure.* Pietermaritzburg: Shuter and Shooter.

twelve

Land Restitution and Community Politics

The Case of Roosboom in KwaZulu-Natal

CHIZUKO SATO

In this chapter I explore the dynamics of land struggles and associated community politics in the Roosboom land claim in the province of KwaZulu-Natal. The former Roosboom residents living in Ezakheni (a township outside Ladysmith, to which they were relocated during apartheid forced removals) constituted one of the first communities in the province to publicly express its desire to return to its land in the early 1990s, and it became a leading community in the emerging nationwide land movement in South Africa (National Land Committee 1993). In spite of strong local leadership and constant support by local nongovernmental organizations (NGOs), however, land reform in Roosboom did not bring about the result that both local leaders and supporting organizations had expected. Broadly, this chapter explores the driving forces behind the Roosboom land restitution movement and the challenges it faced.

Roosboom was an African-owned farm in northwestern KwaZulu-Natal. Its origin dates back to the early twentieth century when a group of Africans formed a syndicate and purchased land as a way of investment. Many, if not all, who subsequently bought pieces of land on the Roosboom farm were Christians known as *amakholwa* (believers). When the apartheid government came into power in 1948, farms owned by Africans were identified as "black spots" in the white countryside and became the targets of forced removals. Between 1975 and 1976, more than seven thousand people from Roosboom were relocated to the Ezakheni Township that had been established to absorb those who were removed from black spots in northwestern Natal. At the time of the removals, Roosboom landowners had accommodated tenants to a point where the tenants outnumbered landowners. Social divisions between landowners and tenants are believed to have weakened the landowners' ability to put up resistance against removals (Mngadi 1981; Sato 2006; Mmutlana 1993).

By the 1950s Roosboom had become a hub of African opposition politics in the area. It produced several African leaders associated with the nonracial Liberal Party, as well as several associated with the African National Congress (ANC) (Sato 2007; Vigne 1997). The most notable figure was Elliot Mngadi who organized African landowners in northern Natal to resist removals. He stayed in politics after their removal from Roosboom and became the first mayor of the Ezakheni Township in 1979, under the administration of the KwaZulu government. However, it cannot automatically be assumed that the spirit of resistance was taken over by later generations after the removals from Roosboom. Nor is it clear to what extent these historical experiences served as a unifying factor among former Roosboom residents in Ezakheni settlement. A few families reoccupied Roosboom in the early 1980s, but they were immediately relocated by the government. It was only a decade later that the demand for land restitution was publicly articulated.

The chapter focuses on land struggles by the former Roosboom residents in the early 1990s and the subsequent process of land restitution in the area. It discusses interactions between the local leadership of Roosboom, land NGOs, and the state in putting forward Roosboom's land restitution demands to the central government. In doing so, the chapter aims to shed light on the community dynamics that unfolded during the land restitution process.[1]

THE ROOSBOOM LAND RESTITUTION MOVEMENT

The main leaders in the land restitution movement of Roosboom were local schoolteachers. They had been teenagers at the time of removal, but by the early 1990s they were in their thirties. Soon after President de Klerk announced his intention to abolish apartheid in 1990, Roosboom activists in Ezakheni called a meeting to discuss the idea of returning to their land. When this first meeting did not attract significant numbers of people, the leaders decided to organize a communal cleaning of the graveyard in Roosboom, hoping that this act would rekindle people's emotional attachment to their land. A group of teachers kept meeting and discussing various ways to invoke people's sentiments about Roosboom. Their ideas always related to the symbolic objects with historical connotations such as fencing the graveyard and renovating the ruined chapel and school at Roosboom (MS interview, 9 July 2002).

Gradually the number of people who came to these meetings increased. Within six months an official representative body known as the Roosboom Interim Committee was formed. Nine people who served on this committee were elected at a meeting attended by about three hundred people (AFRA 1990a). This body was later renamed the Roosboom Board of Overseers (RBO), and it was to lead the Roosboom land movement and subsequent restitution process for more than a decade. The RBO worked closely with the Association for Rural Advancement (AFRA), a Pietermaritzburg-based land NGO. AFRA had been formed in 1979 by a small group of white activists to assist rural communities threatened with forced removals during apartheid. Though several founding members of AFRA worked closely with Mngadi in the 1950s in the Liberal Party, AFRA's network with former residents of Roosboom in Ezakheni hardly existed after Mngadi passed away (PB interview, 2002). In this sense the close working relationship established between RBO and the AFRA in the early 1990s was completely new. Another organization that provided some logistical and strategic assistance to the RBO was the Ladysmith-based Northern Natal Council of Churches (MM interview, 2002).

From the beginning, the RBO considered the reoccupation of Roosboom the most effective strategy but decided to do so quietly instead of doing it en masse. They wanted to be careful not to raise expectations among non-landowners who had been in the majority before the removals. Therefore they insisted to AFRA that meetings concerning the land claim be held exclusively for former landowners (AFRA 1990b, 1990c, 1990d).

Roosboom was not the only community that expressed interest in going back to its land. AFRA found at least two other former black spot communities in Natal, namely Cremin and Charlestown, wanting to do the same. AFRA tried to organize a joint representation among these rural communities. Through AFRA, they repeatedly sent to the government their resolution calling for an official reprieve of removal and for land restitution. Their appeal was partially successful. By mid-1990, the government gave an official reprieve to four Natal rural communities under threat of removal.[2] Nonetheless, it was not prepared to accept the demands for restitution. In October that year, Gerrit Viljoen, the then minister of constitutional development, made it clear that "the government would not consider restoring land to communities which were forcibly removed as this would lead to a worldwide revolution starting in the United States and Australia" (AFRA 1990e).

In the same month that Viljoen made the above statement, the first group of former landowners quietly reoccupied Roosboom. An elderly woman and her three grandchildren were immediately arrested on the charge of trespassing, but were released without bail soon afterward. The magistrate withdrew the case a few days later without any explanation. Although the RBO and AFRA considered this initial reoccupation a "failure," the elderly woman did not share this view. On the contrary, she interpreted her nonprosecution as a sign that they were allowed to return to Roosboom. However, her confidence placed her in a minority among former landowners. At this stage, the RBO was having difficulty mobilizing former landowners to return to Roosboom. Many of them were still worried about the risk of arrest. Indeed, returned families were subjected to continual harassment and intimidation by local farmers, police, and even army personnel from a local army base. Logistical problems such as organizing transport were the other factors preventing some from joining the reoccupation (AFRA 1990f, 1990g).

GOVERNMENT RESPONSE TO THE ROOSBOOM PEOPLE'S DEMANDS

The National Party government's response to the demands of Roosboom claimants and to the reoccupying families in 1991 and for most of 1992 lacked consistency and often caused confusion. At the local level, the Department of Public Works and Land Affairs (DPWLA), the legal owner of Roosboom at the time, agreed to meet with the RBO and negotiate the rights of reoccupation.[3] But the central government's new land policy ruled out the possibility of restoring land to the former landowners. *The White Paper on Land Reform* released by the government in March 1991 argued that a land restoration program for the victims of forced removals "would not be feasible" and "the present position should be accepted" for the sake of "peace and progress" (Republic of South Africa 1991, 6). Nevertheless the DPWLA subsequently implied to the RBO that Roosboom would be dealt with as an exceptional case by the president.[4] When the instructions from the government were finally brought to the RBO, the latter found them contradictory. Although the government had decided to reinstitute the court cases against reoccupiers for trespassing and squatting, it also announced that it was forming a cabinet committee to consider the Roosboom representations (AFRA 1991a).

Confronted with the state's attitude toward their demands, the RBO began to encourage as many landowners as possible to join the reoccupation, to make it difficult for the DPWLA to evict those who had returned to Roosboom. In reality, however, the RBO was losing its grip on the reoccupation process. At a meeting with the DPWLA in mid-1991, the RBO admitted that it could no longer regulate the influx of people onto Roosboom.[5] The strategy of reoccupation was a double-edged sword for former landowners for two reasons. First, the reoccupying people brought with them large numbers of cattle, resulting in competition for grazing land. Second, some landowners brought in new tenants as caretakers for their lands. This was a breach of the earlier agreement that they could take only Roosboom original tenants as their caretakers (AFRA 1991b).

The stalemate in negotiations between the DPWLA and the RBO continued for several months. It was finally resolved in late 1991 when the government set up a new statutory body called the Advisory Commission on Land Allocation (ACLA). The ACLA was to make recommendations for land, which by law belonged to the state for the purpose of settling black people.[6] Black spot communities in Natal were not entirely happy with ACLA's composition and its advisory mandate, but in the end they decided to cooperate as it was better than nothing (AFRA 1992a). *The Roosboom Land Claims Submission to the ACLA* (AFRA 1992b), prepared by AFRA at the request of the RBO, explained the historical background of the Roosboom people's demands for land restitution. It also provided information on possible claimants by including lists of expropriated landowners and landowners who had sold their land to the state fearing expropriation, and the prices and compensation paid to each landowner at the time of removal. According to AFRA, the hardest task in compiling this document was making up the list of people who wanted to return to the land. AFRA managed to collect 158 such names. However, both the RBO and AFRA stressed that this list should not be taken as complete.[7]

In mid-1992, the ACLA organized a public hearing for the Roosboom submission at the Ladysmith Town Hall. More than three hundred people turned up. The RBO specifically asked two elderly women to give evidence there. One was seventy-five years old and had been one of the very first people who joined the reoccupation of Roosboom. She recollected the closure and subsequent demolition of the school where she had been teaching before the removal and emphasized how painful the experience was to her. She continued, "Old as we are, we are eager for our children to return to Roosboom. That is what I pray for every day—that the children will be able to return to the land of our forefathers" ("'Black Spot' Residents Seek Land," *Natal Mercury,* 20 August 1992). Another old woman testified to the brutal manner in which they were removed and added her wish "to die and be buried at Roosboom" ("Give Roosboom Back to Us," *Daily News,* 21 August 1992).

While ACLA was determining the fate of former landowners, Roosboom was filling up with people who had no previous association with the area. The RBO began to feel that people were now seeing Roosboom as "free land" where they could just settle. Neighboring farmers started to lodge complaints to the RBO about wandering animals, theft of firewood, trespassing, and illegal hunting. The RBO and other legitimate reoccupiers tried to distance themselves from the new "squatters," by blaming the latter for such behavior. Two issues particularly troubled the minds of RBO members. On the one hand the RBO was concerned that these incidents might negatively influence the decision of ACLA. On the other hand it was also concerned about losing its authority and influence over people.[8]

INCREASING VIOLENCE AND UNREST IN EZAKHENI

Why it is that Roosboom attracted so many new settlers? Where did they come from and why did they target Roosboom? To answer these questions, we need to look into the intensifying violence and wider unrest that characterized many townships and rural areas in Natal and KwaZulu in the early 1990s. Here two forms of social unrest, both originating from the political transition, were relevant. One was the increasing number of violent attacks against supporters of rival political groups: the ANC and the United Democratic Front (UDF) against the Inkatha Freedom Party (IFP). The fight was over the control of sections of townships, and many activists and ordinary people were assassinated or killed in the process (Jeffery 1997). The other form of unrest was increased farm evictions initiated by white farmers who anticipated undesirable changes during the postapartheid dispensation.

Former residents of Roosboom living in Ezakheni were directly affected by the mounting political tensions and violent attacks. In fact the township manager at the time testified that the fighting was most intense in one section of the township where many of the former Roosboom people (former landowners as well as tenants) lived (BM interview, 2002). People in this area became divided into two factions, with one supporting the IFP and the other the ANC. Due to the close proximity of the residential sites of these two factions, violent attacks in the area were particularly frequent. Many residents in this section, including those who were not openly supporting any political party, did not feel safe sleeping at home. Roosboom, therefore, offered them an alternative shelter.

LAND RESTITUTION AND COMMUNITY POLITICS

Just before the year 1992 ended, ACLA announced that Roosboom would be returned to the former landowners and/or their descendants. Although the Roosboom land restoration movement was developed in an uncertain context, it had succeeded in making the government accept its demands. Following ACLA's announcement, the process of land restitution to Roosboom landowners officially began. Various actors, both government and nongovernment, were involved in the process, which took much longer than originally envisaged.

Land NGO and Development Planning

Several questions can still be asked, including: Why is it that land restitution to Roosboom became prolonged? How did the squatting problem during the period of land struggle affect it? What were the other influences that came to shape the end result of Roosboom land restitution? These questions are dealt with in this section.

In early 1993, AFRA and the RBO called a stakeholder meeting to discuss how to implement ACLA's decision. Two contentious issues emerged from this meeting. One was the repayment of compensation that had been paid out at the time of removal. An official from Pretoria told the meeting that people had to repay it to the government as a lump sum in order for their title deeds to be restored. The RBO spokesperson voiced concerns over the matter and emphasized the hardships that had been endured at the time of removal. Another contentious issue was how to control the influx of people. Theoretically the DPWLA, as a legal owner of the land, could take action against people living in Roosboom illegally, but it was reluctant to do so. Government officials wished the matter be handled by the community and, if possible, amicably. However, the RBO had already lost control of the large number of tenants who ignored its authority.[9]

In this early stage of the implementation of ACLA's decision, AFRA played an important role both in training local leadership and in bringing actual development to people who had already moved back to Roosboom. This was in stark contrast to the Department of Regional and Land Affairs that lacked the will and capacity to implement ACLA's decision. To increase the legitimacy of RBO as the representative body of the Roosboom community and to strengthen its power to control the settlement process, AFRA organized a workshop for members of RBO to draft its constitution.[10] It also held a public workshop to teach people about the importance of land use planning. More than one hundred people attended it.[11] Furthermore, AFRA contracted consultants to identify possible water sources on Roosboom (Hojem 1993). Eleven wells, each fitted with a hand pump, were subsequently installed at Roosboom (BKS [Pty] Ltd. 1995, 1). With help from a local NGO, the RBO also acquired a grant from overseas. Combined with the money collected from landowners, it built two schools in Roosboom (MS interview, 9 July 2002). Thus AFRA and RBO managed to bring some developments to Roosboom.

With the beginning of restitution, the RBO had to transform itself from an activist group into a local leadership structure accountable for the settlement process. This task, though exciting, was new to both the RBO and AFRA, and it brought tension between these two organizations. On the one hand, AFRA began to notice a lack of accountability in the RBO leadership. The number of people who turned up at the meetings called by the RBO had gradually dwindled.[12] On the other hand, the RBO was frustrated at what they called the limited flow of information about the restitution process. A member of the RBO complained to AFRA that they were "being asked to respond to issues that [they] needed guidance on and AFRA was not available to provide this guidance as it ha[d] in the past."[13] Three members of RBO had stopped being active by then. Moreover, when the process of restoring land rights to landowners actually started, individual landowners began to negotiate with the officials of the Department of Regional and Land Affairs directly. The future of local authority in the area was still unclear. It was in this context that the RBO wanted to strengthen the legitimacy of its leadership and adopted the constitution.

In late 1994 the RBO and AFRA convened a community meeting at Roosboom in order to adopt a Roosboom constitution and elect new members for the RBO. It was attended by more than 150 people, of whom 90 percent were landowners and therefore eligible to vote. AFRA showed concern about the exclusion of tenants in voting, but could not change a clause in the draft constitution, which stipulated that "only landowners have the right to vote." However, tenants could become members of RBO if landowners voted for them. A member of the RBO also explained that "by tenants [they] were referring to [their] old tenants of Roosboom not these new troublesome tenants who ha[d] arrived." Most of the outgoing members of the RBO were once again elected to serve on the RBO at this meeting (AFRA 1994). The adoption of the constitution and the election of new RBO members led to the "exit" of AFRA from the Roosboom land restoration process. Although the RBO was shocked to hear of AFRA's decision, the latter reasoned that Roosboom was exceptionally equipped with a strong leadership structure and therefore would be capable of dealing with the land restoration process on its own (AFRA 1995a, 1995b, 1995c). AFRA continued to liaise with the RBO for a while, but gradually its contact became infrequent and eventually stopped.

Difficulty of Title Restoration and the Role of Community Organizations

While AFRA and the RBO were trying to work on the local structure and development of Roosboom, the new government appointed a "land titles commissioner" (outside the ambit of the Commission on Restitution of Land Rights) to take charge of restoring land rights to former landowners. In mid-1995, the Roosboom commissioner submitted the final list of successful and unsuccessful claims to the new Department of Land Affairs (DLA). His list consisted of 256 successful claims, 42 claims needing to be verified, and 131 unclaimed lots.[14]

The Roosboom steering committee, set up by the DLA to administer the new Reconstruction and Development Programme (RDP) fund allocated for the development of Roosboom, examined the list and considered it unsatisfactory for several reasons. First, the number of claims dealt with by the commissioner was too few. Second, it was discovered that the commissioner had accepted untenable claims. The committee thought it problematic that a large number of people had not yet submitted their land claims and decided to temporarily halt the Roosboom restitution process. Apparently the commissioner could not provide records of the facts that supported his recommendations. It was therefore not an easy task for the

DLA to review and correct mistakes, and this was not resolved until a year later.[15] The RBO claimed that it could have managed the title restoration better and demanded that it be granted the status of local government so that it could administer the development of Roosboom through the use of the RDP fund.[16]

One of the major difficulties in title restoration was how to track down possible claimants. As noted above, the list compiled by AFRA and the RBO in their submission to the ACLA was not a complete one. The Roosboom commissioner sent notices to former landowning families by registered mail, but many of the letters were returned (Xulu 1998). Some landowners hesitated to lodge their claims immediately, as they were concerned about the necessity of repaying compensation (GM interview, 24 July 2002). Moreover, the steering committee realized that "while the number of original owners [was] finite, the potential number of claimants, in the form of heirs and descendants, could increase beneficiary numbers significantly."[17] All the leading governmental departments (DLA, Local Government and Housing, and Public Works) for the project were severely understaffed at this stage. Nor was the RBO sufficiently representing the community. Nonetheless, a government official also admitted that without the RBO the process would have been slower and much more difficult.[18]

The socioeconomic survey compiled by the planning consultant for Roosboom in early 1996 reveals the state of settlement in Roosboom at that time. The consultant conducted a questionnaire survey of 663 households (97 percent) of a total of 684 in Roosboom. The number of households that had returned to Roosboom by 1992 was 177. It increased to 230 (1,380 people) by mid-1993 and 684 (4,310 people) in 1996. It was projected that it would increase up to 1,000 households (6,300 people) by 2000 (Urban-Econ and BKS 1996, 2–4). Among the 663 households, the survey found 14.6 percent landowners, 82.5 percent tenants, and 2.6 percent "informal settlers" (squatters). Out of a total of 572 individual lots of varying size in Roosboom, the survey found that only 267 lots had had houses built on them. This meant that there were on average 2.6 households per individual lot. These lots were almost exclusively used for residential purposes, but 23.4 percent of the respondents (117 households) indicated that in the future they would use the land for subsistence agriculture. A further 15.4 percent indicated that they would use the land for farming for the market. More than 35 percent of households surveyed kept cattle, 32.6 percent kept goats, and nearly 60 percent kept poultry. The number of cattle at Roosboom amounted to 1,726, which vastly exceeded the number of livestock recommended for the area by the Department of Agriculture (Urban-Econ and BKS 1996, 11–13).[19] In short, the position at Roosboom was not dissimilar from that of many former homelands.

UNRAVELING THE DIVISION AND COMMUNITY DYNAMICS

In late 1997 the DLA appointed a new land commissioner to resume the Roosboom land restitution process. It also appointed a consultant to meet with individual landowners and administer the overall process. Compared with the previous arrangement, where several governmental departments sent their representatives to the steering committee, this was clearly a downsized engagement in terms of the number of officials involved and the passion of the DLA for the Roosboom restitution project. According to the final report compiled by the consultant in 2000, the transfer of title deeds had been completed for only 187 out of a total of 576 lots at Roosboom (Aitken 2000). Two years later the DLA appointed another consultant to carry on with the project. As an attempt to understand the end result of Roosboom land restitution, in this section I aim to shed some light on the dynamics of reoccupation and community politics in Roosboom that had been unraveling in the process.

The biggest issue was the power relations among landowners themselves, and between landowners and tenants. The beginning of the title restoration process increased the importance of an individual family's actions against that of community organization. Certain landowners saw the title restoration as an opportunity to accumulate financial capital by bringing in tenants and charging them rent. They ignored the RBO's warnings on the possible detrimental consequences of their action on their own land rights, as well as on the interest of the community as a whole. At times quarrels within families also resulted in some of them bringing in tenants to Roosboom (MS, OM, and PD interviews, all 2002). Some tenants took their chances and moved into lots where there was no sign of a landowner's authority. Although most landowners did show interest in their lots in Roosboom and strongly expressed their wish to be buried in Roosboom, they were not in a hurry to return to the land.

Tensions from within came to the surface in late 1998 when the community formed a trust in order to administer the R7.5 million allocated by the government for the development of Roosboom. The RBO convened the annual general meeting (AGM) to elect the first trustees for the new Roosboom Trust. The trust was set up at this meeting, with most of the RBO members elected as trustees (OM interview, 2002). However, after the AGM, the Roosboom Trust effectively split up into two organizations. Two prominent members of the RBO formed separate factions and started to deal separately with outside organizations such as the DLA and the Regional Council, as well as consultants. One faction was alleged by the other faction to be working with tenants, although its leader vehemently denied this (MS interview, 30 July 2002). The leader of the other faction, however, claimed that his faction was against the idea of bringing in tenants and warned landowners of the possibility that tenants might stop paying rents to them. He even went on to say that his faction encouraged tenants not to pay rents to landowners in order to discourage the latter from taking in more tenants (OM interview, 2002).

Internal conflicts weakened the RBO's authority over the people at Roosboom. A consultant noted that the meetings often "end[ed] up being chaotic because the tenants hijack[ed]" them and demanded to discuss the issue of their land rights rather than title restoration to landowners.[20] Several outside organizations dealing with the RBO also noticed that the RBO was split into two, with one faction working with the tenants (MG and CA interviews, both 2002). This incident illustrates that the community dynamics of Roosboom land restitution were much more complex than a simple dichotomy between landowners and tenants that had characterized the removal of "black spots." Landowners themselves were divided, and it is not easy to discern a landowners' interest separately from tenants' interests.

With the demarcation of a new ward for local elections in 2000, another division was introduced to Roosboom. Without taking into consideration the historical background of Roosboom, the demarcation board split Roosboom into two different electoral wards and two different local authorities. Whereas the northern part, known as Roosboom I, became part of the Ladysmith/Emnambithi local municipality, the southern part, known as Roosboom II, was incorporated into the Uthukela District Council. Furthermore, as a result of the election, Roosboom I got an ANC councillor, whereas Roosboom II came to have an IFP councillor. This does not necessarily mean that the political affiliation of residents of Roosboom I and II was divided along the lines of ANC-IFP rivalry, as Roosboom II was amalgamated with another area in forming an electoral ward (OM interview, 2002). Still, elected councillors sparked the emergence of a new leadership among Roosboom residents, who could further strengthen the land rights of tenants who were now a majority of the electoral constituency.[21]

There are other unresolved issues that might have an impact on the end result of the Roosboom land claim. Some claimants, in particular those who submitted their claims earlier, repaid their compensation money, but others did not. Even the DLA does not know who paid, how much money was paid, and to whom it was paid (AS interview, 2002). A second issue was that of unclaimed land. In spite of several publicity campaigns, 39 out of a total number of 576 lots were still unclaimed by mid-2000. This was probably because some of the legitimate claimants were unaware of their stake in Roosboom or had lost interest. The consultant proposed the introduction of a cutoff date for the submission of claims and transferring unclaimed lots to the Roosboom Trust, but the DLA was reluctant to do so (CA interview, 2002). Third, the DLA realized that some legitimate claimants, many living in big cities, had sold their lots to needy purchasers before they legally became the owners through title restoration (AS interview, 2002). For some landowners the value of land was an issue, as tenants were on it. As the land transaction in such cases was done informally and therefore the purchaser could not submit the land claim, the purchaser was not entitled to obtain the title deeds for the land she or he bought.

In this chapter I have discussed the land restitution movement and subsequent land restitution process of Roosboom, a prominent case of popular mobilization for land during the early 1990s. It was one of the earliest cases of land restitution in the country, and thus it was a test case to see how rural land restitution was going to be realized in postapartheid South Africa. The fact that more tenants than landowners returned or came to settle in Roosboom raises the question of what land restitution actually means to people and how the success and failure of land restitution can be defined. It is important to highlight the enormous challenges the Roosboom restitution case presented and the lessons to be gained from it for land reform in postapartheid South Africa.

The Roosboom case clearly showed multiple tensions in determining who could be the rightful owner of a piece of land. Most land at Roosboom was owned by individual landowners, who then claimed the particular lot(s) that he or she or other family members had owned before the removal. As the property belonged to individual families, it was up to them to decide how to use it. This created several unexpected tensions, not only among former landowners and in the landowner-tenant relationship, but also within the household. As most of the original landowners were dead by the 1990s, the determination of who was to inherit their properties became a contentious issue for some landowning families. Tenants were also used by some landowners to stake their claim to a particular piece of land. Land restitution unexpectedly exposed these multiple tensions over the land. At present Roosboom might look as if land restitution has caused the original Roosboom community to disintegrate. It can, however, be also said that exposing the tensions over the land could be a first step to ultimately resolving them.

The community organization that led popular mobilization for land in the early 1990s turned out to be ineffective during the actual restitution process. For outside organizations, including both governmental departments and NGOs, Roosboom was seen to have an exceptionally strong community organization. Roosboom's educated leadership was well-equipped to deal with the government in expressing demands for land restitution. With the commencement of land restitution, however, the role of RBO as a community organization became blurred and weakened. Restitution meant different things to different landowners. What was unfortunate for the RBO was perhaps the fact that the new government institutions were not yet readily available to support a local organization. Still, the limits to the role that community organizations can play in land restitution should be acknowledged as well as the role the government should play.

Finally, it is necessary to point out the importance of not isolating land restitution from regional political and restructuring processes. One of the reasons why Roosboom ended up with tenants and squatters before land restitution began was because of the increasing violence and social unrest in the Ezakheni township and on surrounding white-owned farms. The location of Roosboom, which is on the old main road and much closer to Ladysmith than, say, Cremin, another former "black spot" whose restitution was realized after 1994 (Walker 2004), was another attractive factor for many people who settled in Roosboom. Whether Roosboom develops into a rural agricultural community or a peri-urban settlement will depend largely on the restructuring process of the regional economy. For this reason simply providing "post-settlement support" to the people who have settled in Roosboom will not be enough for the long-term prosperity of the settlement, unless it is linked to an overall development strategy for the region.

NOTES

1. The insights on which this chapter is based were gained during field research in 2002 as part of a doctoral thesis that covered the period from the 1950s to 2002 (Sato 2006). The research drew on field reports of NGO workers who assisted the community in their land claim as well as unstructured interviews with claimant leaders, NGO workers, and government officials. Other useful secondary materials include two dissertations written on the removals in Roosboom, as well as the early phase of its restitution (Mmutlana 1993; Xulu 1998).

2. They were Matiwane's Kop, Steincoalspruit, Tembalihle, and Cornfields.

3. Memorandum, DPWLA and Roosboom, 22 February 1991, ARF.

4. Memorandum, Roosboom Interim Committee and DPWLA, 19 April 1991, ARF.

5. Minutes, meeting between RBO and DPWLA, 20 May 1991, ARF.

6. ACLA was later renamed Commission on Land Allocation (COLA) with a wider mandate. Though the land that COLA could make its decision about was still limited to the state land, its role was very similar to the postapartheid CRLR.

7. AFRA to ACLA, 21 May 1992, ARF.

8. AFRA, meeting with RBO, 20 August 1992, ARF.

9. Notes, Roosboom meeting, 19 February 1993; minutes, Roosboom coordinating committee, 22 April 1993, 2 July 1993, ARF.

10. Roosboom constitution workshop, February 1993, ARF.

11. Roosboom development vision workshop, 6–7 March 1993, ARF.

12. Roosboom meeting, 19 June 1993, ARF.

13. AFRA, report on conversation with Moses Mazibuko, 12 August 1993, ARF.

14. DLA, memorandum: Roosboom, n.d., DLA: Roosboom file, Pietermaritzburg.

15. DLA, memorandum: Roosboom, Ref. CS6/7/2/L3/38, 1 July 1996, DLA: Roosboom file.

16. RBO, report, Restitution of Roosboom and RDP lead project, 4 July 1996, DLA: Roosboom file.

17. Roosboom, final project planning report (draft), n.d. [November 1996], DLA: Roosboom file.

18. Ibid.

19. The report does not clarify the difference between tenants and informal settlers. I assume that the former refers to tenants approved by landowners, whereas the latter just came to live on Roosboom without getting approval from anyone.

20. Minutes, Roosboom meeting, 15 November 1998, DLA: Roosboom file.

21. Eventually the Roosboom Trust was dissolved in 2004, signaling the official ending of the RBO's leadership. Since then, it has been said that a new trust was set up by several landowners in Roosboom, claiming a revival of the original Roosboom syndicate, though the details of this new trust are not known to the author. (PD and IN interviews, both 2004; Thukela Mzinyathi Christian Council, 24 August 2004, Ladysmith.)

REFERENCES

AFRA (Association for Rural Advancement). 1990a. "AFRA Fieldworker's Report, 22 July 1990." Unpublished report, AFRA Roosboom File (ARF). Pietermaritzburg: AFRA.

———. 1990b. "AFRA Fieldworker's Report, 31 August 1990." Unpublished report, AFRA Roosboom File (ARF). Pietermaritzburg: AFRA.

———. 1990c. "AFRA Fieldworker's Report, 16 September 1990." Unpublished report, AFRA Roosboom File (ARF). Pietermaritzburg: AFRA.

———. 1990d. "AFRA Fieldworker's Report, 23 September 1990." Unpublished report, AFRA Roosboom File (ARF). Pietermaritzburg: AFRA.

———. 1990e. "AFRA Press Release, December 1990, Roosboom: Restoration of Land Crisis." AFRA Roosboom File (ARF). Pietermaritzburg: AFRA.

———. 1990f. "AFRA Fieldworker's Report, 24 October 1990." Unpublished report, AFRA Roosboom File (ARF). Pietermaritzburg: AFRA.

———. 1990g. "AFRA Fieldworker's Report, 22 November 1990." Unpublished report, AFRA Roosboom File (ARF). Pietermaritzburg: AFRA.

———. 1991a. "AFRA Report on Roosboom, 23 May 1991." Report, AFRA Roosboom File (ARF). Pietermaritzburg: AFRA.

———. 1991b. "AFRA Fieldworker's Report, 27 January 1991." Unpublished report, AFRA Roosboom File (ARF). Pietermaritzburg: AFRA.

———. 1992a. "AFRA Fieldworker's Report, 5 January 1992." Unpublished report, AFRA Roosboom File (ARF). Pietermaritzburg: AFRA.

———. 1992b. *The Roosboom Land Claims Submission to the Advisory Commission on Land Allocation (ACLA)*. Pietermaritzburg: AFRA.

———. 1994. "AFRA Fieldworker's Report, 30 October 1994." Unpublished report, AFRA Roosboom File (ARF). Pietermaritzburg: AFRA.

———. 1995a. "AFRA Field Report, 2 February 1995." Unpublished report, AFRA Roosboom File (ARF). Pietermaritzburg: AFRA.

———. 1995b. "AFRA Field Report, 12 February 1995." Unpublished report, AFRA Roosboom File (ARF). Pietermaritzburg: AFRA.

———. 1995c. "AFRA Field Report, 16 February 1995." Unpublished report, AFRA Roosboom File (ARF). Pietermaritzburg: AFRA.

Aitken, Chris. 2000. "Crams: Last Title Adjustment and Title Determination Project: Roosboom: Final Progress and Handover Report." Mimeo report. Pietermaritzburg: Department of Land Affairs.

BKS (Pty) Ltd. 1995. "Roosboom Water Supply: Detailed Feasibility Study." Report prepared for RBO and AFRA, Pietermaritzburg, mimeo.

Hojem, G. P. 1993. "Roosboom Water Supply." Report prepared for AFRA, Pietermaritzburg, mimeo.

Jeffery, Anthea. 1997. *The Natal Story: Sixteen Years of Conflict*. Johannesburg: South African Institute of Race Relations.

Mmutlana, Rufus Mokgotlha. 1993. "Forced Removals in Northern Natal: A Comparative Study of the Steincoalspruit and Roosboom Communities in Historical Perspective." MA thesis, University of Natal, Pietermaritzburg, South Africa.

Mngadi, Elliot. 1981. *The Removal of Roosboom*. AFRA special report 2. Pietermaritzburg: AFRA.

National Land Committee. 1993. "Back to the Land." Campaign info pack. Johannesburg: National Land Committee.

Republic of South Africa. 1991. *White Paper on Land Reform*. Pretoria: Government Printer.

Sato, Chizuko. 2006. "Forced Removals, Land NGOs and Community Politics in KwaZulu-Natal, South Africa, 1953–2002." DPhil thesis, University of Oxford, United Kingdom.

———. 2007. "Liberal Opposition to Forced Removals and Non-racialism in South Africa," *Ritsumeikan Annual Review of International Studies* 6 (1): 79–102.

Urban-Econ and BKS (Pty) Ltd. 1996. "Roosboom: Planning for a Settlement, Phase One: Data Collection Report." Durban: Urban-Econ and BKS (Pty) Ltd.

Vigne, Randolph. 1997. *Liberals against Apartheid: A History of the Liberal Party of South Africa, 1953–68*. Basingstoke: Palgrave.

Walker, Cherryl. 2004. "'We Are Consoled'—Reconstructing Cremin." *South African Historical Journal* 51 (1): 199–222.

Xulu, Busisiwe, Barbara. 1998. "Land Reform and Restitution: The Case of Roosboom in Northern KwaZulu-Natal." MA thesis, University of Durban-Westville, South Africa.

INTERVIEWS

CA, consultant to the DLA. Pietermaritzburg, 14 November 2002.
PB, former AFRA chairperson. Pietermaritzburg, 16 July 2002.
PD, RBO member. Ladysmith, 8 November 2002, 24 August 2004 (by telephone).
MG, Thukela Mzinyathi Christian Council. Ladysmith, 7 November 2002.
BM, Ezakheni township manager. Ezakheni, 11 July 2002.
GM, Roosboom landowner. Ezakheni, 24 July 2002, 30 July 2002.
MM, former organizer of the Northern Natal Council of Churches. Pietermaritzburg, 7 May 2002.
OM, RBO member. Ezakheni, 7 November 2002.
IN, Thukela Mzinyathi Christian Council. Ladysmith, 24 August 2004.
AS, DLA district office. Ladysmith, 8 November 2002.
MS, RBO member. Ezakheni, 9 July 2002, 19 July 2002, 30 July 2002.

NEWSPAPERS

Daily News, Durban, South Africa.
Natal Mercury, Durban, South Africa.

part four

Restitution
Policy

*Limits and
Possibilities*

thirteen

Land Claims and Comanagement of Protected Areas in South Africa

Exploring the Challenges

THEMBELA KEPE

Land reform in protected areas is an intensely debated issue and one that continues to challenge many affected governments, agencies, and individuals around the world.[1] The key challenge is how to ensure that both conservation and people's rights to land and natural resources are maintained. In South Africa, following the implementation of a land reform program when apartheid was abolished in 1994, numerous land claims affected protected areas (Wynberg and Kepe 1999; De Villiers 1999; Kepe, Wynberg, and Ellis 2005; Ashley and Freimund 2006). Although there is currently no single database of all land claims in protected areas, it is known that at least twenty-six verified land claims were made on South Africa's twenty-one national parks, of which four had been settled by the time of writing of this paper (Lukhele 2007). Numerous other land claims are known to exist in nature reserves, protected indigenous forests, wetlands, heritage sites, and wilderness areas, to name a few (see Wynberg and Kepe 1999), and many were never officially lodged by the 31 December 1998 deadline but remain a source of conflict between the claiming communities and the managers of the protected areas (Kepe 2001a).

Irrespective of the history, rationale, and type of land reform, research shows that comanagement or joint management between the state and local communities has become the most popular approach for reconciling the goals of biodiversity conservation and land reform in specific geographical areas (Morrison 1997; De Villiers 1999; Magome and Murombedzi 2003; Kepe, Wynberg, and Ellis 2005). In South Africa's land restitution the use of comanagement has gone beyond being merely popular to being the only strategy to reconcile biodiversity conservation and land rights (Magome and Murombedzi 2003; Kepe 2004; Ministry of Agriculture and Land Affairs 2007). Following the settlement of almost all land claims on South Africa's protected areas, comanagement arrangements have been created between the relevant conservation authorities and the successful land claimants. Even though some officials who are involved in the management of protected areas affected by land claims prefer to use concepts such as joint-management or claimant participation rather than comanagement, in policy and in practice there is no difference between these. The creation of these comanagement arrangements has, until recently, been carried out without clear policy or legislative backing. Rather, by the Department of Land Affairs' (DLA's) own admission, they have been based on precedents set by two high-profile land claims—that of the Makuleke community for a section of Kruger National Park and that of the Mbila community for the Greater St. Lucia Wetland Park (DLA 2002).

Establishment of comanagement in these protected areas was motivated by a strong lobby of environmental conservationists who initially opposed the land claims but then opted for a comanagement compromise as a way of saving the protected areas (Cock and Fig 2000; Magome and Murombedzi 2003). It was only in 2002, following numerous complex land claims in many other protected areas, that the DLA formally proposed comanagement as a government policy that should be given political and legal support (DLA 2002). These proposals formally became policy through a "Cabinet Memorandum" (no. 5 of 2002), which was signed on 9 October 2002. However, through a memorandum of understanding between the minister of agriculture and land affairs and the minister of environmental affairs and tourism, signed on 2 May 2007, the two relevant government departments came to a formal, legally binding agreement to use comanagement as the only strategy to guide land reform in protected areas (Ministry of Agriculture and Land Affairs 2007).

Despite there being several comanagement, or joint-management, arrangements in existence in formerly claimed protected areas, research has concluded that the blueprint model of comanagement might be too weak or inadequate a tool for the challenging the land reform process in South Africa (Magome and Murombedzi 2003; Kepe, Wynberg, and Ellis 2005). These authors argue that comanagement has possibly represented a camouflage for the continuation of state hegemony regarding the protected area or national park idea in postapartheid South Africa.

However, in addressing other objectives relating to people and nature in South Africa (e.g., fisheries or ecotourism), comanagement has received fairly positive reviews (Hara and Nielsen 2003; Hauck and Sowman 2003). With regard to dealing with land rights, the only optimistic assessment of comanagement comes from practitioners and researchers who, though admitting that comanagement faces major challenges, plead for patience, arguing that protected area collaborative arrangements are new in South Africa and therefore should not be judged harshly just yet (Reid et al. 2004).

What is puzzling is the absence of a clear justification from government, conservation agencies, and other supporters for suggesting comanagement in resolving land conflicts relating to protected areas. Using the case of Mkambati Nature Reserve's "successful" land claim by local people, in this chapter I explore the shortcomings of the blueprint model of comanagement when it is used to deal with land rights and conservation issues. I identify and discuss three possible reasons for the inadequate performance of comanagement in reconciling land restitution and conservation in South Africa: (1) that the comanagement idea originated in a different context: the conservation of high-value natural resources such as fisheries, forestry, wildlife, and water (Berkes 1997) rather than in concerns for resource rights; (2) that key conditions for successful comanagement have been neglected; and (3) that the terminology and concepts in settlement agreements are ambiguous. I further speculate on why relevant government departments and conservation proponents insist on comanagement arrangements in these land-claim situations despite their questionable track record elsewhere in South Africa.

In addition to a review of the literature, the analysis draws from field research in the Mkambati area over an eleven-year period (1996–2007), including a full-time residence in Khanyayo village for nine months in 1996. I combined observations, interviews, archival research, and a review of secondary sources, including government policy documents and legislation. Another major source of information was a series of workshops held by the DLA, Department of Environmental Affairs and Tourism, and the International Union for Conservation of Nature (IUCN)–South Africa in 1997 and

1998, where key stakeholders were brought together to discuss the resolution of land claims in protected areas (see IUCN 1998).

The next section of the chapter provides an overview of the land claim in Mkambati Nature Reserve, including a brief history of dispossession, lodgment, and settlement of the claim, as well as a postsettlement update. This is followed by a discussion of the three possible reasons for the failure of comanagement in resolving land claims. The paper concludes with a synthesis of key issues emerging from the case study and literature about the appropriateness of comanagement in resolving land claims in protected areas.

THE MKAMBATI NATURE RESERVE LAND CLAIM

The seven-thousand-hectare Mkambati Nature Reserve is situated in northeastern Pondoland between two rivers, Mtentu and Msikaba, in the Wild Coast, Eastern Cape Province (see map 4). It is one of the key biodiversity "hot spots" in southern Africa, supporting numerous rare plants, many of which are endemic—such as the Pondo coconut palm (*Jubaeopsis caffra*) (Tinley 1978; Nel 2003). For many decades ecologists and environmental activists have campaigned for strict conservation of this "pristine" environment (see Briers et al. 1996). It has been pointed out that Mkambati's floral

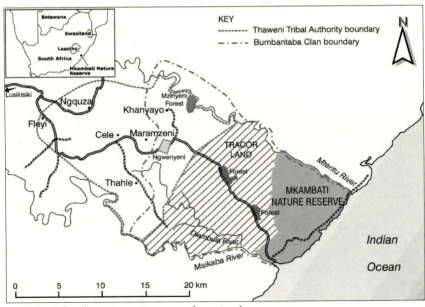

MAP 4. Mkambati Nature Reserve and surrounds

endowments are also important to its ecotourism potential (Kepe 1997). The reserve supports more than two thousand wild herbivores and is also home to a marine reserve.

Adjacent to the nature reserve are seven villages that make up the Thaweni Tribal Authority. As has been the case in many other land claims in South Africa, colonial and apartheid policies and legislation, including the realignment of boundaries that ignored traditional allegiances, have led to tensions among these seven communities. The residents of Khanyayo, the closest village to the reserve, were forcibly removed from an area of about 18,000 hectares in 1920, to make way for a leper colony (Cape Town Archives 1 LSK 13/2/5/2). The Khanyayo are part of the Bumbantaba clan living on both sides of the Mtentu River (see map 4) but were subjected to new boundaries that brought them under a new traditional authority (currently the Thaweni Tribal Authority) following the annexation of Pondoland in 1894. The Khanyayo had previously used the reserve area for settlement, livestock grazing, and the collection of a range of natural resources. For more than seventy years the Khanyayo aggressively attempted to regain their land rights. Despite regulations prohibiting them, they continued to hunt wild game and harvest natural resources within the area. Other villages within Thaweni Tribal Authority also used the area for winter grazing before dispossession. Following the closure of the leper colony in 1976, and its conversion into Mkambati Nature Reserve and Transkei Agricultural Corporation state farm, tension between the state and the Khanyayo increased, particularly over grazing rights. In 1997, the residents of Khanyayo lodged a claim against the state for the restitution of their land rights. However, other villages falling under Thaweni Tribal Authority claimed that they too should be part of the land claim, given that they had previously used the area for winter grazing and that they all currently fall under one chief.

As a way of maintaining peace in the area, officials of the DLA coerced the Khanyayo to withdraw their claim for Mkambati Nature Reserve and permitted only a small number of households whose relatives lost huts in 1920 to be claimants. This deal, proposed in 1999, also went further and included all the six other villages as cobeneficiaries of the land. Following protracted negotiations over several years (1999–2004), the minister of land affairs, through section 42D of the Restitution Act of 1994, formally handed over Mkambati Nature Reserve to Mkambati Land Trust on 17 October 2004. The descendants of people who had lost homesteads in 1920, who numbered 326 in 2004, were given R38,000 (approximately US$5,300) each as compensation. The seven villages became co-owners of the land but agreed to maintain it as a nature reserve, through which they could benefit from ecotourism ventures (Kepe 2004). The agreement that was signed during the handover of the land was that the Mkambati Land Trust, a community legal entity, and the Eastern Cape Parks Board,[2] a conservation agency, would comanage the reserve on behalf of the successful claimants, currently numbering about six thousand households. A community agreement between the community trust, the DLA, and the Provincial Department of Economic Affairs, Environment and Tourism (DEAT) specifies that the land will be comanaged with the Trust, by a comanagement committee, for an initial period of thirty-five years.

One of the key terms of the agreement is that the minister of agriculture and land affairs delegates DEAT to manage the nature reserve on behalf of the state (section 4.2). Five years after the settlement of the land claim, and since the beginning of the comanagement arrangement, there have been numerous conflicts between the Mkambati Land Trust and the Eastern Cape Parks Board, as well as conflicts between the Land Trust and other villagers. Despite having a certificate of ownership, members of the Mkambati Land Trust still disagree with the government, or among themselves, on ownership of the nature reserve. Comanagement has arguably added to a sense of unclear land rights following the successful land claim. The sections that follow attempt to use the progress or absence thereof of the Mkambati comanagement arrangement to explain why comanagement, as used in dealing with natural resource management issues, is not achieving success in resolving land rights issues in the South African context. The first of these sections explores whether the origins of the version of comanagement used in Mkambati and other protected area land claims are in fact responsible or not for the dismal performance of this strategy to resolve land claims.

ORIGINS OF COMANAGEMENT AND ITS RELEVANCE TO RESOURCES

Comanagement as currently used to reconcile land claims in protected areas in South Africa is undoubtedly modeled after the version used in natural resource management (fisheries, forestry, and biodiversity conservation) globally. Even though there has been extensive writing on the benefits of comanagement, there is an equally acknowledged potential for this concept or strategy to be misleading, contested, or abused (Jentoft 2003; Tipa and

Welch 2006). Several things are made to pass as comanagement, depending on the geography, politics, and other social issues (Hara and Nielsen 2003). However, Jentoft's (2003, 3) suggested definition that "comanagement is a collaborative and participatory process of regulatory decision-making between representatives of user-groups, government agencies, research institutions, and other stakeholders" appears to contain most of the key assumptions that are widely seen as fundamentals of comanagement. Essentially, comanagement is seen as suggesting or encouraging participatory democracy, sharing of power, local incentives for local use of natural resources, and decentralization of resource management decisions (Berkes 1997; Jentoft 2003; Plummer and FitzGibbon 2006).

However, even though there are natural resources at stake in the protected areas under claim in South Africa (e.g., Mkambati), there seems to be limited compatibility between the version of comanagement that has been publicized and used globally in the management of natural resources and the resolution of land claims. There are at least three issues consistent with comanagement of natural resources, as cited in the literature, that make it challenging to transfer this strategy to resolving land rights. These are the focus on natural resource sustainability, the goal of the state's gaining legitimacy by involving local people, and the insistence that the state and its agencies are the initiators and key players.

With regard to the first issue, comanagement is seen as a response to a particular *concern*, which is usually connected to perceived, or actual, human impact on natural resources (Tipa and Welch 2006). Jentoft (2003) adds that comanagement is indeed a response to many concerns and is seen as way of rectifying basic flaws in the existing management system. Other authors who support this view suggest that comanagement is developed in cases where there is a resource scarcity or a perception of resource threat (Hauck and Sowman 2001; Hara and Nielsen 2003). If the concern about threats to the biological resource is indeed one of the chief motivations for entering into a comanagement arrangement, as it is suspected to be the case in Mkambati and other similar situations in South Africa, then it means land rights issues are not the main foundation. This could explain the general absence of government departments that deal with land rights in further negotiations or implementation of comanagement. Following the handing over of the certificate of ownership to the Mkambati Land Trust, local people complained that the DLA had practically handed things over to the Eastern Cape Parks Board, a conservation agency. The conservation partner in the comanagement plan is the main government body currently involved in negotiating and restructuring the agreement.

Second, the literature clearly shows that another key motivation for establishing comanagement arrangements is the realization by the state that it cannot protect the resource without involving local people (Plummer and FitzGibbon 2006). In this sense comanagement is often seen as a way of enhancing legitimacy of government with regard to its responsibility to the resource (Jentoft 2003). Others further suggest that by seeking to work with people, rather than against them, in managing the resource, the state is able to deceptively reformulate its existing regulations to make them sound different but keep them the same in practice in order to get the support of the community partners (Hara and Nielson 2003). In other words, co-optation of local people, whereby the state agency retains considerable power, is quite common in a comanagement arrangement (Boonzaier 1996).

Third, and related to the two points made above, state agencies are usually the initiators of and key players in comanagement arrangements (Pomeroy and Berkes 1997). Although this makes perfect sense for resources that are owned and controlled by the state, the same cannot be said for resources whose ownership is vested in the local people. A successful land claim in a protected area, which involves restoration of land, means that the former claimants take over ownership of the area and all the responsibilities that come with it. The question that could be asked is: Should they not then be the ones initiating comanagement arrangements, if they see fit? But biodiversity conservation is a national priority, and the state has to fulfill its obligation by protecting individual guarantees for a protected environment that are enshrined in section 24 of the Bill of Rights. However, government's leading role in most comanagement arrangements could reinforce the previous sense of government as a legal custodian of the area in question.

Magome and Murombedzi (2003) suggest that South Africa's version of comanagement evolved from an apartheid-era strategy of entering into legal agreements with white private landowners to expand national parks. The National Parks Act 57 of 1976 was amended to allow joining of national parks and private farms to the advantage of both private landowners and conservation bodies. Several critics, however, have argued that this model was not meant for poor, powerless black people, many of whom live in rural areas (Magome and Murombedzi 2003; Kepe, Wynberg, and Ellis 2005). The reason for the inappropriateness of this model for the poor and the powerless is twofold. First, poor people are not necessarily interested in or will not voluntarily be giving land for biodiversity conservation when they have other land-use needs that they perceive to be more important to their livelihoods, such as arable farming or livestock grazing (see Songorwa 1999). Second, the poor and powerless always face the danger of being coerced or co-opted into arrangements that do not benefit them but suit those in power, including the state agencies (Boonzaier 1996; Kepe, Wynberg, and Ellis 2005).

NEGLECT OF KEY COMANAGEMENT CONDITIONS

Using the dynamics of the Mkambati Nature Reserve land claim, this section explores the feasibility of the comanagement strategy by analyzing what the literature says versus what happens in practice. In an influential and widely cited article, Berkes (1997, 6) argues that comanagement is feasible only if at least four conditions are met. These are the presence of appropriate institutions, trust between partners, legal protection of local rights, and economic incentives for local people. Starting with the first condition, Berkes maintains that there is a need to ask: "Are there appropriate institutions, both local and governmental?" For South Africa's young democracy, and with the governance status quo in rural areas, this question is pertinent. Although the country has made strides in designing useful legislation and policies, as well as creating relevant institutional frameworks, many critics have pointed to institutional breakdowns during implementation of policies and legislation. Too much or too little political involvement (Parker 2004), poor interdepartmental coordination (Kepe 2001a), and human resource problems are some of the key challenges facing government institutions in implementing their mandates. In the case of Mkambati, the current tentative approach taken by both the Eastern Cape Parks Board and the provincial DLA in Mkambati does not bode well for a robust and successful comanagement arrangement. Local people argue that the absence of key stakeholder government departments in meetings about the Mkambati Nature Reserve land claim, as well as the fact that the focus of interactions appears to be on serving the national interests of the state through conservation, makes it very difficult for them to view comanagement in a positive light.

Local institutions are also facing many challenges. In addition to the lingering confusion in rural local governance in South Africa, where traditional authority institutions are in conflict with democratic institutions, such as elected local government (Ntsebeza 2005), there continues to be a power vacuum in some rural areas. At the core of these problems is the inability of the state to clearly define the roles and powers of traditional leaders. In addition to this, local people are increasingly challenging the legitimacy of traditional authorities in some areas (Kepe 2001a). Ironically, the postapartheid era has also brought about weakened community-based institutions. Influential community leaders in rural areas were drawn into local, provincial, or national political structures, leaving a leadership void in many rural areas (Kepe 1997). With these problems remaining unresolved, representation of local concerns and needs is compromised. Kepe, Cousins, and Turner (2001) have provided detailed accounts of how institutional breakdown in Mkambati has led to both social and ecological misfortunes locally.

Berkes's second condition for successful comanagement is that of "trust between actors" (1997, 6). Although this is not always easy to measure, long-term fieldwork in the area indicates that there is not consistent trust between local people and government officials working for the DLA, Eastern Cape Parks Board, and the O. R. Tambo District Municipality. Besides the current disagreements between the Mkambati Land Trust and the Eastern Cape Parks Board about the terms of the comanagement agreement, the mistrust is mainly historical. Conservationists have traditionally believed that residents of coastal Pondoland, where Mkambati Nature Reserve is located, have environmentally destructive livelihood activities, which need to be controlled (De Villiers and Costello 2006). Similarly, local people have long been suspicious of government intervention, particularly that which involved control of land and natural resources. Kepe (1997, 2005) has reported on how local people were deceived into giving up land for a leper colony in 1920 and how they were subsequently forbidden from using certain natural resources (e.g., medicinal plants and thatch grass). These mistrusts are not confined only to the Mkambati situation. Ntshona, Kraai, and Nomatyindyo (2006) report similar mistrust between government conservation authorities and the people of Dwesa/Cwebe with regard to comanagement of the Dwesa/Cwebe Nature Reserve.

In the case of Mkambati, there is an added dimension to "trust between actors." As mentioned earlier in this paper, the local Khanyayo people, who lost land in 1920, remain suspicious of the actions and motives of the other villagers from Thaweni Tribal Authority. The fact that of the sixteen members of the Mkambati Land Trust only four come from Khanyayo is further ammunition for the mistrust between the two sides. Conflict with the other villagers has been one of the key reasons the Mkambati claim was delayed for many years (Kepe, Wynberg, and Ellis 2005), with the Khanyayo arguing that they should be the sole beneficiaries of the successful land claim and the other villagers arguing that they too should benefit. With all this mistrust and conflict, it is unlikely that comanagement of Mkambati Nature Reserve, which originates from a disputed land claim, would achieve the stated goals. It is important to note that this mistrust or dispute among local people around land claims is not uncommon in South Africa. In some of the well-publicized land claims, such as the Greater St. Lucia Wetland Park in KwaZulu-Natal (Ashley and Freimund 2006) and Kruger National Park in Limpopo (Robins and van der Waal in this volume), internal disputes among local people characterized both the pre- and postsettlement phases of the claim.

The third condition for successful comanagement in Berkes (1997, 6) is that of "legal protection of local rights." In the case of Mkambati, with the certificate of landownership for the Mkambati Nature Reserve in the hands of the Mkambati Land Trust, there should have been minimal concerns. However, two key issues remain unresolved. The first is that—as De Villiers (1999) and others (Magome and Murombedzi 2003; Kepe, Wynberg, and Ellis 2005) have argued—despite successful land claims in protected areas, land tenure rights tend to remain fuzzy in these comanagement arrangements. With land tenure reform not yet implemented in rural areas of South Africa, despite the passing of the Communal Land Rights Act of 2004, it is not clear what the nature of local rights is, as well as what legal recourse local people can take should they feel their rights are infringed. The second issue relates to natural resource use by local people. New legislation and policies on the environment do not explicitly address the rights of local people's access to and control over natural resources (Kepe, Wynberg, and Ellis 2005). For example, considering the history of the "fences-and-fines" model of conservation that has existed in Mkambati for more than one hundred years, it is unclear how the rights of ownership to the reserve land would affect the use of natural resources by local people, and what they could do should they face prosecution.

The fourth condition for successful comanagement in Berkes (1997, 6) is that there should be "economic incentives for local communities to conserve the resource." Given that the very motivation for comanagement is a "concern" for the sustainability of natural resources that are threatened by local users and that one of the key goals is to reverse that situation, it can be argued that comanagement of natural resources seeks less, rather than increased, use of a resource. More often than not, comanagement between the state and the locals tends to involve poor people (Berkes 1997; Hara and Nielsen 2003; Plummer and FitzGibbon 2004). If care is not taken, both these facts mean that comanagement has the potential to leave people worse off, in the sense that the poorest of the poor who might have depended on the "threatened" resources would have to look elsewhere for livelihoods. According to Berkes (1997), comanagement is likely to be successful if there are economic incentives for the local poor to be involved. With Mkambati Nature Reserve being only about seven thousand hectares, but having about six thousand households looking upon it as a key source of their complex and diverse livelihoods, its natural resource base can clearly not support the potential demand. Hence for the last three decades many attempts have been made to turn many coastal areas in the former Transkei, including Mkambati Nature Reserve, into tourist attractions that can generate income for local people (Kepe 2001b). Over the last fourteen years Mkambati Nature Reserve became one of the focal points for a government-initiated ecotourism program, under the banner of the spatial development initiatives program. The government's strategy was to provide infrastructure and create conditions for private sector investment in the formerly marginalized rural areas. However, despite great strides in the provision of infrastructure, private sector investment in ecotourism has not been forthcoming (Kepe 2001a, 2004). Yet the publicized anchor in the Mkambati comanagement agreement, following the resolution of the land claim, is that the landowners will get a share of all revenues from future tourism investment. This is a clear incentive for local people to be content with keeping their returned land a nature reserve, but it is surrounded by many uncertainties: the lack of enthusiasm from potential investors, the sheer numbers of local people who would need to share the revenue, and the absence of strong local institutions to manage equitable distribution of revenues among the local poor. It appears unlikely, then, that the existing conditions create sufficient economic incentives for local users to conserve the resource.

In addition to these four key conditions for successful comanagement described by Berkes (1997), researchers have suggested two further issues that are relevant to the use of comanagement to reconcile land restitution and conservation, which are not mutually exclusive. These are the existence of a common vision among the stakeholders and the willingness of local users to contribute (Plummer and FitzGibbon 2004). The argument here is that if the different stakeholders or partners in a comanagement arrangement have a common vision, there are more chances that all parties, including local people, will contribute toward a common goal. However, although the Mkambati settlement agreement makes a claim of this common vision, the history of the land conflict in the area proves otherwise. Illegal hunting, theft of thatch grass and medicinal plants (Kepe 1997), forceful occupation of buildings (Cousins and Kepe 2004), and burning of forests (Kepe 2005) in Mkambati by local people show that the visions for the use of Mkambati and its surroundings have differed between the local people and government agencies. Local people did all these things in the process of making a living or as a way of showing their dissatisfaction with having been denied their rights to land and natural resources (Kepe 2005). In contrast, government agencies' vision for Mkambati was that of an area conserved for its high levels of biodiversity and ecotourism potential (De Villiers and Costello 2006). Currently there is no evidence that there is a genuine common vision for the future of Mkambati. There is also no evidence of concrete attempts to ensure that this vision exists before embarking on a comanagement arrangement.

AMBIGUITY OF LAND CLAIM SETTLEMENT AGREEMENTS

In addition to the challenges facing comanagement as a key strategy for dealing with land claims in protected areas, the settlement agreements arguably also present a formidable challenge. Almost all the settlement agreements of land claims involving protected areas are similar, and this approach has now been confirmed in a memorandum of agreement between the Ministry of Agriculture and Land Affairs and that of Environmental Affairs and Tourism (Ministry of Agriculture and Land Affairs 2007). Despite the much publicized handover ceremonies and the handing over of a certificate of ownership to the successful claimants, the comanagement model that is currently in use tends to leave land tenure rights unclear (De Villiers 1999; Magome and Murombedzi 2003; Kepe, Wynberg, and Ellis 2005). Besides the fact that the successful claimants undertake to keep the land under conservation, the wording of the documents tends to exacerbate the confusion about land and resource tenure rights.

There are several examples of this. First, in the Mkambati settlement agreement, the section titled "Management Framework" declares that the Provincial Department of Economic Affairs, Environment and Tourism "is the management authority" of the reserve. Second, the section titled "Management of the Reserve" states that the "Department of Land Affairs in collaboration with its delegated management authority, namely the Provincial Department of Economic Affairs, Environment and Tourism, shall assume responsibility for the management, continued use and further development of the Reserve area." These two clauses alone contain enough controversy in terms of land tenure rights to pose a threat to the agreement in the future. The use of the phrase "management authority," at least on paper, seems to reinforce the suspicion that the comanagement arrangement is at best based on inequality, with the state agency being or having a form of "authority" and the successful claimants merely referred to as the "communities" or the "Community Trust." Although the state agency is arguably well positioned to play a significant role in managing the reserve, the "authority" aspect seems to go against the principle of a comanagement arrangement that is based on equality and flexibility.

Another potential problem with the two clauses above is the fact that the DLA delegates "management authority" and "shall assume responsibility for the management . . . of the Reserve Area" (sec. 10.1). Questions could be asked, such as: To whom does the land belong? What powers do the successful claimants have as legal owners? The settlement agreement is full of numerous other ambiguous statements that may come to threaten the comanagement arrangement, but these deserve a separate analysis that is beyond the scope of this chapter. It seems to make sense that a partnership such as comanagement of a protected area between the well-resourced and educated former owners (state authorities) and the poorly resourced, less educated new owners should be as clear, fair, and equitable as it possibly can. Currently, at least in the case of Mkambati, there is a lot of room for improvement.

This discussion of ambiguity in land claim settlement agreements in protected areas would not be complete without acknowledging the nature of negotiations between the different affected parties prior to the actual agreement. This concerns the "decision" by claimants to keep the "returned" land under conservation. In all the documents reviewed for this paper relating to land claim settlements in protected areas there is an unmistakable impression that all the claimants in these cases have agreed to keep the land under conservation. For example, on 6 July 2007 the minister of agriculture and land affairs, Lulama Xingwana, in a speech to the beneficiaries of a land claim in a protected area (Barokologadi Ba Ga Maotwe), reminded the claimants that "you have elected to continue with the current land use [conservation]" (Xingwana 2007a, 2). In another earlier handover celebration of a land claim in a protected area (Hlabisa-Mpukunyoni Community), the same minister said, "I have been told that this community has decided to support bio-diversity and conservation.... You have agreed to the restoration of this land title to you, without your physical occupation of the land. You have decided that this park will be managed in terms of the Protected Areas management plan, in line with the environmental legislation. This is commendable as it fits in snugly with the international debates on "people and parks" (Xingwana 2007b, 4). Although it cannot be disputed that poor, rural land claimants may well choose, out of their own will, to give up their recently acquired land for conservation, there are reasons to doubt that there is always consensus on such issues. First, given what is known about the heterogeneity of rural communities (Li 1996), as well as direct observations in places such as Mkambati, it is doubtful that all the claimants would have the same vision of land use for the area. Kepe and Scoones (1999), for example, have provided detailed examples of how local people's visions of ideal landscapes are rarely consistent and how they change over time, depending on several axes of social difference (e.g., wealth, gender, and location of settlements). Thus a reference such as "this community has decided" (Xingwana 2007b, 4) is likely a misrepresentation of actual reality. Second, in many land claims in protected areas local people had a history of contravening protected areas' regulations, through "illegal" use of natural resources in these areas. Even though this "illegal" use had to do with passive resistance, whereby local people wanted to assert their rights to the areas by contravening state regulations, there is little doubt that this use of protected areas served an important function in people's livelihoods, with Mkambati (Kepe 2001a) and Dwesa-Cwebe nature reserves (Ntshona, Kraai, and Nomatyindyo 2006) serving as good examples of this. It is therefore unlikely that when people get their land back, the livelihood needs that were previously fulfilled by the protected area simply cease to exist, especially in the case of the poorest of the local community.

Land claim settlement agreements rarely reflect the complexities of the preceding negotiations, whereby the negotiating local elite, seeing opportunities for themselves, may enter into agreements with state agencies that do not necessarily reflect the needs of the majority (Kepe 2004). Similarly, the role played by hegemonic conservation discourses, with the help of state officials who are part of the negotiations, is not widely known by those who are not part of the negotiations. It is therefore critical that assumptions about the transparency and authenticity of the agreements be understood in the light of nuances of the negotiations that precede the land claim settlement.

In this chapter I have argued that the current comanagement model being encouraged and implemented by the state (Ministry of Agriculture and Land Affairs 2007) is not appropriate to meet land restitution and conservation goals (see also Magome and Murombedzi 2003; Kepe, Wynberg, and Ellis 2005). The case study of comanagement in Mkambati demonstrates unresolved tensions in attempts to deal with land claims in protected areas. First, there is the issue of limited models for resolving land claims in protected areas. Although it should be appreciated that biodiversity conservation is a national and international imperative, the current comanagement model has emphasized conservation interests over the land rights of claimants. If this is the case, then land reform as a key government policy faces more challenges, perhaps including its very legitimacy among claimants and within certain government agencies.

Second, even if comanagement were a suitable model for reconciling land claims and conservation, the apparent neglect of factors that make comanagement work in other situations is strange, to say the least. There are possibly many reasons for the neglect of these preconditions, but the one most relevant here is the inability of conservation agencies to deal with such complex matters. The Mkambati case and others have shown that the respective conservation authorities often take the lead role in negotiating with local communities following the settlement of the claim. Yet many of the issues that are being neglected, such as the absence of appropriate institutions and legal protection of local rights, need to be dealt with at other levels in government. The question is: Why are these not addressed? The answer may lie in the possibility that South Africa's new democracy is still battling with coordinating its policy implementation mandate. But it is clear that if comanagement is to have any meaningful chance to reconcile land rights and biodiversity conservation, then there is a need to invest in thinking about a new model that genuinely considers issues of appropriate power-sharing arrangements that give landowners more say.

Third, given the high levels of ambiguity in settlement agreements in land claims affecting protected areas, it can be speculated that the ambiguities serve the interests of certain constituencies, including state agencies. It may be that the relevant state agency does not know how to deal with the situation properly or that the agency knows that there are problems but hopes that the ambiguity could provide a loophole in the future should things not work according to plan. Another way of looking at how ambiguity may serve the state is the apparent disjuncture in the country's Constitution, where both land rights and biodiversity conservation are enshrined, but without any clarity on which of the two has priority over the other. Berkes and Henley (1997, 29) have argued that crisis-based comanagement is "an *ad hoc,* and possibly temporary policy response to crisis." It would appear that the current comanagement in claimed protected areas does qualify as being crisis-based comanagement. What remains to be seen is whether the crisis is about a threat to natural resources or a threat to the state from people who seek to regain their land rights. If nothing changes in the long run, it would appear that the crisis could indeed be about a threat to all—biodiversity, human rights, and the state.

NOTES

1. This chapter is an adapted version of an article of the same title that was published in *Environmental Management* 41 (3) (2008): 311–21). It is reproduced here with kind permission of Springer Science and Business Media. I thank Ruth Hall, Cherryl Walker, and the three independent reviewers for useful comments on earlier drafts of this paper. I am grateful to the Norwegian Centre for Human Rights for financial support that allowed me to do fieldwork. I take responsibility for all the views presented here.

2. Eastern Cape Parks Board has since changed its name to Eastern Cape Parks.

REFERENCES

Ashley, L., and W. Freimund. 2006. "Land Restitution and Protected Area Conservation in KwaZulu-Natal: The Challenge of "Ownership." Paper presented at the conference Land, Memory, Reconstruction and Justice: Perspectives on Land Restitution in South Africa. Houw Hoek, 13–15 September.

Berkes, F. 1997. "New and Not-So-New Directions in the Use of the Commons: Co-management." *The Common Property Resource Digest* 42 (March): 5–7.

Berkes, F., and T. Henley. 1997. "Co-management and Traditional Knowledge: Threat or Opportunity?" *Policy Options* 18 (2): 29–31.

Boonzaier, E. 1996. "Local Responses to Conservation in the Richtersveld National Park, South Africa." *Biodiversity and Conservation* 5 (3): 307–14.

Briers, J. H., M. Powell, J. M. Feely, and P. M. Norton. 1996. "Identification and Preliminary Evaluation of Potential Conservation Areas along the Pondoland

Coast." Ministry of Economic Affairs, Environment and Tourism, Directorate of Nature Conservation, Port Elizabeth, South Africa.

Cape Town Archives. Volume 1 LSK, File 13/2/5/2: Mkambati Leper Institution—Reservation of Site.

Cock, J., and D. Fig. 2000. "From Colonial to Community-based Conservation: Environmental Justice and the National Parks of South Africa." *Society in Transition* 31 (1): 22–35.

Cousins, B., and T. Kepe. 2004. "Decentralisation When Land and Resource Rights Are Deeply Contested: A Case Study of the Mkambati Eco-tourism Project on the Wild Coast of South Africa." *European Journal of Development Research* 16 (1): 41–54.

DLA (Department of Land Affairs). 2002. "Principles That Would Guide Settlement of Restitution of Land Claims in Proclaimed Protected Areas." Pretoria: Department of Land Affairs.

De Villiers, B. 1999. *Land Claims and National Parks: The Makuleke Experience.* Cape Town: HSRC Press.

De Villiers, D., and J. Costello. 2006. *Mkambati and the Wild Coast: South Africa and Pondoland's Unique Heritage.* Singapore: Tien Wah Press.

Hara, M., and J. R. Nielsen. 2003. "Experiences with Fisheries Co-management in Africa." In *The Fisheries Co-management Experience: Accomplishments, Challenges and Prospects,* ed. D. C. Wilson, J. R. Nielsen, and P. Degnbol. Dordrecht, Netherlands: Kluwer Academic.

Hauck, M., and M. Sowman. 2001. "Coastal and Fisheries Co-management in South Africa: An Overview and Analysis." *Marine Policy* 25 (3): 171–85.

———, eds. 2003. *Waves of Change: Coastal and Fisheries Management in South Africa.* Cape Town: University of Cape Town Press.

IUCN (International Union for Conservation of Nature). 1998. "Workshop on Land Claims on Conservation Land." Record of Proceedings, 3–4 September 1998, Aloe Ridge Hotel, Gauteng, South Africa.

Jentoft, S. 2003. "Co-management: The Way Forward." In *The Fisheries Co-management Experience: Accomplishments, Challenges and Prospects,* ed. D. C. Wilson, J. R. Nielsen, and P. Degnbol. Dordrecht, Netherlands: Kluwer Academic.

Kepe, T. 1997. "Communities, Entitlements and Nature Reserves: The Case of the Wild Coast, South Africa." *IDS Bulletin* 28 (4): 47–58.

———. 2001a. "Waking Up from the Dream: The Pitfalls of 'Fast-Track' Development on the Wild Coast of South Africa." Bellville: Programme for Land and Agrarian Studies, University of the Western Cape (Research Report no. 8).

———. 2001b. "Tourism, Protected Areas and Development in South Africa: Views of Visitors to Mkambati Nature Reserve." *South African Journal of Wildlife Research* 31 (3) and (4): 155–59.

———. 2004. "Land Restitution and Biodiversity Conservation in South Africa: The Case of Mkambati, Eastern Cape Province." *Canadian Journal of African Studies* 38 (3): 688–704.

———. 2005. "Grasslands Ablaze: Vegetation Burning by Rural People in Pondoland, South Africa." *South African Geographical Journal* 87 (1): 10–17.

Kepe, T., B. Cousins, and S. Turner. 2001. "Resource Tenure and Power Relations in Community Wildlife: The Case of Mkambati Area, South Africa." *Society and Natural Resources* 14 (10): 911–25.

Kepe, T., and I. Scoones. 1999. "Creating Grasslands: Social Institutions and Environmental Change in Mkambati Area, South Africa." *Human Ecology* 27 (1): 29–53.

Kepe, T., R. Wynberg, and W. Ellis. 2005. "Land Reform and Biodiversity Conservation in South Africa: Complementary or in Conflict?" *International Journal of Biodiversity Science and Management* 1 (1): 3–16.

Li, T. M. 1996. "Images of Community: Discourse and Strategy in Property Relations." *Development and Change* 27 (3): 501–27.

Lukhele, L. 2007. Personal Communication. E-mail to author, 14 August 2007.

Magome, H., and J. Murombedzi. 2003. "Sharing South African National Parks: Community Land and Conservation in a Democratic South Africa." In *Decolonizing Nature: Strategies for Conservation in a Post-colonial Era*, ed. W. M. Adams and M. Mulligan. London: Earthscan.

Ministry of Agriculture and Land Affairs. 2007. "Memorandum of Agreement between the Minister of Agriculture and Land Affairs and the Minister of Environmental Affairs and Tourism." Pretoria: Ministry of Agriculture and Land Affairs.

Morrison, J. 1997. "Protected Areas, Conservationists and Aboriginal Interests in Canada." In *Social Change and Conservation: Environmental Politics and Impacts of National Parks and Protected Areas*, ed. K. B. Ghimire and M. P. Pimbert. London: Earthscan.

Nel, M. 2003. "The Extraordinary Floral Riches of Pondoland: Working towards a 'Pondo Park.'" *Veld and Flora* 89: 96–99.

Ntsebeza, L. 2005. *Democracy Compromised: Chiefs and the Politics of Land in South Africa*. Leiden: Brill Academic.

Ntshona, Z., M. Kraai, and N. Nomatyindyo. 2006. "Rights Enshrined but Rights Denied? Post-settlement Struggles in Dwesa-Cebe in the Eastern Cape." Paper presented at the conference Land, Memory, Reconstruction and Justice: Perspectives on Land Restitution in South Africa, Houw Hock, 13–15 September.

Parker, G. 2004. "The Challenge of Sustainable Land-based Local Economic Development in Poor Communities of South Africa: The Case of Groblershoop, Northern Cape." MPhil thesis, University of the Western Cape, South Africa.

Plummer, R., and J. FitzGibbon. 2004. "Co-management of Natural Resources: A Proposed Framework." *Environmental Management* 33 (6): 876–85.

———. 2006. "People Matter: The Importance of Social Capital in the Co-management of Natural Resources." *Natural Resources Forum* 30 (1): 51–62.

Pomeroy, R. S., and F. Berkes. 1997. "Two to Tango: The Role of Government in Fisheries Co-management." *Marine Policy* 21 (5): 465–80.

Reid, H., D. Fig, H. Magome, and N. Leader-Williams. 2004. "Co-management of Contractual National Parks in South Africa: Lessons from Australia." *Conservation and Society* 2 (2): 377–409.

Songorwa, A. N. 1999. "Community-Based Wildlife Management (CWM) in Tanzania: Are the Communities Interested?" *World Development* 27 (12): 2061–79.

Tinley, K. L. 1978. "Mkambati Nature Reserve: An Ecological and Planning Study." Pretoria: Farrel and van Riet Landscape Architects and Ecological Planners.

Tipa, G., and R. Welch. 2006. "Co-management of Natural Resources: Issues of Definition from an Indigenous Community Perspective." *The Journal of Applied Behavioral Science* 42 (3): 373–91.

Wynberg, R., and T. Kepe. 1999. *Land Reform and Conservation Areas in South Africa—Towards a Mutually Beneficial Approach.* Pretoria: IUCN.

Xingwana, L. 2007a. "Speech for the Land Hand-Over Celebration for the Barokologadi Ba Ga Maotwe Land Claim: North West Province, 06 July." Pretoria: Department of Land Affairs.

———. 2007b. "Speech for the Land Hand-Over Celebration for the Hlabisa-Mpukunyoni Community Claim, Hluhluwe, 08 June: Kwazulu-Natal." Pretoria: Department of Land Affairs.

fourteen

Restitution in Default

Land Claims and the Redevelopment of Cato Manor, Durban

CHERRYL WALKER

The historical Cato Manor of the early 1950s is celebrated in literature and liberation historiography as a symbol of popular resistance to apartheid. Nationally not as iconic in the popular imagination as District Six and Sophiatown, this Durban suburb enjoys a prominent reputation nonetheless. Today the reemerging Cato Manor is also lauded for its contribution to urban renewal in the postapartheid era. In 2002 the Cato Manor Development Association (CMDA) described it thus:

> In the eight years since the end of apartheid, Cato Manor has experienced significant and exciting change across all sectors. Today, around 93,000 people live, work and enjoy a normal life in Cato Manor. New houses, buildings, facilities, roads and engineering works have been and continue to be developed. Cato Manor's economy and its people, especially the urban poor, have benefited from the integrated development process.
>
> The Cato Manor Development Project (CMDP) has achieved worldwide acclaim as a model for integrated development. Within South Africa it has become a model of post-apartheid sustainable urban development practice.

> Once divided by race, Cato Manor's people are being united in a vibrant cross-cultural identity and integrated into the activities and life of the rest of the city of Durban. (CMDA 2002, 1)

Strikingly absent from the public celebration of this area is a serious engagement with its history of land restitution—despite the fact that the forced removals of the apartheid era feature prominently in accounts such as CMDA's above. In this respect the Cato Manor restitution process has followed a notably different trajectory from that in District Six, where despite critical differences among stakeholders, redevelopment is premised on the overriding legitimacy of restitution claims (Beyers, this volume). Given that Cato Manor involved one of the largest sets of individual land claims lodged with the Commission on Restitution of Land Rights (CRLR) nationally, this reticence is even more surprising.

Taking this apparent anomaly as the starting point for this chapter, first I write the history of restitution back into the post-1994 reconstruction of Cato Manor, and, second, I highlight the significance of this history for an assessment of the larger restitution program.[1] I suggest the metaphor of "default" as a useful way for thinking about this case. "Default" is a multilayered term pointing not only to the failure to perform or honor a commitment (to default on a debt) but also, in the language of computers, to an underlying operating system that prevails if alternatives are not actively supported. Although I use the term primarily in its dictionary definition as a "failure in performance" or "an imperfection, defect, blemish, flaw,"[2] I also use it to invoke the sense of underlying forces shaping the outcome. I am not suggesting that the metaphor applies to the restitution program as a whole, but I am arguing that an understanding of the dynamics in Cato Manor is important for that larger analysis.

My discussion is organized as follows. The first three sections provide brief overviews of the history of the area, the struggles of the early 1990s over its future, and the outcome of the land claims process. The fourth section then explores the idea of restitution in default across several intersecting themes that find echoes in other chapters in this volume. The first theme concerns the way in which urban claims dictated much of the CRLR's agenda in its critical first term (1995–2000), despite the lack of attention to urban removals in the design of the restitution program. This disconnect not only had negative implications for urban claims, caught as they were in a policy gap, but also negatively affected rural restitution, which found itself crowded off the CRLR's agenda in practice if not in principle in this critical period. A second theme is the very limited way in which the public interest in restitution has been integrated with other public goods since 1994, in this case low-cost housing for the urban poor. A third is the failure of the restitution program to develop alternative forms of redress for the nonmaterial dimensions of dispossession. In the case of Cato Manor these shortcomings manifested themselves in a contest that erupted between land restitution on the one hand and housing delivery on the other, a contest in which the latter emerged as dominant, trumping the land claims of former landowners and other residents. One consequence is that the redevelopment of the area has consolidated, not undermined, the ethnic divisions entrenched in Durban under apartheid.

HISTORICAL BACKGROUND: CATO MANOR TO THE 1960S

The area that is loosely described as Greater Cato Manor covers some eighteen hundred hectares, seven kilometers from Durban's central business district (CMDA 2002, 2). At the time that it was proclaimed a white group area in 1958 it was a socially diverse cluster of overlapping settlements—formal, semiformal, and informal—that had rooted themselves over the course of the twentieth century on the hills beyond the city center. Its total population was estimated at between 100,000 (Fitchet et al. 1997, 9) and 160,000 (SPP 1983, 234).

The name reflects its colonial beginnings in an 1845 land grant to George Cato, who subsequently became Durban's first mayor in 1854. In the late nineteenth century the original farm underwent a process of subdivision, and by the early 1920s Cato Manor had transformed into a peri-urban area where landowners from more marginalized sectors of Durban were establishing new communities. Most were market gardeners of Indian descent, but there were small numbers of African landowners who had acquired plots before the 1913 Natives Land Act shut off such opportunities. In 1932 the area was incorporated into the Durban municipality. Settlement patterns became denser as many landowners turned to leasing their land to tenants (primarily but not exclusively African). Cato Manor's favorable location near the city center and port, its relative autonomy from state control, and the general lack of black housing in the city—all combined to make it an attractive base for the city's working class.

After the Second World War the pace of informal development accelerated as African urbanization gathered momentum. Some sections developed into dense, unserviced settlements that alarmed the local authority—as public health threats, but also as centers of subversive political activism and unregulated economic activity, including illegal beer-brewing by women. Other parts retained a market-garden character, whereas the area around Mayville developed into a more formal and relatively self-sufficient urban space, with its "own schools, shops and bazaars, temples, churches and mosques" as well as "social and sporting amenities" (Govender 1996, 11).

The "Durban riots" of 1949 had a huge impact on the social landscape of Cato Manor, just as the advent of apartheid was posing new threats. Previously an area where Africans and Indians had coexisted in relative, if not unproblematic, harmony, Cato Manor was convulsed by two days of anti-Indian violence that led many Indian families to flee the area altogether and sharpened ethnic polarization around the future development of the area. In intriguing ways landowner responses then prefigured restitution debates in the 1990s:

> In the wake of the riots, the Cato Manor Ratepayers' Association at first called for repatriation of Africans from Cato Manor, the institution of curfews on them, and a ban on the construction of shacks. The 1950 annual conference on the Natal Indian Congress "opposed the expropriation of Indian-owned [but not in fact occupied] land in Cato Manor for the purpose of a temporary African housing scheme" only to agree to such a scheme a year later because "if the shack development in Cato Manor is not checked, then the shack settlements will overflow into adjacent areas now occupied by Indians." (Freund 1995, 70)

During the 1950s the Durban City Council intensified efforts to assert its authority over what it regarded as an increasingly unruly area. By 1950 the number of shacks had grown to 6,000, housing 45,000 to 50,000 people (Maharaj and Makhathini 2004, 30). The authorities responded by instituting an Emergency Camp for African residents on expropriated land in the vicinity of the Mkhumbane river, some of it abandoned in the wake of the 1949 riots. Then, in 1958, Cato Manor and eight other racially mixed suburbs of Durban were proclaimed white group areas (SPP 1983, 227–28). By then landownership was divided almost equally between Indians on the one hand (48 percent of the area)[3] and whites and the city council on the other (28 percent and 22 percent respectively). People classified as African constituted two-thirds of the population but a tiny proportion (2 percent) of landowners (Fitchet et al. 1997, 9).

The enforcement of the apartheid vision took several years to effect. State land acquisition took the form of expropriation or forced sales with the state the only buyer. Officials used a complex formula to calculate compensation for landowners, resulting in a process that, in the careful words of a 1997 panel of valuers, "falls short of what today would be regarded as just and equitable compensation. . . . That [compensation] might have succeeded in certain cases could only have been the result of coincidence or tenacious litigation by claimants. . . . With few exceptions, mute acceptance or acceptance due to financial duress was the common response" (Fitchet et al. 1997, 3).

By the mid-1960s almost all the black residents of Cato Manor were gone. Those classified as Indian were moved mainly to Chatsworth and Phoenix, two new group area townships on the fringes of Durban's white suburbia. Those classified as African were officially relocated beyond the formal boundaries of the city altogether, into the new townships of Umlazi and KwaMashu being built on land designated within the emergent bantustan of KwaZulu. However, many Umkhumbane residents "disappeared" from official view into the margins of the city or beyond.

For the next twenty-five years Cato Manor stood largely vacant, apart from isolated properties where former owners clung tenaciously to their land as tenants of the city. In the early 1980s the Surplus People Project (SPP) (1983, 234) put this group at some five hundred Indian families. The University of Natal bought a substantial piece, but for the most part the state struggled to sell land to approved (i.e., white) buyers other than the city council. Former landowners strongly resisted efforts to redevelop Cato Manor as a white group area, forming the Cato Manor Residents' Association in 1979 and lobbying for the return of their land throughout the 1980s. In 1979, partly in response to this sustained lobbying, the state rezoned a small section as an Indian group area, on which a housing project was built. Thus most of Cato Manor remained state land. Over time the numerous small plots making up the previous cadastre were consolidated into much larger properties, and the earlier history of landownership was erased.

CONTESTED SPACE: CATO MANOR IN THE EARLY 1990S

The transition to democracy triggered three major interventions around the future of this large swath of now undeveloped land within the inner core of the city.

The first was a series of land invasions by extralegal settlers, with significant local political backing from the recently unbanned African National Congress (ANC).[4] By 1992 there were an estimated one thousand shacks in the area (Makhathini 1994, 56); three years later the number of residents classified as "informally housed" had increased to "at least" twenty-eight thousand (CMDA 2002, 3). According to the CMDA (2002, 3) "roughly 50% . . . had been displaced by violence" whereas others "were seeking accommodation closer to employment centres." Their leaders and sympathetic officials boosted their legitimacy by emphasizing that significant numbers had historic ties to the area.

Makhathini (1994, 56, 57) has described the "squatter invasion" of Cato Manor as "quite distinct from those on the peripheries of Durban," involving "staged, selective invasions of pockets of land" that "seem[ed] to coincide with periods of intense instability on the city periphery" but were also precipitated by "township overcrowding, changes in the political climate, and skewed distribution of resources." He described how the "constant threat of demolition . . . result[ed] in a desire to multiply and become a strong united front" and consolidated a sense of community and entitlement. Successive rounds of negotiations between the authorities and the strong men who emerged as community leaders led to the official numbering of shacks, with very different meanings for the different players: "For the authorities they are a means of control and identification, while for squatters they signify legitimacy and a degree of permanence. The numbers represent the transition to the open stage of squatting, and are a public statement of their victory" (Makhathini 1994, 57).

The second intervention was a major redevelopment initiative that the Transitional Metropolitan Council of Durban (later renamed the eThekwini municipality) launched under the auspices of the CMDA in 1993. The CMDA was established after several years of negotiations involving local government and civil society. In 2002 its primary objective was described as "the creation of an efficient and productive 'city-within-a-city' aimed mainly at the poor and the marginalised . . . through the provision of affordable housing and security of tenure . . . and the integration of Cato Manor into the eThekwini Municipality—spatially, politically, economically and socially" (CMDA 2002, 4).

This redevelopment program had strong national and international backing. Designated a Presidential Lead Project in 1995, it drew substantial international donor support, in particular from the European Union.

CMDA's core staff consisted of a cohort of progressive urban planners (mainly white), who were subjected to "a severe baptism of fire" as they battled a "seemingly endless series of challenges . . . related to staffing and capacity; land claims; invasion of land and houses; and a loss of confidence in CMDA" (Robinson and Forster 2004, 63). They worked with a spatial planning framework that was informed by a metropolitan overview and the urgency of economies of scale. Although their vision of a future Cato Manor invoked social values, project targets were cast in concrete and quantifiable terms: twenty-five thousand housing units and twenty-five thousand permanent jobs (CMDA 2002, 4).

This was not a context receptive to deviations from tightly managed plans; it did not easily accommodate the individual or the intangible. From the beginning the CMDA regarded the residents of the informal settlements as its primary constituency. The relentless pressure to manage huge infrastructural projects in impoverished, politically volatile, and violence-wracked communities, within the regulatory frameworks set by donor and state funding, relegated any additional demands to the sidelines, from where they could become threats to the agency's success. In the early 1990s this was how land restitution came to be seen. For the CMDA, land claims were something to be neutralized as quickly as possible to prevent the disruption of its structure plan and project cycles. Claimants also tended to be stereotyped as members of a politically conservative, relatively wealthy, relatively privileged section of society (i.e., Indian and middle class), who were far less deserving of state attention than the new settlers.

In 1993 a group of 419 dispossessed landowners lodged land claims for Cato Manor and neighboring Bellair with the de Klerk government's Commission on Land Allocation (COLA) (CRLR 1996, 17). This precipitated vigorous objections from the Durban City Council on behalf of CMDA: "If the Association were to be required to re-purchase the land from the previous owners . . . the whole scheme [of low-cost housing] would be jeopardized" (quoted in COLA 1993, 4). In response COLA made an ineffectual recommendation that the parties should attempt to negotiate a settlement among themselves, whereby former owners should be given "preference" to acquire land within the framework of CMDA's plan (COLA 1993, 5). Then, in early 1994, as the outline of the postapartheid restitution program began to take shape, CMDA took the lead in lobbying the drafters of the Restitution Act to include a clause—later section 34 of the act—that would enable state bodies to apply to the Land Claims Court (LCC) to rule out restoring land to claimants in areas under their jurisdiction, when such an order was deemed to be in the public interest.

This was the context for the third major intervention around the future of Cato Manor, one couched in the language of land restitution. In early 1995, the year the CMDA initiative was declared a Presidential Lead Project, the regional land claims commissioner (RLCC) for KwaZulu-Natal opened her office in Pietermaritzburg, some eighty kilometers away. Like the CMDA, the CRLR was under immense pressure from the start. Its regional office was launched initially without staff or operational policies but with an inherited backlog of unresolved COLA claims, as well as extremely high expectations of restitution on the part not only of land claimants but also the broader public.

From the start Cato Manor dominated the RLCC's agenda in the province. By May 1998 a total of 6,639 of the approximately 7,000 claims lodged in KwaZulu-Natal were urban, of which 4,871 were for greater Durban and 3,412 for Cato Manor alone—that is, at that stage Cato Manor accounted for half the claims in the province and 70 percent of Durban claims (Walker 2008, 157). By the time the 1998 deadline for lodging claims was reached, Cato Manor claims had risen to approximately 5,000, or one-third of all claims lodged in KwaZulu-Natal. They were divided between some 2,000 former landowner families, mostly but not exclusively of Indian descent, and 3,000 former tenant families, mostly but not exclusively of African descent (CRLR 2000, 16). For the most part claimants constituted a geographically dispersed, socially fragmented agglomeration of people, with little to bridge their different histories and identities. Only a minority were organized—the group of former landowners who had long been campaigning for the return of their land and were well placed to dominate the forums in which claimant interests were now articulated.

This group, constituted as the Cato Manor Action Group, subsequently formed a significant block of claimants in the negotiations around the place of restitution in the redevelopment of Cato Manor. They and their lawyers adopted a rigid understanding of claimant rights and were deeply hostile to the development agenda of the CMDA, which they regarded as having cruelly preempted their prospects for land restoration at the last moment; not only were their claims legally and morally compelling, but they had been fully feasible in the early 1990s, when much of Cato Manor was still unoccupied. For many former landowners, the post-1994 restitution process was an opportunity to restore more than family rights to land. It was also an opportunity to restore a former community and its historical and cultural authority over the area. Whereas the new settlers asserted their claims in the present, and the CMDA projected an imagined future made tangible in the form of maps and plans and tables of data, these claimants looked back to a particular reconstruction of the past, for which indisputable evidence could still be found in the abandoned streets and rundown buildings scattered across the hillsides and encroaching shack settlements.

This was the community lamented by the writer, Ronnie Govender, in a poem in a 1996 collection of short stories from his youth:

> no more Discovery Road
> no more Trimborne Road
> no more hopscotch
> no more ripe mangoes from Thumba's yard
> Cato Manor, you have done your penance
> amid crumpled eviction notices.[5]

RESTITUTION: THE SECTION 34 COURT APPLICATION

In June 1996 the CMDA served notice on the RLCC of a court application in terms of section 34 of the Restitution Act. This precipitated a head-on clash between the formal restitution process and the redevelopment ambitions of the informal settlers (who were rapidly consolidating their presence), the CMDA, and their backers in the local authority. Yet although the contestation was played out formally through a courtroom drama, a much wider constellation of social forces underpinned its outcome.

An immediate challenge for the CRLR was to ensure that as many potential claimants as possible were aware of the restitution process so that they might identify themselves as "interested parties" in the case. In February 1996 the RLCC launched a campaign calling on all potential Cato Manor claimants to lodge claims within the next three (later five) months. Whereas CMDA was required to serve notice of its case on all identified claimants, the responsibility for locating them and then assisting them with their applications (if they wished), including through the provision of legal aid, fell to the RLCC.

In this time some 2,000 new claims were lodged, bringing the total for Cato Manor to 2,765 by late 1996 (CRLR 1996, 16) and "placing considerable strain on the RLCC's personnel and resources" (CRLR 1997a, 56). However, in the end less than 10 percent of the final number of Cato Manor claimants—a total of 434 former residents, both landowners and tenants—formally objected to the application when legal proceedings began in November 1996.[6] They were represented by twelve different legal firms, among them the public-interest Campus Law Clinic, which represented a quarter of the claimants and played an important facilitative role in the subsequent negotiations.

The ensuing court hearing was an adversarial and emotional affair, made still more complicated by the number of legal firms involved and the "winner takes all" approach of lawyers on both sides of the table. From the start the legal process accentuated disparities in power and vision. The Cato Manor Action Group split into two main factions, one of which adopted a legal strategy that was particularly hostile to any suggestion that claimants should acknowledge the legitimacy of the new settlers' demands for inclusion in the redevelopment of the area. For its part, the CMDA was impatient with the objectors, at one stage applying for legal costs against them although subsequently backing down. It was also frustrated by the inability of the RLCC to supply it with speedy, accurate information about the claimants, the validity of their claims, and the precise location of their lots on its reconfigured cadastre. The CMDA regarded its application as an "elegant solution" to the threat of land claims (Cole, Smyly, and Hazel 2004, 395), but the RLCC was critical of the way it glossed over the history of the Group Areas Act and presumed "that the argument for low-cost housing speaks for itself" (CRLR 1996, 27). The RLCC report to the LCC urged CMDA to affirm restitution "as a matter of major public interest" and commit to "the possibilities for accommodation of . . . claims for restoration within the development framework" (CRLR 1996, 39, 29).

As the limitations of the court process for resolving the contestation became increasingly apparent, the parties agreed to enter into negotiations, which finally resulted in an agreement that became an order of court in April 1997 (LCC 15/96). In terms of this the CMDA agreed to review its structure plan to determine whether it was feasible to restore the land rights of each of the 434 claimants before the court; where the parties disagreed, they were committed to a compulsory process of mediation and arbitration facilitated by the RLCC.

For the court this was a happy recognition of two expressions of the public interest that were, thereby, merged into one:

> In determining what was in the public interest in this matter, it was taken as almost axiomatic that, given the history of dispossession in Cato Manor and the resultant devastation and hardship suffered by the removed community, restoration would be in the public interest. Blanket restoration in the area would, however, have necessitated a refusal of the section 34 application and the resultant loss of the development. So, against the advantages to the public interest of restoration there had to be weighed and balanced the advantages to the public interest of development. . . . [which] include: (a) the provision of affordable housing for the disadvantaged communities of Greater Durban near places of potential employment; (b) the opportunities for employment as a result of the development; (c) the upgrading of informal settlements; (d) foreign investment; (e) economic upliftment of the greater Durban area with the possibility of spilling over into the entire KwaZulu-Natal area; (f) obviating potential violent strife between the informally settled communities and land claimants. (LCC 15/96)

The judges were, however, careful not to pronounce conclusively on "the meaning to be given to the concept of public interest in section 34," as this was not argued in the case (LCC 15/96).

At the time the CMDA, the RLCC, and eleven of the twelve claimant lawyers also hailed the agreement as a genuine attempt to balance "the rights of the historically dispossessed and the imperatives of development."[7] However, the mediation process turned out to be yet another protracted, bad-tempered, and costly affair, further complicated by an ultimately unsuccessful court challenge by lawyers representing 178 hardliners in the Cato Manor Action Group, in which the city, the RLCC and the minister of land affairs were all cited as respondents (LCC 9/98). A 1998 consultants' report noted how "in most mediations the CMDA has not been prepared to concede that restoration is feasible" (Bosch 1998, 3), leading to frequent deadlock.

The outcome saw just twenty-two claimants winning the formal right to restoration of their land, of whom only seven finally decided to proceed with that option (Cole, Smyly, and Hazel 2004, 400). A group of approximately one hundred former tenants who had not been party to the original section 34 application were subsequently incorporated into a CMDA housing project by means of a "social clause" that the RLCC and Campus Law Clinic had managed to tag onto the main section 34 agreement. But for the overwhelming majority of claimants, including objectors to the initial court application and the several thousand who were never before the LCC, restitution took the form of different levels of financial compensation, depending on the original land right that was claimed. The impact of the restitution process on the reimagining of Cato Manor as a postapartheid urban space has thus proved insignificant.

For the advocates of restitution this outcome was deeply unsatisfactory. Not only was the process extremely costly to the state; it had also not seen a meaningful incorporation of either individual land claims or the larger social reality that they represented into the redevelopment of the area. From the perspective of the CMDA, however, their project was saved. From being "by far the most significant external threat" to their plans in 1996 (Robinson and Forster 2004, 80), by 2003 the land restitution program had become "a really, really small part of the Cato Manor programme . . . much smaller than . . . anybody anticipated" (Forster interview, 2003).

RESTITUTION IN DEFAULT

At its simplest, the metaphor of restitution in default describes the experience of most claimants. Here a failure in performance is fairly easy to demonstrate, even without assuming that the majority of claimants necessarily wanted to return to the Cato Manor of the 1990s. Claimants were initially totally disregarded in the redesign of the area. Subsequently most were also excluded from the formal legal process that set the parameters within which their claims would be processed—even the minority who were before the court were totally, and not always happily, dependent on the expertise, commitment, and integrity of their lawyers to represent them and keep them informed about what was going on.

The shortcomings extended beyond individual claimants, however, to the challenges of how to give content to redress in an area such as Cato Manor, as well as how to engage its fractured past. CMDA's vision of urban integration was a restricted one, more successful in a technical than a social sense, but the CRLR's vision of restitution also faltered in its practical application. As noted elsewhere in this volume, urban claims were never comfortably accommodated within the restitution program in the 1990s, even though major cases such as Cato Manor dominated the work of the CRLR, especially in its first five years, to the detriment of other claims. In 1998 the authors of a ministerial review of the land claims process identified urban restitution as a major reason for the CRLR's problems:

> In the rush to show progress in cases, what was too easily disregarded was the mismatch between the institutional legal and policy framework and the scope and nature of demand. The Restitution programme, originally a programme for land reform, aimed at addressing historical injustice and promoting economic empowerment in South Africa's rural areas, was swiftly overwhelmed by a huge flood of urban restitution claims. According to figures made available by the Commission, urban claims now make up some 85% of the case load of the Commission. This initially unforeseen eventuality is one of the key causes for the frustration experienced in the Restitution Programme. (du Toit et al. n.d., 11)

Although the suggestion that the "eventuality" of urban claims was initially unforeseen is not entirely accurate (see Walker 2008; Cole, Smyly, and Hazel 2004), the general point remains pertinent. The national debate on urban claims was always thin, both in the initial design of the restitution program and the subsequent development of operational policy within the CRLR and the Department of Land Affairs (DLA). Certainly when the CRLR took office in early 1995 it was unprepared for the deluge of urban claims that ensued. Its subsequent response was fragmented across the different regions, cobbled together in a context of crisis, insufficient resources, and a slow-moving national bureaucracy. In the words of Cole, Smyly, and Hazel (2004, 393), "The reality was that the CRLR was thrown headlong into an implementation phase with an act that did not fit an urban reality, that it had no support on urban claims in the DLA, and that it had no guidelines or leadership in place to support and advise an approach to urban claims."

In the case of Cato Manor, the consequences extended to other restitution claims in the region, including rural claims that were overshadowed by the demands of this case on CRLR resources during the formative years of the restitution program. This had negative repercussions for the credibility of the program overall. The Cato Manor process was extremely taxing on the RLCC's office, exacerbating debilitating tensions between it and the office of the chief land claims commissioner (CLCC) about the centralization of authority and management of budgets within the national office. A 1997 report by the RLCC to the CLCC highlighted these problems: "Implementing the Cato Manor Agreement has put this office under pressure and exposed many of the institutional, infrastructural and resource weaknesses of the Commission. I am sure that many of the problems experienced in this office are not unique to it and believe there is an urgent need for the Commission to embark upon a serious evaluation of its structures, management systems, administrative processes, and resource needs" (CRLR 1997b, 2).

The problems derived not simply from the pressure of thousands of claims on limited resources and fragile procedures. More challenging was the design and implementation of settlements that could accommodate the rights of very diverse groups of claimants in urban environments that generally had changed dramatically since claimants were dispossessed of their land. Not only had claimant communities changed enormously in the intervening years, along with the built environment, property market, and broader urban economy; other urban constituencies had also emerged in this time, particularly after the demise of apartheid blocks on urbanization unleashed a new generation of rural immigrants, placing huge demands for housing and service delivery on unprepared municipalities.

Crucially absent in the thinking around restitution was a set of principles for how to engage other public goods: in the case of Cato Manor, low-cost housing for the urban poor. The restitution program suffered from a certain insularity in its conceptualization—at its simplest an insistence that redress and land restoration were morally coterminous, which often blinkered its advocates against more complex realities on the ground yet still shapes the policy debate on financial compensation. Despite the prominence of urban dispossession in the history of apartheid, responsibility for restitution was allocated to the primarily rural portfolio of the minister of Land and Agricultural Affairs. At the same time, little was done to link the restitution project to the broader debates on reparations within the Truth and Reconciliation Commission (TRC) (see also Dhupelia-Mesthrie in this volume). This body has been criticized for the narrowness of its focus "on direct acts of political repression, to the exclusion of the far more widespread and numerous abuses of apartheid, including forced removals and the expropriation of land, the pass laws, racial classification, and the whole host of legislative cruelties imposed upon millions of citizens in the name of apartheid" (Fullard and Rousseau 2003, 84). Less attention has been directed at the narrow way in which the CRLR and DLA understood their own constitutional mandate to provide for "restitution of property *or equitable redress*" (act 108 of 1996 clause 25[7], emphasis added). Attempts to broker some discussion between the TRC and the CRLR when their terms overlapped (1996–1998) never got off the ground.[8] This limited the possibilities for more imaginative responses to land claims in contexts where land restoration was not necessarily feasible or where the underlying claim concerned violations of human dignity or loss of community rather than simply or primarily the loss of land or land-based livelihoods (Cole interview, 2002).

A further consequence has been that the redevelopment of Cato Manor since 1994 has entrenched rather than shifted the ethnic divisions of apartheid within Durban. From time to time observers have expressed concern at the failure of rural land reform to break down the spatial legacies of the past—Is rural land reform in effect simply "growing the bantustans"? The Cato Manor process poses a similar question in the urban context (Cole interview, 2002). Contrary to CMDA's upbeat claim reported at the start of this chapter, here the apartheid-era divisions of "race" have largely been confirmed, if not strengthened, by the restitution process. During the section 34 negotiations there were instances when social barriers were temporarily lowered among groups of African and Indian claimants, in joint debates at public meetings over rights, history, and legal strategy (Ramgobin interview, 2002; Walker 2008). In general, however, the process did not facilitate such encounters, and the outcome hardened rather than softened the ready suspicions against "the other" circulating among the participants in the case.

In Cato Manor—unlike District Six—land restitution never enjoyed a clear local political legitimacy, in part because of the way in which historically structured ethnic divisions continued to inform social relationships and material interests in the transition period of the early 1990s. In this regard the informal settlers were more successful in reinserting themselves into the center of the city than claimants. The outcome of the Cato Manor restitution project thus has implications for Durban and its council's ambitious plans for reintegrating the apartheid city not only spatially but socially. It can be seen as a missed (albeit difficult) opportunity for building a less fragmented postapartheid city.

In Cato Manor the restitution program defaulted on its promise of redress—not maliciously, but as a result of imperfections in design and implementation in relation to the social forces swirling around this part of the city in the 1990s. Cato Manor was multiply contested land—contested not only by different groups of ethnically divided restitution claimants, including former landowners and tenants, but also and more significantly by the informal claimants who had settled on the land from the late1980s. In contrast to other celebrated restitution sites (District Six, Sophiatown), the local authority and key national departments regarded these new settlers, not former residents, as the primary constituency that should benefit from the redevelopment of the land. Here land restitution was cast as a political obstacle, not an opportunity, for urban renewal.

Understanding this process of "restitution by default" is important, I am arguing, not only for understanding local dynamics in the Durban metropolitan region but also for assessing the significance of the restitution program more widely, as a national endeavor. At a very early stage the process pitted different visions of the public interest against each other and exposed the weaknesses of a land claims process premised largely on a presumption of (rural) land restoration as the proper form of redress. More clearly than in many restitution projects, perhaps, Cato Manor also revealed the difficulty of drawing a clear line around which experience of dispossession qualified for state restitution. At one level it can be seen as a struggle between two different categories of claimants—on the one hand, formal claimants in terms of the Restitution Act and, on the other, informal claimants able collectively, through land invasions, to capitalize on their extreme marginality in the fluid moment of transition in the early 1990s.

The restitution process in Cato Manor offered an opportunity for a more imaginative approach to redevelopment than the agencies entrusted with this responsibility could grasp. Whether a more visionary and inclusive approach was actually possible, given the enormous pressures on the CMDA and CRLR at the time is, of course, open to debate. Nevertheless, this case study highlights the significant ambiguities of purpose that emerged within the restitution program in the course of its translation from constitutional ideal to implementation—a progression that required both officials and claimants to engage with more complex, case-specific contexts and constructions of the public interest than they were ready to imagine or allow. It also points to certain continuities with struggles over land and identity that were already under way in Durban in the 1950s, at the time of removals.

NOTES

1. The author was regional land claims commissioner (RLCC) for KwaZulu-Natal from 1995 to 2000; this chapter draws on that experience. An expanded version of this article appears as a chapter in Walker 2008.

2. The Compact Edition of the Oxford English Dictionary (Oxford: Oxford University Press, 1971).

3. This total includes a handful of families classified as "coloured"; 193 of the more than 16,000 households in the area were classified as white.

4. Xaba (2004, 114) dates the first large-scale settlement to 1987, in Cato Crest, but Cole et al. (2004, 390) date it to 1991, involving three hundred families.

5. Excerpted from the Epilogue of Govender 1996.

6. Loopholes in the settlement agreement meant that the total number of claimants who were party to the settlement agreement finally numbered more than five hundred.

7. Press statement issued by the RLCC and other parties, n.d., copy in the possession of the author.

8. The author recalls discussing the value of meeting with the TRC within the CRLR; a limited hearing on land issues was convened by the TRC commissioner in Durban.

REFERENCES

Bosch, Dawie. 1998. "Interim Report on the Work of the Facilitation Group: Cato Manor Mediations (FAGCamm) April to July 1998." Unpublished report, author's copy.

CMDA (Cato Manor Development Association). 2002. *Cato Manor Development Project: Review 1994–2002.* Durban: CMDA.

Cole, Josette, Dave Smyly, and Neil Hazel. 2004. "Land Claims and Conflict Resolution." In *Urban Reconstruction in the Developing World; Learning through an International Best Practice,* ed. Peter Robinson, Jeff McCarthy, and Clive Forster, 389–402. Sandown: Heinemann.

COLA (Commission on Land Allocation). 1993. "Bellair and Part Bellair—Report for Purposes of Recommendation to Deputy Minister of Land Affairs." Pretoria: Department of Land Affairs.

CRLR (Commission on Restitution of Land Rights). 1996. "Report of the Commission on Restitution of Land Rights in Terms of Section 34(2) of the Restitution of Land Rights Act in Respect of the Land Commonly Known as Greater Cato Manor, Durban." (LCC15/96). Randburg: Land Claims Court.

———. 1997a. *Annual Report 1997.* Pretoria: Commission on Restitution of Land Rights.

———. 1997b. "RLCC's Office: KwaZulu Natal, Monthly Report: July 1977." Unpublished report, Pretoria: Commission on Restitution of Land Rights.

———. 2000. *Annual Report April 1999–March 2000.* Pretoria: Commission on Restitution of Land Rights.

———. 2001. Honouring the Promise of Our Constitution. Annual Report April 2000–March 2001. Pretoria: Commission on Restitution of Land Rights.

du Toit, Andries, Peter Makhari, Heather Garner, and Alan Roberts. N.d. [1998]. "Report. Ministerial Review of the Restitution Programme." Bellville: Programme for Land and Agrarian Studies, University of the Western Cape.

Fitchet, M., D. Bristow, Y. Moolla, and C. Bradshaw. 1997. "Report to the Commission on Restitution of Land Rights on Historical Valuations Research. Cato Manor: Durban." Unpublished report. Pietermaritzburg: Commission on Restitution of Land Rights.

Freund, Bill. 1995. Insiders and Outsiders: The Indian Working Class of Durban, 1910–1990. Pietermaritzburg: University of Natal Press.

Fullard, Madeleine, and Nicky Rousseau. 2003. "An Imperfect Past: The Truth and Reconciliation Commission in Transition." In *State of the Nation: South Africa 2003–2004,* ed. John Daniel, Adam Habib, and Roger Southall, 78–104. Cape Town: HSRC Press.

Govender, Ronnie. 1996. At the Edge and Other Cato Manor Stories. Pretoria: Manx.

Maharaj, Brij, and Maurice Makhathini. 2004. "Historical and Political Context: Cato Manor, 1845–2002." In *Urban Reconstruction in the Developing World: Learning through an International Best Practice,* ed. Peter Robinson, Jeff McCarthy, and Clive Forster, 27–49. Sandown: Heinemann.

Makhathini, Maurice. 1994. "The Case of Cato Manor." In *Here to Stay: Informal Settlements in KwaZulu-Natal,* 55–64, ed. Doug Hindson and Jeff McCarthy. Durban: Indicator Press.

Robinson, Peter, and Clive Forster. 2004. "Unfolding of the Project—Institutional and Planning History of Cato Manor's Redevelopment 1992–2002." In *Urban Reconstruction in the Developing World: Learning through an International Best Practice,* ed. Peter Robinson, Jeff McCarthy, and Clive Forster, 56–87. Sandown: Heinemann.

SPP (Surplus People Project). 1983. Forced Removals in South Africa: The SPP Reports. Volume 4. *Natal.* Cape Town: Surplus People Project.

Walker, Cherryl. 2008. *Landmarked: Land Claims and Land Restitution in South Africa.* Cape Town: Jacana Media; and Athens: Ohio University Press.

Xaba, Thokozani, with Clive Forster and Willies Mchunu. 2004. "Urban Development and Land Invasions." In *Urban Reconstruction in the Developing World: Learning through an International Best Practice,* ed. Peter Robinson, Jeff McCarthy, and Clive Forster, 111–19. Sandown: Heinemann.

INTERVIEWS

Cole, Josette, independent consultant. Cape Town, 27 August 2002.
Forster, Clive, chief executive officer of the CMDA, 1996–2003. Durban, 23 July 2003.
Ramgobin, Asha, former director of the Campus Law Clinic. Durban, 18 July 2002.

CASE LAW

Dhanpaul Singh and 177 Others v the Two Councils, being the North Central and the South Central Local Councils, the Inner West Local Council, the Commission on the Restitution of Land Rights, and the Minister of Land Affairs and Agriculture, 1998 (9/98) (LCC).

North Central and South Central Metropolitan Substructure Councils of the Durban Metropolitan Area and another, Ex Parte 1998 (1) SA 78 (15/96) (LCC).

fifteen

Unfinished Business

*The Role of Governmental Institutions
after Restitution of Land Rights*

ALAN DODSON

What has become plain since the promulgation of the Restitution of Land Rights Act is that the processing and adjudication of land claims is a complex task. Yet the end result of a successful claim for land restoration is merely the return of one component of what was lost. As pointed out by Andries du Toit:

> The problem is . . . that land is not the only thing that was lost. What was destroyed . . . was a whole way of being, a set of community relations, a system of authority and . . . a broader system of economic relations and livelihoods of which the land was but a part, and which gave it its function and its value. The terrible truth of restitution has thus been that the moment of return to the land is often a moment of disappointment and anti-climax. To settle on the spot from which one's forbears—or even a younger, more vigorous, more hopeful self—were once removed, is not necessarily to return to that more authentic, more dignified, more hopeful mode of existence. (Quoted in *In re Kranspoort Community*)[1]

Is the restitution program designed to ensure a dignified, hopeful, and sustainable return to land? And if so, whose job is it to secure this?

This chapter addresses these questions primarily from the perspective of the Commission on Restitution of Land Rights (CRLR), although the role of other institutions is considered. It looks first at the constitutional basis for restitution, then the extent to which the Restitution Act provides for circumstances following restoration of land, and how the Land Claims Court (LCC) has dealt with the postrestoration scenario. Thereafter I explore the CRLR's role against the backdrop of the Constitution, the Restitution Act, and the decisions of the LCC, and draw conclusions about future steps that could ensure the sustainable resettlement of restored land.

THE CONSTITUTION

The right to restitution is enshrined in section 25(7) of the 1996 Constitution, which provides that "A person or community dispossessed of property after 19 June 1913 as a result of past racially discriminatory laws or practices is entitled, to the extent provided by an Act of Parliament, either to restitution of that property or to equitable redress."

Although the constitutional right is circumscribed by an act of Parliament, the reference to "restitution . . . or . . . equitable redress" must bear some core range of meaning within its constitutional setting.[2] In *Dulabh & Another v. Department of Land Affairs*[3] the LCC was called upon to consider the meaning of "restitution" in section 123 of the 1993 Interim Constitution and said the following:

> [44] The term "restitution" has a variety of different meanings in different legal contexts. Given that the concept of restitution of a right in land is a novel one in South African jurisprudence, it is hardly surprising that South African legal dictionaries offer no definition of restitution in this context, but only that of *restitutio in integrum* in relation to the law of contract.
>
> [45] Black's *Law Dictionary* lists other meanings of restitution . . . :
>
> "restitution—an equitable remedy under which a person is restored to his or her original position prior to the loss or injury or placed in the position he or she would have been in had the breach not occurred. The act of making good or giving equivalent for any loss, damage or injury. The act of restoring something to the rightful owner. Compensation for the wrongful taking of property. . . ."

[46] To fully determine the ambit of restitution, one should reach beyond the immediate linguistic context of the word "restitution," its ordinary and grammatical meaning, as contained in the Interim Constitution . . . and the [Restitution] Act . . . , to its wider legal and jurisprudential context so as to give effect not only to the purpose of the legislation, but also to the sense, spirit, ethos, morality and fundamental principles of the Interim Constitution and the Act.

The LCC then goes on to prefer a purposive and generous interpretation of the right to restitution. Although it expressly distinguished the provisions of the Interim Constitution from those in section 25(7) of the final Constitution,[4] the LCC provided guidance on the broad interpretation of the constitutional provisions created to address racial dispossessions of property.[5] The facts in the Dulabh case concerned whether or not a claimant who had secured restoration of his dispossessed land by buying it back before the Restitution Act came into force could still claim financial compensation. Underlying the court's judgment is a clear intention to ensure that claimants are properly and fully restored to the position before the racial dispossession of property. This principle is clearly capable of application in different factual circumstances.

Section 39(1) of the Constitution, furthermore, obliges a court interpreting the Bill of Rights to consider international law and allows it to consider foreign law. Although not yet constituting binding international law, the recently published "Principles on Housing and Property Restitution for Refugees and Displaced Persons," also known as the "Pinheiro Principles," may thus be considered in ascribing a meaning to the concept of restitution (UNESCO 2005). Principle 10.1 provides that "All refugees and displaced persons have the right to voluntarily return to their former homes, lands or places of habitual residence, in safety and dignity." Principle 10.4 provides that "States should, where necessary, request from other States or international organisations the financial and/or technical assistance required to facilitate the effective, voluntary return, in safety and dignity, of refugees and displaced persons." Principle 12.4 provides that "States should establish guidelines which ensure the effectiveness of all the relevant housing, land and property restitution procedures, institutions and mechanisms."

These principles require that restitution must provide for the viable and effective reestablishment of displaced communities. Emphasis is also placed on the protection of the dignity of displaced persons. The Constitutional

Court has emphasized the particular significance to be given to the right to human dignity in the South African Constitution.[6] This too is a relevant consideration in establishing the range of meaning contemplated for restitution. It is unlikely that the framers of the Constitution would have wished the beneficiaries of this right to receive nothing more than being dumped once more upon a bare parcel of land. Rather, a purposive and generous interpretation of the right requires that claimants are, as far as reasonably possible, restored to the position they would have been in had the dispossession not occurred.

THE RESTITUTION ACT

Given the broad conception of restitution emanating from the Interim Constitution, the Restitution Act that followed makes surprisingly limited provision regarding the implementation of restitution orders and settlement agreements.

The term "restitution of a right in land" is defined in section 1 of the act as meaning either the restoration of a right in land or equitable redress. "Restoration of a right in land" is then defined to mean the return of a right in land. "Equitable redress" is defined broadly to include any equitable redress other than the restoration of a right in land, including a right in alternative state-owned land and the payment of compensation. Section 6 sets out the "general functions" of the CRLR. All but one of the provisions deal with powers designed to ensure that the CRLR is able to receive, investigate, mediate, settle, and process claims. Only one of the powers listed in this section applies to the situation following an order restoring possession—section 6(2)(a), which empowers the commission to "monitor and make recommendations concerning the implementation of orders made by the Court under section 35." However, this power is given to the commission only in relation to a court order, not in cases settled administratively in terms of section 42D of the Restitution Act or by ministerial expropriation in terms of section 42E. (I return to this aspect below.) Beyond that, the act is silent on the possible role of the commission in postrestoration situations.

Section 42C of the Restitution Act allows the minister of agriculture and land affairs to provide grants or subsidies "for the development or management of, or to facilitate the settlement of persons on, land" restored to claimants (including for planning purposes). The LCC is also expressly given limited powers in relation to postrestoration developments. It may, in terms of section 35(1)(d) of the Restitution Act, "[order] the State to include the claimant as a beneficiary of a State support programme for housing or the allocation and development of rural land"; "determine the manner in which the rights [in land restored] are to be held" (sec. 35[2][c]); "give any other directive as to how its orders are to be carried out, including the setting of time limits for the implementation of its orders" (sec. 35[2][e]); and "make appropriate orders to give effect to any agreement between the parties regarding the finalisation of the claim" (sec. 35[2][fA]).

Section 35(3) of the Restitution Act also provides as follows:

> An order contemplated in sub-section (2)(c) shall be subject to such conditions as the court considers necessary to ensure that all the members of the dispossessed community shall have access to the land or the compensation in question, on a basis which is fair and non-discriminatory towards any person, including a tenant, and which ensures the accountability of the person who holds the land or compensation on behalf of the community to the members of such community.

Given the function of the LCC to interpret the Restitution Act, one must also consider how it has interpreted the act in relation to the postrestoration situation.

LCC INTERPRETATIONS OF THE RESTITUTION ACT

The decisions of the LCC reflect an increasing concern over time with the postrestoration situation of claimants. From the outset, the court was mindful of its obligation to ensure equitable access to the land restored. It did so primarily by requiring that land be restored to communal property associations (CPAs) established in terms of the Communal Property Associations Act (28 of 1996), which has built-in provisions to ensure equitable access to and control of land owned by a community.

Initially the LCC had the power in terms of section 35(2)(d) of the Restitution Act to "recommend to the Minister that a claimant be given priority access to State resources in the allocation and development of housing and land in the appropriate development programme." It relied on this power to make a recommendation, in the first claim where it ordered the restoration of land,[7] that resources be allocated to replace the housing and infrastructure that were destroyed at the time of the forced removal. This section was, however, deleted by the Land Restitution and Reform Laws Amendment Act of 1997, probably because of overlap with section 35(1)(d) of the Restitution Act.

In the case of *In re Farmerfield Communal Property Trust*[8] the court, in an informal manner during the pretrial conference proceedings, raised the issue of the claimant community's ability to reestablish itself successfully on the restored land. Inputs were obtained from the relevant government departments about making agricultural extension and other services available to the community upon resettlement.[9] Moreover, in the final paragraph of its judgment, the court made a recommendation that the claimant community be given priority access to state resources for development of the land, despite the repeal of section 35(2)(d).[10] It was able to do so because the parties consented to such an order.

As pointed out above, section 35(1)(d) of the Restitution Act allows the court to "order . . . the State to include the claimant as a beneficiary of a State support programme for housing or for the allocation and development of rural land."[11] The question arises whether this may be granted only as an alternative to other restitution awards or whether it may form part of a hybrid order, together with an order for land restoration. At first blush, it may seem difficult to argue that a community should be allocated additional rural land. However, where, as is often the case, a community has grown substantially since its forced removal, additional land may be the only way of making resettlement of its land a viable proposition. In the case of *Richtersveld Community v. Alexkor Ltd & Another* the LCC held that the relief granted by the court in terms of section 35(1) could include more than one form of relief (in that case a combination of restoration, compensation, and land rehabilitation).[12] By parity of reasoning, then, relief in terms of section 35(1)(d) could be included in addition to other forms of relief granted—an aspect that legal representatives of claimant communities should consider in acting on behalf of their clients.

In the case of *In re Kranspoort Community*[13] the court confronted the postrestoration scenario more directly. It introduced the issue in the following manner:

> [107] Paragraphs (a), (c) and (e) of s35(2) and s35(3) [of the Restitution Act] give the Court further wide powers to devise appropriate conditions to ensure that the order will be implemented

fairly and will bring about a workable and practical result. In considering how these provisions should be applied, I have had regard to some emerging literature regarding the aftermath of restoration orders and agreements. It appears . . . that there is a trend of serious problems . . . related to—

(1) lack of coordination between the restitution process and the planning, budgeting and development programmes of provincial government;

(2) shortage of land;

(3) absence of proper planning before resettlement of the land;

(4) disputes over entitlement to membership of the community; and

(5) shortage of skills and resources needed to redevelop the land.

Concerned that similar problems might arise at Kranspoort, the court identified four potential problem areas: organizational matters, decision making on the basis of insufficient information, absence of planning, and the risk of unsustainable depletion of renewable resources. It then addressed each of these by including in its order appropriate conditions under section 35(2)(a) of the Restitution Act. The organizational concerns were addressed by requiring the formation of a CPA to take transfer of the restored land. To ensure adequate information for decision making, the court required the RLCC and the DLA to provide information at a community meeting about the financial aid and governmental agricultural and environmental services which would be available to facilitate resettlement and development. To deal with the absence of proper planning, the court imposed a condition in terms of section 35(2)(a) requiring that before any restoration could take place, it should first approve a "suitable" development plan for the farm. Arguing that this would "act as a strong incentive for the planning process to proceed," the LCC indicated that:

In scrutinising that plan, the Court will not act as a super-planner judging the merits of the plan which was presented. Rather it will satisfy itself that:

(1) a reasonable degree of planning has taken place,

(2) on the basis of a sufficiently participatory planning process, and

(3) there is a clear commitment to the implementation of the plan or plans formulated.

Taking note of the sensitive ecological status of the land and a history of overgrazing on the part of the claimant community, the court also imposed the requirement that the CPA constitution include provisions prohibiting the grazing of livestock in excess of the official carrying capacity for the area.[14] It gave specific functions to the regional land claims commissioner (RLCC) in relation to the provision of information to the CPA on various government services (including financial aid in terms of the Restitution Act, agricultural extension, and access to housing), and the enlisting of the assistance of other government departments. Both the RLCC and the Department of Land Affairs (DLA) were requested to "endeavour to secure the attendance of representatives of national, provincial and local government who are able to inform the claimant community about any forms of State assistance which may be available for the use and development of the farms."[15] After rejecting an initial version of the development plan, the court ultimately ordered that, subject to certain reservations, it was sufficiently satisfied with the development planning and allowed restoration of the land to proceed.[16] This was pursuant to a requirement that the claimants apply to the court within six months of its initial order for a further order confirming compliance with the various conditions that it had imposed.[17]

According to the community's legal representative, by September 2006 the Kranspoort community had reached the final stages in the process of obtaining the necessary approvals in terms of the Development Facilitation Act for its proposed developments on the farm and had commenced limited forms of agricultural production. The community was planning to return only after housing and services had been developed on the land. Its CPA continued to be a vibrant and effective institution.[18] A similar order was made by the Land Claims Court in the matter of *The Gamawela Community v. Government of the Republic of South Africa & Others*.[19]

However, although the LCC's concern about the impact of its orders is to be welcomed, there are difficulties with this approach. As the court itself observed in the *Kranspoort* case,[20] judges are not development planners. The court was fortunate to have a qualified development planner as its assessor in this particular case, but this is not always possible. There is also a fatigue factor. As other chapters in this volume attest, it is usually difficult enough for claimants to get to the point of proving the validity of their claim. An enormous amount is expected of claimants and their legal representatives if they are also to anticipate the issue of postrestoration planning and resettlement, formulate their pleadings accordingly, and present the necessary expert evidence to guide the court in this regard. This is illustrated by the decision of the LCC in *Mphela & Others v. Engelbrecht & Others*,[21] in which the claimants persuaded the court that the imposition of development conditions was not necessary, given the then availability of the Department of Agriculture's Comprehensive Agricultural Support Programme to the claimants. Nonetheless, in my view and notwithstanding the claimants' submissions, in this case the court ought to have imposed conditions that obligated at least a certain level of planning and coordination with other government departments.

The other context in which the LCC has addressed questions around postsettlement support has been in assessing whether or not the dispossessed community received "just and equitable" compensation as contemplated in section 2(2) of the Restitution Act at the time of its original forced removal. Here the court has taken the position that for compensation to have been just and equitable, it would have to have included provision of the necessary resources for the community to reestablish itself successfully on the land to which it had been forcibly removed. The gap between the estimated value of such resources and the compensation actually provided is then taken as an element of the undercompensation. In the case of *Mphela v. Engelbrecht*[22] a witness who was an expert on resettlement presented evidence on behalf of the claimants outlining the standards set by the World Bank's Operational Policy on Involuntary Resettlement. In the event, the court did not consider it necessary to rely on these guidelines but summarized their content in its judgment. Although developed for an involuntary process, they represent a good starting point in the debate about appropriate standards for current resettlement initiatives. Although aspects of this judgment were overturned on appeal by the Supreme Court of Appeal, the latter court accepted the relevance of the expert evidence as well as the LCC's approach to determining whether or not just and equitable compensation had been received.[23]

Another difficulty associated with the provision of substantial postrestoration support by the government, is that it may generate perceptions of unequal treatment between claimants who receive restoration of rural land on the one hand and claimants who receive restoration of urban land or financial compensation on the other. In a slightly different context, in *Mphela v. Engelbrecht* the LCC was prepared to accept that a successful claimant community could, over and above its restored land, retain ownership of the compensatory land to which it had been removed in order to improve its prospects of successfully using the restored land.[24] However, this approach was rejected by the Supreme Court of Appeal, which overruled the LCC and deprived the claimant community of part of the land that it was claiming back, because of the compensatory land it had received at the time of its forced removal. The Supreme Court of Appeal was not prepared to accept that claimants could end up with substantially more land than they had originally lost, despite the state's having waived any claim to the compensatory land in this case, expressly to promote successful resettlement through an element of land redistribution.[25]

These decisions show that, at least on the part of the LCC, there is a real concern to interpret the Constitution and the Restitution Act in a manner that will allow claimants to return to their land on a sustainable basis. This jurisprudence runs counter to the criticism of commentators who have suggested that the LCC has adopted an unduly formalistic approach and promoted antipoor outcomes.[26]

However, the somewhat different approach of the Supreme Court of Appeal in the *Haakdoornbult Boerdery CC* case[27] shows the inadequacy of the legislation in addressing clearly and unambiguously the rights of claimants, particularly community claimants, and the powers and duties of the state in relation to relief aimed at sustainable resettlement. A further problem is that the bulk of land claims are now settled under the auspices of the CRLR, without the LCC playing a role. The scope for it to influence the approach to sustainable resettlement is therefore limited, unless the legal precedents it has set influence the CRLR and other organs of state. Nevertheless, those few provisions in the Restitution Act that do confer postrestoration powers on the LCC provide claimants with a legal platform for addressing problem situations that develop after resettlement. The jurisprudence suggests that creative court applications to the LCC under these circumstances will be well received.

THE ROLE OF THE CRLR

I have argued that, properly interpreted, section 25(7) of the Constitution envisages restoration in a form that gives rise to a sustainable and dignified return to land taken under apartheid. That, in turn, imposes a constitutional duty on the state to ensure that the necessary institutions are in place to achieve this.

Under the Restitution Act the primary role of the CRLR is the receipt of claims, their investigation, attempted settlement, and, failing settlement, their referral, either for expropriation in terms of section 42E or adjudication in terms of section 14(1) of the act. Section 6(2)(a) of the Restitution Act confers upon the CRLR a potentially important role in carrying out monitoring and advisory work, to ensure the successful implementation of orders providing for the restoration of land. This function is enhanced where the LCC is able to impose conditions regulating the situation after restoration and assign particular responsibilities to the commission. However, there is no reason why section 6(2)(a) should not also provide the CRLR with the authority to play such a role in the absence of the court.

In the context of settlement agreements, the minister of agriculture and land affairs has similar powers to those of the LCC and may use them to introduce conditions into the settlement agreement that enhance the prospects for sustainable resettlement on the restored land. Thus, in terms of section 42D of the Restitution Act, the settlement agreement may provide for "the manner in which the rights awarded are to be held" or "such other terms and conditions as the Minister considers appropriate." Moreover, the minister's powers under section 42D may be delegated to an RLCC who, provided that he or she acts within the terms of the delegation, may similarly incorporate appropriate provisions into the settlement agreement to achieve a workable solution. Another mechanism for conferring a postrestoration role on the CRLR is to make the settlement agreement an order of court. Rule 62(1)(b) of the LCC Rules allows a party or parties to bring an application to make a deed of settlement an order of court. That, in turn, would bring into play the powers given to the CRLR in terms of section 6(2)(a) of the Restitution Act.

Unfortunately, however, the Restitution Act as currently formulated does not come close to providing a comprehensive legislative and institutional framework for addressing the demands of sustainable resettlement. An additional potential impediment was the government's earlier decision that the CRLR should complete its work by 31 March 2008, whereupon it would be wound down. Fortunately, however, reality prevailed—the date came and went, and there is no suggestion that the CRLR is to close down soon. Although it is important that targets be set for the completion of its work, this particular target was both unrealistic in terms of its aims and potentially disruptive as it would have left an institutional vacuum for post-settlement support.

At the same time, the finite nature of the restitution process needs to be respected. The CRLR needs to work according to a clear vision for its role in the final phases of the restitution process. Such a vision should embrace at least the following elements:

> New, realistic targets should be set for the resolution of complex urban and rural claims, based on a clear understanding of the number of claims involved and the degree of their complexity, along with realistic assessments of the procedures to be followed to bring about their final resolution and the time that this will take (including appeals to higher courts);
>
> Arrangements should be in place for the CRLR to have the staff and resources to process complex claims and achieve its target dates;
>
> The Restitution Act should be amended to confer upon the CRLR, or another institution created specifically for the task, a new and separate role to ensure the ongoing sustainable and dignified resettlement of land restored in the restitution process;
>
> Legislative provision should also be made for intergovernmental cooperation in achieving this goal, with the responsibilities of the different levels of government and organs of state clearly delineated and the forums established within which they might cooperate;
>
> With respect to this mandate the CRLR, or the other institution created for the task, should be staffed with persons appropriately qualified to focus on development of resettled communities, as opposed to claims processing;
>
> The appropriate life span for this initiative should be realistically assessed based on the need to reestablish viable communities—some guidance in this regard is to be found in the World Bank's policy on involuntary resettlement.

In this chapter, I have examined the extent to which the Restitution Act makes provision for the sustainable resettlement of restored land and sought to identify where institutional responsibility for this lies. It is clear that the sustainable implementation of restitution orders and settlement agreements will require the redesign of elements of the legislative and institutional framework, as well as different kinds of expertise and coordinated participation by all spheres of government. The process should be guided by legislation along the lines suggested above, executed by personnel with appropriate qualifications in development, and coordinated in terms of the principles of cooperative government set out in chapter 3 of the Constitution. With a newly designed focus, the CRLR could yet play a vital role in this process.

It is only in this way that there can be a realistic prospect of making restitution work. It requires recognition from the government that restitution cannot simply be treated as a passing (or past!) phase in the development of a more just society. It needs to remain a developmental priority for many years to come.

NOTES

1. 2000 (2) SA 124 (LCC), para 108.
2. Although in *Minister of Health and Others v. Treatment Action Campaign and Others (No 2)* 2002 (5) SA 721 (CC) the Constitutional Court rejected a "minimum core" argument regarding socioeconomic rights (paras 26–39), the context here is different. The right to restitution is not one that the state is to make available progressively, as with socioeconomic rights. Arguably, the provision of a right to restitution that does not allow for a viable and dignified return is unreasonable and any statute that fails this test is deficient.
3. 1997 (4) SA 1108 (LCC).
4. At para 43.
5. The LCC has held that the changes between the Interim and Final Constitutions did not fundamentally change the basis for restitution and were largely the consequence of a change in drafting style.
6. See, for example, *S v. Makwanyane and Another* 1995 (3) SA 391 (CC) at paras 144, 327–29.
7. *In re Elandskloof Vereniging* 1999 (1) SA 176 (LCC) at 180 B–181 A.
8. 1999 (1) SA 936 (LCC).
9. This is not apparent from the written judgment but derives from the author's involvement in the case as one of the presiding judges.
10. *In re Farmerfield Communal Property Trust*, at para 15.
11. This discussion does not address the precise meaning of this subparagraph or the range of programs that might be included.
12. [2004] 3 All SA 244 (LCC), paras 25–33.
13. 2000 (2) SA 124 (LCC) at para 106 ff.
14. See para 3.2 of the order.
15. See para 4 of the order.
16. Unreported judgment of the LCC, Case No. LCC 26/98, 13 June 2001.

17. Above at p185 G–186 A.
18. Interview with the community's legal representative, 13 September 2006.
19. Unreported order of the LCC, Case No. LCC 29/01, 4 June 2004.
20. Above at para 116.
21. [2005] 2 All SA 135 (LCC).
22. Above at p177–178 and p181. See also *The Baphiring Community v. Uys & Others* 2007 (5) SA 585 (LCC), paras 20–22.
23. *Haakdoornbult Boerdery CC v. Mphela* 2007 (5) SA 596 (SCA) at para 49.
24. Unreported judgment of the LCC, Case No. LCC 66/01, 1 June 2005, paras (d)–(f).
25. *Haakdoornbult Boerdery CC v. Mphela* above. The Supreme Court decision was confirmed in most respects on appeal to the Constitutional Court, although the Constitutional Court preferred to characterize the reason for not restoring all the claimed land as restoration not being feasible, primarily because of the irrigation equipment installed on the land in question.
26. See, for example, Roux 2004, where unwarranted conclusions are drawn about the LCC's performance on the basis of an unrepresentative sample of decisions. Nor were the outcomes in the cases referred to by Roux necessarily anti-poor. In *In re Macleantown Residents Association: re Certain Erven and Commonage in Macleantown* 1996 (4) SA 325 (LCC), the agreement that the LCC declined to sanction was probably incapable of passing transfer of ownership to the claimants as worded and potentially excluded a group of legitimate claimants.
27. *Haakdoornbult Boerdery CC v. Mphela* above.

REFERENCES

du Toit, Andries. 2000. "The End of Restitution: Getting Real About Land Claims." In *At the Crossroads: Land and Agrarian Reform in South Africa into the 21st Century*, ed. Ben Cousins, 75–91. Bellville: Programme for Land and Agrarian Studies, University of the Western Cape.

Roux, Theunis. 2004. "Pro-poor Court, Anti-poor Outcomes: Explaining the Performance of the South African Land Claims Court." *South African Journal of Human Rights* 20 (4): 511–43.

UNESCO. 2005. "Economic, Social and Cultural Rights. Housing and Property Restitution in the Context of the Return of Refugees and Internally Displaced People. Final Report of the Special Rapporteur, Paulo Sërgio Pinheiro." Commission on Human Rights: Sub-Commission on the Promotion and Protection of Human Rights. E/CN.4/Sub.2/2005/17. New York: United Nations.

STATUTES

Constitution of the Republic of South Africa, Act 200 of 1993. Pretoria: Government Printers.

Constitution of the Republic of South Africa, Act 108 of 1996. Pretoria: Government Printers.
Restitution of Land Rights, Act 22 of 1994. Pretoria: Government Printers.

CASE LAW

The Baphiring Community v. Uys & Others 2007 (5) SA 585 (LCC).
Dulabh & Another v. Department of Land Affairs 1997 (4) SA 1108 (LCC).
The Gamawela Community v. Government of the Republic of South Africa & Others 2001. Case No. LCC 26/98, 13 June 2001.
Haakdoornbult Boerdery CC v. Mphela 2007 (5) SA 596 (SCA).
In re Elandskloof Vereniging 1999 (1) SA 176 (LCC).
In re Farmerfield Communal Property Trust 1999 (1) SA 936 (LCC).
In re Kranspoort Community 2000 (2) SA 124 (LCC).
In re Macleantown Residents Association: re Certain Erven and Commonage in Macleantown 1996 (4) SA 325 (LCC).
Minister of Health and Others v. Treatment Action Campaign and Others (No 2) 2002 (5) SA 721 (CC).
Mphela & Others v. Engelbrecht & Others [2005] 2 All SA 135 (LCC).
Richtersveld Community v. Alexkor Ltd. & Another [2004] 3 All SA 244 (LCC)
S v. Makwanyane and Another 1995 (3) SA 391 (CC).

sixteen

Restitution, Agriculture, and Livelihoods

National Debates and Case Studies from Limpopo Province

MICHAEL ALIBER, THEMBA MALULEKE,
MPFARISENI THAGWANA, AND
TSHILILO MANENZHE

Although the main objective of South Africa's land restitution program has been restorative justice and reconciliation, its rural component has always had a recognized role within a broader rural development strategy. In the African National Congress's (ANC's) 1994 Reconstruction and Development Programme (RDP), restitution and redistribution together are identified as "the central and driving force of a programme of rural development," requiring in equal measure the support one associates with agricultural development (ANC 1994, s2.4.2) The *White Paper on South African Land Policy*, similarly, speaks of land restitution as part of, rather than separate from, rural development (DLA 1997).

For the bullish authors of the RDP, what justified this optimism was the belief that anything replacing the agricultural status quo could only be for the better: "[The improved quality of rural life . . .] must entail a dramatic land reform programme to transfer land from the inefficient, debt-ridden, ecologically-damaging and white-dominated large farm sector to all those who wish to produce incomes through farming in a more sustainable agricultural system" (ANC 1994, s4.3.8). This statement is buttressed by other passages that extol the virtues of small-scale farmers and the massive employment opportunities they represent.

However, within ten years this way of thinking had been turned on its head. By 2004, government's predominant concern had become how to transfer land from white people to black people without damaging commercial agriculture, a trend that has continued to the present. This gradual about-face can be roughly traced through a series of programmatic changes and public statements. For example, from around 2000 the Commission on Restitution of Land Rights (CRLR) became demonstrably more concerned about the economic viability of rural restitution projects, evidenced by the sudden increase in uptake of the Settlement Planning Grant, together with the introduction in that year of the Restitution Discretionary Grant of R3,000 per household. Around 2001–2002, the CRLR set up a central Development Planning and Facilitation Unit, which was replicated in the regional land claims commissioner's (RLCC's) offices, and in 2003, a Development Grant was introduced, set at a maximum of 25 percent of the land value.

Initially a concern about project sustainability, the approach evolved into a particular interpretation of what was going wrong, which went beyond inadequate funding at project level. Even though there were acknowledgments of the inadequacy of extension support and planning, what is remarkable about public statements by senior politicians and officials from around 2002 is that they lay most of the responsibility for the economic shortcomings of land restitution at the feet of the beneficiaries themselves. In her budget vote speech in April 2003, Thoko Didiza, the minister of agriculture and land affairs, declared: "It is important for us also to highlight the fact that new challenges have emerged as we proceed with the implementation of the Restitution Programme. One of these challenges is a lack of capacity among the beneficiary communities to effectively manage the projects that they have taken over, where some of the legal entities that have been established—such as the communal property associations—are finding it difficult to maintain the projects as viable going concerns" (Didiza 2003). Shortly afterward the CRLR's *Annual Report* expressed the same idea by way of a pseudohistorical explanation: "The most regrettable effect of apartheid spatial planning is that previously highly productive victims of racial land dispossession were either forced onto uneconomic pieces of land . . . in the homeland areas, or to townships as job seekers. In this process, the victims lost their agricultural skills. The challenge is to identify the skill and to revive the interest in agriculture" (CRLR 2004, 5). Although one does not want to take the textual analysis of public utterances too far, what is interesting about these statements is the contrast they suggest between "viable going concerns" on the one hand, and "uneconomic pieces of land" on the other. Increasingly the former referred, first and foremost, to large-scale commercial agriculture, far from the vision of peasant farmers conjured by the RDP.

The reason for this about-face is partly related to the lackluster performance of land restitution projects to date. But it is also found in the tone of defiant defensiveness that some senior government officials adopted in reaction to external criticism:

> The challenge is to all people of goodwill, including current land owners, the private/public sector, local and international donors, to join hands with the South African government, in working towards a better life for all in the area of land reform, in general, and land restitution, in particular. . . . Such a well-considered, well planned and well-resourced approach, will bring sobriety to the fire-eaters, who want to push recklessly for land invasions, with dire consequences for all involved. (CRLR 2001, 7)

At a 2006 restitution ceremony the new minister of agriculture and land affairs, Lulu Xingwana, explained how in the short term the claimants were going to lease their land back to the former owner: "During this lease period [the former owner] has committed to the total skills transfer to the new landowners. Go out and tell those prophets of doom that those farmers who sold us the land for land reform purposes still have an important role to play in the agricultural sector of this country" (Xingwana 2006). In practical terms, the minister seems to suggest that commercial farmers possess the skills that land restitution claimants need to make it in agriculture; by the same token, therefore, they represent the benchmark for the kind of agriculture to which land restitution now aspires. This claim, more implied than explicit, is arguably the focal point of current debates regarding land reform and livelihoods.

This chapter contributes to this debate by reviewing the literature on the implications of rural land restitution for livelihoods and then surveying four case studies from Limpopo Province. The purpose is to use these disparate case studies to propose a more nuanced interpretation of the evidence. Our tentative conclusion is that the debate currently raging in policy circles also takes place within restitution projects; furthermore, understanding the rather different factors propelling this level of the debate promotes an appreciation of the complexity of our policy choices that could move the analysis beyond starkly delineated camps.

RURAL RESTITUTION AND LIVELIHOODS

A recent review of the impact on livelihoods of rural land restitution notes with concern that "the central problem in assessing the impact of land reform on livelihoods is the paucity of post-settlement evaluation studies. . . . [I]mpact evaluation is hampered by the absence of baseline data . . . , a lack of agreed indicators, and the lack of longitudinal panel data" (PLAAS 2006, 3). Indeed, in terms of rigorous, quantitative impact evaluations, there has been little. The Department of Land Affairs (DLA) commissioned a "Quality of Life Survey" in 1999, but only seven restitution projects were included in the sample (encompassing 130 household interviews), of which four had been settled in the year prior to the fieldwork (May et al. 2000). At best this could be regarded as limited baseline data for future longitudinal evaluation, as was envisaged at the time, but in the event the data were lost. The next Quality of Life Survey, for which fieldwork was conducted in 2000/01, included nine restitution projects, but did not report distinct findings for restitution (Ahmed et al. 2003). The most recent Quality of Life Survey went to field in 2006, but at the time of writing this chapter the results had not yet been released.

Despite this dearth of quantitative evidence regarding the livelihoods impact of restitution, there is a rapidly growing body of project case studies. Some are stand-alone, whereas others, potentially more useful, have adopted a common strategy with a view to comparative analysis. The most noteworthy of these are studies by the Community Agency for Social Enquiry (CASE) and the Programme for Land and Agrarian Studies at the University of the Western Cape (PLAAS), the first commissioned by the DLA, and the second undertaken on behalf of the CRLR.

The CASE study is noteworthy in that it covered all 179 restitution projects involving a settlement and/or development component at the time. It was thus able to quantify patterns of success and failure based on qualitative assessments at project level in a manner that smaller studies were not. One of the study's main findings, for example, was that "[o]f the 128 projects with agricultural developmental aims, 83 percent have not achieved these developmental aims. Approximately nine percent (12) have partially achieved their agricultural developmental aims but are not generating any income. A further five percent have partially achieved their agricultural developmental aims and are generating income. However, these five percent of projects are not making a profit and are not sustainable yet" (CASE 2006, 21). The study thus provides a valuable bird's-eye-view of rural restitution in general and the majority of projects whose developmental goals center on agriculture in particular. The study does not focus on the implications for livelihoods; rather, it is implied that successful projects will contribute positively to livelihoods and unsuccessful projects will not. Analytically, the study seeks to identify factors that contribute to success or failure at project level. With respect to failure, the usual suspects are fingered: lack of money and equipment; lack of skills (both technical and managerial); lack of "postsettlement support"; lack of appropriate legal structures; and infighting. As with much of the literature on land reform in South Africa, failure is overdetermined, and the sense is that if government carried through with its commitments to sound project planning and adequate support, we would see success. For all its value, this is where the study falls short: although it makes sense to assess project performance in relation to goals in view of the patent inadequacy of so many of the projects, there is surely a need to ask whether there is not something wrong with the formulation of the goals.

The PLAAS study is an interesting counterpoint in terms of methodology, more particularly in that it addresses the question of goals head-on. The study integrates six case studies of rural restitution projects with an analysis of recent literature, including that on land redistribution. The central conclusion is stated as follows: "The most striking finding . . . is that the majority of beneficiaries across all the restitution projects have received no material benefit whatsoever from restitution, whether in the form of cash income or access to land" (PLAAS 2006, 16). Whether one can justify the implied generalization to all rural restitution on the basis of so few case studies is open to question. Nonetheless, the analysis is conducted with sensitivity and skill, drawing attention not just to the failure to make good on "project business plans" but to deficiencies with the plans themselves. One problem is paramount—the tendency to discourage "self-provisioning," whereby beneficiaries get on with agricultural production in the manner in which they are accustomed and with the resources they have. Thus at the core of the PLAAS analysis is the debate about the agricultural model, in particular doubt about the efficacy of "strategic partnerships" with current and former commercial farmers.

Two other studies are worth mentioning, if for no other reason than the remarkable contrast between them. The first is Philip du Toit's 2004 angry polemic, *The Great South African Land Scandal,* which, although not claiming academic rigor, presents similar desultory case study material. Ironically, du Toit's perspective has much in common with the government's analysis of the problems facing land reform in general and restitution in particular, although he is critical of its attempts to address the problems: "In a covert way, it appears the SA government has come to realize that handing over a farm to subsistence farmers is a failure, but they are slow to admit this. Instead, they quietly bring in managers and consultants who rectify—if possible—the damage done, and the patched-up project is again given to the same beneficiaries" (du Toit 2004, 4).

In contrast, the well-meaning and sometimes insightful anthology of "seven successful case studies" by de Villiers and van den Berg (2006) seeks to counterbalance the apparently excessive focus on bad news on land reform. Three of the seven case studies are restitution projects. The study emphasizes the importance of good planning, good communication, and realistic expectations. It also advocates the use of strategic partners and mentors (each of the three restitution projects involved strategic partners), and implicitly supports the idea that projects should maintain commercial farmland, even though it recognizes that it may be strategic to allow some land to be used for subsistence.

The common denominator among these studies is that land restitution projects struggle to perform in commercial agriculture. However, the studies differ with respect to two key questions: first, whether and how these challenges can be successfully addressed; and second, whether commercial agriculture is the most appropriate goal. In principle, both questions are amenable to empirical investigation, but at present the latter appears to be more the subject of presumption and ideological debate than objective research.

FOUR CASE STUDIES

This section presents four case studies of projects in Limpopo province. The projects are Shimange, Mavungeni, Munzhedzi, and a cluster of seven land claims in the Levubu Valley.[1] All are in the eastern part of Makhado Local Municipality and were settled after 2000. However, despite their geographical proximity, their circumstances differ enormously. These differences allow us to sharpen our questions about the challenges facing restitution in making a positive impact on livelihoods.

Shimange

The Shimange community comprises Shangaan- and Venda-speaking people who were scattered across the homelands of Gazankulu and Venda after being removed from their land between 1965 and 1972 to make way for two white-owned farms. In the mid-1970s the Venda homeland government acquired the land, from which time it was not actively used apart from unauthorized grazing by members of a nearby community. In 1998, 366 Shimange households claimed the land. The claim relating to the farm Syferfontein (719 hectares) was finalized in March 2002; however, the claim to the adjacent farm Uitschot (311 hectares) was somehow overlooked by the RLCC and remains in limbo. Since the finalization of the claim to Syferfontein, about five claimant households have settled there, whereas three claimant households have settled on Uitschot despite its unresolved status.

On Syferfontein, development has been paralyzed, ostensibly owing to the dysfunctionality of the communal property association (CPA) committee as well as to differences between the committee and other claimants. The committee does not hold regular meetings because a number of its members stay in Gauteng and KwaZulu-Natal. It is dominated by those who think that the farm should be run as a single entity under centralized management, to generate profits, and oppose the idea of land allocation for semisubsistence and settlement purposes, evidently the preference of many other members of the claimant community. The practical implication of this impasse is that the RLCC has deferred release of about R2 million earmarked for development of Syferfontein. However, there is also a less palpable dimension of the paralysis: because a detailed development plan centered on commercial farming has already been drawn up and CRLR funding is not forthcoming, claimants are waiting for the process to resume. Thus, only the households who have settled on Syferfontein are actively using the land, mainly in terms of modest home gardens and low-intensity grazing. Meanwhile, two of the households at Uitschot are producing field crops at a scale well beyond the usual homestead garden and, more significantly, well beyond anything happening at Syferfontein. One of them is also engaged in small-scale irrigated vegetable production. The ability of these households to farm on this scale is related to the fact that they have the personal resources to do so, in addition to taking advantage of cheap Zimbabwean labor. However, they are by no means well-off, and there are certainly other claimant households who in principle have similar resources to invest at Syferfontein. Tentatively, we ascribe the greater willingness to invest in production at Uitschot to the fact that there is no pending plan with which to interfere. Rather than a hindrance, the lack of formal blessing from the RLCC to develop Uitschot has left a vacuum that some claimant households are using to their advantage. Still, they represent only a handful of the approximately forty Shimange households who claim a particular historical link to Uitschot. Why is it not more?

Mavungeni

Mavungeni CPA comprises two hundred households who lodged a claim in 1998 for the restoration of a 745-hectare portion of the farm Vleifontein, from which their community had been removed between 1930 and 1968. Because of uncertainty about the restitution process, in 1998 they also applied for a redistribution grant with which to purchase another portion of Vleifontein, comprising 561 hectares. By coincidence, the redistribution and the land restoration awards took place within months of each other, in 2002, but in the meantime the community had already started accessing the redistribution portion. This land included an equipped dairy as well as some grazing and nonirrigated arable land, whereas the restored portion included about 25 hectares of irrigated avocado, mango, and macadamia orchards. The balance of the redistribution grant was used to purchase a tractor, and the Limpopo Department of Agriculture provided a "starter pack" including a second tractor, a trailer, a planter, and two plows.

In 2002 the CPA purchased nine dairy cows, but seven died within a year from heart water disease. The CPA could also not afford to pay for an electricity connection with which to operate the dairy equipment. In 2002/03, the CPA committee allocated two- to three-hectare plots to approximately forty households. In that year, some households did well in terms of producing sufficient maize meal for their own needs, but in subsequent years members have generally not done as well owing to drought and damage from uncontrolled livestock. The CPA allows its members to graze their own livestock freely, but this is a source of some internal discontent because some members benefit more than others: for example, one member whose herd exceeds one hundred cattle. In addition, the CPA leases some grazing camps for R1,000 per month to a well-off nonmember residing in a nearby township; however, for lack of an adequate perimeter fence, other nonmembers from adjacent communities regularly graze their livestock on the land without permission.

As for the orchards, for a time these were leased to a CPA member who arranged to pay the CPA 10 percent of his profits per year. However, in early 2007 the CPA committee canceled this arrangement because, although the lessor had paid over R30,000 for the use of the orchard over the previous year, he had fueled suspicions by failing to disclose his profits. The CPA committee thereafter entered into an arrangement with a local company that is managing the orchard on the CPA's behalf and hiring some CPA members as workers.

Apart from agricultural activities, the Mavungeni CPA hoped to establish a township on the property. This plan, however, has not been acted upon pending provision of bulk infrastructure by the municipality. In 2004 a dissident group of CPA members organized an occupation of the land, ostensibly out of frustration with the lack of visible progress with the township establishment, but also alleging that the CPA committee was making decisions regarding the proposed township without proper consultation. To date about forty makeshift dwellings have been erected, by both CPA as well as nonmember households. These are the only households presently residing on either portion of the Mavungeni community's land.

Munzhedzi

The Munzhedzi community was forcibly removed from its land in 1936. In 1998 six hundred households lodged a claim for the restoration of their land, which had been owned by the homeland government of Venda but scarcely used since the early 1980s. In 2000 some claimants became impatient and occupied the land illegally. The following year the claim was finalized with the return of 1,400 hectares to the claimant group. However, to date fewer than two hundred claimant households have settled on the land, whereas over seven hundred nonclaimants have. As of early 2008 some 1,130 residential sites were demarcated, of which about 930 were settled, and by all accounts the number of sites is still growing. The rapid settlement of Munzhedzi is largely thanks to a local self-proclaimed chief who allocates land to virtually anybody willing to pay a small fee. This is despite the fact that the land is officially held by a CPA. Residential sites are reasonably large at around 30 by 50 meters, for which nonbeneficiaries pay a onetime fee of R150 to R300.

Although there is a poultry project as well as a piggery project supported by a local nongovernmental organization, these involve very few people. By contrast, around 60 percent of resident households do some gardening on their sites, and about 3 percent are engaged in additional field crop production elsewhere on the land. There remains a fair amount of unused arable land, but this is steadily declining as more households plant and more land is allocated for settlement. Some residents praise the fact that agricultural conditions are better than where they come from (mostly overcrowded settlements nearby), but as many cite the fact that they are now closer to transport routes, affording better access to piece jobs in Makhado. In essence, Munzhedzi is a re-creation of a communal area in settlement patterns and land use but more favorably located and with better agricultural conditions than many.

The Levubu Valley Cluster

The Levubu Valley east of Makhado town and north of Elim constitutes the most significant concentration of subtropical commercial production in the municipality. It is also the site of seven recently concluded land claims involving land from about ninety-three farms (though many of these had been effectively consolidated over time). As described in detail by Derman, Lahiff, and Sjaastad (this volume), the RLCC took a firm stand that these claims would be handled in a manner that would ensure continuity of agricultural production, or, put another way, that would prevent collapse. This would be accomplished by means of introducing "strategic partners," that is, private sector entities who would provide the farm and business management while sharing the returns and to some extent the risks. Two strategic partners were formally appointed in 2005, the one taking responsibility for two-thirds of the farms and the other for the balance. Both have the responsibility to develop internal capacity within the claimant groups to enable complete devolution of responsibility within ten years.

The reason the RLCC has proceeded in this manner is no secret. It followed the demise of some restored farms in Letsitele Valley in the neighboring municipality, which government officials described as a "wake-up call." The presence of strategic partners is to avert a repeat of this experience. The expected benefits to claimants include a guaranteed annual rent calculated as 1.25 percent of the total land value (which works out to about R2,700 per household per year), sharing of profits (if any) at the end of the year (which most communities have decided to invest in community infrastructure rather than distribute to households), and first preference for new on-farm employment opportunities.

DISCUSSION

These four case studies do not allow a precise quantification of the economic impacts of restitution in the respective projects (and in any event it is a very small sample). However, they do provide a qualitative picture of the overall implications and a rich tableau of complex and contrasting experiences. We first summarize and compare the livelihoods impacts and then discuss what the case studies reveal about the choices made by restitution claimants and the debates they engage in regarding those choices.

The actual and potential benefits include various combinations of cash profits, own-consumption benefits (food produced and consumed by beneficiaries), increased wealth (e.g., through livestock and tree stock, and land itself), rental income, and improved residential circumstances. At Shimange a few claimant households are deriving significant own-consumption and some modest cash profits (particularly on Uitschot, where some have settled illegally), but at present the vast majority are deriving no benefits at all. At Mavungeni, a somewhat larger fraction of claimant households are deriving own-consumption benefits, and a handful are building their wealth based on access to improved grazing. Although the group receives some rental income, it is modest and not distributed to member households. At Munzhedzi, a very large number of households are benefiting in terms of mostly modest own-consumption benefits and many more from improved residential circumstances, notwithstanding the lack of services. And finally, claimants in the Levubu cluster are or will be deriving rental income, which, although not substantial, is nonetheless significantly more than on Mavungeni. In a perverse manner, one of the ostensible aims of the strategic partnership is to preserve jobs that might otherwise be under threat if the restored land were not well managed—including farm jobs and associated agro-processing jobs. This is not a benefit of restitution per se, but, rather, of the strategic partner model; furthermore, these benefits do not accrue only or even particularly to the claimant households.

Does this mean that Munzhedzi is the preferred model for what should happen on restored farmland, as though vindicating the original vision of the RDP? Indeed, with proper support—both for settlement and for agriculture—what is apparently a modest success could realistically be a significant one. However, the majority of those benefiting are not technically part of the claimant group, an issue to which we return below. Moreover, what distinguishes the projects from one another is the different circumstances from which they began, with the Levubu farms being a conspicuous outlier in terms of their endowment and the arrangement instigated by the RLCC. A Munzhedzi-type approach to Levubu might well have resembled the very disaster that the strategic partnership model was designed to avoid. Were we to examine these "disasters" more closely, we might find that, from a livelihoods perspective, they are not such disasters after all—but as Shimange and Mavungeni remind us, they might well be so.

What emerges clearly from the case studies is that the debate between a unified, commercial farming model or a household-based semisubsistence model is taking place not only in government and academic circles; for Shimange and Mavungeni, this debate is at the center of the groups' problems. For Shimange, it is tempting to interpret the strong preference of the CPA committee for commercially oriented unified production as a reflection of their physical remoteness from the project. However, it does not appear as simple as this; after all, at least on the Uitschot land, there is nothing stopping interested claimant households from planting, and yet only three households are there. At Mavungeni, differences on whether to lease out or divide up appear to reflect different views as to the best way of ensuring that benefits are derived from the land. Leasing may even be perceived as more equitable than the divide-it-up option, because the latter favors those with more resources to begin with, such as the project member who previously leased the CPA's orchards.

A second observation is that the debate at project level is equally about the question of settlement versus agriculture. To be more precise, the debate positions settlement with semisubsistence production—i.e., rural homesteading—against the unified commercial agriculture option. It is not immediately obvious why the trade-off is portrayed this way: does unified commercial agriculture require more space than household-based subsistence production? Some members clearly perceive settlement as antithetical to unified commercial farming because it may lead to the bulk of the land being taken over by homesteads; as stated by some Shimange claimants, "We don't want to go the way of Munzhedzi."

The third observation concerns the striking contrast between Munzhedzi, on the one hand, and Shimange and Mavungeni, on the other. Earlier we remarked on the fact that, of the four case studies, Munzhedzi has by far the largest number of people benefiting from the land, not because of the size of the land, but because of the rapid pace of settlement. This is largely because claimant households did not have an effective mechanism to prevent the chief from allocating sites to nonclaimants. In physical terms, Munzhedzi and Shimange are separated by only a boundary fence, but their development trajectories are fundamentally different because at Munzhedzi, the local demand for land was allowed to express itself, whereas at Shimange (and for that matter Mavungeni) this was not the case. The question is, why not?

We offer a rather simple hypothesis backed up with some secondary evidence. We suggest that the reason so much of Shimange and Mavungeni remains unsettled and uncultivated goes beyond the dysfunctionality of their CPAs or other forms of infighting. Rather, given a claimant group of a certain size, only some group members will have a strong interest in either relocating or farming. Even so, the group as a whole may well wish to exclude nongroup members. At Munzhedzi, this control function was never effectively exercised, so the property has attracted settlers from far and wide, that is, people who have self-selected according to their need, for whom, presumably, even the undeveloped state of Munzhedzi is an improvement over where they have come from. This is to such an extent that new arrivals at Munzhedzi are exerting pressure on the common boundary with Shimange, which remains mostly vacant and unused.

The secondary evidence comes from a 2005 household survey in three provinces (Limpopo, Free State, and Eastern Cape), which, among other things, sought to understand who wants land and why (HSRC 2005a). The pertinent finding for our discussion here is that 48 percent of respondents who indicated that they or their families had experienced land dispossession wanted or needed additional land (although not necessarily the particular land that was taken), whereas among those who did not regard themselves as victims of land dispossession, the figure is 41 percent. Thus the experience of land dispossession may boost the likelihood of demanding land, although not by much. Among all respondents who indicated that they wanted or needed land, only about 2 percent indicated that their main motivation was to get back what was taken from them. By extension, being a restitution claimant does not necessarily imply that one has a particularly strong demand for land. This is not to imply that claimants do not have an earnest interest is seeing their claims settled or that they lack a keen interest in deriving some kind of material benefit from the restored land, only that this is not equivalent to a personal interest in gaining access to the claimed land for day-to-day purposes.

For many Munzhedzi claimants (as with those at Shimange and Mavungeni), the experience of the claims process has been entirely different from that of nonclaimants settling there. Apart from how they know about the land in the first place, the biggest difference, arguably, is that they have had their expectations raised and then unfulfilled at different stages of the restitution process. It appears that for many what these projects have to offer is insufficient to attract them away from where they are presently settled and what they are currently doing. Apart from the long, drawn-out process of false starts and waiting, it is also reasonable to suppose that for many claimant households there is something attractive about the unified commercial farm model. This is a partial explanation for what we observed at project level, where the debate about the best mode of land use is at least as fierce as that in policy circles, albeit for different reasons. Quite simply, the attractiveness of the unified commercial farming model is that it offers claimants a benefit from their land without their committing to actual day-to-day involvement.

Does this imply that the strategic partnership approach is appropriate? Possibly. However, much will depend on whether the partnership works out as planned and in particular whether meaningful project dividends materialize. The experience from share equity schemes and strategic partnerships in South Africa is not altogether encouraging, as shown in both the PLAAS and CASE studies noted above. Explaining why this approach has produced such uneven and often woeful results is not the focus of this chapter, but drawing on the Levubu study, the dearth of appropriate strategic partners who can do this type of work is very likely a component of the answer. A curious feature of the Levubu cluster is government's initial willingness to appoint one strategic partner for the entire cluster of claims, which represents a massive effective consolidation of operational units. Even after the claimants requested more choices and a public invitation for bids, the RLCC ended up with only two strategic partners. As claims to much of the rest of Levubu reach finalization, not to mention other high-value properties in Limpopo, will it be possible to replicate the strategic partnership model on a much larger scale, and what will it effectively mean for the agrarian structure of the province?

We conclude this section by returning to the question of why the government's insistence on strategic partners and other kindred mechanisms appears to be more intense in the realm of rural restitution than in that of land redistribution. The reasons are not difficult to fathom. The first is that, whereas the redistribution program has successfully managed to bring down the average size of beneficiary groups—large group size being seen as one of the main culprits for poor performance among the first generation of redistribution projects (i.e., roughly from 1995 to 2000)—this remedy is generally not available for restitution. In restitution, group size is largely a function of history and not amenable to change through program design. The second reason is that, relative to redistribution, a greater proportion of properties transferred to restitution beneficiaries involves high-value, irrigated horticulture production. This again links to history, in the sense that these are the properties from which claimants were removed, which should be restored to them. The current design of the redistribution program makes acquisition of such properties more or less impossible. The seven Levubu claims are a case in point: to date the total land cost for the restored farms is a staggering R240 million, which is almost half the national grant budget for redistribution for 2006/07 and works out to an average cost per claimant household of about R215,000. Although such an amount per beneficiary is technically possible under the Land Redistribution for Agricultural Development grant structure, it is unlikely because to access the maximum grant of R100,000 per adult, the beneficiary must contribute four times as much, which is rarely possible for sizable groups.

The third reason why restitution is different concerns the different textures of land demand. Redistribution is more readily self-selecting for people with an interest in agriculture. Although many redistribution projects have a number of obliging family members or neighbors associated with them, who add their names to the application for the sake of boosting the final grant award, these hangers-on do not play much of a role following the transfer of the land. Rural restitution projects are often different from redistribution projects. Following claimants' dedicated participation in community meetings leading up to the finalization of the transfer, they still very much regard the land as theirs. But if our case studies are anything to go by, participation in the claims process is not the same as self-selecting for participation in resettlement or agricultural production. The reasons why people are involved make a difference, and this has implications for how they articulate their preferences regarding the economic function of their land.

In this chapter we have sought to summarize what is known about the implications of rural land restitution for livelihoods, and in so doing we have engaged a debate about how agriculture should be organized on restored land. We have recounted the rather cheerless circumstances giving rise to this debate at the national level, summarized perspectives from other studies, and then sought to explore how the debate plays out in actual restitution projects. Key to the analysis were the contrasts among four case studies from Limpopo Province. Although many of the surface facts of these cases are familiar enough—malfunctioning communal property associations, poor planning, inadequate government support—what emerged as most revealing was the juxtaposition of rapid settlement by nonbeneficiaries where no effective claimant control prevented it to the largely unused land belonging to claimant communities generally riven by internal conflict.

The tentative conclusion is that the misfortune of rural restitution is only partly about the technical and ideological differences that preoccupy policymakers and implementers; at least as significant are differences regarding land use options within claimant groups themselves. One of the factors conditioning rural restitution that has received insufficient attention is apathy among claimants, not about having land restored, but about day-to-day involvement in agriculture on the restored land. For those claimant households who, presumably for perfectly good reasons, have no great enthusiasm either for relocating or for farming, arranging to have the land farmed commercially by a small core of interested individuals makes perfect sense. But other claimants face different circumstances and needs, and thus the scene for conflict is set. One solution is that suggested by de Villiers and van den Berg (2006, 38), whereby provision is made for both subsistence and commercial farming models within the same project, as well as for settlement where this is a particular need. As for how to make the commercial component work better than has generally been the case to date, it remains to be seen whether the strategic-partner approach is either viable or replicable on a large scale.

But beyond project level, the questions are even more daunting. What will it mean if, as the data suggest, two-thirds of the commercial farming area of Limpopo could be transferred through the restitution process? (e.g., SDC 2007, 17), Ultimately the question comes back to the impact of land reform on the role of agriculture in the economy and in relation to food security in particular. Critics of land reform allege that the prospect of widespread project failure represents a threat to food security, whereas those in favor argue that there is much underused land in the commercial farm sector and that, in a context of declining jobs, land reform can render direct benefits to food-insecure households. Given so little consensus as to what represents a good project, and how to design one, it is not surprising that this issue remains far from resolved.

NOTE

1. The first three case studies build on previous work of the authors alone or in collaboration with others. The Shimange study comes largely from Lahiff et al. (2008), the Mavungeni study from Manenzhe (2007), and the Munzhedzi study from HSRC et al. (2005b). Each case study also draws on more recent fieldwork conducted for this chapter.

REFERENCES

Ahmed, A., P. Jacobs, R. Hall, W. Kapery, R. Omar, and M. Schwartz. 2003. "Monitoring and Evaluating the Quality of Life of Land Reform Beneficiaries, 2000/01." Unpublished report prepared for the Department of Land Affairs.
ANC (African National Congress). 1994. *The Reconstruction and Development Programme: A Policy Framework*. Johannesburg: Umanyano Press.
CASE (Community Agency for Social Enquiry). 2006. *Assessment of the Status Quo of Settled Land Restitution Claims with a Developmental Component Nationally*. Pretoria: Department of Land Affairs.
CRLR (Commission on Restitution of Land Rights). 2001. "Land Restitution in South Africa—Honouring the Promise of Our Constitution; The Contribution of the Land Restitution Process to Sustainable Development." http://land.pwv.gov.za/restitution. Accessed 7/19/2007.
———. 2004. *Annual Report 2003–04*. Pretoria: Government Printers.
De Villiers, B., and M. van den Berg. 2006. *Land Reform: Trailblazers; Seven Successful Case Studies*. Johannesburg: Konrad Adenauer-Stiftung.
Didiza, T. 2003. "Address by the Minister of Agriculture and Land Affairs, Ms. Thoko Didiza, to the National Council of Provinces on the Occasion of the Budget Vote, 10 April 2003 Cape Town." http://land.pwv.gov.za. Accessed 7/19/2007.
DLA (Department of Land Affairs). 1997. *White Paper on South African Land Policy*. Pretoria: Government Printers.
Du Toit, P. 2004. *The Great South African Land Scandal*. Centurion, South Africa: Legacy Publications.
HSRC (Human Sciences Research Council). 2005a. "Auditing the Realisation of Democracy and Human Rights in the Context of Rural Land Reform in South Africa: Technical Report." Report for the multicountry OECD study on Measuring Human Rights, Democracy, and Governance (METAGORA). Pretoria: HSRC.
———, University of Fort Hare, University of KwaZulu-Natal, and Nkuzi Development Association. 2005b. "HIV/AIDS, Land-Based Livelihoods, and Land Reform

in South Africa." Report commissioned by the International Food Policy Research Institute and the Department of Land Affairs, South Africa. Pretoria: HSRC.

Lahiff, E., T. Maluleke, T. Manenzhe, and M. Wegerif. 2008. "Land Redistribution and Poverty Reduction in South Africa: The Livelihood Impacts of Smallholder Agriculture under Land Reform." Bellville: Programme for Land and Agrarian Studies, University of the Western Cape (Research Report 36).

Manenzhe, T. 2007. "Post Settlement Challenges for Land Reform Beneficiaries: A Case Study of Munzhedzi, Mavungeni and Shimange Communal Property Associations." Unpublished master's thesis, Programme for Land and Agrarian Studies, University of the Western Cape.

May, J., B. Roberts, J. Govender, and P. Gayadeen. 2000. "Monitoring and Evaluating the Quality of Life of Land Reform Beneficiaries, 1998/1999." Unpublished report prepared for the Department of Land Affairs. Pretoria: Department of Land Affairs.

PLAAS (Programme for Land and Agrarian Studies). 2006. "The Impact of Land Restitution and Land Reform on Livelihoods." Report commissioned by the Sustainable Development Consortium, Cape Town. Bellville: Programme for Land and Agrarian Studies, University of the Western Cape.

SDC (Sustainable Development Consortium). 2007. *A Settlement and Implementation Support Strategy for Land and Agrarian Reform in South Africa.* Pretoria: Commission on Restitution of Land Rights.

Xingwana, L. 2006. "Speech Delivered by the Hon. Minister for Agriculture and Land Affairs Ms. Lulu Xingwana, Land Hand-Over Celebration, Elim Mission Community, Paddock, Kwa-Zulu Natal, 15 July 2006." http://land.pwv.gov.za. Accessed 7/19/2007.

seventeen

Strategic Questions about Strategic Partners

Challenges and Pitfalls in South Africa's New Model of Land Restitution

BILL DERMAN, EDWARD LAHIFF,
AND ESPEN SJAASTAD

The South African land reform program has been lauded for its consensual and transparent approach—particularly the eschewing of the powers of expropriation granted under the Constitution—but it has also been widely criticized for the slow pace of land transfer and the failure of many land reform projects to make productive use of their land (Borras 2003; Hall 2007). Between 1994 and 2006 less than 5 percent of white-owned land was transferred through land reform to new black owners, making it unlikely that the state will achieve its target of 30 percent by 2014 and increasing pressure on it to seek innovative solutions to land acquisition and posttransfer development (Lahiff 2007).

Particularly challenging has been the restoration of highly developed commercial farms to their former owners under the restitution program. Most affected is Limpopo Province, where upwards of 50 percent of white-owned farmland is reported to be under claim.[1] Widespread concerns have been raised about the likely impact on South Africa's export economy, to which the province contributes substantially through production of fruit, nuts, and vegetables, and on employment and other economic activities.

Although the government is under pressure to maintain the productivity of the agricultural sector with land reform, its ability to do so has been severely compromised by a restitution policy that focuses on the purchase of fixed assets and inhibits the acquisition of associated business enterprises as "going concerns." As a result, functioning commercial farms may be effectively shut down, and claimants, working with a variety of state and private-sector organizations, may find themselves having to re-create businesses virtually from scratch.

This combination of issues has, since about 2004, led the state to attempt a new restitution model in Limpopo. According to this, successful claimant communities, organized in communal property associations (CPAs) or trusts, must form joint ventures with private entrepreneurs (often with a small share reserved for farmworkers) in which the entrepreneur—the so-called strategic partner—invests working capital and takes control of farm management decisions for a period of ten years, with the option of renewal for a further period. The potential benefits to the claimant communities include rental income for use of their land, a share of profits, preferential employment, training opportunities, and the promise that they will receive profitable and functioning farms at the termination of the lease agreements.

This new model raises many questions about the direction of the restitution program, the realization of benefits among claimants, and the extent to which the original objectives of the South African land reform program are being achieved. Also in question is the capacity of the state to plan and implement complex commercial deals on such a scale, as well as provide the necessary support to claimants and their commercial partners, and, over the longer term, safeguard the interests of communities and their individual members.

In this chapter we analyze the application of this model in Limpopo's subtropical Levubu Valley, where the transfer of over four hundred farms, amounting to almost thirty thousand hectares, to various communities, in alliance with two strategic partners, is under way (see also Aliber et al. in this volume). Levubu is an important test for restitution because of its highly developed agricultural economy, its integration into both national and international markets, and the unprecedented scale of land restoration envisaged. It also offers potential lessons for other land and rural development projects based on commercial enterprises by large community groups. Research for this study involved extensive interviews from 2005 to 2007 with all the parties, including local and regional representatives of the

Provincial Department of Agriculture (PDOA) and the regional land claims commissioner's (RLCC's) office, senior managers within the two companies designated as strategic partners, leaders and members of claimant communities and the lawyers who represent them, commercial farmers and their legal representatives, farmworkers, and employees of nongovernmental organizations (NGOs) active in land reform in Levubu. In this time we also observed numerous community workshops and meetings between various parties and analyzed the negotiations documentation.

Reaching agreement on the details of the strategic partnership arrangements has taken longer than anticipated, and by July 2007 (the end date for the field work reported on here) the contractual agreements between claimants, strategic partners, and the state were yet to be signed. This chapter is thus largely forward-looking, aimed at identifying key challenges and possible pitfalls in the model for claimants in particular. Developments since then, which are reported on briefly in the conclusion, point also to potential problems for strategic partners in an uncertain market environment, but this is not the primary focus of this chapter.

LEVUBU VALLEY: BACKGROUND

The upper Levubu valley is one of a number of pockets of high-value irrigated land in Limpopo province, situated close to the town of Makhado (formerly Louis Trichardt). Before 1898 the military strength of local tribes and the presence of malaria meant the area was not occupied by white settlers (Harries 1989; Mulaudzi 2000; Nefale 2000), who only arrived in significant numbers starting in the 1920s. The government at the time established an irrigation scheme for poor white farmers in the 1930s, which only became fully operational with the construction of the Albasini dam in the 1950s. The African population of the area—speaking mainly Venda and Shangaan (or Tsonga)—was gradually removed from the best agricultural land and later from adjacent hillsides that were planted to forestry. Sizable numbers were incorporated into the white-controlled agricultural economy, mainly as labor tenants and wage laborers, through a variety of repressive measures (Platzky and Walker 1985; Lahiff 2000; Fraser 2007).

The date of white settlement is of particular significance, falling as it does after 19 June 1913, the specified cutoff date for restitution claims. Land claims at Levubu are based on acts of dispossession stretching from 1913 up to the 1970s, when African people were forcibly removed from land through the establishment and later the abolition of labor tenancy, and the social engineering that accompanied the formation of the ethnic bantustans of Venda and Gazankulu. Given this history, a number of factors are contributing to the pressure for return of ancestral land at Levubu. These include the relatively recent date of dispossession, which means that many members of claimant communities have personally lived on the land in question; the continued existence of claimant groups as distinct (and sometimes well-organized) communities living in close proximity to the claimed lands; a history of contestation of dispossession, stretching up to the present day; the continued involvement of many members in agriculture; and the fact that the land under claim continues to be used for high-value agriculture. Taken together, they offer strong political and practical grounds for the restoration of land to claimants, as opposed to the cash compensation that has predominated elsewhere.

Some claims were still under investigation in mid-2007, but it was already clear that virtually the entire irrigated area in the valley—up to 420 properties—would be affected. The first phase of investigation and settlement (in 2005–2006) involved a total of seven claimant communities for farms whose landowners accepted the purchase offers made by the state. Other landowners, however, have rejected the initial offers from the state and stated their intention to resist any attempts at expropriation.

This first phase involved the transfer, in freehold title, of approximately 5,382 hectares of private land, in sixty-three parcels, purchased at a total price of R219 million.[2] The Department of Land Affairs allocated an additional R5 million in the form of Settlement Planning Grants and Restitution Discretionary Grants, and may make further funding available for development of the land. Additional private land is likely to be transferred in the near future, through either negotiated purchase or expropriation. A further area of approximately 2,600 hectares of state-owned land, mostly plantation forests, has also been earmarked for restoration to three of the seven claimant communities. It is not known exactly how many workers are currently employed either directly on the farms or in the upstream and downstream businesses linked to them, but the estimate for Levubu as a whole is in the order of ten thousand (Lahiff et al. 2006).

The Levubu claimants are all self-defined communities, identified by their tribal names—Ravele, Tshakuma, Ratombo, Shigalo, Tshivhazwaulu, Masakona, and Tshitwani. They vary in size from approximately 78 households in the case of Tshitwani to 324 households in the case of Ravele.

The land claimed ranges from 344 hectares (Ravele) to 1,330 hectares (Ratombo). Some communities, such as Tshakuma, remained on small fractions of their former land after the original dispossession, whereas Ravele and Shigalo were moved to drier areas up to fifty kilometers away. Interviews with members of these communities suggest that many see the restoration of tribal land as key to the reinvigoration of tribal identity and the power and status of tribal leaders. It is not therefore surprising that tribal chiefs ("traditional leaders") are at the forefront of most claims, including holding key positions within the CPAs and trusts.[3]

Despite the compelling arguments for it, restoration presents numerous challenges. First and foremost is the scale of the claims. Transferring such an extensive resource to a new set of owners is unprecedented and presents enormous practical challenges for the Commission on Restitution of Land Rights (CRLR), which has limited staff and technical resources. Furthermore, the change in landownership could potentially be highly disruptive of the local economy—in terms of productivity, farm employment, upstream and downstream industries, and property values. Such concerns have been voiced by political leaders across the spectrum, including the African National Congress, and local business interests. Third, it is unclear whether the new representative institutions (CPAs or trusts) are sufficiently strong or democratic to ensure effective and principled management of community interests. Fourth, although the government has belatedly threatened uncooperative landowners with expropriation, it still faces strong opposition from many. Fifth, the spectacular failure of a few early restitution projects (and the widespread underperformance of many more) has attracted much negative publicity and added to the pressure on the CRLR to come up with "sustainable" solutions that preserve the productive capacity of the farms and ensure a reasonable degree of material benefits for the claimants over time.

It is in this context that the concept of strategic partnerships has emerged. The factors contributing to the emergence of this model can be summarized as follows:

> An *economic* imperative to maintain the productivity of commercial farms and minimize the impact on employment and the local export economy
>
> A *developmental* imperative to ensure long-term benefits to claimants, over and above the symbolic value of the return of the land or

the limited benefits perceived to flow from alternative land uses (e.g., " subsistence" agriculture)

A *political* imperative to preserve the image of the government—in the eyes of political opponents, potential investors, and international commentators—as competent, dependable in fulfilling its promises, and responsible in the use of state resources

THE STRATEGIC PARTNERSHIP MODEL

The strategic partnership model has evolved gradually since it was first proposed around 2001, but it is important to note that it requires no changes in legislation or dramatic break with past policy. Initially, some landowners—known as the Group of 23—attempted to become the strategic partner for some of the Levubu claimant communities, but the Limpopo RLCC turned down their proposal, reportedly because it represented too great a continuity with the old order. The RLCC, working closely with the PDOA, then proposed that a single firm, South African Farm Management (SAFM), would become the strategic partner for all the claims in the Levubu Valley. This company was owned by established (white) interests in the agricultural sector and new black empowerment partners. It had a close working relationship with the PDOA through its management of the former state-owned Zebediela citrus estate in the province, now regarded as a successful example of a strategic partnership within restitution. Under pressure from Levubu claimants, the RLCC then undertook to identify other potential partners, which resulted in the selection of Mavu Management Services, a company formed by a number of white farmers from Levubu with black partners. Eventually, SAFM ended up as the nominated strategic partner for five of the seven claimant communities at Levubu (with a total of 3,336 hectares, in forty-four portions, under phase 1), with Mavu the nominated partner for the remaining two communities (2,045 hectares, in nineteen portions).

The farms to be restored are mainly planted with fruit and nut orchards. In addition to primary production, they produce oils from macadamias and avocados and juice from citrus, litchis, guavas, and mangoes. Approximately half the farms are reported to have unused portions of land, but it is not clear whether these are suitable for high-value crops.

Under the strategic partnership model, ownership of the land is vested in the claimant CPA or trust. Land is transferred directly from the landowner once agreement is reached with the RLCC on a purchase price.[4] Land transfers and the release of state grants are specified in a settlement agreement signed between the claimant communities and the state, represented by the minister of Agriculture and Land Affairs. Each claimant community and its strategic partner are required to form an operating company, in which farmworkers may also be given a small share through a specially created farmworkers' trust. In Levubu, the proposed allocation of shares is 50 percent to the claimant community, 48 percent to the strategic partner, and 2 percent to the farmworkers' trust. Specific responsibilities and rights regarding the company and its operations are spelled out in a shareholders' agreement, a lease agreement, and a management agreement between the parties. Profits are to be paid as dividends to shareholders according to their shares, or reinvested in the company.

Although the operating company is jointly owned, day-to-day management of the farms is in the hands of the strategic partner, who, in terms of the shareholders' and management agreements, has control of all financial and operational matters. For this, the partner charges the operating company a management fee. This fee, combined with the salaries of key managers provided by the strategic partner, may not exceed 8 percent of the turnover of the operating company. Since the restitution program does not pay for movable property, such as tractors, trucks, packing machinery, or pumps, the transferred farms no longer have the equipment required for production. This, therefore, has to be obtained by the strategic partner, either through leasing arrangements or the purchase of new machinery.

According to the model, claimant communities benefit through a combination of rental income for their land, a share in profits, training opportunities, and preferential employment opportunities in the enterprise. Although, with the exception of rent, the full value of these benefits has not generally been specified during the negotiation phase, community members are expecting significant material benefits from the restoration of their land and their involvement in these business ventures. Rent has been tentatively set at 1.25 percent of the land purchase price per annum (indexed to inflation), meaning that communities will potentially receive both dividends on their shareholding and rent, although the latter is below market rates for agricultural land in the area. In a move to protect the long-term interests of the communities, the settlement agreement specifies that they may neither sell, mortgage, nor otherwise put their land at risk.

For the strategic partner, as discussed further below, the benefits lie in the management fee (more or less guaranteed as long as turnover is maintained), a share in the profits of the company, and exclusive control of upstream and downstream activities, with potential benefits exceeding that of the farming enterprise itself. Also, by entering into partnerships with multiple communities, strategic partners have the possibility of consolidating and rationalizing production in a way that was not generally open to the farms' previous owner-occupiers.

A significant development in the negotiations was an intervention by Nkuzi Development Association, a local land rights organization known for its defense of landless people and its advocacy of radical land reform, to secure legal representation for claimants. It was clear that complex legal and business matters were at stake, and that the prospective strategic partners—experienced corporate players with extensive legal and financial experience—were in a strong position to dictate terms to both the CRLR and the claimant communities. Nkuzi, which had assisted many of the communities lodge their claims in 1997–98, now secured the services of one of South Africa's leading business law firms, on a pro bono basis, to represent five of the seven Levubu communities. Since September 2006, these lawyers have proposed numerous changes to the draft agreements to introduce elements that would give claimant communities greater control of the joint operating company and direct access to unused portions of land.

STRATEGIC QUESTIONS

Our research to date raises six critical questions about the strategic partnership model, which we set out below.

Who Makes the Key Decisions?

The strategic partnership model arises out of the assumption that relatively poor black rural communities possess neither the skills nor the capital necessary to operate highly developed agricultural enterprises successfully. The commercial operators that take on the role of strategic partner are assumed to have both the expertise and access to markets and capital, and are also attracted by the opportunities for profit. The partnership is thus highly asymmetrical and will obviously require careful handling from all sides to ensure that it functions smoothly and its benefits are shared equitably.

The agreements and process thus far, however, suggest that inequalities in information and power were being entrenched from an early stage. A recurring complaint in our interviews with both members and leaders of claimant communities was a lack of understanding of the process and poor communication with the office of the RLCC and, to a lesser extent, the strategic partners.[5] Early drafts of the shareholders' agreement—prepared by the RLCC and PDOA, in consultation with the strategic partners but with little or no input from the claimants—granted 50 percent of seats on the board of directors to the community, but it also granted an effective veto to the strategic partner over all aspects of strategic and financial management.[6] All matters affecting the company in any substantial way—including dissolution, changes in the composition of the board of directors, or changes in shareholding—would require a 75 percent majority at a general meeting of shareholders, voting according to their allocation of shares. However, on operational matters, including financial matters, the managing director, whose appointment is under the control of the strategic partner, would have effective control over the company, provided he or she consults with the management team and the board from time to time.

These issues were challenged by the lawyers acting on behalf of the communities since their intervention. Revised proposals included greater representation for communities on the board of directors and a phased approach, under which the strategic partner has effective control over operational matters for an initial three years, after which strategic decisions would be made by the board.

What Will Happen to Revenue?

Whether the new companies will show a profit is an open question. Certainly, the strategic partners expect a net gain from this process, which involves considerable costs in terms of negotiations, community liaison, management time, and capital expenditure.

The distribution of profits according to fixed shares may, at first glance, appear incentive-compatible. The allocation of 50 percent of the shares—and thus of the profits—to the community acts, from the perspective of the strategic partner, as a tax on net revenues, and there is no immediate incentive not to maximize profits. For the strategic partners, however, on-farm production is just one element in a vertically integrated process up and down the supply and market chains. Even though they are required to share profits from on-farm production with the communities, no such requirement applies to other parts of the value chain, over which they have exclusive control. It is here where conflicts of interest are likely to arise.

It is not insignificant that the first draft agreements made repeated provision for the strategic partner to be the sole decision maker in terms of purchasing and sales. There clearly exists both the incentive and the means for strategic partners to deflect profits away from the farming enterprise by transferring value to the companies they own upstream and downstream. This could be achieved relatively easily by hiking farm input prices or reducing output prices for transactions between the different companies they control, or through the supply of movable capital. Furthermore, because the farms lack movable machinery and equipment, a logical solution for the strategic partner was to set up a company from which to rent such machinery, as was done. Currently the communities are purchasing some of that equipment with government grant monies.

Depending on product differentiation and local supply and demand structures for farm inputs and output, price discrimination practices within established output categories may be relatively easy to detect (although still difficult to prevent). More subtle may be the manipulation of output grades, which would effectively disguise price discrimination as quality differentiation. More generally, strategic partners with vested interests in agricultural processing may make farm management choices, such as planting and harvesting schedules, that maximize profits in processing at the expense of profits in farming, and such practices will be virtually undetectable.

A further and potentially highly lucrative source of revenue for the strategic partners is their management fee, which is based on a percentage of annual turnover (i.e., independent of profit). According to an early draft of the shareholders' agreement, this fee, with salaries to senior managers, "will not exceed" 8 percent of turnover, and there seems no reason why this upper limit will not become the effective norm.[7] This arrangement clearly creates an incentive for the strategic partner to maximize turnover, which may not be compatible with maximizing on-farm profits or deflecting value up or down the market chain. Strategic partners may, for example, find it advantageous to increase turnover by maximizing output, particularly toward the end of their contracts. Although it is impossible to predict what strategies will be adopted at points throughout the business cycle, it is worth noting that the contractual agreements grant strategic partners a range of mechanisms for manipulating costs, revenues, turnover, and, ultimately, profits, with a range of potential outcomes. Community partners have recognized the value of upstream and downstream activities and have sought various means to ensure that the profits are shared property. This represents the growing sophistication of community leadership.

What Are the Implications for Scale of Production and Risk Management?

Traditionally, commercial farmers in Levubu have hedged against risk by diversifying production within an individual farm. From the perspective of the two strategic partners, it would make sense to think of their respective restitution farms as single estates.[8] This would avoid bottlenecks related to labor demand but could also likely to lead to a lower net demand for labor. Given the gains from specialization that are available—related to management, crop-soil combinations, labor skills, marketing, and equipment—as well as the opportunity to spread risk over a much larger management unit, the transition to larger, more specialized production units seems inevitable.[9] This is likely to be to the advantage of the strategic partner but may lead to three specific problems for claimants.

First, because of their vested interests in upstream and downstream industries, strategic partners are likely to favor crops that require the particular inputs their companies can provide and, even more important, those crops that supply the processing plants that they control. Indeed, one of the partners has already begun to eliminate forestry on the farms under its control and turn the area over to fruit trees because it lacks capacity for wood processing. The interests of the strategic partner and the communities are not necessarily aligned around such choices.

Second, although the strategic partners themselves may be well protected against risk, through the enlarged scale and associated variety of the production unit, the same will not necessarily be true of the individual communities. Putting multiple farms under bananas, for example, may bring economies of scale but will expose the owner-community to a degree of risk not shared by the strategic partner, who controls a range of products over several claims. It is possible, indeed likely, that an optimal insurance strategy for strategic partners (across multiple claims) will expose particular claimant communities to greater production and price risks, leading to substantial differentiation and fluctuation in net income.

Third, the combination of multiple claims may also provide opportunities for deflecting costs—and thereby manipulating profits—between communities, in the overall interest of the strategic partner. As in other areas of operations, the strategic partner may be able to choose between boosting revenues (e.g., by pushing up costs) or boosting profits, depending on which option best serves its interests. Transportation schedules, machinery rentals, and deployment of management staff all provide opportunities for cost manipulation across communities.

Who Will Benefit from Employment Opportunities?

Given the lack of direct access to land by community members and the limited (and indirect) benefits likely to flow via their CPAs and trusts, direct employment on the farms is one of the principal ways in which individuals might benefit. Yet employment opportunities for community members are likely to be extremely limited and could lead to tensions between the relatively few who gain employment and the many who do not, as well as create scope for patronage by community leaders. Employment of a small number at higher ranks—in management or as members of the board of directors—will introduce a further degree of inequality, and potential tensions, among members.

In addition, the position of existing farmworkers is far from secure, and many would already appear to have lost their jobs. For example, at Applefontein, due for takeover by Mavu, all former workers have been laid off. In other cases, interruptions to production due to the drawn-out negotiations process has led to loss of jobs by default, as unpaid workers have drifted away from the farms, with no guarantees that they will be reemployed by the new operators. Even where workers are retained, operating companies are likely to come under pressure to employ members of the claimant community, either as additional workers or in place of existing workers. This tension is already evident in the negotiations around the extent of shares to be allocated to workers, which was reduced from the 10 percent proposed by the CRLR to just 2 percent in draft agreements.[10]

The draft shareholders' agreement assumes the existence of a workers' trust to represent workers in the employment of the company. No such trusts have been established at Levubu to date, and it is unclear where responsibility for forming them now rests. Although these trusts were originally intended to benefit prerestitution workers on the farms, the layoffs that have already taken place make it is highly unlikely that they will benefit from this arrangement. Switching from the existing labor force to a new one is also likely to bring multiple tensions and disruptions on the operational side. Most workers live on or near the farms, which cannot be said for most community members, who might end up commuting over long distances. The skills of existing farmworkers are also unlikely to be matched by the claimants.

How Will the Handover to the Communities Be Implemented at the End of the Contract Period?

Community-owners are expected to acquire full control of the operating companies after the initial ten (or fifteen) years of the joint-venture agreement. Given proper training and work experience during this initial phase, it is assumed that they will be in a position to operate the farms commercially, but this will obviously depend on a range of factors, not least continued access to capital and produce markets.

An immediate concern is whether a time span of ten (or even fifteen) years will affect strategic partner choices with regard to crop selection and investments. It may, for example, be rational for them to plant short-term crops such as bananas or vegetables, rather than a crop such as macadamia nuts, which will not reach maturity during the first contract period, even though the latter may be more profitable from a longer-term (i.e., community) perspective. There is also an incentive to let reinvestment in physical capital lapse toward the end of the contract.

A further concern is whether sufficient funds for working capital, capital maintenance, and capital renewal will have been set aside at the conclusion of the joint-venture phase for the farms to remain operational. A key function of the strategic partner is to secure capital for the operating company, either from its own resources or from the banks, which will be lent on to the joint company. The repayment of loans from the strategic partner (or loans guaranteed by it) at the end of the partnership can come only from community funds (or, less likely, from further state grants). This requires the community to accumulate funds equivalent to the debt owed to the strategic partner—itself an onerous requirement given the inevitable pressure to distribute benefits to members over time. Opportunities to raise finance (for instance by taking up an additional loan or by liquidation of assets), however, are effectively denied by the prohibition against using land as collateral and the control of farm management decisions by the strategic partner.

How Will Communities and Their Members Benefit?

The potential benefits of land restoration to communities can be divided into five categories: the symbolic value of regaining ownership of ancestral lands; direct access to land for settlement and productive use; a flow of revenue and associated material benefits; opportunities for employment among individual beneficiaries; and access by individual community members to training and acquisition of skills in farm management and labor.

The strategic partner model clearly has the ability to provide some of these benefits, but not all, and it is important to consider the trade-offs that are being made, knowingly or otherwise. The model provides considerable scope for training of community members in the skills of farming and farm management, probably more so than any alternative approach, barring extensive and prolonged state involvement. Given sufficient commitment by the two main shareholders, this is perhaps its most promising aspect. The model also provides employment prospects for community members, albeit at the probable expense of existing farmworkers and possibly, through consolidation, at the expense of net farm employment in the area.

In terms of monetary and associated material benefits, however, the model is likely to make a limited contribution, at least over the initial ten or fifteen years. The amount that the communities will receive annually as rent—the benefit that is most likely to materialize—will amount to between R658 per household and R3,639 per household, based on available membership lists. One strategic partner, SAFM, did not pay rent due to its financial insolvency. Other rental monies have been used to purchase trucks, computers, and offices for the CPA committee. Profits seem distant for the moment as all community farms are currently losing money. Future profits where they materialize are, according to various community leaders, likely to be reinvested in the company rather than paid out to shareholders. Claimant groups at Levubu have yet to develop detailed proposals for income distribution, but the arrangements proposed to date center on provision of public goods, such as a community hall, roads, and student scholarships. It appears unlikely that there will be any individual cash payments to community members, not least because this is being actively discouraged by state officials and many community leaders.

As a means of fulfilling the promise of returning land to the original holders, the model is likely to deliver only in the narrow sense of restoring formal ownership, at least in the short to medium term. The joint-venture agreements focus narrowly on the continuation of core commercial agricultural activities, which fall under the effective control of the strategic partner. Little or no attention has been paid to the wider land needs of communities, such as land for housing or for small-scale food production. (See also Aliber et al. this volume.)

Strategic partnerships represent a new departure for land restitution in South Africa. The key policy shift is away from an emphasis on *land access* by claimants and toward the maintenance of *agricultural productivity*. Although this has potential benefits for claimants, and for the wider economy in terms of employment and trade, it also carries considerable risks for all parties, as the questions raised here have shown.

In late 2008, the restitution process in Levubu suffered a serious setback when SAFM was placed under liquidation with debts reported to amount to some R100 million. In addition to managing a majority of the Levubu claims, SAFM was also responsible for numerous restitution projects elsewhere in Limpopo Province and South Africa. This development points up risks and problems not highlighted in this chapter. In particular, trusting a single strategic partner with a majority of restitution projects makes the entire process vulnerable to overextension and mismanagement within that firm. More generally, the failure of SAFM highlights the problems that may emerge when the responsibility for land reform is transferred to a private-sector company whose interests may be at odds with the land reform objectives envisaged in the Constitution and whose capabilities may not match the scale of the responsibilities transferred. Delays in the transfer of government grant monies have been suggested as a contributing factor in the collapse of SAFM; the partnership, lacking accumulated capital of its own, was unable to make investments and adjustments necessitated by a recent downturn in relevant agricultural markets and the neglect of farm assets during the process itself.

The overreliance on SAFM is not a simple reflection of cronyism and bad decision making within government. The fact is that the South African private sector is unable to meet the challenges contained within the strategic partner model of restitution because of a shortage of firms willing to enter this process on the stipulated terms.

From the point of view of claimants, the impact on land rights and livelihoods of a "successful" strategic partnership arrangement is likely to be extremely limited, in the short to medium term in particular. Lack of direct access to the restored land means that most members may be no better off in terms of land for housing and small-scale farming, the need for which is clearly expressed in all the communities. Indirect benefits, in terms of income from shareholding, is unlikely to materialize for many years, and income from land rental is likely to be used for the CPA's own expenses, perhaps including salaries, rather than redistributed to community members. Any distribution of benefits is likely to be tightly controlled by community leaders, including unelected tribal authorities.

The most likely benefits in the short term are employment and training opportunities for community members, including participation in management and on the boards of directors for a lucky few. The generally low wages on offer for farmworkers, however, have already caused discontent among claimant communities. The impact on net employment also looks set to be negative, at least in the short term, as production slumped during the transition to new ownership. The big losers in this regard are the existing workforce, whose interests have effectively gone unprotected throughout the restitution process, despite lip service from various quarters and promises of a stake in the reconstituted farming enterprises. Although not specified in the draft agreements, it appears likely that selected entrepreneurs from within the claimant communities may be given preference in terms of contracts to supply fuel and other services to the farms, a potentially valuable benefit but one that is unlikely to be shared with the majority of community members.

The problems and weaknesses inherent in the current version of the strategic partnership model cannot primarily be blamed on the commercial partners themselves who are, by their own account, motivated by commercial incentives. The failure to shape the contractual arrangements more closely to the needs of the communities involved, especially their poorer members, and to protect existing workers can in large part be attributed to the haste with which the state institutions involved—the Limpopo office of the RLCC and the PDOA—have developed the model and the lack of meaningful consultation with claimants around its implementation. Lack of capacity within communities and a poor record of democratic decision making have also meant that the intended beneficiaries have not been as involved in the process as they should have been. This has manifested itself in a growing divide between some community leaders, who are keen to conclude the deals with their new partners and take their places on the board of directors, and the majority of members who understand little about the process or how they are likely to benefit.

Postsettlement support has emerged as one of the major challenges facing land reform in South Africa. The creation of strategic partnerships is viewed by the CRLR and politicians at the provincial and national levels as the solution, to the extent that this function has now effectively been privatized. Strategic partners will become responsible for the development of economic activity on the restored land, including the provision of working capital and training for community members. Nonetheless, there remains a clear need for continued involvement by government and NGOs in monitoring the performance of these new joint ventures in the interests of claimants, and supporting CPAs with capacity (knowledge and skills), business advice, dispute resolution, and equitable distribution of benefits. A postsettlement support unit has been created with membership from the Limpopo Department of Agriculture and the CRLR. It has been functioning but under severe pressure because of SAFM's bankruptcy and the number of farms in poor condition.

The social, political, and economic factors influencing the South African restitution process suggest that some variant of the strategic partnership model is likely to be implemented across more claims on high-value agricultural land for the foreseeable future. The emerging model at Levubu has proven problematic from many perspectives, especially that of poor and unemployed community members, but there is scope for improving it. Probably the most important modification, which would bring the most immediate benefit to the most people at relatively little cost, would be to allow for limited settlement (combining both housing and small-scale agriculture) on noncore land. A greater emphasis on training of beneficiaries in farm management, business management, and corporate and marketing activities, including more specific targets in terms of numbers to be trained and timescales, would also help. Communities need greater power to terminate agreements and assume control of operating companies when contracts expire, without being obliged to repay all debts owed to the strategic partner immediately.

Finally, there is a need for the state, and NGOs, to put mechanisms in place to monitor the performance of both operating companies and community leaders with regard to business decisions and the distribution of benefits. Above all, emerging models of restitution must deliver significant material benefits and substantive rights in land if they are to be sustainable and meet their constitutional obligations.

NOTES

1. "No Turning Back for SA as Minister Pulls Pin on Expropriation." *Business Day*, 10 June 2005.

2. In December 2006 US$1 was worth approximately R7.

3. See Ntsebeza (2006) and Oomen (2005) for detailed discussions on traditional leaders, and Hellum and Derman (2009) for a detailed account of chiefs and CPAs in Levubu.

4. Expropriation may legally be invoked if no agreement is reached, but as yet this has not been considered at Levubu.

5. Claimant communities have also complained that Nkuzi and their lawyers have not kept them well informed of developments.

6. Draft Shareholders' Agreement, 2006.

7. Draft Shareholders' Agreement, 2006.

8. For accounting purposes, each claim (i.e., each joint venture) has to be run separately, but there is no bar to full consolidation of farm units within a claim. Some degree of integration may also be possible across claims, but this will be complicated by the presence of different owners and different operating companies.

9. One of the strategic partners interviewed insisted on the necessity of larger, more specialized production units for economic reasons.

10. Draft Shareholders' Agreement, 2006; Draft Shareholders' Agreement, 16 May 2007.

REFERENCES

Borras, S. M. 2003. "Questioning Market-led Agrarian Reform: Experiences from Brazil, Colombia and South Africa." *Journal of Agrarian Change* 3 (3).

Fraser, Alistair. 2007. "Hybridity Emergent: Geo-history, Learning, and Land Restitution in South Africa." *Geoforum* 38 (2): 299–311.

Hall, Ruth. 2007. "Transforming Rural South Africa: Taking Stock of Land Reform." In *The Land Question in South Africa: The Challenge of Transformation and Redistribution,* ed. L. Ntsebeza and R. Hall, 87–106. Cape Town: HSRC Press.

Harries, Patrick, 1989. "Exclusion, Classification and Internal Colonialism: The Emergence of Ethnicity Among the Tsonga-Speakers of South Africa." In *The Creation of Tribalism in Southern Africa,* ed. Leroy Vail, 82–110. London: Currey; Berkeley: University of California Press.

Hellum, Anne, and Bill Derman. 2009. "Government, Business and Chiefs: Ambiguities of Social Justice through Land Restitution in South Africa." In *Rules of Law and Laws of Ruling,* ed. Franz and Keebet von Benda Beckmann and Julie Ebert, 125–51. London: Ashgate.

Lahiff, Edward. 2000. *An Apartheid Oasis? Agriculture and Rural Livelihoods in Venda.* London: Frank Cass.

———. 2007. "Willing Buyer, Willing Seller: South Africa's Failed Experiment in Market-Led Agrarian Reform." *Third World Quarterly* 28 (8): 1577–98.

Lahiff, E., M. Wegerif, T. Manhenze, J. Quan, and M.Aliber. 2006. *The Area Based Land Reform Initiative in Makhado, Limpopo Province.* Natural Resources Institute, University of Greenwich. Land and Territory Research Paper No. 4. December 2006.

Mulaudzi, Maanda. 2000. "'U Shuma Bulasi': Agrarian Transformation in the Zoutpansberg District of South Africa, up to 1946." PhD diss., University of Minnesota.

Nefale, M. M. 2000. "The Politics of Land in Levubu, Northern Province, c. 1935–1998." Unpublished MA thesis (history), University of Cape Town.

Ntsebeza, Lungisile. 2006. *Democracy Compromised: Chiefs and the Politics of Land in South Africa.* Cape Town: HSRC Press.

Oomen, B. 2005. *Chiefs in South Africa: Law, Power and Culture in the Post Apartheid Era.* London: James Currey.

Platzky, Laurine, and Cherryl Walker. 1985. *Surplus People: Forced Removals in South Africa.* Braamfontein: Ravan Press.

Contributors

Michael Aliber, Institute for Poverty, Land and Agrarian Studies, University of the Western Cape, South Africa

Chris Beyers, Department of International Development Studies, Trent University, Canada

Anna Bohlin, Centre for Public Sector Research, University of Gothenburg, Sweden

Angela Conway, Southern Cape Land Committee, South Africa

Chris de Wet, Department of Anthropology, Rhodes University, South Africa

Bill Derman, Noragric, Norwegian University of Life Sciences, Aas, Norway, and Michigan State University, United States of America

Uma Dhupelia-Mesthrie, History Department, University of the Western Cape, South Africa

Alan Dodson, Advocate, Johannesburg Bar, South Africa

William Ellis, Department of Anthropology and Sociology, University of the Western Cape, South Africa

Derick Fay, Department of Anthropology, University of California, Riverside, United States of America

Ruth Hall, Institute for Poverty, Land and Agrarian Studies, University of the Western Cape, South Africa

Deborah James, Department of Anthropology, London School of Economics, United Kingdom

Thembela Kepe, Geography Department, University of Toronto, Canada

Edward Lahiff, Trinity International Development Initiative, Trinity College, Dublin, Ireland

Contributors

Themba Maluleke, Department of Rural Development and Land Reform, South Africa

Tshililo Manenzhe, Parliament of the Republic of South Africa, South Africa

Eric Mgujulwa, Chatha Village, Eastern Cape Province, South Africa

Hanri Mostert, Department of Private Law, University of Cape Town, South Africa

Steven Robins, Department of Sociology and Social Anthropology, University of Stellenbosch, South Africa

Chizuko Sato, Institute of Developing Economics, Japan External Trade Organization, Chiba, Japan

Espen Sjaastad, Noragric, Norwegian University of Life Sciences, Aas, Norway

Mpfariseni Thagwana, Human Sciences Research Council, South Africa

Kees van der Waal, Department of Sociology and Social Anthropology, University of Stellenbosch, South Africa

Cherryl Walker, Department of Sociology and Social Anthropology, University of Stellenbosch, South Africa

Marc Wegerif, Economic Justice Campaign Coordinator for the Horn, East and Central Africa Region, Oxfam International, Tanzania

Tim Xipu, Southern Cape Land Committee, South Africa

Index

A page number in italic type indicates a map, table, or figure on that page. The letter *n* following a page number indicates a note on that page.

Abolition of Racially Based Land Measures Act of 1991, 19
Abrams v. Allie, 73, 75
Advisory Commission on Land Allocation (ACLA), 219–20
AFRA. *See* Association for Rural Advancement (AFRA)
African National Congress (ANC), 126, 146, 201
  agricultural economy and, 310
  in Cato Manor, 260
  in Chatha, 201, 203
  "coloured" identity and, 126
  Land Manifesto of 1992, 20
  land reform and, 2
  private property and, 19
  Reconstruction and Development Programme (1994), 288
  in Roosboom, 216
African Wildlife Foundation, 176
Alexkor, 66
Alexkor Ltd & Another, Richtersveld Community v., 278
Allie, Abrams v., 73, 75
ANC. *See* African National Congress (ANC)
Association for Rural Advancement (AFRA), 217, 221–23

Bain's Bushmen, 186
bantustans, *xi*, 10, 18, 107, 198, 269, 309
Barnard, Cecil S. (Bvekenya), 167
Bastervolk Organisasie, 182
Berkes, F., 243–46
Berzborn, Suzanne, 47
betterment planning, 10, 24, 34, 198–99
  See also Chatha case study
Black Communities Development Act of 1984, 72

Black River, Cape Town, 83–87, 97–98
  financial compensation and, 87, 90, 91, 93, 94, 97
  individual narratives and, 87–89, 89–91, 91–93, 93–96
  meaning of restitution and, 86
  restoration of property and, 88–89
  scope and limits of restitution and, 96–97
  tenants and, 90, 96
  urban restitution and, 86–87
Bleek, Dorothea, 185
Bohlin, Anna, 97
Border Rural Committee (BRC), 202, 209–11, 212–13
Brazil, 47, 53
  Constitution, 113–14
Brown, Marj, 85
Bulpin, T. V.: *Ivory Trail*, 167
Bunn, David, 166

Campus Law Clinic, 264, 265
Cape Town
  Group Areas Act and, *xii*, 144
  political turbulence and, 146–47
  restitution and local government and, 147–49
Cape Town Community Land Trust (CTCLT), 147–48, 152, 156
Cato Manor case study, 265
  Cato Manor Action Group and, 262–63
  CMDA redevelopment initiative and, 260–61
  contested space in the early 1990s and, 259–63
  default and, 256, 266–69
  dispossession and relocation and, 258–59
  Durban riots of 1949 and, 258

327

Cato Manor case study (cont.)
  historical background of, 257–59
  low-cost housing and, 268
  as Presidential Lead Project, 262
  reparations and, 268
  restitution and ethnicity and, 269
  restitution process and, 270
  RLCC and, 262
  section 34 court application and, 263–66, 269
  squatter invasion and, 260
  See also District Six case study
Cato Manor Development Agency (CMDA). See Cato Manor case study
Cayuga Nation, 51
chapter overview, 5–13
Chatha case study, 210–12
  ANC and, 203–4, 208
  betterment planning and, 199–200
  BRC and, 202, 209–11, 212–13
  DLA ruling and, 203
  forestry project confrontation and, 206–7
  Keiskammahoek Rural Survey and, 199
  moral ambiguities and, 205–6
  opposition to restitution terms and, 203–4
  partisan politics and, 201
  polarization and conflict, 2002 to 2006, 204–9
  rearrangement of residential areas and, 201
  residents' relationship to the land and, 200
  restitution and, 202
  restitution awards and, 209–10
  restitution-based development 2007 to 2009 and, 210–12
  sources of polarization and conflict and, 207–9
  South African National Civic Organization (SANCO) and, 201
  UDM and, 208–9
  village politics and, 200–201
Chennels, Roger, 182, 194–95
Coeur d'Alene Indians, 56n3
Cole, Josette, 267
comanagement of protected areas
  agreement ambiguities and, 250–51
  ambiguity of land settlement agreements and, 247
  common vision among stakeholders and, 246–47
  complexity of issues and, 250
  economic incentives to conserve resources and, 245–46
  involvement of local people and, 242
  legal protection of local rights and, 245
  management of land claims and, 250
  natural resource sustainability and, 241–42
  origins of concept of, 240–41
  presence of appropriate institutions and, 243–44
  prior negotiations and, 248–49
  protected areas, land claims and, 236
  reviews of, 237
  state agencies as initiators and key players in, 242
  trust between actors and, 244–45
  See also Mkambati Nature Reserve case study
commercial agriculture, 133, 289, 290, 293, 299
Commission on Land Allocation (COLA), 261
Commission on Restitution of Land Rights (CRLR), 2, 21, 135, 183
  amount and cost of land and, 30
  Annual Report (2004), 289–90
  cash or financial compensation and, 24, 27, 268
  claims lodged and, 28–29
  claims received and, 23
  claims settled and, 29–30
  definition of, 241
  DLA and, 27
  expansion of role of, 27
  funding and, 31–32
  LCC and, 27, 63
  necessary vision of, 284
  number and type of claims filed with, 2–3
  primary roles of, 282–84
  Restitution Act and, 276
  rural claims and, 31
  strategic partnerships and, 36
  sustainable resettlement and, 282–83
  urban claims and, 3–4
  See also restitution program in South Africa; specific case studies
Communal Land Rights Act of 2004, 245
communal property associations, 35, 165, 277, 303, 307
Communal Property Associations Act of 1996, 277
Community Agency for Social Enquiry (CASE) study, 291–92
Community Development Board, 134–35

Index

Constitutional Court, 63–64
Constitution of South Africa, 20–21
  human dignity and, 276
  Interim and Final differences and, 285n5
  land reform and, 62, 145
  prior compensation and, 25
  private property and, 20, 24–25
  property clause and, 62–63, 100, 112–13
  restitution definition in, 274
  right to restitution and, 274–76, 282–83
  role of local government and, 145
  See also specific cases
Cousins, B., 244
Covie case study, 132–40
  claimant unity and, 139
  Covie Claimant Committee and, 135–36
  CPA and, 138–39
  development of appropriate plans and arrangements, 137–38
  incremental dispossession and, 133
  NGOs and, 139
  settlement process and, 136–37, 139–40
CRLR. *See* Commission on Restitution of Land Rights (CRLR)
Crook's Corner, 167

Daniel, J. B., 198
Davhana, Chief, 109
Democratic Alliance (DA), 146
Department of Land Affairs (DLA), 27
  ≠Khomani San and, 186–87
  Cato Manor and, 268–69
  Chatha community and, 202–3
  claims and, 2
  comanagement and, 236
  commercial farming and, 112–13
  CRLR and, 27, 112–13
  Eastern Cape Parks Board and, 241–42
  Levubu Valley settlement grants and, 309
  Mkambati Nature Reserve and, 239–40, 248
  National Land Summit of 2005 and, 61–62
  postsettlement support and, 21
  Quality of Life Surveys, 291
  Roosboom and, 225, 227
  tenancy claims policy and, 120
  White Paper on South African Land Policy (1997), 22, 24, 70, 218–19, 288
  See also specific case studies
Department of Land Affairs, Dulabh & Another v., 274–75
Department of Land Affairs, In re The Farm UAP 28A, Jacobs v., 73–74
Department of Land Affairs v. Witz, In re Various Portions of Grassy Park, 74
Department of Public Works and Land Affairs (DPWLA), 218–19
Department of Water Affairs and Forestry (DWAF), 132
de Tolly, Peter, 150, 153
Development Bank of South Africa, 177
de Villiers, B., 245, 303
  Land Reform, 293
Dhupelia-Mesthrie, Uma, 33–34
Didiza, Thoko, 23, 202, 289
District Six case study, 47, 50
  Beneficiary and Redevelopment Trust and, 144, 153–55, 159
  Cato Manor and, 159
  City of Cape Town and, 150–51, 152–53, 159
  Civic Association and, 148
  compaction in line with market principles and, 152–53
  disagreements over decision making and development costs, 158
  dispossession and, 143–44
  District Six Museum and, 153–54
  establishing the primary public and, 147–49
  Ex-Residents and Traders Association and, 148
  housing question and, 155–57
  integrated development and, 154
  land development priorities and, 158–59
  Metropolitan Spatial Development Framework and, 152
  N2 Gateway Project and, 157–58, 159
  negotiations and planning after 1998, 149–52
  ongoing arguments and, 157–58
  Record of Understanding of 1998, 148
  restitution claims and, 144
  restructuring of local government and, 151–52
  section 34 of the Restitution Act and, 147–49
  social redress for the dispossessed and, 153–55
DLA. *See* Department of Land Affairs (DLA)
Dominy, Michelle, 54
Dulabh & Another v. Department of Land Affairs, 274–75
du Toit, Andries, 47, 97, 273

329

du Toit, Philip: *Great South African Land Scandal*, 293
Dwesa-Cwebe, 46, 52

Eastern Cape Parks Board, 240, 241, 243, 244
Eastern Europe, 45, 54
Ellis, William, 46
Endangered Wildlife Trust, 176
Engelbrecht & Others, Mphela & Others v., 281–82
Erasmus, Justin, 85
expropriation, 25, 26, 44, 54, 61, 74, 306, 309, 310
    Cato Manor and, 258, 259, 268
    Restitution Act and, 276, 283
    Roosboom and, 219

Farmerfield Communal Property Trust, In re, 278
financial compensation. *See* restitution program in South Africa
Ford Foundation, 176
Freedom Charter of 1955, 19, 20
Free State, 31
Friedman, J., 168

Gamawela Community v. Government of the Republic of South Africa & Others, 280
Goldfields, 176
Government of the Republic of South Africa & Others, The Gamawela Community v., 280
Great Limpopo Transfrontier Park (GLTP), 163–64, 165
Group Areas Acts, 18, 65, 72, 96, 117
GTZ, 176
Gwanya, Tozi, 23–24

Haakdoornbult Boerdery CC v. Mphela, 282
Hanekom, Derek, 86
Harries, Patrick, 167
Hazel, Neil, 267
Heidevallei, 118, 121–22

identity, 4, 42, 43, 46, 87
    African, 156
    in Cato Manor, 256, 270
    in Chatha, 207
    "coloured," 126, 146, 156
    community, 50
    San, 9, 181, 195
    Shangaan, 163
    tribal, 163, 310

Inkatha Freedom Party (IFP), 220
Institute for Poverty, Land and Agrarian Studies (PLAAS), 164–65, 291, 292–93
Ivory Trail (Bulpin), 167

Jacobs v. Department of Land Affairs, In re The Farm UAP 28A, 73–74
Junod, Henri, 168
justice, 33, 41, 45, 49, 53, 68, 85–86, 94–95, 97, 148–49
    redistributive 156, 159
    restorative 3, 20, 156, 159, 288
    retributive 164
    social, 54, 76, 156

Kagga Kamma group, 186, 187, 188–89, 191
Kakhathini, Maurice, 260
Kalahari Gemsbok National Park (KGNP), 182
Kalk Bay case study, 122–25
    Group Areas proclamation and, 123
    lodging of claims and, 122
    settlement and, 125
Kepe, T., 244
Khanyayo, 239
≠Khomani San case study
    authenticity and, 193–95
    conceptualization and framing of the claim and, 182
    delivery of social services and, 189
    identification of, 185
    ≠Khomani San Communal Property Association (CPA) and, 185
    livelihood goals and, 187–89
    livestock farmers and, 189–91
    meaning of restitution and, 193–94
    membership in the claiming San community and, 185–87
    N/u language and, 186, 192
    resistance to and resolution of the claim and, 182–83
    restitution package and, 184
    return to the old ways and, 192–94
    traditional versus western cultures and, 191–92
    western/westernized San and, 187, 189, 191, 194
Khumalo, Daniel, 105
Khumalo v. Minister of Land Affairs, 73, 75
Kingwill, Rosalie, 85
Kluane First Nation, 51–52

Knott and Another v. Minister of Land Affairs, 74–75
Knysna case study, 117–22
   drawn-out negotiations and, 119–20
   initial land claims and, 118
   lack of policy and, 120
Knysna Community Forum, 121
Koch, Eddie, 174
Kranspoort Community, In re, 65, 70, 278–80
Kruger National Park (KNP), 163, 166
   removal of the Makuleke and, 166–68
Kruiper, Dawid, 182, 187, 189, 194–95
Kuper, Adam, 49

Land Claims Commission (the commission). *See* Commission on Restitution of Land Rights (CRLR)
Land Claims Court (LCC), 4–5, 21–22, 27, 63, 261–62
   Cato Manor case study and, 264–65, 283
   the Constitution and, 285n5
   discrimination and dispossession and, 71–75
   Dulabh; Witz; Randall and Knot and, 73–75
   Khumalo; Allie and, 73
   Kranspoort and, 65
   "land" and "community" and, 64–71
   Ndebele-Ndzundza and, 68–70
   Restitution Act interpretations and, 277–82
   "restitution" definition and, 274–75
   Richtersfeld case and, 65–68, 72–73
   role of, 63
   Slamdien and, 71–72
   See also specific cases
Land Claims Working Group, 20
land reform
   civil society organizations and, 5
   key issues of, 100
   state institutions and, 5
   See also land restitution, comparative study of; South African restitution program
Land Reform (de Villiers, van den Berg), 293
land restitution, comparative study of
   Australia and, 55
   beyond restitution and, 48
   Brazil and, 47, 51, 53
   Canada and, 45, 55
   citizenship and, 51
   claim staking and, 46–47
   community and governance and, 49–51
   community formation and, 46–47
   complex meanings of, 4
   demands of the state and, 47
   disjuncture and social change and, 42–43
   dispossession and, 44, 266
   duration of, 48–49
   Eastern Europe and, 45, 54
   historical and political context of, 18–21
   improvement and, 53
   indigeneity and, 50
   institutionalization of property and, 51–53
   judicial activism and, 4–5
   land claims and, 45–46
   negotiation and litigation and, 46
   New York State, 45, 52
   New Zealand and, 54, 55
   Peru and, 46, 47
   policy formation and, 44–45
   post-dispossession period and, 44–45
   as process, 2
   resettlement and, 48
   rights and wrongs and, 53–54
   role of the state and, 43
   Romania and, 55
   social relationships and, 42
   South Africa and, 55
   stakeholders in, 46
   study of, 42
   Zimbabwe and, 54
LCC. *See* Land Claims Court (LCC)
Legal Resources Centre (LRC), 164–65
Levubu Valley case study (Limpopo), 306–7
   background of, 308–11
   improvement possibilities and, 322
   restoration challenges and, 310
   strategic partnership model and, 311–13
   strategic questions and, 313–19
   See also strategic partnerships
Levubu Valley Cluster case study (Limpopo), 297–98
Liberal Party, 216

Mabo v. Queensland, 67
Macleantown Residents Association: re Certain Erven and Commonage in Macleantown, In re, 286n26
Magome, H., 242
Mahlahuvani case study, 101–6

community organization and, 109
conflict and ethnicity and, 111–12
nature of production and, 110
occupation overview, 107–9
principal crops and, 108
production and political leadership and, 110–11
Makuleke case study
background to, 166–70
borderland entrepreneurs and the culture of improvisation and, 170–71
communal property association and, 173–74, 177
conservation and community development and, 164–65, 177–78
continuing complexities and risks, 178
definition of community and, 172–73
development-orientation and, 164
Friends of Makuleke and, 176
gender equity and, 173, 174
issues of land and chieftancy and, 168–70, 171–73
Makuleke Tribal Authority and, 173
Makuleke village and, 169
principles of constitutional democracy and, 164–65
recent legislation and, 178
reconciling chieftancy, democracy, and conservatism, 173–77
Restitution of Land Rights Act and, 171–72
SANParks settlement and, 174–75
significant developments and, 176–77
Transfrontier Park concept and, 175–76
Maluleke, Lamson, 164
Mandela, Nelson, 1, 95, 126
Mavu Management Services, 311
Mavungeni case study (Limpopo), 294–95
Mayson, David, 85
Mbeki, Thabo, 163–64, 173
memory, 43, 47, 56, 83, 87
Mgoqi, Wallace, 86, 119, 120, 160n
Mhinga, Chief, 166, 176–77
counterclaim of, 168
Mier Residents Association, 182–83
Minister of Health and Others v. Treatment Action Campaign and Others, 285n2
Minister of Land Affairs, Khumalo v., 73, 75
Minister of Land Affairs, Knott and Another v., 74–75
Minister of Land Affairs, Randall and Another v., 74–75
Minister of Land Affairs v. Slamdien, 71–72

Minkley, G., 198
Mkambati Nature Reserve case study
ambiguity of settlement agreements and, 248–50
background of, 238–40
comanagement origins and relevance to resources, 236, 240–43
Eastern Cape Parks Board and, 240, 241, 243, 244
Land Trust and, 239, 240, 241, 244, 245
management authority and, 248
neglect of key comanagement conditions and, 243–46
Provincial Department of Economic Affairs, Environment, and Tourism (DEAT) and, 240
restitution agreement, 239–40
See also comanagement of protected areas
Mngadi, Elliot, 216
Mphela, Blessing, 24
Mphela, Haakdoornbult Boerdery CC v., 282
Mphela & Others v. Engelbrecht & Others, 281–82
Mpumalanga, 23, 30, 31
Mugakula, Phahlela Joas, 163
Munzhedzi case study (Limpopo), 296–97
farming types and, 298–99
Murison, Isgak, 151
Murombedzi, J., 242
Murray, Colin, 85

Nagia, Anwah, 148
National Forest Act, 133
National Land Summit of 2005, 23, 61–62
National Party (NP), 19, 20, 146
Natives Land Act of 1913, 18, 20, 69, 257
Ndebele-Ndzundza Community & Others, Prinsloo & Another v., 68–70
communal nature of restitution claims and, 69
ownership as a bundle of rights and, 69–70
New National Party (NNP), 146
NGOs. *See* nongovernmental organizations (NGOs)
Nhlapo Commission, 168, 169
Nkuzi Development Association, 107, 313
nongovernmental organizations (NGOs), 5, 8, 19, 139, 322
≠Khomani San and, 190–91, 194
Chatha and, 10, 202, 212, 213
Makuleke and, 176–77

restitution and, 42
Roosboom and, 215, 221–23, 228
Stake Your Claim campaign and, 26–27
See also Association for Rural Advancement (AFRA); Border Rural Committee (BRC); Nkuzi Development Association; Southern Cape Land Committee (SCLC); Surplus People Project (SPP)
Northern Cape, 31
Northern Natal Council of Churches, 217
N/u language, 186, 192

O. R. Tambo District Municipality, 244

Peace Parks Foundation, 175
Pillay, In re, 74
Pinheiro Principles, 275–76
PLAAS (Programme for Land and Agrarian Studies). *See* Institute for Poverty, Land and Agrarian Studies (PLAAS)
Preliminary Survey of the Bantu Tribes of South Africa (Van Warmelo), 168
"Principles on Housing and Property Restitution for Refugees and Displaced Persons" (UNESCO), 275–76
Prinsloo & Another v. Ndebele-Ndzundza Community & Others, 68–70
  communal nature of restitution claims and, 69
  ownership as a bundle of rights and, 69–70
property clause. *See* Constitution of South Africa
property rights, 6, 17, 19, 20, 22, 35, 44, 48, 70, 113
  Black River, Cape Town and, 85
  Makuleke and, 166
  restitution and, 24–26, 55
protected areas, 18
  land claims and, 235
  See also comanagement of protected areas; Mkambati Nature Reserve case study

Queensland, Mabo v., 67

Ralushai Commission on Traditional Leadership, 168, 169
Randall and Another v. Minister of Land Affairs, 74–75
regional land claims commissioners (RLCCs), 21, 30, 149
  See also specific case studies
Regopstaan, 182, 194–95

Resources Africa, 176
Restitution of Land Rights Act of 1994, 1–5, 21, 22, 62–63
  CRCLR functions and, 276
  development planning and, 280–81
  development subsidies and, 276–77
  discrimination and, 277
  equitable redress and, 276
  just and equitable compensation and, 281
  Land Restitution and Reform Laws Amendment Act of 1997 and, 278
  LCC interpretations of, 277–82
  Makuleke and, 171–72
  rural versus urban claims and, 281–82
  section 34 (*see* Cato Manor case study; District Six case study)
restitution program in South Africa, 125–26
  1998 review of, 27–28
  aging and, 125–26
  cash versus land and, 24–25, 27–28, 30, 33, 94, 97, 116–17, 120–21, 125–29
  claims deadlines and, 36–37
  competing claims and, 34
  conflict and, 9, 25, 26, 35, 85
  constitutional background and statutory parameters of, 62–63
  Constitution of 1996 and, 274–76
  discrimination and dispossession and, 71–75
  disruptive effects of, 97
  economic impacts of, 298–99
  eligibility parameters and, 22–24, 63–64
  expropriation and, 25
  farming types and, 298–99
  financial (cash) compensation and, 3, 7, 30, 33, 87, 97, 116, 117, 120–21, 125–26, 128–29, 203, 266, 268, 275, 281, 309
  healing and, 17, 85, 86, 97, 119
  "land" and "community" and, 64–71
  land versus property and, 25
  legislation and institutions and, 21–22, 27
  new dispossessions and, 34–35
  objectives of, 61
  parameters and, 24
  payment and, 26
  postsettlement support and, 321–22
  price of, 33
  progress of, 1995 to 1999, 26–28
  reconciliation and, 38
  reconstituting community and, 35

333

restitution program in South Africa (cont.)
- reconstituting tradition and, 34
- reparations and, 33–34
- restitution definition and, 274–75
- rights and development and, 35–36
- rural land claims and, 23, 29–32, 36, 64, 267
- rural land reform and, 38
- rural restitution and livelihoods and, 291–93
- scope and limits of, 96–97
- settlement versus agriculture and, 299
- state interventions and, 47
- strategic partnerships and, 36, 301–2
- suffering and, 25
- sustainability and, 273–74
- symbolic dimensions of, 6, 7, 17, 38, 41, 44, 49, 55, 87, 94, 135, 147, 184, 217, 310, 318
- temporality and, 44–48, 125–28
- transparency and, 37
- trust in the process and, 126–28
- urban land claims and, 11, 29–33, 86–87, 116, 120, 256, 266–67
- "western"/westernized San and, 4
- *See also specific agencies and organizations; specific case studies*

Restonia Trust, 121–22

Richtersveld case, 25, 65–68, 72–73, 74, 75
- aboriginal title doctrine and, 66–67, 76
- beneficial occupation and, 67
- date of dispossession and, 66
- indigenous law ownership and, 67–68

Richtersveld Community v. Alexkor Ltd & Another, 278

Robins, S., 192

Roodt, Monty, 85

Roosboom case study
- background of, 215–16
- black spots and, 215–16
- community dynamics and, 225–27
- DPWLA and, 218–19
- *Land Claims Submission to the ACLA* and, 219
- land NGO and development planning and, 221–23
- land restitution and regional restructuring processes, 228
- land restitution movement and, 216–18
- repayment of compensation money and, 227
- Roosboom Board of Overseers (RBO) and, 217
- Roosboom Trust and, 225–26
- socioeconomic survey and, 224–25
- title restoration and, 223–24
- unclaimed land and, 227
- violence and unrest in Ezakheni and, 220–21
- weakness of RBO and, 228

Salt River, 118, 121

SANCO. *See* South African National Civic Organization (SANCO)

SANParks. *See* South African National Parks Board (SANParks)

Schulz, Kathleen, 118, 120

Shimange case study (Limpopo), 294–95
- farming types and, 298

Slamdien, Minister of Land Affairs v., 71–72

Smyly, Dave, 267

South Africa, locality of major case studies in, x

South African Farm Management (SAFM), 311, 320, 322

South African Forestry Company Limited (Safcol), 133–34

South African National Civic Organization (SANCO), 201, 203, 207–9, 212

South African National Parks Board (SANParks), 134, 136
- ≠Khomani San land claim and, 182, 183–84
- Makuleke settlement and, 168, 174–75
- Tsitsikamma National Park and, 134

Southern Cape and Karoo Land Restitution Forum (SKKLRF), 135

Southern Cape Land Committee (SCLC), 117, 132

Southern Kalahari Land Claims Committee, 182, 185, 186

Stake Your Claim campaign, 26–27

Standard Settlement Offers (SSOs), 27, 90

Steyn, H. P., 195

strategic partnerships, 36, 301–2
- community benefits and, 318–19
- contributing factors and, 310–11
- employment opportunities and, 317, 321
- handover to communities and, 318
- impacts on revenue and, 314–16
- implications for scale of production and risk management and, 316–17
- key decisions and, 313–14
- model of, 311–13
- *See also* Levubu Valley case study (Limpopo)

Index

Supreme Court of Appeal, 5, 21, 62, 63–64, 68, 71, 281–82
  Richtersfeld case and, 76
Surplus People Project (SPP), 18, 259

Thaweni Tribal Authority, 239
Traditional Leadership and Governance Framework Act, 173
Treatment Action Campaign and Others, Minister of Health and Others v., 285n2
Truth and Reconciliation Commission (TRC), 4, 33–34, 53, 85, 86, 164, 193, 268–69
Tsapekoe Estates, 107
Turner, S., 244

United Democratic Front, 19

van den Berg, M., 293, 303
van der Walt, A. J., 62–63
Van Vuuren, Chris J., 168, 169
Van Warmelo, N. J.: *Preliminary Survey of the Bantu Tribes of South Africa,* 168

Verdery, Kathleen, 45, 54
Viljoen, Gerrit, 218
Vula Masango Singene campaign, 213

Walker, Cherryl, 23, 87
Welkom, 182
Westaway, A., 198
White Paper on Land Reform (Republic of South Africa, 1991), 70
White Paper on South African Land Policy (Department of Land Affairs, 1997), 19, 22, 24, 70, 218–19, 288
Wits expedition, 185
Witz, In re Various Portions of Grassy Park, Department of Land Affairs v., 74
Wolmer, William, 167
Women's Rural Movement, 173

Xingwana, Lulama, 248, 290

Zille, Helen, 158
Zimbabwe, 54, 171
Zuma, Jacob, 47

Land, Memory, Reconstruction, and Justice